DATE DUE

HF 15 00			
JY 1 3 '09			

DEMCO 38-296

This book is dedicated to Nariaki Suzuki,
our dear Dōzō Bāchi

Published by
Princeton Architectural Press
37 East 7th Street
New York, New York 10003
212.995.9620

For a free catalog of books, please call 1.800.458.1131

Editing and design: Clare Jacobson
Special thanks to: Seonaidh Davenport, Caroline Green, Sarah Lappin,
Bill Monaghan, Allison Saltzman, and Ann C. Urban of Princeton
Architectural Press—Kevin C. Lippert, publisher

Cover photograph: Botond Bognar
Page 17, fig. 11, Kawasumi Architectural Photograph Office, courtesy
Kenzo Tange
Page 18, fig. 13, courtesy Kisho Kurokawa
Page 20, fig. 19, Y. Takase, Y. Futagawa and Associated Photographers,
courtesy Arata Isozaki
All other photographs in this volume have been taken by the author dur-
ing the last twenty-two years. All drawings are courtesy of the architects.

Library of Congress Cataloging-in-Publication Data
Bognár, Botond, 1944–
    The Japan guide / Botond Bognar.
    p.cm.
    Includes bibliographical references and index.
    ISBN 1-878271-33-4
    1. Architecture—Japan—Guidebooks. 2. Architecture—
20th century—Japan—Guidebooks. 3. Japan—Guidebooks.
I. Title.
NA 1555.B526 1995
720˙.952˙0904—dc20   94-17609
                                                                 CIP

12

The Japan Guide

Botond Bognar

Princeton Architectural Press

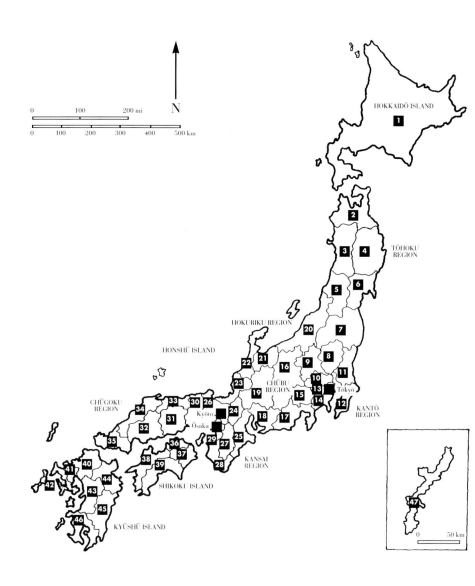

0   100   200 mi

0   100   200   300   400   500 km

N

HOKKAIDŌ ISLAND

1

2

3   4

TŌHOKU
REGION

5   6

HONSHŪ ISLAND

HOKURIKU REGION

20

7

22   21

16   9

8

11

23

CHŪBU
REGION

10
13

19

15   14

Tokyō

12

KANTŌ
REGION

CHŪGOKU
REGION

33   30   26

34

31   Kyōto   24

32   Ōsaka

18   17

25

35

36

29   27

KANSAI
REGION

38   39

28

41   40

37

44

SHIKOKU ISLAND

42

43

45

46   KYŪSHŪ ISLAND

47

0   50 km

CONTENTS

MAP OF JAPAN

ACKNOWLEDGMENTS

In my work of compiling *The Japan Guide* throughout the years, I have been helped, assisted, or otherwise supported by many people to whom I am truly grateful. To list the names of all is impossible, but a few need to be acknowledged as the most important ones. These include, first of all, the architects themselves, who provided invaluable information, material, as well as encouragement, extending even their friendship.

Specifically, I would like to thank my friends Tadao and Yumiko Ando, Takefumi Aida, Hiromi Fujii, Hiroshi Hara, Itsuko Hasegawa, Kunihiko Hayakawa, Toyo Ito, Atsushi Kitagawara, Akira Komiyama, Kisho Kurokawa, Fumihiko Maki, Yasumitsu Matsunaga, Toshio Nakamura (chief editor of *A+U*), Yasuhiro Teramatsu and Masato Nakatani (editors of *The Japan Architect*), Kayoko Ota (editor of *Telescope*), Kazunari Sakamoto, Kazuyo Sejima, Ryōji Suzuki, Shin Takamatsu, Minoru Takeyama, Kōji Yagi, Riken Yamamoto, Kazumasa Yamashita, Hajime Yatsuka, and Shōei Yoh.

In addition, I am also much indebted to Professor Hiroyasu Fujioka of Tōkyō Institute of Technology and the architects Arata Isozaki, Kiyonori Kikutake, Kazuo Shinohara, and Kenzo Tange.

Very special thanks to Shoji Hayashi, Deputy President, and Kunihiro Misu, Director of International Operations, both of Nikken Sekkei Company, for all their generous support and cooperation.

Much of my appreciation goes to Nariaki Suzuki, our dear Dōzō Bāchi, president of Seikō Kōgyō Company and a long-time friend of my family; without his continuing help, assistance, and personal attention, much of the work would have been impossible to accomplish. In a similar way Yasuhiko Matsushiro and his wife Yoshiko Matsushiro have extended their friendship and assistance over many years.

I am grateful also to R. Alan Forrester, Director of the School of Architecture at the University of Illinois, Urbana-Champaign, for his continuing support of my work. Tracy Tieman and Jane Cook have proven to be again, as always, invaluable with their typing the manuscript in the most professional way possible. Thank you.

Nana Ito, a graduate student and research assistant of mine, drew all the maps, helped with some of the translation, and assisted in many other ways in the preparation of the book, and I am very grateful to her.

Also, I have to acknowledge with great appreciation the generous grants I received from the Northeast Asia Council (NEAC) for the initiation of the project, and from the Research Board of the University of Illinois for the completion of the last stages of the work.

Moreover, I want to thank Kevin Lippert and Clare Jacobson of Princeton Architectural Press for their substantial contributions to the book during the entire production.

Finally, my family deserves credit for all the patience and endurance during all these years when instead of going on summer vacations, "we all" were collecting material.

INTRODUCTION

Contemporary Japanese architecture has achieved in the short time of the past few years an important leading position on the international scene, and it appears that this position will be maintained in the years to come. The reasons behind this phenomenal success are complex and include various basic features that characterize Japan in general as it approaches the twenty-first century. These often indirect but by all means significant features include: the strength of the economy (which, despite the recent recession, still qualifies the country as an "economic superpower"), the strongly future-oriented predisposition of the society, the leading role of technological progress, the Japanese dedication to high quality, the rapid development of the information society, the particular qualities of the Japanese urban environment, and the Japanese penchant for experimentation and innovation that has always characterized people's conduct beyond their ongoing dialogue with traditions.

The last decade has witnessed a heretofore unparalleled increase of interest in Japan and Japanese architecture by the rest of the world. Many foreigners find it important to visit the country and witness the growing number of outstanding examples of contemporary design. Moreover, in addition to the connoisseurs or interested laypersons, more and more Western architects now not only closely follow the developments of contemporary Japanese architecture, but also seek the opportunity and challenge of working in Japan and taking advantage of the special conditions there. Indeed, in our age of an increasingly global economy, the information exchange and the mutual interest between Japan and the West is more intense than ever before.

Yet, the unusual conditions in Japan do pose considerable difficulties for both interested visitors and professionals alike. These difficulties ensue from the basic differences that exist between Western and Japanese cultures (languages, customs, etc.) and, more importantly for architects, between the varying physical contexts of the built environment—that is, the qualities of the urban fabric. The overly dense and chaotic Japanese city constitutes, with almost no exception, the context of all representatives of Japanese architecture today, and this context is unquestionably indispensable for understanding the works proper. It is also an unavoidable condition through which one has to navigate daily in order to reach various destinations. This urban environment is evidenced rather poignantly on some of the photographs that follow; these photos, nevertheless, fall far short of preventing even the more knowledgeable travelers from the "shock" they may experience upon first landing in Tōkyō. Therefore, considering all these circumstances, the publication of an up-to-date guidebook to Japanese architecture, having been long overdue, is now timely.

The Japan Guide has been compiled with several specific intentions in mind. First, it wants to provide a brief, general introduction to the background—that is, the development and present course—of contemporary Japanese architecture. Second, it aims to introduce a large number and broad spectrum of buildings and complexes that represent the best, as well as the peculiar or the unusual, examples of this tremendously creative and fascinating architectural culture, covering material from the mid-nineteenth century until today. To this end, more than 280 selected buildings as main entries are documented by textual, graphic, and photographic material, in addition to over 360 other projects which, as secondary entries, are also listed in the volume. Both types of entries include buildings that, based upon their historic or cultural/ architectural value, have been designated as "Important National Cultural Properties" by the Japanese government.

As the third and most important goal of the guidebook, every effort has been made to supply as detailed information as possible to facilitate a relatively easy on-site visitation of *all* the entries. Therefore every building is listed by both its English and, when different, Japanese names—as they appear in international literature on the one hand, *and* as the Japanese know or call them on the other. The name is followed by its date of completion and precise address. The entry also includes the means of transportation or the way to reach the location, including public transportation lines—train, subway, bus—with names of stations, points of transfer, etc., and/or the length of taxi ride or walk involved. Japanese names are transcribed into English, reflecting the Japanese pronunciation with the appropriate accents. When relevant, visitation hours are also indicated.

Public buildings such as museums, galleries, libraries, and temples are open in general from 9:00 or 9:30–17:00 with little variation, although *the last admittance is usually 30 minutes before closing.* Many of them are closed on Mondays or, occasionally, on another day of the week, or the next day if the regular day is a national holiday; most of them are also closed on national holidays, and all are closed around the new year from 28 December through 3 January.

Public transportation is exceptionally widespread and effective in Japan, and so most locations discussed in *The Japan Guide* can be reached by using only trains, subways, and municipal or long-distance bus service. The reliability of the system is well exemplified by the elaborate timetables and the on-time accuracy it follows. Such timetables (*jikokuhyō*) are published in bilingual version (*JTB Speed Jikokuhyō*), and are available in larger bookstores.

Yet, a word of *caution*: before using public transportation, one should be well advised to double check, by asking the driver or the platform attendant, if the vehicle or train is indeed destined to the stop/station one intends to go. This may be necessary, because from the same platform many different trains can depart; express trains do not stop at every station; sometimes, after a certain point, one *part* of the train may continue in another direction; and not every train runs the entire length of the line.

Entries are introduced according to their geographic location, that is to say, by regions, prefectures, and urban areas, starting with Hokkaidō in the north, then proceeding south and west on Honshū, Shikoku, and Kyūshū main islands, finally reaching Okinawa in the far south. To make visitations more convenient within such geographic areas and cities, closely located buildings have been "grouped" together, or arranged sequentially, along the same train or subway line, or as they may add up to shorter or longer walking tours. For easy overview and reference, an index in the back of the book lists architectural examples in alphabetical order by their designers; another lists all buildings introduced in the volume in chronological order.

In order to better locate and find some of the buildings, there are over thirty maps that indicate the name and location of prefectures, major train lines, national roads, expressways, important cities and towns, and featured buildings. These sketch maps, however, work only in conjunction with more detailed, commercially available maps, which can be purchased in bilingual versions in Kinokunya or Maruzen bookstores and some other major bookshops in larger cities of Japan.

Although finding one's way in Japan has become much easier in recent years, it is still more difficult than in countries where the Roman alphabet is used. (An increasing number of written information is bilingual now, but not all.) Yet, the different writing system, and the fact that most streets, roads, and sometimes even large avenues do not have names, are only relatively minor sources of difficulty. The more important ones are attributable to a "new" pattern of urbanism, an amorphous urban nexus, wherein the labyrinthine network of streets, and all the systems of "codes," signs, and landmarks seem to consistently defy the ones by which a foreigner, most especially a Westerner, "reads" and comprehends the city and the larger human environment. I point out these characteristics not as necessarily negative features, and certainly not to discourage potential visitors, but in order to engender a heightened awareness about important cultural differences that, fortunately, still characterize Japan. Such differences, unfamiliar as they may be to a foreigner, provide not only the challenge but also the fascination one experiences when abroad. And Tōkyō makes by all means one of the most exciting, if not the most beautiful, cities in the world.

Nevertheless, the fact remains that many of the buildings featured here, though they may be prominent public structures, are buried in the densely built, kaleidoscopic, radically heterogeneous urban fabric that deprives them from both easy accessibility and good, commanding visibility. Some small, private structures have even more "precarious" settings. For better results in finding these buildings, their entries note easily identifiable nearby structures wherever possible. Such landmarks give better points of reference for taxi drivers as well.

For the above-mentioned reasons, photographing some of the buildings is very difficult, if not impossible. In other cases, and far more often than in the United States or European countries, photography is not permitted, although one can, of course, freely take photos from streets and other *outside* public places. However, sometimes such buildings as banks, courthouses, and certain offices are located within demarcated compounds, within which photography is prohibited. Moreover, and more importantly, *inside* any bank, museum, art gallery, exhibition hall, and government and private office buildings—and often in some ordinary public structures as well—no photography is allowed.

As for the selection of the buildings that are included in this volume, indeed my most important goal was to introduce as broad a range of representative works of the one-and-one-half century of contemporary Japanese architecture as possible. Several limitations immediately arose. The further one goes back in history, the less extant important examples one can find. Unfortunately, relatively few structures remain from the Meiji Era (1868–1912), and the number increases only slightly when it comes to the Taishō (1912–1926) or early Shōwa (1926–1989) periods, that is, the prewar developments of Japanese architecture. Most buildings from these times were either destroyed in the 1923 Tōkyō earthquake, or in World War II, or were simply pulled down for a variety of reasons.

Many noted representatives of Japan's prewar, but also postwar, architecture, including Frank Lloyd Wright's Imperial Hotel (1923) in Tōkyō and Kenzo Tange's Old Tōkyō City Hall (1957), have fallen victim of more recent outbursts of real-estate boom and/or speculation, and the vicissitudes of today's accelerated consumerist urbanism. Wright's building, after surviving the above-mentioned devastating earthquake, had to give way to a new, high-rise hotel in 1965, although the central section of the old hotel was reconstructed in Meiji-mura, an open air village museum north of Nagoya, in 1980. Tange's landmark design, on the other hand, is being replaced by the Tōkyō International Forum, designed by Rafael Vinoly, winner of an international competition.

It is true that many of the prewar and early postwar buildings had been poorly constructed by today's standards and were only a few stories high while occupying very expensive pieces of land. Yet such rapid turnover of the built landscape has continued, perhaps even increased, in the case of recently completed and "physically perfectly fit" buildings. Masaharu Takasaki's Crystal Light, a company guest house (1987) in Tōkyō, is a case in point. It was pulled down after but a few years of hardly any use; in its place now stands another building of a more profitable kind. Although this is obviously an extreme example, it dramatizes well the growing volatility of the Japanese urban environment in today's commodity culture. Moreover, some significant projects, such as facilities of expositions, including the Ōsaka Expo '70, had been erected *a priori* as temporary edifices, and were pulled down after the shows closed.

There are, however, other reasons why many well-known or important works could not be included in the list of featured buildings. In most part, respecting the privacy of tenants, individual residences have been excluded from coverage; only in exceptional cases—where they can be seen well and viewed in decent circumstances from public roads and areas—have they been listed. A large number of both private and public structures are indeed located in areas wherein they are hardly visible, if at all, from easily accessible places. Others, long after their completion, now find themselves in radically altered conditions; they have been remodeled beyond recognition by their owners, like Itsuko Hasegawa's Bizan Hall (1984) in Shizuoka, or their surrounding urban environment has changed to the extent that it now "buries" or otherwise seriously obscures them. Among the numerous such examples Tadao Ando's Wall House (Matsumoto House) in Ashiya (1976) and Toyo Ito's U-House in Nakano, Tōkyō (1976) stand out.

While several buildings had to be left out, work of foreign architects who were, have been, or still are active in Japan, starting with the beginning of Japan's modern era in the middle of the nineteenth century, have been included. Most of these architects are internationally recognized, outstanding designers who have produced works in Japan that often surpass their achievements in their own native countries. Zaha Hadid completed her first building, the interior of the Moonsoon Restaurant, in Sapporo (1990); the Il Palazzo in Fukuoka (1989) is acknowledged as one of Aldo Rossi's best works; and Steven Holl and Rem Koolhaas each designed a unique and innovative type of residential block at the Nexus World Housing project in Fukuoka (1991). All of these buildings, although not the

Shibuya Station Plaza in Tōkyō with Minoru Takeyama's 109 Building (1978) in the center.

View of a dense residential district in Tōkyō's Ōta-ku.

products of Japanese architects, are now part of the Japanese cultural landscape to which they contribute in a significant way; their inclusion therefore is amply justified.

Beyond these objective aspects, inevitably some subjective ones have played a role in the selection of examples. The inclusion and number of buildings, other than the most outstanding ones, have been guided by several personal considerations. The overall number has been limited by the volume of the book. In order to provide a balanced coverage with regard to geographical locations, as many as possible regions or urban areas in the country have been included. Moreover, when in the near vicinity of a major or important architectural piece, other, lesser-known structures have also been listed, in most cases.

Finally, although in the preparation of *The Japan Guide*—the result of more than two decades of work—I have made every attempt to assure the accuracy and up-to-dateness of the extensive amount of information, the more-than-usual volatility of the Japanese urban conditions prevents a guarantee that every piece of data will hold valid in the time to come, perhaps even in the near future. This should be kept in mind when planning any major tours to visit the listed architectural sites. Nevertheless, in the end it does not matter much if one has to miss one or two targeted examples; the remaining plenty will certainly make up for the loss by providing personal experiences that are, more often than not, as exhilarating and pleasantly rewarding as they are professionally instructive. Good luck.

THE COURSE OF CONTEMPORARY JAPANESE ARCHITECTURE

Japanese architecture since the middle of the nineteenth century has to be viewed in the context of contemporary political and economic upheavals, as well as related intellectual and cultural developments. Some of these have been experienced in common with other countries, while others have been unique to Japan. The Meiji restoration in 1868 and the following rapid modernization of Japanese society, together with remarkable industrial and commercial growth, the Sino-Japanese War in 1894–95 and the Russo-Japanese War in 1904–05, plus the worldwide recession of the late 1920s and the 1930s all had a profound impact on the direction and quality of prewar architecture in Japan. Similarly, the aftermath of World War II and the subsequent establishment of democracy in Japan, the postwar need to rebuild the country and redefine its national identity, the economic boom of the 1960s, the oil crisis of 1974–75 and concurrent recession, the steady recovery and progress of the 1980s and, last but not least, the unprecedented urbanization along with the evolution of an unusually dynamic urban culture in the past decade have been indispensable agents in the shaping of Japan's new architecture. This architecture is as much renown in the world today as its traditional counterpart has always been.

The Japanese commitment to advanced technology and innovation has induced the erection of many significant buildings in recent years. A whole technological armory has been used in the service of architecture through the joint efforts of various government agencies, progressive private developers, numerous outstanding designers, and giant construction companies that have built a range of structures: museums and art galleries, town halls and festival halls, universities, offices, and buildings for recreation, commerce, and transport. Moreover, the Japanese have consistently taken the opportunity to demonstrate their innovative ideas—and celebrate a close collaboration between engineering, applied technology, and architecture—at such events as the Olympic Games in Tōkyō of 1964 and the World Expositions at Ōsaka in 1970 and 1990, Okinawa in 1975, Tsukuba in 1985, and Tōkyō in 1996. Yet, it is important to emphasize that all this would not have been possible to achieve without the talent, knowledge, and sensitive capability of consecutive generations of dedicated architects, who justly deserve recognition for the growing success of their work.

Meiji Era and Prewar Developments

Throughout its history Japan has actively sought to enrich its culture through "Japanization," a process by which ideas from abroad are transformed, refined, and absorbed into Japanese life. As a result, Japan has been able to match, and frequently even surpass, the accomplishments of the very origins of its inspirations. The Chinese and Korean civilizations were the most important early sources for Japan.[1] This influential period was followed by more than two centuries of isolation during the Tokugawa (or Edo) Era (1603–1868). The Meiji Era (1868–1912) once more opened up the country to extensive influence, this time from the West. Understanding modernization as a matter of its survival as a sovereign nation, Japan was determined to catch up to Western social, commercial, political, and cultural developments. The Japanese government enacted a national policy for the modernization of the country, a process that in effect became synonymous with Westernization.[2]

To expedite these rapid changes, the Japanese invited many foreign experts, including specialists to design and supervise the construction of major public buildings and lay the foundations for a Western system of architectural education. Among them was the British architect Josiah Conder (1852–1920) after coming to Japan in 1877—not only designed such prominent buildings as the Old Ueno Imperial Museum (1882) and the Mitsubishi Building 1 (1894), both in Tōkyō, but also taught the first generation of Western-trained architects, including Kingo Tatsuno (1854–1919) and Tokuma Katayama (1853– 1917) at Tōkyō Imperial University. These newly trained Japanese architects soon took over the difficult task of meeting the growing demand for new types of buildings: schools, banks, hotels, and the like. In order to further their knowledge and experience, many young designers studied or worked abroad, at first primarily in Europe: the United Kingdom, Germany, Italy, and France.

Patterned after contemporary European models, Japanese architecture at the turn of the century was similarly eclectic and conservative, as can be seen in the Italianate Bank of Japan in Ōsaka (1896) by Tatsuno (fig. 1) and the French-inspired Akasaka Detached Palace and Hyōkeikan in Tōkyō (fig. 2) (both 1909) by Katayama. The Ōsaka Library (1904), the Sumitomo Bank (1926), both by the Sumitomo Eizen Design Office in Ōsaka, and the Parliament Building (National Diet Building) in Tōkyō, designed by the Architecture Department of the Ministry of Finance and completed in 1936 after much debate, are further examples of Western eclecticism in Japan.[3] Increasingly, however, architects began to question the appropriateness of anachronistic academicism. Criticism came from two opposing directions.

2. Hyōkeikan, Tōkyō, 1909, Tokuma Katayama

1. Bank of Japan Ōsaka Branch, Ōsaka City, 1903, Kingo Tatsuno

The first camp favored an attitude to design—called *wakonyosai* in Japanese—that, although benefiting from Western technology, was supposedly of "Japanese spirit." In reality this search for a national expression produced nothing more than another kind of eclecticism, which became known as the Imperial Crown Style or *teikan-yoshiki*. This style, often using the formal elements of traditional Japanese and other Asian architectures, notably the tiled roof of Buddhist temples, was promoted by the historian Chuta Ito (1867–1954) and exemplified first in Shinichirō Okada's (1883–1932) rebuilding of the Kabuki Theater in the Ginza area of Tōkyō (1924), then in Ito's own Soldiers' Hall (1934) and, to some degree, Tsukiji Hongan-ji Temple (1935), and more so in Hitoshi Watanabe's (1887–1973) Tōkyō Imperial Museum in Ueno (now Tōkyō National Museum) (1937) (fig. 3). *Teikan-yoshiki* was favored also by the increasingly nationalistic and fascist powers in Japan in the later 1930s.

The second, smaller group consisted of young architects who were growing dissatisfied with the revision and recycling of historical styles and who distanced themselves from such past architecture, whether Western or Japanese. In 1920 several graduates of the Tōkyō Imperial University formed the Japanese Secessionist Group or *Bunri Ha Kenchiku Kai,* which, although limited to ten years of activity, exerted a liberating effect on the contemporary architecture of Japan. Among its founding members were Sutemi Horiguchi (1895–?), Mamoru Yamada (1894–1966), and Kikuji Ishimoto (1894–1963), all of whom came under the influence of both Viennese Secessionism and German Expressionism. Since the original impulse of *Bunri Ha* was to reject all prevailing, mainly stylistic, tendencies, the group slowly paved the road toward the introduction of the International Style. Thus, the early expressionist buildings produced by the group—Yamada's Central Telegraph Office (1925) and Ishimoto's Asahi Newspaper Building (1927) and Shirokiya (now Tōkyū) Department Store (1931) (fig. 4), all in Tōkyō—were soon followed by rather rational designs representing a more genuine modernism—such as the Dental College (1933) by Bunzō Yamaguchi (1902–78) and Teishin Hospital (1937) by Yamada, both in Tōkyō.[4]

3. Tōkyō Imperial Museum in Ueno (now Tōkyō National Museum), Tōkyō, 1937, Hitoshi Watanabe; detail of main entrance.

4. Shirokiya (now Tōkyū) Department Store, Tōkyō, 1931, Kikuji Ishimoto; after a substantial redesign of the facade by Junzo Sakakura in 1957.

5. Sōgō Department Store, Ōsaka City, 1935, Togo Murano

Change was conspicuous not only in the works of Yamada, Horiguchi, and Yamaguchi, but also in those of a talented group of designers working for municipal and other public offices, such as the architectural departments of the Metropolitan Government and the Ministry of Communications in Tōkyō. In this context Tetsuro Yoshida (1894–1956) became a leading figure; the central post office buildings in Tōkyō (1931) and Ōsaka City (1939) are among his most celebrated works. Another architect, Togo Murano (1891–1984), whose long, independent, and free-spirited career began in 1930, also made a few contributions to a new, non-historicist mode of design. His Morigō Shōten Office Building (now Kinsan Building) in Tōkyō (1931), Sōgō Department Store in Ōsaka (1935) (fig. 5) and, most especially, Public Hall in Ube (1937) are among the noteworthy early examples of modern Japanese architecture.

Foreign architects who lived and practiced in Japan may have influenced these changes. In 1916 Frank Lloyd Wright (1867–1959) arrived to build the new Imperial Hotel in Tōkyō (1923) (fig. 6), while simultaneously working on several smaller projects, such as the Yamamura House in Ashiya

(1924). More significant than Wright's highly individualistic architecture, however, was that of his
assistant, the Czech-born American architect,
Antonin Raymond (1888–1976). Raymond, even
before the completion of the Imperial Hotel, established a design office of his own in Tōkyō, which he
maintained, with the exception of a few years during World War II, until his death. His own house in
Reinanzaka, Tōkyō (1924), the Rising Sun Petrole-
um Company Office Building in Yokohama (1926),
and residences for members of the Akaboshi family
are among the most notable examples of his early
work. Raymond's office was also the "training
ground" for several well-known modern architects,
such as Kunio Maekawa (1905–86).[5]

6. Imperial Hotel, Tōkyō, 1923, Frank
Lloyd Wright; reconstructed central
section in Meiji Mura, Aichi Pref., 1980

7. Katsura Imperial Villa, Kyōto City,
seventeenth century

Other Europeans drawn to Japan included Bruno
Taut (1880–1938), who spent the years 1933–36
there and contributed to the reevaluation of traditional Japanese architecture through his writings,
such as the opulently illustrated book *Houses and
People of Japan* (1937). Taut's publications, while
drawing world-wide attention to such historic monuments as the Katsura Villa, Kyōto (seventeenth
century) (fig. 7) and the Ise Shrine (third century),
also served to foment the theories of modernism in
Japan immediately prior to World War II.[6]

8. Daiichi Life Insurance Building,
Tōkyō, 1938, Hitoshi Watanabe

Another way in which the achievements of modernism reached Japan was
through those Japanese architects who went abroad to study or work with
leading European architects; Bunzō Yamaguchi and Chikatada Kurata
(1895–?) worked with Walter Gropius, for example, while Kunio Maekawa,
Junzo Sakakura (1904–69), and Takamasa Yoshizaka (1917–80) were
employed, at different times, in Le Corbusier's office in Paris. In addition, the
magazine *L'Esprit Nouveau* and publications such as Gropius' *Internationale
Architektur* (1925, 1927) spread progressive ideas in Japan.

The most significant foreign acknowledgment of prewar Japanese architecture came with Sakakura's Japanese Pavilion at the Paris World's Fair (1937);
the building elicited high praise from the historian and theoretician of modernism, Sigfried Giedion. Yet, despite all the progress—particularly in regard
to its variety—modernism achieved in Japanese architecture by this time, the
militarization of Japan and the rise of nationalism in the 1930s demanded that
major, new buildings be conceived in an "Asian-Japanese style." For example,
Maekawa's and others' numerous design competition entries were systematical-
ly rejected as being in the International Style of Le Corbusier.[7] Even so, a still-
tolerated rational "classicism"—that could, curiously, forward the ideologies
and traits of both national socialist (fascist) and modernist architectures—
managed occasionally to produce outstanding designs, such as the Daiichi Life

Insurance Building in Tōkyō (1938) (fig. 8) by Hitoshi Watanabe, the architect of the Tōkyō Imperial Museum in Ueno (1937), epitomizing the *teikan-yoshiki* style.[8] Eventually, however, a combination of politics, ideological suppression, and the advent of the war ensured the collapse of the modern architectural movement in Japan.

Postwar Reconstruction and the Metabolism Movement of the 1960s

Japan's rebirth after World War II as a democratic society removed most obstacles to the rapid spread of progressive architecture. The task of urgent reconstruction and the goal of an "architecture for democracy" demanded the effective rationalization and industrialization of building and design. First Maekawa and Sakakura emerged as architectural leaders; in his Kamakura Prefectural Museum of Modern Art (1951), Sakakura recaptured the delicacy of his Japanese Pavilion in Paris (1937). Equally significant was Antonin Raymond's Reader's Digest Building in Tōkyō (1951); returning to Japan after the war, Raymond designed this two-story structure on a simple, *T*-shaped plan with deep eaves and balconies, and used steel and exposed concrete, metal louvers for sunlight control, and such technological innovations as acoustical tiling, fluorescent lighting, heat-pump systems, and floor-to-ceiling glazing.

Kenzo Tange (b. 1913), who in effect entered the architectural scene only after the war, came to prominence with the completion of his Hiroshima Peace Center in 1955, which signaled the beginning of widespread use of reinforced concrete in Japan. The influence of Le Corbusier was felt increasingly, and eventually he was invited to design the National Museum of Western Art in Ueno, Tōkyō (1959). Japanese architecture of the 1950s also reflected architects' growing concern for tradition and local character. Among others, Maekawa, Tange, and Kiyosi Seike (b. 1918) showed their remarkable ability to synthesize modern technology and design with traditional Japanese architecture without reverting to nationalist clichés. Seike established a reputation for domestic architecture; his early houses, including the Mori (1951) and Saitō (1952) houses in Tōkyō, make notional use of ancient residential styles while also forwarding the ideals of modern architecture. Among public buildings that best represent this new synthesis, now often referred to as the "New Japan style," are Tange's Old Tōkyō City Hall (1957) (fig. 9), Kagawa Prefectural Office Building in Takamatsu (1958), Old Kurashiki City Hall (1960), and Olympic Gymnasia, Tōkyō (1964), as well as Maekawa's Kyōto Hall (1960) and Metropolitan Festival Hall in Tōkyō (1961).[9] Sachio Otani's (b. 1924) Kyōto International Conference Hall (1966) is another good, though late, example.

9. Old Tōkyō City Hall, Tōkyō, 1957, Kenzo Tange (now demolished)

The 1960s marked the "Japanese miracle," an unparalleled period of progress in industrialization and technology, yielding the greatest economic boom in the history of the country. This called for a new approach to architecture and urbanism and simultaneously offered the means for its realization. Architects became increasingly preoccupied with systematic design and building methodologies. Large-scale and mostly utopian urban schemes provided models for an architecture that was regarded, theoretically at least, as a testing ground for the latest technology. As early as 1958 Maekawa's Harumi Apartments and Kiyonori Kikutake's (b. 1928) own Sky House (fig. 10), both in Tōkyō, did already reveal, if only partially, this new mode of design.

10. Sky House, Tōkyō, 1958, Kiyonori Kikutake

Tange's Tōkyō Plan (1960) (fig. 11) proposed a linear extension of the city over Tōkyō Bay, forming a civic axis along which growth and change would be possible. In 1961 Tange founded URTEC, a team of architects and urbanists with whom he developed systematic planning methods applicable to both individual buildings and the layout of cities. Megastructures became prominent in planning circles during the 1960s, and Tange's Yamanashi Press and Broadcasting Center in Kōfu (1966) with its powerful, cylindrical shafts rising through and supporting the entire building, is perhaps the most relevant archetype.[10] Surprisingly, in light of the result, one of Tange's aims in this project was to provide flexibility of use. Other designs by Tange, in which related ideas with similar solutions were explored, include the reconstruction of Skopje City Center, Yugoslavia (1966), the Shizuoka Press and Broadcasting Offices in Tōkyō (1967), plans for the Yerba Buena Center, San Francisco (1968), the Kuwait Embassy and Chancery Building in Tōkyō (1970) (fig. 12), and the Fiera District Center in Bologna, Italy (1974).

11. Tōkyō Plan, 1960, Kenzo Tange (photo courtesy of K. Tange)

12. Kuwait Embassy and Chancery Building, Tōkyō, 1970, Kenzo Tange

Under the personal influence of Tange, the movement known as Metabolism was formally launched at the World Design Conference held in Tōkyō in 1960. The Metabolists believed that architecture should not be static but be capable of undergoing "metabolic" changes; instead of thinking in terms of fixed form and function, these architects concentrated on changeability of space and function. Their ideas call to mind futuristic statements about new, modern cities with moving and variable parts; thus the Metabolist designs, with their interchangeable elements, and often capsules, can also represent a high-technology realization of the speculative work by the contemporary Archigram Group in London.[11] While the mutual influence and a similarity in intentions between the two groups are evident, the Metabolists were carried along by Japan's healthy and expanding economy and a spirit of vigorous—often even naive—optimism. As opposed to their British counterparts, they actually were able to realize many of their ideas. The original members of the Metabolism group included the architects Kiyonori Kikutake (b. 1928), Fumihiko Maki, Masato Otaka (b. 1923), and Kisho Kurokawa (b. 1934), plus the architectural critic Noboru Kawazoe (b. 1926) and the industrial designer Kenji Ekuan (b. 1929).

In the group Kikutake played a key role, both as a theorist and architect. He designed numerous futuristic urban projects, most of which, such as the Floating City (1960), were to be located over the sea.[12] One such project was partly realized in his Aquapolis of the Okinawa Marine Expo '75, which acquired a shape reminiscent of an oil rig. These schemes, taking up Tange's proposals for Tōkyō (1960) in general, tried to fuse city planning with technological possibility. In his use of exposed reinforced concrete at the Izumo Shrine Office Building (1963) and the Hotel Tōkōen in Yonago (1964), Kikutake explored further the logical expression of structure with remarkable results.

Although Kikutake's buildings are clearly of the twentieth century, it was the young Kurokawa who captured the essence of Metabolism, and whose work typified the movement's aspirations in striking science-fiction-like forms. Furthermore, his numerous writings provided an important theoretical buttress for the Metabolists.[13] Kurokawa's early explorations for a visionary Agricultural City (1960) and Helix City (1961) (fig. 13) were followed by his completed design for the Nitto Food Company Cannery in Sagae (1964), which represented an adaptable architecture of high technology. This commitment is evinced most potently in Kurokawa's fascination with capsules—which were to reflect a flexible but close relationship between humanity and technology—as demonstrated in his Takara Beautillion of the Ōsaka Expo '70, the Nagakin Capsule Tower in Tōkyō (1972), and the Sony Tower in Ōsaka (1976). In later years he has turned towards a more historicist, postmodern mode of

design, which is subtler—more sophisticated yet less dramatic, as can be seen in his Saitama Prefectural Museum of Modern Art, Urawa (1982), the Wacoal Kōjimachi Building, Tōkyō (1984), and the Nagoya City Museum of Modern Art (1987). Kurokawa's rapidly growing international recognition is also expressed in numerous commissions abroad, such as the Sporting Club Illinois Center in Chicago (1988) and the Melbourne Central, a skyscraper and atrium complex in Australia (1991).[14]

Maki, although he belonged to the group that launched Metabolism, did not himself share the utopian speculations of Kikutake and Kurokawa. His work was characterized not so much by the sculptural forms and technical inventiveness of

13. Helix City, 1961, Kisho Kurokawa

other Metabolists, but by a reticent language and a

THE COURSE OF CONTEMPORARY JAPANESE ARCHITECTURE

flexible articulation of both architectural and urban spaces. His early architecture recalled the buildings of his teacher at Harvard, Josep Lluis Sert, then became increasingly preoccupied with the elaboration of a new and more sensitive mode of urban design. This can be noted, for instance, in his Risshō University Kumagaya Campus (1968), Hillside Terrace Apartments in Tōkyō (1969–92) and Senri New Town Center Building in Toyonaka, near Ōsaka City (1970) (fig. 14). Later works of Maki, such as the Keiō University Library in Tōkyō (1981), YKK Guest House in Kurobe (1983), and the Kyōto National Museum of Modern Art (1986) display an enrichment in architectural vocabulary and a sophistication in detailing and craftsmanship that are comparable to the ones found not only in traditional Japanese architecture, but also in the designs of Carlo Scarpa, for example.[15]

14. Senri New Town Center Building, Toyonaka, Ōsaka Pref., 1970, Fumihiko Maki

15. Space frame of the Theme Pavilion, Ōsaka Expo '70, Suita, Ōsaka Pref., 1970, Kenzo Tange (now demolished)

The Ōsaka Expo '70 marked the climax and culmination of the Metabolism Movement with numerous innovative projects: Tange's Theme Pavilion (fig. 15) consisted of a giant space frame alluding to the idea of a city in the air, which Isozaki had expressed in his seminal project of 1961, while Kikutake's Landmark Tower recalled Peter Cook's futuristic Montreal Tower project (1964). With its several capsule buildings by Kikutake and Kurokawa, and various, new, large-scale, pneumatic structures, the Ōsaka Expo embodied the ideas of a wide range of visionaries, including the Archigram Group, Paolo Soleri, and

16. Sanwa Bank, Tōkyō, 1973, Nikken Sekkei Company

Buckminster Fuller, as well as the Metabolists. At the same time, it also revealed many limitations of the overwhelmingly technology-oriented architecture of the previous decade.

Events in the 1960s were conducive to the rapid expansion of large construction firms in Japan. The Shimizu, Ōbayashi, Takenaka, Taisei, and Kajima corporations strengthened their already well-established design departments, while Nikken Sekkei Company emerged as a large and comprehensive, but independent, design company with several branch offices across the country.[16] The novel designs of these companies, especially those of Nikken Sekkei Company, often incorporated elements and features inspired by Metabolism and were executed with the highest possible professionalism, occasionally to the extent of craftsmanship. Among such structures, the company's San-Ai Dream Center (1963), Palaceside Building (1966), Pola Home Offices (1971), Nakano Sun Plaza (1973), Sanwa Bank (1973) (fig. 16), and Long Term Credit Bank of Japan (1993), all in Tōkyō, are perhaps the most prominent.

Japanese Postmodernism of the 1970s

The energy crisis and the subsequent worldwide recession in the 1970s eventually slowed down Japan's progress, and the boom of the 1960s was largely dampened. An optimistic faith in the unlimited benefits of technology gave way to disillusionment, and an increased concern for the environment. The ideological basis of modernism and its last representative in Japan—Metabolism— were challenged, and a new approach to both architecture and urbanism emerged. The 1970s ushered in an unprecedented diversification in design, heralding the advent of the postmodern era in Japanese architecture.

Yet even before the demise of Metabolism there had been architects who were unwilling to see architecture in terms of rigid or rational systems and industrial processes. In particular, Togo Murano, Seiichi Shirai (1905–83), Takamasa Yoshizaka, and Kazuo Shinohara (b. 1925) were all determined to follow their own independent courses of design.[17] The individualistic tendencies in Murano's work can be seen in his World Peace Memorial Cathedral in Hiroshima (1953), the New Kabuki Theater in Ōsaka (1958), the Takarazuka Catholic Church (1967), and the Industrial Bank of Japan in Tōkyō (1974), while Shirai's explicitly mannerist and symbolistic approach to architecture is displayed in his Shinwa Bank Buildings in Sasebo (1967–75) and the Noa Building (1974) and Shōtō Museum (1980) (fig. 17), both in Tōkyō. Yoshizaka's buildings, including the Athene Française in Tōkyō (1962), demonstrate a powerful sculptural quality, which reflects the influence of Le Corbusier, for whom he worked from 1950–52.

Shinohara, who insisted that "a house is a work of art,"[18] specialized until recently in small residential buildings in which he reinterpreted certain qualities of traditional Japanese architecture and space. The abstraction and symbolism of these buildings gave them both a unique, geometrical, formal quality and a poetic intensity, as manifested in the Umbrella House (1961) and House in White (1966), both in Tōkyō. Later, especially after the mid-1970s, young architects came to regard Shinohara as their role model, particularly as the work of Tange, Maekawa, Kikutake, and their followers became less striking.

17. Shōtō Museum, Tōkyō, 1980, Seiichi Shirai

18. Joint Core System, 1960, Arata Isozaki

19. City in the Air, 1961, Arata Isozaki

Another important architect who emerged during the 1960s was Arata Isozaki (b. 1931). Beginning his career as a disciple of Kenzo Tange, and, so, an initial sympathizer with the ideas of Metabolism, Isozaki produced numerous large-scale and innovative urban projects like the Joint Core System (1960) (fig. 18), the City in the Air (1961) (fig. 19), and Future City (1962). Yet, even these early, unrealized designs revealed features that pointed beyond the Metabolists' preoccupation with technology and "mechanical changeability" toward unique form of mannerism Isozaki was to fully develop in the 1970s. Isozaki's works of the 1960s: the Ōita Medical Hall (1960; addition 1972), the Old Ōita Prefectural Library (1966), and the Fukuoka Sōgō Bank Ōita Branch (now Fukuoka City Bank) (1967), all in Ōita, and the Fukuoka Sōgō Bank Ropponmatsu Branch (now Fukuoka City Bank) in Fukuoka (1971) (fig. 20) combined reinforced concrete technology, as well as other, high-tech aspects, with strikingly new spatial and formal configurations. His fascination with a new "rhetoric" of architecture[19] is also exemplified by his exhibition installation, the Electric Labyrinth, at the 1968 Milan Triennale in Italy.

20. Fukuoka Sōgō Bank Ropponmatsu Branch (now Fukuoka City Bank), Fukuoka, Fukuoka Pref., 1971, Arata Isozaki

With the bankruptcy of Metabolism, the new generation of Japanese architects turned from large-scale utopian projects to the design of small-scale buildings, primarily residences, in existing towns and cities. There was a fresh concern for context and a renewed attempt to generate urban symbolism. Even large design companies showed themselves more sensitive to the qualities of the environment. Two buildings by the Nikken Sekkei Company illustrate this: the Yamaguchi Municipal Center in Yamaguchi (1971) (fig. 21), which connected to a busy city intersection by means of a semi-enclosed public plaza, and the Besshi Copper Mine Memorial Museum (1975), which blended with its hilly surroundings by means of sloping roofs covered with earth and vegetation.

21. Yamaguchi Civic Center, Yamaguchi, Yamaguchi Pref., 1971, Nikken Sekkei Company; axonometric drawing

22. Diagrams of various types of "Collective Forms": Compositional, Mega, and Group Forms, 1964, Fumihiko Maki

More than anyone, it was Fumihiko Maki—an erstwhile Metabolist, but educated partly at Cranbrook Academy of Art and Harvard Graduate School of Design—who showed the keenest interest in the spatial relationship between architecture and the city. Japan has a historical tradition that, in lack of Western-type urban plazas and piazzas, emphasizes the significance of the street, where city life is enacted. Inspired by various traditional types of urbanism and working from his notion of "group form," Maki became the leading proponent of Japanese contextualism (fig. 22).[20] By responding sensitively to both physical and cultural contexts, such buildings of his as the Ōsaka Prefectural Sports Center (1972), National Aquarium of Okinawa Marine Expo '75, and the Hillside Terrace Apartments in Tōkyō (1969–92) successfully mediate between the divergent urban and natural areas around them.

In Japan, even large cities such as Tōkyō and Ōsaka retain their historically evolved labyrinthine street pattern while providing a stage for the Japanese fascination with signs; indeed the French semiologist Roland Barthes aptly called Japan an "Empire of Signs."[21] Among those who investigated the systems of signs in the city, along with a new understanding of "architecture as language," was ArchiteXt, a loose-knit association of young architects who first exhibited in Tōkyō in 1971. ArchiteXt had five members: Minoru Takeyama (b. 1934), Takefumi Aida (b. 1937), Mayumi Miyawaki (b. 1936), Takamitsu Azuma (b. 1933), and Makoto Suzuki (b. 1935). All five maintained separate offices, but were united in their rejection of Metabolism and interest in urban semiology. Takeyama, the unofficial spokesman of ArchiteXt, summed up its common philosophy as "discontinuous continuity"[22]—a description as paradoxical as the group's own activities.

Takeyama's pursuit of architectural "heterology" and Azuma's concern for "polyphony" express the diversity of approach that characterized ArchiteXt; in addition, the group was responsible for promoting so-called "pop architecture," "defensive architecture," "vanishing architecture," and what Aida named the "architecture of silence."[23] Takeyama's Ichiban-kan Building (1969) and Niban-kan Building (1970) in Tōkyō's Shinjuku area and the Hotel Beverly Tom (now Hotel East Japan) in Tomakomai (1973), are examples of populist schemes in urban locations. Aida's most provocative work of this period includes the Nirvana House in Fujisawa

23. Blue Box, Tōkyō, 1971, Mayumi Miyawaki

(1972) and the earth-covered PL Institute Kindergarten in Tondabayashi, Ōsaka (1974). By using concrete in simple geometric shapes, Suzuki completed the Ryōkoku-ji Temple (1979) and the Studio Ebis (1981), both in Tōkyō. The small concrete houses by Azuma and Miyawaki—such as Azuma's own house (1967) and Miyawaki's Blue Box (1971) (fig. 23), both in Tōkyō—reveal an introverted or defensive attitude towards their neighborhoods; in this respect they were forerunners of the residential architecture of such younger architects as Toyokazu Watanabe (b. 1938), Toyo Ito (b. 1941), and especially Tadao Ando (b. 1941).

Other architects who devoted attention to architectural communication include Kiko (Monta) Mozuna (b. 1941) and Team Zoo—Atelier Zo (established 1971). Mozuna's symbolism, rooted in his reinterpretation of Asian philosophy and mythology, resulted in a "cosmic architecture" filled with ritualistic spaces and shapes. This was already evident in his radical early work, such as the Anti-Dwelling Box (Mozuna House) in Kushiro (1972), the Constellation House in Wakayama (1976), and the Mirror Image Hall in Tōkyō (1980). Similarly, although in a vernacular vein, Team Zoo—Atelier Zo has designed buildings with a playful but ritualistic quality, as can be seen in the Domo Celakanto in Kamakura (1974), the Miyashiro Community Center (1980), the Nago City Hall (1981), and the more recent projects of the Yufuin Art Museum and the Kuma High School of Industry, Traditional Architecture Workshop in Hitoyoshi, both of 1991.

Along with the rapid megalopolitan developments in Japan in the mid-1970s, commercialism began to dominate the city; it was first seen as at odds with the traditions of Japanese architecture and urbanism (fig. 24). In this situation, aggravated by worsening urban conditions of pollution, and congestion, many architects felt that the established relationship between buildings and the city, or between the private and public realms, was difficult—even impossible—to maintain. Thus the exteriors of many new buildings—usually small houses built of reinforced concrete—turned their backs on the city, though inside they were imaginative and challenged customary perceptions and habitual relationships.

24. Urban landscape in Tōkyō's Shinjuku Area, 1985

Tadao Ando demonstrated his concern for these issues in his unique, minimalist designs, which emphasized, in a reinterpreted form, the calm of traditional *sukiya*-style architecture and the courtyard-like arrangement of the urban residence or *machiya*. Ando's designs thus revealed a strong affinity with the simplicity and "primitivism" of vernacular architecture, and so his Azuma House (Row House in Sumiyoshi), Ōsaka City (1976) (fig. 25), among many others, may be viewed as a criticism of the increasingly hedonistic and conformist Japanese lifestyle. Other houses by Ando, designed around tiny inner courtyards, are poetic essays in their ways of reintroducing nature and natural phenomena, such as light-and-shadow effects captured on extensive wall surfaces, into architecture. Some of the best examples of this are the Matsumoto (1977) and Koshino (1981) (fig. 26) houses in Ashiya, Hyōgo Prefecture, and the Tezukayama (1977) and Glass Block (1978) houses in Ōsaka.

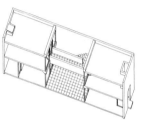

25. Azuma House (Row House in Sumiyoshi), Ōsaka City, 1976, Tadao Ando; axonometric drawing

26. Koshino House, Ashiya, Hyōgo Pref., 1982, Tadao Ando; interior of living room

Kazuo Shinohara, Toyo Ito, Hiromi Fujii (b. 1935), and Hiroshi Hara (b. 1936) pursued similar aims in the 1970s, as they too rejected the chaotic and hostile urban environment. Externally Shinohara's House in Uehara (1976) and House on a Curved Road (1978) (fig. 27), Ito's U-House in Nakano (1976) (fig. 28), and Fujii's Miyajima House (1973) are all "alienated objects" within the confines of Tōkyō, but internally they are poetic, although apparently simple, in their use of space. Inside Hara's "reflection houses," such as his own residence in Machida, Tōkyō (1974), there are various axial spaces, shaped as symbolic public or urban streets and stairways, and lined with miniature "urban" fragments: squares, monuments, intersections, and the facades of inward-looking rooms (fig. 29). Similar intentions of "burying the trove of the

27. House on a Curved Road, Tōkyō, 1978, Kazuo Shinohara; interior of living room

28. U-House in Nakano, Tōkyō, 1976, Toyo Ito

29. Hara House, Machida, Tōkyō, 1974, Hiroshi Hara; interior view

30. Kitakyūshū City Museum of Art, Kitakyūshū, Fukuoka Pref., 1974, Arata Isozaki

city in architecture"[24] can be seen in the "fissure spaces" within Shinohara's Incomplete House (1970) and Repeating Crevice House (1971), both in Tōkyō, and in many of Isozaki's public buildings such as the Old Ōita Prefectural Library (1966), Fukuoka Sōgō Bank Home Offices (now Fukuoka City Bank), Fukuoka (1971), and its branches. Importantly, these and other works by Isozaki and Shinohara provided much of the incentive and vocabulary of Japanese architecture of the 1970s.

At this time, when architects were rapidly becoming polarized between a "professionalist" majority and a "conceptualist" minority, Isozaki played a crucial role in leading the conceptualists. Together with Shinohara, he became the most influential designer of his generation in the so-called "new wave" of Japanese architecture. Isozaki's designs, along with his new mannerist approach, combined diverse intentions, experiments, motifs, quotations, and metaphors into a unique form of symbolism. While some aspects of his symbolism were being reflected and examined in the works of many other Japanese architects, such as Fujii, Aida, Takeyama, and even Shirai, Isozaki's architecture remains largely unparalleled in contemporary Japanese architecture.

Isozaki's best works of the 1970s include several buildings of the Fukuoka Sōgō Bank in Fukuoka (1971) (fig. 20), the Gumma Prefectural Museum of Modern Arts in Takasaki, the Kitakyūshū City Museum of Art (fig. 30), the Fujimi Country Clubhouse in Ōita, all three of 1974, the Kitakyūshū Central Library and the Shūkōsha Building in Fukuoka, both of 1975, and the Kamioka Town Hall (1978). By implication they simultaneously criticized the trivializing commercialism of the city while endorsing its potential and vitality. Arguably this is also represented by the more recent Tsukuba Center Building (1983) and the Shufunotomo Plaza in Tōkyō (1987), with their references to French neoclassicism. His latest work, such as the projects for Paternoster Square in London (1988) and Art Tower Mito (1990) continue to reflect Isozaki's response to historical/classical postmodernism, although the design of the tower seems to point beyond this declining paradigm in architecture. He has also achieved broad international recognition; many of his recent works are designed for foreign countries: the Museum of Contemporary Art in Los Angeles (1987) (fig. 31), the Disney World Headquarters Building in Orlando, Florida (1991), and the San Jordi Sports Hall for the 1992 Olympics in Barcelona.

31. Museum of Contemporary Art, Los Angeles, 1987, Arata Isozaki

A New Age of Experimentation: Toward the End of the Century

The early 1980s witnessed yet another change of direction in Japanese architecture. Prompted by the rapidly rebounding economy, the quickly advancing consumer and information societies, and the evolution of another urban renaissance that can be called a new, "accelerated urban culture"[25] in Japan, the previous aversion toward the city softened, while its flexibility, vitality, and resilience were discovered anew. This change in architects' attitudes has by now led to a new "form" of urban architecture in which a broadening range of interpretations of, and approaches to, the city are brought to play; these include poststructuralism, deconstructivism, and new modernism, among others. Divergent as they are in their concerns, these new urban sensibilities share a basic position, namely that the radically heterogeneous, volatile, and chaotic conditions of the Japanese city, best represented by Tōkyō, can be the source of not only destructive forces, but also tremendously creative energies, and even of poetic inspiration.

The architecture of the 1980s in Japan can be characterized by an important shift of emphasis from the previously dominant industrial technology, or "hardware," toward a highly sophisticated electronic and communication technology, or "software." As a result, recent designs, while not abandoning the tectonic culture and engineering bravura of earlier modernism, manifest an increased fascination with the ephemeral and phenomenal or, in short, the sensual in architecture. With their image-value multiplied, buildings in growing numbers appeal to the human senses as much as, and often far more than, they challenge the speculative or critical mind: instead of striving for monumental permanence, they foster ambiguity and perceptual instability with an implicit indeterminacy of meaning.

In recent years, architects have increased the use of lighter, yet "ordinary" industrial materials (Teflon-fiber fabrics, stainless steel, perforated aluminum, wire mesh, etc.) to erect buildings that, by virtue of their lack of heavy materiality or substantial corporeality, and by way of their fragmentary compositions, are intended as parts of the rapidly changing environment rather than as dominant, permanent objects with deterministic forms. In a characteristic Japanese manner, boundaries are frequently defined without being rigidly established. Areas are surrounded by multiple layers of screens and other thin elements, which take advantage of lightweight and translucent/transparent materials (LCD glass, synthetic films, infrared-reflecting polycarbonate membranes, etc.) as well as the latest technologies in lighting, including lasers, and various computer-controlled spatial articulations. In this way buildings can be more effectively engaged in, but also protected from, their environments. Similarly, architects' critical intentions are not necessarily relinquished or neutralized; while partaking in the life of the city, these designs are often capable of resisting the increasingly trivializing practices of consumerist urbanism.[26] However, this also means that Japanese architecture has become as paradoxical as the urban culture in which it is inescapably conceived.

Since the mid-1980s the flourishing economy and the related real-estate boom in Japan have prompted many "enlightened" developers and, even more importantly, government agencies to initiate and promote large-scale urban projects with high-quality architecture. The Momochi (1989) and Nexus Kashii (1991), both in Fukuoka, and especially the unique and still-ongoing Kumamoto Art Polis (K.A.P.) (1987 onward) in Kumamoto Prefecture have already proven to be highly successful, setting the trend for similar future projects elsewhere in the country.[27] They were pursued with the purpose of finding innovative solutions to the problems of contemporary and future modes of urban living, public housing, etc., and realized through the leadership of Arata Isozaki (as commissioner of these projects) and with the contributions of numerous invited leading Japanese and foreign architects.

Many of the older generation architects, such as Kurokawa, Takeyama, Maki, and Aida, have altered course and thus continue to be active as part of the vanguard: Maki's Fujisawa Municipal Gymnasia (1984), Spiral Building (1985) and Tepia Science Pavilion (1989), both in Tōkyō, and Nippon Convention Center in Chiba (1990)—as well as his receipt of the Pritzker Prize, the most prestigious international award in architecture—attest well to this leadership. In 1991, Takeyama completed his most outstanding work to date, the Tōkyō Port Terminal, which was inspired, partially at least, by Russian constructivist architecture. The ever-prolific Kurokawa, now following his new "philosophy of symbiosis," has designed such award-winning projects as the Hiroshima City Museum of Contemporary Art (1988) and the Nara City Museum of Photography (1992), while Tange has completed the heavily monumental and highly controversial New Tōkyō City Hall (1991). Kazuo Shinohara also has maintained his influential position; his unique Tōkyō Institute of Technology Centennial Hall (1987) (fig. 32) is surely among the milestones of late-twentieth-century Japanese architecture.

32. Tōkyō Institute of Technology Centennial Hall, Tōkyō, 1987, Kazuo Shinohara

33. Kazama House, Kawaguchi, Saitama Pref., 1987, Takefumi Aida; view from nearby cemetery

Hiromi Fujii, who continues to be involved in academia, has resumed his architectural practice and produced the Ushimado International Arts Festival Building (1985) and Project Mizoe 1 in Iizuka (1988). Though largely derivative of his previous experimentation with semiology and structuralism in architecture, these new works point toward poststructuralist interpretations. Concluding his Toy Block House series of the late 1970s and early 1980s, Takefumi Aida presently produces his "architecture of fluctuation"[28] in the Kazama House in Kawaguchi (1987) (fig. 33), the Tōkyō War Dead Memorial Park (1988), and the Saitō Memorial Hall of Shibaura Institute of Technology in Ōmiya (1990), among others. Hiroshi Hara's recently developed design philosophy based on "modality in architecture"[29] has found expression in several large and spectacular works, including his Yamatō International Building in Tōkyō (1987), Iida City Museum (1988), and Umeda Sky Building in Ōsaka (1993).

Continuing his interest and artistry in modulating and layering architectural spaces and introducing natural phenomena in buildings of unfinished concrete, Tadao Ando has expanded his repertoire by successfully transcribing many features of his earlier designs into larger, public complexes, quickly increasing in number. Yet, similar to most other Japanese architects, he has attenuated his explicitly negative stance toward the city, while not abandoning an implicitly critical position altogether. Therefore, although the courtyard arrangement reappears in various configurations in many of his urban projects, it is now articulated so as to assure more open overall spatial compositions than before. As the Rokkō Housing in Kōbe (1983 and 1993), Festival in Naha (1984), Time's in Kyōto (1984 and 1991), Galleria Akka in Ōsaka (1988), and Collezione in Tōkyō (1990) best exemplify, Ando's new architecture engages the built environment more actively, although still selectively.

Ando has also undertaken significant cultural and ecclesiastical commissions: three Christian churches and a Buddhist temple, in addition to numerous museums and art galleries. In the designs of the Chapel on Mount Rokkō in Kōbe (1986), Church on the Water in Tomamu (1988), Water Temple on Awaji Island (1991), Children's Museum Hyōgo in Himeji (1989), Forest of Tombs Museum in Kaō-machi, Kumamoto (1992), and the Chikatsu-Asuka Historical Museum, near Ōsaka (1994), he has complemented his previous modes of integrating architecture into its natural environment by responding to both the landscape and the land. Many of these projects incorporate the increased use of not only light, wind, and water, but also earth as "architectural" element, insofar as these buildings are designed with sunken courtyards and extensive subterranean realms and/or are buried considerably in the ground. Today Ando is recognized as one of the most accomplished architects in both Japan and the world (fig. 34).

34. Tennōji Fair Main Pavilion, Ōsaka City, 1987, Tadao Ando

The 1980s witnessed the maturation of not only Ando, but also his entire generation. Many of them had been previous disciples of older masters, such as Shinohara and Hara, while others followed their own, independent paths from the very beginning. Among the latter, Yoshio Taniguchi (b. 1937) emerged as the most remarkable example. His growth as an architect and urbanist is well represented by a series of significant public buildings that began with the much-acclaimed Ken Dōmon Museum of Photography in Sakata (1983), and

35. Keiō Shōnan-Fujisawa Junior-Senior High School, Fujisawa, Kanagawa Pref., 1992, Yoshio Taniguchi

has led to such recent masterpieces as the Marugame Genichirō-Inokuma Museum of Contemporary Art in Marugame (1991) and the Keiō-Shōnan-Fujisawa Junior-Senior High School in Fujisawa (1992) (fig. 35). Although a straightforward approach to design and the "simplicity" of the modern language of architecture—along with a heightened sensibility toward the natural environment and phenomena—continue to characterize Taniguchi's work, his latest projects reveal an increased sophistication in spatial articulation and skill in shaping the urban fabric in which they either find themselves or, alternatively, what they intend to create.

The so-called Shinohara School of the early 1970s "graduated" several outstanding architects; among them Itsuko Hasegawa (b. 1941) and Toyo Ito became leading figures and have achieved by now both national and international reputations. The novel lines of their designs are guided by their theories and unique sensibilities toward contemporary life and urban society. Hasegawa has developed an approach that regards "architecture as another nature"[30]; Ito, on the other hand, has come to understand the dynamics, volatility, and mobility of today's Japanese city as the domain or stage of "urban nomads."[31] In her recent architecture, best represented by the Bizan Hall in Shizuoka (1984) (fig. 36), House in Nerima, Tōkyō (1986) and the highly acclaimed Shōnandai Cultural Center in Fujisawa (1991), Hasegawa combines her concern for the natural environment with a keen interest in new materials and technologies, all filtered through what she calls a "feminine"[32] sensibility. Changing the course of his architecture in the 1970s, Ito initiated a new direction of design with the completion of his own house, the Silver Hut in Tōkyō (1984), which alluded to the lightweight, "primitive" and, above all, mobile structures of the nomads. In his consecutive projects of increasing scale and

36. Bizan Hall, Shizuoka, Shizuoka Pref., 1984, Itsuko Hasegawa

37. Egg of Winds (Okawabata River City 21, Town Gate B), Tōkyō, 1991, Toyo Ito

significance, he has further elaborated this "architecture as phenomenalism"[33] by taking advantage of both natural phenomena, such as topography, light, and wind, and the latest information, media, and even computer technology, as first seen in the Tower of Winds, Yokohama (1986). The Guest House for Sapporo Breweries in Eniwa, Hokkaidō (1989), Egg of Winds in Tōkyō (1991) (fig. 37), Yatsushiro Municipal Museum (1991), and Shimosuwa Municipal Museum (1993), among others, are characterized by the extensive application of lightweight, ferrous materials, screens, and structures as well as systems of softly undulating, thin, and reflective metallic roofs aspiring to the aesthetics of some industrial buildings.

A similar strain of "industrial vernacular" is manifest in the work of numerous other architects, including Kazunari Sakamoto (b. 1943)—an early follower of Shinohara—who, in the House F in Tōkyō (1987) (fig. 38) and most especially the large-scale Hoshida Common City Housing in Katano, Ōsaka (1991), provides other convincing examples of this straightforward yet responsive contemporary mode of design. Riken Yamamoto (b. 1945), a former student of Hiroshi Hara, attracted national as well as international attention with his residential complexes, the Rotunda Building in Yokohama (1987) and the Hamlet, Residential Complex in Tōkyō (1988), where he first applied his new design theories interpreting "the city as topography."[34] These, and more recent projects—Hotakubo Public Housing in Kumamoto (1991) and Ryokuen-toshi Interjunction City in Yokohama (1992–94)—feature a range of new materials (Teflon-fiber, translucent acrylic sheets, etc.) in addition to a remarkably fresh spatial quality and explore new forms of urban living.

38. House F, Tōkyō, 1987, Kazunari Sakamoto

39. Inscription House, Tsukuba, Ibaraki Pref., 1987, Yasumitsu Matsunaga

40. K House, Tsukuba, Ibaraki Pref., 1993, Yasumitsu Matsunaga; general view in the evening

Among those who have broadened in a significant way the spectrum of architectural intentions within this generation are Shōei Yoh (b. 1940), Yasumitsu Matsunaga (b. 1941), and, with a new approach to design, Kiko (Monta) Mozuna. Yoh's preoccupation with a renewed architectural tectonic culture and high technology is exemplified by his Aspecta Outdoor Concert Hall (1987) and Misumi Ferry Terminal (1990), both in Kumamoto Prefecture, and Saibu Gas Museum of Phenomenart in Fukuoka (1989). Matsunaga's Inscription House (1987) and K House (1994) in Tsukuba (figs. 39 and 40), Housing in Daita, Tōkyō (1990), and Y's Court Nakahara in Kawasaki (1991) reveal an architecture that aspires as much to the recent modern "industrial vernacular" as to a "cosmic" phenomenology.[35] On the other hand Mozuna, toning down his previous obsession with mythology and cosmology and mobilizing a broad variety of technological innovations together with a new spirit in design, has produced the remarkable Notojima Glass Art Museum and Noto Monzen Family Inn, both of 1991, in Ishikawa Prefecture.

Younger architects, many of whom only began their architectural education after the demise of Metabolism, are even more individualistic than their immediate predecessors in the new wave. Their architecture ranges between extensive symbolism at one end, displayed in the singularly monumental buildings by Shin Takamatsu (b. 1948), and an anti-symbolist, "deconstructivism" at the other, seen, for example, in the exceptionally fluid and ethereal spatial designs of Kazuyo Sejima (b. 1956). The unusually large number and stunning, science-fiction quality of Takamatsu's buildings—including the Origin buildings (1981–86), the Week Building (1986) (fig. 41), and the Syntax (1990), all in Kyōto, the Kirin Plaza in Ōsaka (1987), and the Kunibiki Messe,

41. Week Building, Kyōto City, 1986, Shin Takamatsu

42. Platform 2, Summer House, Kitagoma-gun, Yamanashi Pref., 1990, Kazuyo Sejima

43. Y House, Katsuura, Chiba Pref., 1994, Kazuyo Sejima

44. House in Higashikurume, Tōkyō, 1987, Ryōji Suzuki; interior

Convention Hall in Matsue (1993)—have assured this Kyōto-based designer growing attention and worldwide recognition. Sejima, a former assistant of Toyo Ito, has only a few completed buildings on her record as of now, but the continued skill and sophistication with which she has shaped her two Platform Houses in Katsuura, Chiba Prefecture (1988) and Kitagoma-gun, Yamanashi Prefecture (1990) (fig. 42), Saishunkan Seiyaku Women's Dormitory in Kumamoto (1991), and Y House in Katsuura, Chiba Prefecture (1994) (fig. 43) among others, are sure to guarantee her a significant role in Japanese architecture in the years to come.

Emerging in the late 1980s as other important players on the stage of architecture are Ryōji Suzuki (b. 1944), Hajime Yatsuka (b. 1948), Atsushi Kitagawara (b. 1951), and Kiyoshi Sei Takeyama (b. 1954). Suzuki's highly conceptual, avant-garde architecture—which nevertheless stimulates human sensibility as much as it appeals to the intellect—is represented by his Azabu Edge in Tōkyō (1987) and numerous residential buildings, such as the House in Higashikurume (1987) (fig. 44) and House at Sagi (1991). Yatsuka's interest in the "acceleration of modernism"[36] combined with traits of deconstructivism is shown in his Angelo Tarlazzi Building (1987) and House in Komae (1988) (fig. 45), both in Tōkyō, and Wing Building in Nishinomiya (1991). Kitagawara, in his rapidly growing number of buildings, including the Rise Cinema Complex (1986), Metroca Apartment Building (1989) (fig. 46), and Scala Building (1992), all in Tōkyō, and Santō in Kyōto (1991), pursues a design that is guided by both artistic expression and technological innovation, often reaching the qualities of surrealism. Finally, Takeyama's somewhat Ando-inspired architecture is well exemplified in his Oxy Nogizaka (1987) and Terrazza (1991), both in Tōkyō (fig. 47). Representing the emergence of an even younger generation, the outstanding early work of Hiroshi (b. 1953) and Akiko (b. 1958) Takahashi invites commentary. Previous disciples of Kazuo Shinohara, this husband and wife team achieved its first spectacular success with the designs of the Sakamoto Ryōma Memorial Hall in Kōchi (1991) (fig. 48). Winner of a national competition, the Takahashis' proposal is impressive not only because of its boldly elegant structural solution, but also, and more importantly, because of its remarkably sensitive response to the challenges of the site, situated above a steep segment of the seashore in the south of Shikoku Island. Moreover, the memorial hall has managed to bypass the traps of both the anonymity of universal modernism and historicist, shallow postmodernism; curiously, while floating above the land, almost literally, it is also rooted in it, thereby establishing a truly memorable place of its own.

It is only inevitable that, upon coming of age, this generation, along with its immediate predecessors, including the new wave, will largely be responsible for shaping the character of Japanese architecture at the end of the twentieth century and beyond. Since the 1970s and, more so, 1980s Japanese architects have shown that, after having been influenced by the West for so long, Japanese architecture and design have the qualities and capacity to exert a profound impact on the architecture of the West and even challenge many of its prevailing ideals. At the same time, by achieving leading positions in the world of international architecture in the age of information and globalization, Japanese designers are prompted to free themselves from the obligation of paying homage to the *formal* traditions of their own past.

In this process, however, not every development ensured forward-looking and viable alternatives. The 1980s, especially the latter part of the decade, fueled by anxieties and the ethos of the so-called "bubble economy" in Japan, could be likened to a huge, fast-running, and surrealistic experimental urban laboratory that has yielded, also in the field of architecture, as much excessiveness and cultural nihilism as it has also produced truly innovative results and new possibilities for future explorations. It is only reassuring that many of the emerging directions today appear to build upon the positive results of the 1980s. Yet, while the "burst of the bubble" and the slow down of the economy is likely to curtail further the scope of unrestrained adventures, it will not alleviate all the problems and

45. House in Komae, Tōkyō, 1988, Hajime Yatsuka

46. Metroca Apartment Building, Tōkyō, 1989, Atsushi Kitagawara

47. Terrazza, Tōkyō, 1991, Kiyoshi Sei Takeyama

48. Sakamoto Ryōma Memorial Hall, Kōchi, Kōchi Pref., 1991, Akiko and Hiroshi Takahashi

contradictions that have characterized Japan and its process of modernization and progress from the very beginning. It is therefore safe to say that continued fermenting and paradoxical conditions constitute an overall climate in which, at the end of the century and that of the millennium, Japan's future social, economic, and cultural values will be both nurtured and questioned.

Notes

1. From China, starting in the mid-sixth century AD, Japan imported its writing system; Buddhism, Taoism, and Confucianism; and much of its early architecture, city planning, building types, and construction methods. Korea, that is, the contemporary Kingdom of Paekche, played an important role in transmitting much of the influence coming from China, and, by modifying them, contributed substantially to shaping the early development of Buddhist culture in Japan.
2. The most important aspect of Japan's modernization process was the acquisition of Western technologies and a keen interest in technological progress has been the kernel of Japan's success throughout the twentieth century as well.
3. Initially, after the Meiji restoration in 1868, there were no private or independent architectural offices in Japan. The first such office was established in 1903 by Kingo Tatsuno (1845–1919); others followed, but their number grew slowly before World War II. At the turn of the century much of the design and supervision of buildings, including the Parliament Building, were carried out by the architecture departments of various companies and/or government agencies.
4. The architecture of the *Bunri Ha* was a unique mixture of Viennese Secessionism and European Art Nouveau, blended later on with traits of Russian constructivism. Finally, influenced by functionalism and rationalism, it produced representatives of modernism and even precursors of the International Style in Japan.
5. However, David Stewart argues that Raymond's influence on the evolution of modern Japanese architecture was more limited than has been generally accepted. David Stewart, *The Making of a Modern Japanese Architecture* (Tōkyō and New York: Kōdansha International, 1987): 142.
6. Taut, though recognizing the greatness of the Katsura Villa and Ise Shrine, interpreted them with a somewhat modernist bias and considered them to be the outcome of only purist and functional/rational ideals, and so the direct predecessors of Japanese modernism.
7. One such example was the national competition for the Tōkyō Imperial Museum, Ueno, which was won by Hitoshi Watanabe's project, designed in the Imperial Crown Style (1937) (fig. 3).
8. Such "stripped classicism" in the 1930s, derived from a strongly rational paradigm in architecture, often served the ideological purposes of fascism, yet yielded excellent examples of high-modernism in both Japan and Europe, best represented by Giuseppe Terragni's Casa del Fascio in Como (1936).
9. The "New Japan Style" was coined by Robin Boyd in his *New Directions in Japanese Architecture* (New York: George Braziller, 1968), 28.
10. The Yamanishi Press and Broadcasting Center in fact transplants ideas from the City in the Sky, one of the numerous futuristic urban plans by the Metabolists. Tange's design methodology of this time was also influenced by the principles of structuralism as they were first elaborated in linguistics.
11. These two groups, both formed in 1960, obviously influenced each other but, despite their similarities, there were differences between them. Archigram was not only more theoretical in orientation, but also ideologically more oppositional toward the prevailing establishment of the profession and other aspects of society. The Metabolists, on the other hand, were riding on the "establishment" of a quickly developing, technology-oriented society, plus the growing eagerness and capability of large construction companies. Japanese designers, as opposed to their European counterparts, were more preoccupied with the structural and formal potentials of a new, man-made, urban realm often envisioned and built over the sea or on artificial land, including landfill.
12. The futuristic, large-scale proposals of the Metabolists were also propelled by the designers' intention to alleviate the worsening congestion, lack of available land, and overpopulation brought about by the explosive urban developments of the 1960s in Japan.
13. A few of Kurokawa's early books are:
Urban Design (Tōkyō: Kinokunya Shōten, 1965)
Action Architecture: The Aesthetics of Metabolism (Tōkyō: Shōkokusha, 1967)

Homo Movens (Tōkyō: Chūō Kōron Shinsho, 1969)
Conception of Metabolism (Tōkyō: Shiratori Shuppan, 1972)
14. Most probably Kurokawa leads the list of those Japanese architects who have a growing number of commissions abroad. He has completed buildings on all five continents, in the United States, Western and Eastern Europe, Australia, Korea, China, France, Germany, and Bulgaria.
15. Some of Maki's recent projects display, in addition to the basic rationality of design, a strain of mannerism that is often related to his increased attention to detailing and craftsmanship.
16. Most of these large construction companies in Japan can trace back their origins to the large carpenter families or "guilds" of the Edo Era (1603–1868). In the mid-nineteenth century they were transformed into quickly developing, contemporary contractors, which, like their predecessors, continue to provide services in both architectural design and construction. Nikken Sekkei Company's predecessor, the Sumitomo Eisen (later on Hasebe and Takegoshi) Design Office was first established as the Architecture Department of Sumitomo Conglomerate (*zaibatsu*) in 1900.
17. Although Shinohara had the most profound impact of the new generation of architects, the other three designers too had considerable influence on their juniors.
18. Kazuo Shinohara, "A House is a Work of Art," *Shinkenchiku* (May 1962): 25.
19. Arata Isozaki, "Rhetoric of the Cylinder," *The Japan Architect* (April 1976): 61–63.
Arata Isozaki, "From Manner, to Rhetoric, to . . ." *The Japan Architect* (April 1976): 64–67.
20. In his theoretical investigations, Maki distinguished among three types of morphologies that constituted the basis of various architectural paradigms. The "compositional form" informed the aesthetic sensibilities of modernism, among others; while the "megaform" guided much of the intentions of the Metabolists in Japan. Maki's own "group-form" was derivative of certain urban vernacular architectures and guided the evolution of his contextual design.
21. Roland Barthes, *Empire of Signs*, trans. Richard Howard (New York: Hill and Wang, 1982).
22. Minoru Takeyama, on the exhibition installation of ArchiteXt in Tōkyō, 1971.
23. All quotes are from the architects themselves first spelled out at the 1971 ArchiteXt exhibition and repeated in various publications thereafter. See for example *ArchiteXt, Japan Architect* (June 1975).
24. Hiroshi Hara, "Anti-Traditional Architectural Contrivance," ed. Kenneth Frampton, *A New Wave of Japanese Architecture* (New York: IAUS, 1978), 39.
25. Botond Bognar, "Between Reality and Fiction: Japanese Architecture in the 1990s or the New Fin de Siècle," in Botond Bognar, ed., *Japanese Architecture 2 (Architectural Design Profile* 99) (London: 1992): 9.
26. Such resistance is forwarded in a variety of ways: by virtue of "the aesthetics of minimalism," "industrial vernacular" and, ultimately, through a criticism of prevailing modes of representation.
27. Within K.A.P. projects on various urban and rural locations in the prefecture, many small- and large-scale public complexes have been completed. The unique and high-quality designs of museums, office buildings, schools, public housing, parks, toilets, and bridges are meant to promote an architectural and environmental culture with an increasing standard. Since the beginning of the slowing-down of the economy in 1991, similar programs have been cut back, but the K.A.P. continues even on a reduced scale.
28. Takefumi Aida, "From Toy Blocks to an Architecture of Fluctuation," *Shinkenchiku* (June 1987): 203.
29. Hiroshi Hara, "Modality—Central Concept of Contemporary Architecture," *The Japan Architect* (November–December 1986): 24.
30. Itsuko Hasegawa, "Architecture as Another Nature and Recent Projects," *Aspects of Modern Architecture: Architectural Design Profile* 90, ed. Andreas Papadakis (1991): 14.
31. Toyo Ito, "Architecture Sought After By Android," *The Japan Architect* (June 1988): 9.
32. Hasegawa, "Architecture as Another Nature," 15.
33. Toyo Ito, "Vortex and Current—On Architecture as Phenomenalism," in Botond Bognar (ed.). *Japanese Architecture 2, Architectural Design Profile* 99 (London: 1992): 22.
34. Riken Yamamoto, "The City as Topography," *The Japan Architect* (November–December 1986): 42.
35. About his Daita Housing Project, Matsunaga writes that its "configuration reminds one of the model of the bubblelike structure of the universe which the latest cosmic theory has verified." Correspondence with author, 23 August 1990.
36. Hajime Yatsuka, "Angelo Tarlazzi, Tōkyō, 1987" in Botond Bognar, *The New Japanese Architecture* (New York: Rizzoli, 1990): 213.

BUILDINGS BY GEOGRAPHICAL LOCATION

Japanese addresses are written in the reverse order of English addresses; that is, starting with the largest entity and proceeding to the smallest one. In this book, however, the addresses follow the Western order. Moreover, Japanese addresses rarely identify names of streets or roads because the Japanese traditionally do not name them; only recently do some major avenues (*-dōri*) carry names, and even then they are seldom, if at all, used in addresses. What are named are the areas: zones, districts, wards, municipalities, etc. Numbers refer to smaller units—blocks and buildings—yet the numbering of buildings does not follow an order of location; rather, buildings are numbered in the order of their completion and therefore appear in a random sequence.

The most important terms that are used in addresses:

-chihō = region (such as Chūbu-chihō = Chūbu Region)
-ken = prefecture (Nagano-ken = Nagano Prefecture)
-to = prefecture (only in the case of Tōkyō, Tōkyō-to = Tōkyō Metropolis)
-fu = prefecture (only in the cases of Ōsaka and Kyōto, such as Ōsaka-fu and Kyōto-fu = Ōsaka and Kyōto prefectures)
-gun = county (Yufutsu-gun = Yufutsu County—on Hokkaidō)
-shi = city (Nagano-shi = Nagano)
-machi = town (Shimosuwa-machi = Shimosuwa) or quarter (in large cities)
-ku = ward (in larger cities, such as Shibuya-ku—in Tōkyō)
-chō = small town, or municipality, or district (in large cities)
-mura = village (Toga-mura = Toga Village)
-chōme = block (such as 1-chōme, 2-chōme, etc.)

In the case of Hokkaidō, where the entire island is a prefecture, the reference to prefecture is dropped by the Japanese. In the case of Tōkyō, Japanese addresses are written as "Tōkyō-to," "Tōkyō" (Prefecture), or "Metropolitan Tōkyō," and the various wards (-ku) indicate that the location is within the twenty-three-ward Tōkyō city itself. In this guide, "Tōkyō" alone always indicates Tōkyō City. When the location is outside this area, the town or municipality is followed by "Tōkyō Prefecture." In the case of Ōsaka and Kyōto, when the location is within these two cities, Japanese addresses are indicated by "Ōsaka-shi" and "Kyōto-shi," that is, Ōsaka City and Kyōto City, and omit Ōsaka-fu and Kyōto-fu (Ōsaka Prefecture and Kyōto Prefecture). In this guide, we follow the same system, thus "Ōsaka Prefecture" and "Kyōto Prefecture" appear only when the location (municipality) is outside of Ōsaka and Kyōto cities. In the following entries, "(see map)" indicates that the location of the building is marked on the relevant city map preceding the entry.

SAMPLE ENTRIES

Municipalities are introduced by the following symbols:

郡   *gun* = county

都   *to* or *miyako* = capital, metropolis

市   *shi* = city

町   *chō* = ward, sector; *machi* = town

村   *son* or *mura* = village

市 **MUNICIPALITY**

**Major Entry
(in black type)
Date**
Name of building in Japanese
Architect Name
Address Number, Street,
District, City, Prefecture
Transport By train, streetcar,
and/or bus; includes addition-
al time by taxi or foot
Visitation Days and hours
open to public; phone number

**Minor Entry
(in shaded type)
Date**
Name of building in Japanese
Architect Name
Address Number, Street,
District, City, Prefecture
Transport By train, streetcar,
and/or bus; includes addition-
al time by taxi or foot
Visitation Days and hours
open to public; phone number

The image or images and corresponding large-print
text refer to the major entry on the page (minor
entries are not pictured in this book). The image or
images and corresponding large-print text refer to
the major entry on the page (minor entries are not
pictured in this book). The image or images and
corresponding large-print text refer to the major
entry on the page (minor entries are not pictured in
this book). The image or images and corresponding
large-print text refer to the major entry on the page
(minor entries are not pictured in this book).

HOKKAIDŌ REGION

Hokkaidō, the northernmost and second largest of the four main islands of Japan, was the last to join the country in the sixteenth century, and also the last to be fully settled. Even today, Hokkaidō, with only slightly more than 5.5 million inhabitants, is the most sparsely populated region. As a last frontier, it features the largest wide-open landscapes in Japan. Although there are ranges of mountains, the extensive plains offer the best uninterrupted areas for agriculture. The climate includes four seasons and is more continental-like than the rest of the country; the summer is mild and short, with less rain, while the winter is rather long and cold with plenty of snow.

Hokkaidō was originally populated by the Ainu, whose race and culture, unlike those of the Japanese, have close ties with the continent, particularly Siberia. Discriminated by the Japanese for a long time, the Ainu today form a distinct though shrinking minority on the island. Therefore, the limited number of historic sites and structures on Hokkaidō do, only in small part, include references to the Ainu past; the remaining are related to the early developments of the region after the Meiji Restoration in the mid-nineteenth century. These involve settlements around important ports, such as Hakodate and Otaru, where some of the Meiji Era (1868–1912) urban districts and/or significant pieces of architecture are preserved. One interesting example is the massive wall structure of Goryōkaku, the only Western-style fortress in Japan, which was constructed with a pentagon layout near Hakodate in 1864.

Hokkaidō's industrial, urban, and cultural developments entered a new, rapid stage after World War II, and were given fresh impetus with the advent of the economic boom in the 1980s. The 1985 completion of the famous 33.4 mile/53.9 kilometer Seikan Tunnel—the longest underwater tunnel in the world, providing direct train service between Honshū and Hokkaidō—further contributed to the progress of this northern island. Yet, the number and size of important cities here still cannot be compared to those on the main island of Honshū. The few major urban areas in the Hokkaidō region include Hakodate, Kushiro, Tomakomai, Asahigawa, and, the largest of all, Sapporo (population 1.66 million), one of Japan's growing number of international cities. Significant architectural examples are also relatively few, most of them located around or within urban areas such as Sapporo and Kushiro. Minoru Takeyama (b. 1934, Sapporo) and Kiko Mozuna (b. 1941, Kushiro), both natives of Hokkaidō, are the most active contemporary architects here, but others, including Toyo Ito and Tadao Ando, also have completed outstanding projects in this region, and the number of prominent architectural examples is growing.

HOKKAIDŌ PREFECTURE

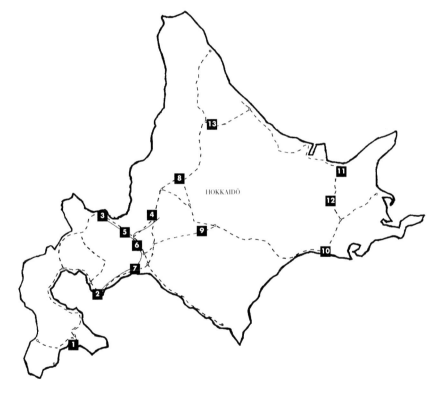

1 Hakodate, page 38
2 Muroran
3 Otaru, page 39
4 Mikasa, page 39
5 Sapporo, page 40

6 Eniwa, page 45
7 Tomakomai, page 46
8 Asahigawa
9 Tomamu, page 47
10 Kushiro, page 48

11 Kiyosato-chō, page 51
12 Teshikaga-chō, page 51
13 Shimokawa-chō, page 51

Hakodate Khristos Orthodox Church 1916

Hakodate Harisutosu-Sei Kyōkai
Architect Izo Kawamura
Address 3–13 Motomachi, Hakodate, Hokkaidō
Transport From JR Hakodate Station: streetcar to Jujigai stop and 8-minute walk uphill
The church is an Important National Cultural Property.

The slopes of the Motomachi area are the site of numerous Western-type buildings. After Japan's opening to the rest of the world, many foreign traders settled in Hakodate, the southernmost part of Hokkaidō. The Old Russian Consulate and Old Public Hall are also in the vicinity.

Founded in 1861, the Church burned down in 1907, after which the present structure was completed by 1916. The white walls and Byzantine domes of the small masonry structure reveal its Russian origin and denomination.

Hakodate Ward Old Public Hall 1910

Hakodate-Ku Kyū-Kōkaidō
Architect Asajiro Konishi
Address 11-13, Motomachi, Hakodate, Hokkaidō

Transport From JR Hakodate Station: streetcar to Jujigai stop and 12-minute walk uphill (6-minute walk from the Hakodate Khristos Orthodox Church)
The hall is an Important National Cultural Property, and a well-maintained, colonial, two-story, wooden building.

**Old Japanese Mail
Shipping Company
Otaru Branch (now
Otaru City Museum)
1906**
*Kyū Nippon Yūsen Otaru
Shiten,* now *Otaru Shiritsu
Hakubutsu-kan*
Architect Shichijiro Sadachi
Address 7-8, Ironai-chō
3-chōme, Otaru, Hokkaidō
Transport Train—JR Hako-
date line to Otaru Station:
north exit and 8-minute walk
The museum is a two-story
stone building.

**Bank of Japan
Otaru Branch
1912**
Nihon Ginkō Otaru Shiten
Architects Kingo Tatsuno and
Uheiji Nagano
Address 11–16, Ironai-chō
1-chōme, Otaru, Hokkaidō
Transport Train—JR Hako-
date line to Otaru Station:
north exit and 5-minute walk
The bank is a two-story
masonry building.

**Hotel Otaru Marittimo
(interior)
1989**
Architect Nigel Coates (U.K.)
Address 3-1, Ironai-chō
1-chōme, Otaru, Hokkaidō
Transport Train—JR Hakodate line to Otaru Station:
north exit and 5-minute walk

市 **MIKASA**

This small group of buildings is dominated by a
cylindrical glass volume with an inverted conical
roof. The design is further enlivened by the visibility of the radial, lacy steel structure and the applied
primary colors. While the circular plan expresses
the designer's intention to blend this industrial
building in its natural environment, it generates
images—stadium, amphitheater, etc.—that seem to
conflict with its function as a factory. Takeyama
calls this a "counter-positional" design method.

**Pepsi Cola Company
Bottling Plant
1972**
Pepsi Kōjō
Architect Minoru Takeyama
Address 127, Okayama,
Mikasa, Hokkaidō
Transport From JR Sapporo
Station: Train—Hakodate
main line to Iwamizawa Station
and 10 minutes by taxi (the
plant is along Route 12)

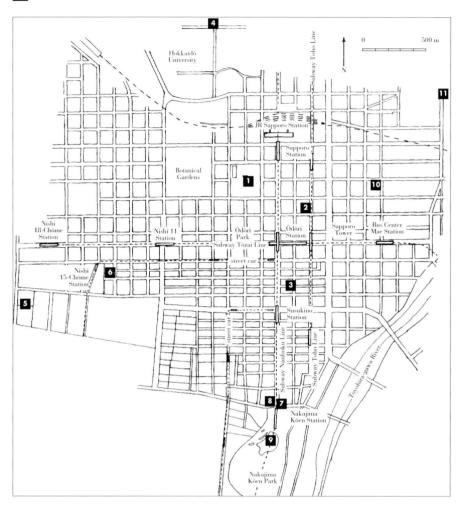

1. Old Hokkaidō Government Building (Dochō), page 41
2. Clock Tower (of previous Sapporo Agricultural College), page 41
3. Tattoo Building, page 41
4. Model Barn of Hokkaidō University, page 41
5. Atelier Indigo, page 42
6. Nakamura Memorial Hospital, page 43
7. Moonsoon Restaurant, page 43
8. Noah's Ark Restaurant, page 43
9. Hōheikan, page 44
10. Sapporo Factory, page 44
11. Sapporo Beer Brewery and Museum, page 44

Patterned after American baroque architecture, the red brick building of the Old Hokkaidō Government Building is an important landmark in downtown Sapporo, and an excellent representation of Western-style eclectic architecture of the Meiji Era (1868–1912). Its construction followed the demise of its predecessor, which burned down in 1879. The new structure, too, was badly damaged in a 1909 fire, but was rebuilt in 1911 and served as the Prefectural Offices of Hokkaidō until a larger modern building was constructed next to it in 1969. At that time the old brick building was restored to its original form and opened to the public. The entire complex (the new administration center and the preserved old building in front) is located in a large enclosed garden, which features many trees and two ponds in an area of four city blocks.

Old Hokkaidō Government Building (Dochō) 1888

Hokkaidō Kyuhon Chōsha
Architect Seijiro Hirai
Address Kita-3, Nishi-5, Chūō-ku, Sapporo, Hokkaidō (see map)
Transport From JR Sapporo Station: south exit and 5-minute walk
Visitation Building: 9:00–17:00, Saturday 9:00–13:00 (closed Sundays and national holidays); Garden: 8:00–21:00 (June–September); 8:00–18:00 (October–May)
The building is an Important National Cultural Property.

Clock Tower (of previous Sapporo Agricultural College), 1877

Tokeidai
Architect William Wheeler (U.S.)
Address Kita-1, Nishi-2, Chūō-ku, Sapporo, Hokkaidō (see map)
Transport From JR Sapporo Station: Subway—Nanboku line to Ōdōri Station and 2-minute walk; or from JR Sapporo Station: south exit and 6-minute walk southeast
Visitation 9:00–16:00 (closed Mondays and the day after national holidays)

Tattoo Building 1989

Five Fox-Tattoo
Architect Shin Takamatsu
Address 11-4, Nishi-3, Minami-3, Chūō-ku, Sapporo, Hokkaidō (see map)
Transport Subway—Nanboku line to Susukino Station and 5-minute walk
Visitation Open daily, tel: (011) 221-6014
The Tattoo Building, less than twelve feet/four meters wide but about seventy-two feet/twenty meters high with two slim, vertical skylights, is between two larger structures.

Model Barn of Hokkaidō University 1871

Hokkaidō Daigaku Daini Nōjō
Architect William Wheeler (U.S.)
Address Kita-8, Nishi-5, Kita-ku, Sapporo, Hokkaidō (see map)
Transport From JR Sapporo Station: north exit and 10-minute walk to the campus entrance (building is within the campus)
The barn is an Important National Cultural Property.

市 SAPPORO

Atelier Indigo
1976

Architect Minoru Takeyama
Address Minami-4, Nishi-18,
Chūō-ku, Sapporo, Hokkaidō
(see map)
Transport Subway—Tōzai
line to Nishi 18-chōme Station and 5-minute walk south

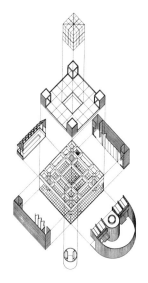

The small building is Takeyama's own Sapporo branch office; it was designed with some unusual features that include a group of mobile elements above the roof. The Atelier Indigo is also used on occasions for invited performances and small concerts, while the rooftop device in various configurations is often used for temporary exhibitions and art shows. Therefore the flexibility for rearrangement of spaces, derivative of the crisply modular design, was of primary importance. With its "space synthesizer"—a manually operable hinged system of large, cubical, wooden "boxes"—Takeyama's design is capable of yielding "in an ad hoc fashion the constantly altering combinations of architectural language" with different meanings, as he himself described the project (Minoru Takeyama, "Atelier Indigo," *JA* [January 1978]: 21).

Born in Sapporo, but now living in Tōkyō, Takeyama has completed several projects in Hokkaidō.
Among them the largest is this hospital that spe-
cializes in neurosurgery. The complex is comprised
of two blocks: a fifteen-story patient ward and a
five-story operating room ward. The design makes
extensive use of curving lines and vaulted roofs,
reminding the observer of the forms of the human
skull. In between the two blocks a multistory public
space is arranged; with its crossing bridges, stairways, and natural lighting, it is the most impressive
part of the architecture.

Nakamura Memorial Hospital 1980

Nakamura Kinen Byōin
Architect Minoru Takeyama
Address Nishi-14, Minami-1,
Chūō-ku, Sapporo, Hokkaidō
(see map)
Transport Subway—Tōzai
line to Nishi 11-chōme Station and 3-minute walk to
southeast; or streetcar to
Nishi 15-chōme stop and a
few steps to the east

Moonsoon Restaurant (interior), 1990

Architect Zaha Hadid (U.K.)
(with Studio 9)
Address 287-4, Minami-9,
Nishi-4, Chūō-ku, Sapporo,
Hokkaidō (see map)
Transport Subway—Nanboku line to Nakajima Kōen
Station and 3-minute walk to
southwest to Kita Club
Building.
The fragmentary, colorful
composition—Hadid's first
completed work—is located
within the Kita Club, a building by Mitsuru Kaneko.

Noah's Ark Restaurant 1988

Architect Nigel Coates (U.K.)
Address Minami-9, Nishi-4,
Chūō-ku, Sapporo, Hokkaidō
(see map)
Transport Subway—Nanboku line to Nakajima Kōen
Station and 3-minute walk to
southwest (across the road
from Moonsoon)
As if directly lifted from some
fairy-tale picture book for
children, the Ark is designed
as a stage set and stands for
an explicitly representational
or "narrative architecture."

🏛 SAPPORO

Hōheikan
1880

Architect Yoshiyuki Adachi
Address Nakajima Park,
Minami-11, Nishi-4, Chūō-
ku, Sapporo, Hokkaidō
(see map)
Transport Subway—Nanbo-
ku line to Nakajima-Kōen
Station and 7-minute walk to
southwest
Visitation 9:00–17:00 daily
The building is an Important
National Cultural Property.

A prominent representative of Western-style wood-
en clapboard architecture, Hōheikan was built as a
hotel. Soon after its completion, it was used as the
residence of the visiting Meiji Emperor. The building originally faced Ōdōri Park, but in 1958 was
relocated to its present site in the Nakajima Kōen
Park. The structure exemplifies how Japanese
builders in the early Meiji Era, who had no training
in Western-style architecture, used Japanese construction methods in imitating a foreign design.
The blending of Western and Japanese design elements, rather than diminishing the quality of architecture, resulted in an attractive building.

Sapporo Factory
1992

Architect Minoru Takeyama
Address Kita-2, Higashi-4,
Chuō-ku, Sapporo, Hokkaidō
(see map)
Transport From JR Sapporo
Station: 10 minutes by bus,
or 5 minutes by taxi, or
15-minute walk
Takeyama created the large
commercial complex of shops,
restaurants, and health clubs
by reconstructing the old
brick buildings of a previous
Sapporo factory (1876) and
adding some new wings and a
huge and spectacular atrium
space.

Sapporo Beer Brewery
and Museum
1890

Architect Anonymous
Address Kita-7, Higashi-9,
Higashi-ku, Sapporo,
Hokkaidō (see map)
Transport Municipal Bus 3
to Kitahachijō, Higashinana-
chōme stop and 5-minute walk
Visitation Brewery: 11:00–
21:00; Museum: 9:00–15:40
(September–May), 8:40–
16:40 (June–August)
The complex, established in
1876 by the Commissioner of
Colonization (*Kaitakushi*),
was built in its present form
in 1890.

Historic Village of
Hokkaidō, Village
Museum of Meiji and
Taishō Eras
1868–1926

Hokkaidō Kaitaku-no Mura
Address 50-1, Onopporō,
Atsubetsu-chō, Atsubetsu-ku,
Sapporo, Hokkaidō
Transport From JR Sapporo
Station: Train—JR Chitōse
line to Shin-Sapporo Station;
or Subway—Tōzai line to
Shin-Sapporo Terminal and
5 minutes by taxi
Visitation 9:30–16:30 (closed
Mondays)
The museum features excel-
lent Hokkaidō architecture.

Guest House for Sapporo Breweries 1989

Sapporo Bīru Hokkaidō Kōjō Gesto Hausu
Architect Toyo Ito
Address 542-1, Toiso, Eniwa, Hokkaidō
Transport From Chitōse Airport: 15 minutes by taxi; from JR Sapporo Station: Train—JR Chitōse line to Eniwa Station and 5 minutes by taxi (the brewery with its guest house is located along Route 36)

The earth-covered building is integrated into its hilly natural environment—reminiscent of Scandinavian landscapes—which unfolds as a large "dishlike" sunken garden behind the curving contour of the guest house. The entranceway, skylights, and ventilating towers are highlighted by "airplane wings" floating above them. In a similar manner, the elevation facing the garden is shaded from the sun by an "independent" metallic screen. In addition to using earth as an architectural element, Ito employed the latest products of media and high technology; the "garden of light" features a series of stainless steel, triangular, prismatic columns with speakers to bring recorded music to the visitors and large blocks of liquid crystal glass, which seem to flicker as they change from transparent to a frosted, milky, translucent quality according to the rhythm and intensity of the music.

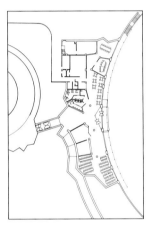

Hotel Beverly Tom (now Hotel East Japan) 1973

Architect Minoru Takeyama
Address 69, Nakano, Tomakomai, Hokkaidō
Transport From JR Tomakomai Station: 5 minutes by taxi (the hotel is along Route 36)

The Hotel Beverly Tom, with its cylindrical guest-room tower and *L*-shaped, low-profile wings housing a reception area, restaurants, and other public facilities, marks the corner of a busy intersection. At the front of the hotel, a vertical segment one quarter of the cylinder is "removed" to open up the building toward the residential areas and the range of mountains in the far distance, while the rear of the block toward the nearby industrial port remains relatively closed. The originally black cast-aluminum-covered tower is capped with an open, geodesic dome that defines an attractive rooftop space and terrace. Moreover, the numerous light bulbs placed at every intersection of the dome's structural elements evoke the image of a curious planetarium. Regrettably, the hotel's new owner has painted the entire exterior white, significantly altering its appearance.

Church on the Water
1988
Mizu no Kyōkai
Architect Tadao Ando
Address Tomamu, Shimu-
kappu-mura, Yufutsu-gun,
Hokkaidō (the Church is within the compound of Hotel
Alpha Tomamu)
Transport From JR Sapporo
Station: Train—JR Sekishō line
to Tomamu Station (2 hours)
and 5 minutes by the hotel's
own shuttle bus to the hotel
Visitation Inquire at hotel
reception; daily guided tours to
see interior at 17:00 (except
during wedding ceremonies)

One of Ando's most spectacular projects, the small chapel, owned by Hotel
Alpha Tomamu, is used primarily for wedding ceremonies. Located in a pastoral landscape of the northernmost island of Japan, the design takes advantage of this setting by integrating the structure with nature in a profoundly
poetic manner. Ando's articulation of all the project's elements—the concrete
walls, the shallow, stepped pool, the opening of the interior toward the exteri-
or, and the positioning of the cross in the water in front of the chapel—reveals
both traditional Japanese and Nordic sensibility, best represented by the work
of Gunnar Asplund and Kaija and Heikki Sirén. Particularly attractive is the
approach and entrance to the church: along the extended and intricate path
one experiences, in a multiplicity of ways, both the landscape and the architecture, which, by virtue of Ando's artistry, mutually enhance each other.

🕌 KUSHIRO

1 Kushiro Castle Hotel,
page 48

2 Anti-Dwelling Box
(Mozuna House), page 48

3 Kushiro Fisherman's
Wharf Moo, page 49

4 Kushiro City Museum,
page 50

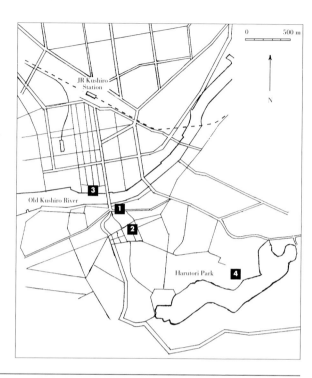

Kushiro Marshland Museum and Observatory 1984

Kushiro Shitsugen Tembōdai
Architect Kiko (Monta) Mozuna
Address 6-11, Hokuto, Kushiro, Hokkaidō
Transport From JR Kushiro Station: Bus—Tsurui-sen or Kawayū-sen line to Shitsugen-Tembōdai
Visitation Open daily, tel: (0154) 56-2424

The horizontally stretching, brick-faced building overlooking an open plateau and marshland is dominated by a three-story central section crowned by a flat dome.

Kushiro Castle Hotel 1987

Architect Kiko (Monta) Mozuna
Address 2-5, Kawa-chō, Kushiro, Hokkaidō (see map)
Transport From JR Kushiro Station: south exit and 12-minute walk (4-minute walk from Fisherman's Wharf Moo, across Nusamai-bashi Bridge)
Visitation Open daily, tel: (0154) 43-2111

Anti-Dwelling Box (Mozuna House) 1972

Architect Kiko (Monta) Mozuna
Address 5-5, Fujimi-chō 1-chōme, Kushiro, Hokkaidō (see map)
Transport From JR Kushiro Station: south exit and 15-minute walk (4-minute walk from Kushiro Castle Hotel
Visitation Private residence, seen only from the outside.

The Kushiro Fisherman's Wharf Moo is a large commercial complex that provides year-round indoor facilities. The design articulates two volumes. A large, multistory building features two atrium spaces, various shops, restaurants, and game parlors. The smaller, yet still extensive, glass structure—like a giant greenhouse or indoor park with trees and other vegetation—serves as a recreational space for Kushiro even during the long and severe winter season. By virtue of careful arrangement as well as special articulation, many details and formal elements of the composition, such as the large, winglike steel construct in front of the main elevation, evoke a unique symbolism. Mozuna's design, inspired as much by his interest in mythology and cosmology as by an industrial architecture, matches the colorful environment of the busy port and adds further excitement to the waterfront.

Kushiro Fisherman's Wharf Moo
1989

Architects Kiko (Monta) Mozuna (with Nikken Sekkei Company)
Address 2-4, Nishiki-chō, Kushiro, Hokkaidō (see map)
Transport From JR Kushiro Station: south exit and 8-minute walk (the Complex is along the north bank of Kyū-Kushiro-gawa River)
Visitation Open daily, tel: (0154) 23-0600

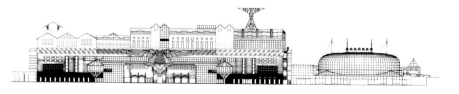

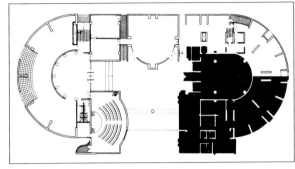

Kushiro City Museum, 1984

Kushiro Shiritsu Hakubutsukan

Architect Kiko (Monta) Mozuna

Address Harutori Park, 1-7, Shunkodai, Kushiro, Hokkaidō (see map)

Transport From JR Kushiro Station: south exit and Bus 8, 15, 17, 21, or 22 to Kagaku-kan-dōri stop and 3-minute walk

Visitation 9:30–17:00 (closed Mondays and national holidays), tel: (0154) 41-5809

A three-story symmetrical building, the Kushiro City Museum stands atop a hill within the Harutori Urban Park. The two halves of the building are identically composed of layers of telescoping circular shapes alluding to what the designer calls a large "bird-with-eggs." Moreover, both the "wings" and the central space of the "egg" are articulated according to Mozuna's interpretation of the Asian world views of "earth-man-heaven," geomancy, and *feng-shui*. In this interior cosmic world of past, present, and future, a double helix staircase acts as a sort of pilgrimage path, and at the same time is reminiscent of the human genetic structure, the DNA.

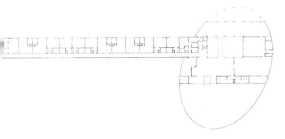

The unusual design of the Hotel P is the result of combining a one-story, oval-shaped block with an interpenetrating, two-story, elongated volume. The former features inner courtyards, reception, and public facilities, while the latter contains twenty-eight guest rooms. Located along a country highway, in an attractive natural environment, Ito's design provides intimate interior spaces while taking advantage of the views of the open landscape. The lobby is approached through a small forecourt filled with a shallow pool of water and enclosed by the softly curving, smooth, concrete walls of the lower block. Thus the entryway is shaped as a "bridge" under an equally long and narrow canopy. The corridors, from which the guest rooms open, are articulated with story-high glass-block walls that comprise the street elevation of the higher hotel block. Contrasting with the intimacy of the "inner landscapes" of the courtyards and the light-filled, but otherwise inward-oriented, corridors, the guest rooms are designed with large windows that overlook the pristine green fields and woods. The hotel is a simple yet very impressive work by Ito.

▥ KIYOSATO-CHŌ

Hotel P in Shari
1992
Hotēru Poluinya
Architect Toyo Ito
Address 815, Aza Kami-Shari, Kiyosato-chō, Shari-gun, Hokkaidō
Transport From JR Kushiro Station: Train—JR Senmo line to Kiyosato Station and 5 minutes by taxi, or call (01522) 5-3800 for hotel's shuttle bus (for guests only)

▥ TESHIKAGA-CHŌ

Ainu Ethnic Museum
1982
Ainu Minzoku Shiryōkan
Architect Kiko (Monta) Mozuna
Address 276-1, Kussharō-kotan, Teshikaga-chō, Kawakami-gun, Hokkaidō
Transport From JR Kushiro Station: Train—JR Kunmo line to Teshikaga Station and 30 minutes by taxi
Visitation Open daily, tel: (01548) 4-2128

▥ SHIMOKAWA-CHŌ

Shimokawa City Tower
1991
Shimokawa Furusatō Kōryūkan
Architect Kiko (Monta) Mozuna
Address 1046, Nishimachi, Shimokawa-chō, Kamikawa-gun, Hokkaidō
Transport From JR Nayōro Station: bus bound for Okoppe or Monbetsu to Shimokawa (35 minutes) and 5-minute walk, or 20 minutes by taxi. By car: Route 40 to Nayōro then Route 239 to Shimokawa.
Visitation Open daily, tel: (011655) 4-2627

TŌHOKU REGION

Despite Japan's growing, nationwide industrialization and urbanization, this region—the northern part of Honshū, the main island of Japan—still remains almost as rural and agricultural as Hokkaidō. Yet Tōhoku, because of its long but slow development, has better preserved certain aspects of traditional lifestyles. Therefore, traditional examples of architecture in Tōhoku, while falling short of other regions to the south, are more frequent than on Hokkaidō and include such significant buildings as the seventeenth-century feudal castle in Hirosaki (1611; rebuilt in 1810), the ancient and much-revered Buddhist monasteries of Yamadera near Yamagata (founded circa AD 860) and Chūson-ji in Hiraizumi (1124), and numerous traditional villages and small towns, such as Tōno, Ōuchi-juku, Yonezawa, Kuroishi, and Kakunodate.

Perhaps with the exception of Sendai (population 900,000), most urban districts are centered around small, regional towns rather than large metropolitan areas. Among these towns, Aomori, Morioka, Akita, Sakata, Yamagata, and Fukushima are the more important. Outstanding pieces of contemporary architecture and urban projects are also fewer and more scattered in the region, when compared to other areas. Kisho Kurokawa, Yoshio Taniguchi, and Kunihiko Hayakawa are among those architects who have designed various, mainly small complexes here.

The climate of Tōhoku, somewhat similar to that of Hokkaidō, has long and rather severe winters and warm summers, although the summers here are more humid than those on that northernmost island.

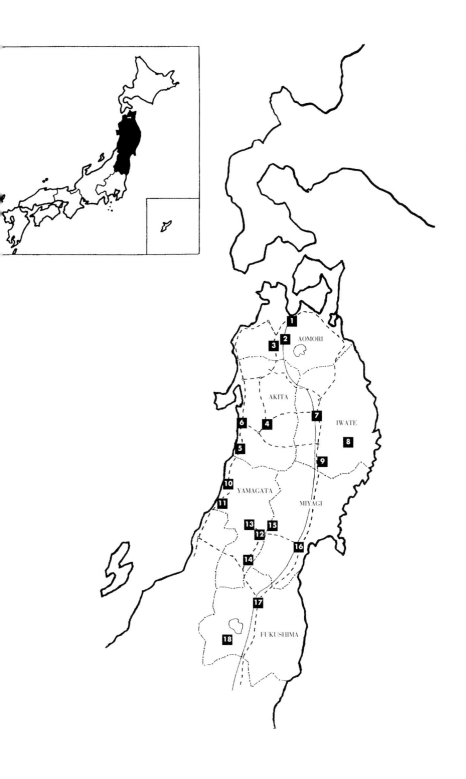

AOMORI

AKITA

IWATE

YAMAGATA

MIYAGI

FUKUSHIMA

🏙 HIROSAKI

Aomori Bank Memorial Hall, 1906
Aomori Ginkō Kinenkan
Architect Sakichi Horie
Address 26, Motonaga-chō, Hirosaki, Aomori Pref.
Transport Train—JR Ou line to Hirosaki Station: west exit and 15-minute walk or bus or taxi (near the southeast corner of Hirosaki-jō Castle)
The hall is an Important National Cultural Property. The architecture of the two-story masonry building displays a mixture of European classical and Russian Orthodox Christian stylistic elements.

🏘 KONOURA-CHŌ

Memorial Hall for Shirase Expeditionary Party of the South Pole 1990
Shirase Nankyoku Tankentai
Architect Kisho Kurokawa
Address 15-3, Iwagata, Kurokawa-Aza, Konoura-chō, Yuri-gun, Akita Pref.
Transport Train—JR Uetsu line to Konoura Station and 6 minutes by taxi
Visitation 9:00–17:00 (March–October) and 9:00–16:00 (November–February) (closed on Mondays and 29 December–3 January), tel: (0184) 38-3765

🏘 KAKUNODATE-MACHI

Nishinagano Primary School, 1992
Kakunodate Chōritsu Nishinagano Shōgakkō
Architect Toyokazu Watanabe
Address 402, Nakadomari, Nishinagano Aza, Kakunodate-machi, Akita Pref.
Transport From JR Morioka Station: Train—JR Tazawako line to Kakunodate Station and 15 minutes by bus or 10 minutes by taxi
The symmetrical building with a *U*-shaped plan and a front court is dominated by various roof elements, all covered with aluminum plates.

🏘 KAKUNODATE-MACHI
Akita Sogo Bank, Kakunodate Branch, 1976

Akita Sogo Ginko Kakunodate Shiten
Architect Mayumi Miyawaki
Address 43-1, Kamishin-machi, Kakunodate-machi, Akita Pref.
Transport From JR Morioka Station: Train—JR Tazawako line to Kakunodate Station and 12-minute walk west

In the 1970s, Miyawaki designed a series of small but innovative branch office buildings for the Akita Sogo Bank, including those in Morioka (1970), Futatsui (1971), and Honjō (1974). They were all shaped according to Miyawaki's theory of "primary architecture," with simple or primary geometric forms painted in primary colors. The articulation of this branch in Kakunodate slightly deviates from the strictly abstract forms of the previous branches in the series to respond to the traditional townscape of Kakunodate, with special regard to the surrounding old, white plastered, urban, merchants' residences/shops called *machiya*.

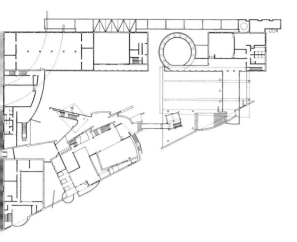

Akita Nissan Complex (La Cage) 1990

Architect Kunihiko Hayakawa
Address 1-59, Dojōnuma-chō, Yabase, Akita, Akita Pref.
Transport From JR Akita Station: west exit and 10 minutes by taxi, or 20 minute by bus bound for Dojōnumachō or Akita-kō to Mazda-mae stop and 2-minute walk north on Akita Shinkokudō Road
Visitation Open daily during working hours, tel: (0188) 63-2323

Located along a national highway in a suburban setting, the complex houses a variety of functions (bank, post office, restaurant, and shops) in addition to the Nissan auto showroom, service facilities, and offices, all centered around a reflective pool. While these activities are arranged in five "zones" with different articulation for each, the layered spatial composition defies the trivialized hodge-podge of its suburban surrounding and adds up to a small, but more meaningful, "urban" environment.

Ken Dōmon Museum of Photography 1983

Dōmon Ken Shashinkan
Architect Yoshio Taniguchi
Address 301, Ii-Moriyama, Miyanoura, Sakata, Yamagata Pref.
Transport Train—JR Uetsu line to Sakata Station and 25 minutes by bus bound for Ii-Moriyama Bunka Kōen; or 10 minutes by taxi
Visitation 9:00–16:30 (closed Mondays and 29 December–3 January, but no holidays in July and August). tel: (0234) 31-0028

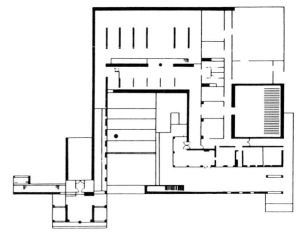

Both the Ken Dōmon Museum of Photography and the nearby Kokutai Kinen Gymnasium are located in Ii-Moriyama Park at the outskirts of Sakata. The museum, featuring the work of the well-known photographer Ken Dōmon, faces a small pond. Much of the design is the outcome of the architect's sensitive response to its natural environment. An attractive entranceway, intimate passages, and tranquil spaces wrapping around semi-enclosed courtyards (one marked with a sculpture by Isamu Noguchi), in addition to the sophisticated handling of natural light and of the transition between outside and inside, make this piece of architecture worth visiting.

市 SAKATA

Sakata Kokutai Kinen Gymnasium 1991

Sakata Kokutai Kinen Taiikukan
Architect Yoshio Taniguchi
Address 296-1, Ii-Moriyama, Miyanoura, Sakata, Yamagata Pref.
Transport Train—JR Uetsu line to Sakata Station and 25 minutes by bus bound for Ii-Moriyama Bunka Kōen; or 10 minutes by taxi (the gymnasium is about 500 feet/150 meters from the museum in the Ii-Moriyama Park)

The gymnasium is comprised of two distinct parts: a large arena and a smaller training hall. Both are covered by uniquely shaped, vaulted roofs. These large-span roofs with extensive overhangs are composed of a series of tension cable-reinforced frames, whose elegantly slim steel structure is exposed directly to the spaces below and, through glass finishing underneath, to the outside. The walls of the structure are finished with a thin, corrugated metallic membrane. The complex also features an archery range, a small library, an audio-visual room, and other service facilities.

市 TSURUOKA

Old Nishidagawa District Office 1881
Kyū-Nishidagawa Gunyakushō

Old Tsuruoka Police Station, 1884
Kyū-Tsuruoka Keisatsushō
Architect Kenkichi Takahashi
Address 10-18, Ienaka Shin-hō, Tsuruoka, Yamagata Pref.
Transport Train—JR Uetsu line to Tsuruoka Station; south exit and 15-minute walk or taxi (near Tsuruoka Castle and the surrounding park)

Both buildings are Important National Cultural Properties and are examples of Meiji Era wooden architecture patterned after European Renaissance or classical styles.

市 YAMAGATA

Yamagata Museum of Local History 1879
Yamagata-shi Kyodokan
Architect Hiroyuki Haraguchi
Address 1-1, Kasumijō Kōen, Yamagata, Yamagata Pref.
Transport Train—JR Yamagata Shinkansen or JR Ou line to Yamagata Station; west exit and 6-minute walk to the Kasumi-jō Park around the castle

An Important National Cultural Property, the building is and an attractive wooden structure with a three-story tower. It is another outstanding representative of early Meiji Era architecture that combined Western and Japanese styles.

市 SAGAE

Sagae City Hall 1967
Sagae Shichōsha
Architect Kisho Kurokawa
Address 9-45, Chūō 1-chōme, Sagae, Yamagata Pref.
Transport Train—JR Aterazawa line to Sagae Station and 10-minute walk

Supported solely by four huge, reinforced concrete, quadrilateral shafts, the Sagae City Hall is an early but good example of Kurokawa's Metabolist architecture.

AMAGATA PREFECTURE   **57**

KANTŌ REGION

With Tōkyō as its center, Kantō is Japan's most densely populated, industrialized, and built-up region. While much of the area is covered by mountains, Tōkyō and many of the surrounding urban communities are located on the large Kantō Plains. This setting allowed Tōkyō to expand almost limitlessly. With a population of 8.1 million in its twenty-three inner wards (*-ku*), this capital city of Japan is one of the world's largest metropolises, yet it is merely a part of the even greater Tōkyō area (*Tōkyō-to*) that, by the inclusion of many other, smaller adjoining municipalities, houses more than 12 million inhabitants. Moreover, Tōkyō is also inseparably grown together with such similarly large cities, such as Kawasaki (1.15 million) and Yokohama (3.21 million), to form not only one of the most extensive conurbations (23 million), but also the beginning of perhaps the largest megalopolitan development in the world, insofar as this urban sprawl continues all along the Pacific seaboard, connecting the metropolitan areas of Shizuoka, Nagoya, Kyōto, Ōsaka, Kōbe, and even Hiroshima and beyond.

As the most urbanized region in the country, Kantō is obviously also the place where the majority of contemporary architectural examples is concentrated. In this respect, Tōkyō, by virtue of its sheer size and extreme dynamism, leads the way. Most Japanese architects live in and work out of Tōkyō, and even if a growing number, including Tadao Ando, Shin Takamatsu, Shōei Yoh, Toru Murakami, and Team Zoo—Atelier Zo, are based elsewhere, just about all of them are represented here by some outstanding piece of design. Therefore, although today Tōkyō is not the only center of the various developments in the country, it still provides, with its innumerable new projects, an excellent introduction to contemporary Japanese architecture; in addition, with its unique urban qualities, undogmatic and innovative spirit, and constant and rapid transformations, it qualifies for one of the most exciting and futuristic cities today.

In this respect, some areas are especially exemplary: they are the districts around the numerous urban centers that, in an interconnected yet random network, populate the vast metropolitan area of Tōkyō. Historically, Ginza is the oldest and most established business district with many exclusive and expensive department stores, shops, and restaurants. Yet today, it is by no means the

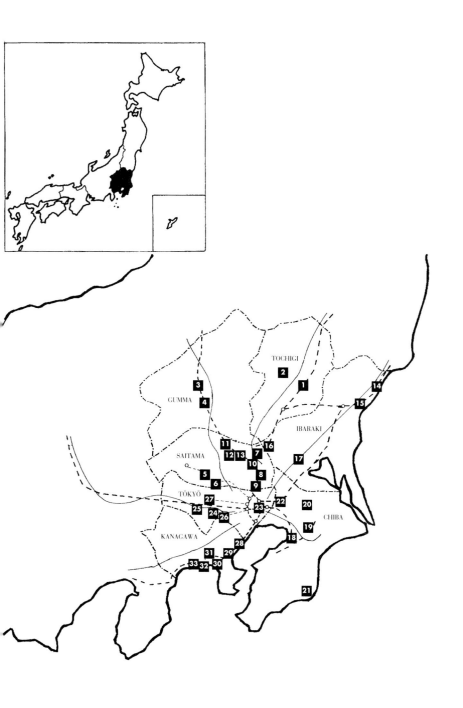

only downtown area in the city. In the rapid urbanization during the postwar decades, and especially in the 1980s, many other districts have grown up to this status: some, like Shibuya, Shinjuku, Aoyama, Harajuku, Roppongi, Akasaka, Akihabara, Ueno, and Ikebukuro, are now even larger, flashier, more dynamic, more futuristic, and more popular than Ginza, Nihonbashi, and Marunouchi. These quickly developing commercial, business, cultural, and entertainment districts, with their kaleidoscopic, chaotic, urban matrix, electronic dreamscapes of desire, and extreme volatility, effectively blur the distinction between reality and fiction. They are surely on the cutting edge of outlining the process of urbanization in our age of global information, media, and commercialization, while representing both their benefits and disadvantages.

An entirely new waterfront subcenter of Tōkyō, the Tōkyō Teleport Town, is now under construction in Tōkyō Bay. The first stage, to be completed in 1996 and to open with the World City Exposition Tōkyō '96, Urban Frontier, this most futuristic urban development is built on extensive landfill area and artificial islands. It aims to respond to the future demands of an even more globalized, information-oriented society in the twenty-first century. When completed early in the next century, it will accommodate 63,000 inhabitants and a working population of 106,000 on a 1,120-acre area. The 1996 exposition, as well as the Tōkyō Teleport Town, will provide opportunities to experience far-reaching urban services and facilities connected with living, working, and relaxing in the cities of the future.

On the other hand, Tōkyō and the entire Kantō area is less known for its surviving traditions and historic architecture than Kyōto, Nara, and even Ōsaka in the Kansai Region. Among the few famous ancient monuments in the region, the Tōshōgu Shrine (1636) in Nikko, and the old Shintō and Buddhist structures in Kamakura (fourteenth to fifteenth centuries), should be pointed out. In Tōkyō the Meiji Shintō Shrine (1920) and the Asakusa Kanon Buddhist Temple, or *Sensō-ji* (seventeenth century), are the largest but, like many others, they too were destroyed in World War II, then both (re)built in 1958, the former in wood, like the original, and the latter, in large part, in *reinforced concrete*, a new material. (There are, of course, numerous less significant or smaller temples and shrines in the region.)

The climate of the region is temperate and, like most of this island country, under the influence of the prevailing monsoon. This means that the summer is introduced by a six-to-seven-week rainy season, while the beginning of autumn in September is frequented by heavy typhoons. But the climate shows some differences between the northern and southern parts. The north, centered around the mountains of Gumma and Tochigi prefectures, has cold winters and plenty of snow, while the summer is somewhat cool. The southern part, including the Kantō Plains and Tōkyō, well protected from the north by the high mountain ranges, is dominated by the effect of the Pacific Ocean. Here the summer is hot and humid, whereas the winter is mild and relatively dry with very little, if any, snow. For the majority of visitors, as well as natives, however, the most pleasant seasons remain the spring and fall: from mid-March to early June and from mid-September to late November.

Perhaps Otaka's most successful design, the Tochigi Prefectural Conference Hall combines two spatially different sections and two different construction methods. The first, the large volume of the auditorium, is wrapped on three sides by the second, the horizontal wings of smaller rooms and offices in a modular arrangement. This organization provides a multistory entrance hall in between the two volumes. While the auditorium is of monolithic concrete, the structure of the wings is comprised of a pair of huge *in situ* reinforced concrete beams, each on four massive columns, and a system of prefabricated frames suspended from these beams on the second floor and surmounted on these beams on the third floor. Shaped by important structural considerations as well as elevated over attractive pilotis, the building offers both three-dimensional facade articulation and spatial depth that challenge the flat volumes and anonymous designs of many of its contemporaries. The hierarchy of supporting structures—a large-scale primary and smaller secondary and tertiary systems—was often used by Metabolist architects. Their preoccupation reveals the influence of structuralist theories on their designs. This can also be seen in Otaka's Motomachi and Chōjuen High-rise Apartment Blocks (1973) (see page 250).

Tochigi Prefectural Conference Hall 1968

Tochigi-ken Gikai Tōchōsha
Architect Masato Otaka
Address 1-20, Hanawada 1-chōme, Utsunomiya, Tochigi Pref.
Transport Train—JR Tōhoku main line to Utsunomiya Station: west exit and 15-minute walk to west; or 5 minutes by taxi

🏛 UTSUNOMIYA

Tochigi Prefectural Museum of Fine Arts
1972

Tochigi Kenritsu Bijutsukan
Architect Kiyoshi Kawasaki
Address 2-7, Sakura 4-chōme, Utsunomiya, Tochigi Pref.
Transport Train—JR Tōhoku main line to Utsunomiya Station: west exit and 10 minutes by taxi

A prismatic, reflective-glass volume and connecting low-profile wings that surround a pool and courtyard for sculpture exhibitions form the essential elements of the museum. They engage in a serene dialog not only with one another but also with the trees within the compound. Entry to the complex is provided through the first floor of the three-story glass structure, which, in addition to the lobby, houses such service facilities as offices, lecture and seminar halls, and storage spaces. The horizontal wing features the exhibition halls. The outside pool within a sunken and stair-stepped part of the courtyard adjoins the complex at the first basement level, where it continues behind the slanting glass wall of the cafeteria. This arrangement, while assuring an attractively intimate transition between inside and outside spaces, also defines the focal point of the entire architectural composition.

🏛 SHIBUKAWA

Hara Museum ARC
1988

Hara Bijutsukan ARC
Architect Arata Isozaki
Address 2844-1, Kanai-ono, Shibukawa, Gumma Pref.
Transport From JR Shibukawa Station: bus bound for Ikaho Onsen to Green-Bokujō-Mae stop (20 minutes) or 10 minutes by taxi
This symmetrical small building is covered by darkened wooden clapboard; its central section is capped with a pyramidal skylight.

🏛 TAKASAKI

Gumma Music Center
1961

Gumma Ongaku Sentā
Architect Antonin Raymond (U.S.)
Address 29-30, Takamatsu-chō, Takasaki, Gumma Pref.
Transport From Ueno Station in Tōkyō: Train—JR Takasaki line or Jōetsu Shinkansen line to Takasaki Station: west exit and 15-minute walk to northwest
This reinforced concrete building has folded, zig-zagging walls.

Gumma Prefectural Museum of History, 1979
Gumma Kenritsu Rekishi Hakubutsukan
Architect Masato Otaka
Address Gumma-no-mori, 239, Iwahana-chō, Takasaki, Gumma Pref.
Transport From Ueno Station in Tōkyō: Train—JR Takasaki line or Jōetsu Shinkansen line to Takasaki Station and 10 minutes by taxi or bus bound for Gumma-no-mori (east of Isozaki's Gumma Prefectural Museum of Modern Art)

Isozaki's most outstanding work from the 1970s, the Gumma Prefectural Museum of Modern Art is built out of a series of gigantic cubical frames, forming both the tectonic and theoretical deep structure of the intriguing architectural composition. This rectangular system, with a wing housing the gallery of traditional Japanese art skewed at 22.5°, is further amplified by the 4-foot/1.2-meter subdivisions of the cubes, expressed in an endless network of squares of highly polished aluminum panels, tiles, and window mullions. Within this dazzling perceptual field—akin to the experimental designs of the Italian Superstudio and the American conceptual artist Sol Lewitt and minimalist Donald Judd—yet simultaneously contrasting with it, the design introduces numerous paradoxical elements that seem to float without destination or predetermined relation to one another and the abstract grid. Such elements include the illusive spaces of the main stairway, the huge, stepped, sculptural volume (designed by Isozaki's wife, the sculptor Aiko Miyawaki) in the lobby, and the tearoom. The interior of the large gallery, on the other hand, is a series of simple but well-lit spaces. Set against the lush green of the Gumma Forest Park and reflected in a shallow pool, the glittering museum appears as an elusive mirage or, as Kōji Taki put it, "a world in a mirror."

Gumma Prefectural Museum of Modern Art
1974

Gumma Kenritsu Gindai Bijutsukan

Architect Arata Isozaki
Address Gumma-no-mori, 239, Iwahana-chō, Takasaki, Gumma Pref.
Transport From Ueno Station in Tōkyō: Train—JR Takasaki line or Jōetsu Shinkansen line to Takasaki Station and 10 minutes by taxi or bus for Gumma-no-mori Park

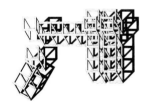

🏙 IRUMA

**Eishin Higashino
High School
1985**
*Eishin Gakuen Higashino
Kōtō-gakkō*
Architect Christopher
Alexander (U.S.)
Address 112-1, Nihongi,
Iruma, Saitama Pref.
Transport From Ikebukuro
Station in Tōkyō: Train—
Seibu Ikebukuro line to
Irumashi Station and bus to
Nihongi stop and 5-minute
walk.

🏙 TOKOROZAWA

**Waseda Seminar
1989**
*Waseda Semināru
Tokorozawa-kō*
Architect Yuzuru Tominaga
Address 16-4, Kita-chō,
Tokorozawa, Saitama Pref.
Transport From Seibu
Shinjuku Station in Tōkyō:
Train—Seibu Shinjuku line to
Kōkū Kōen Station (one stop
after Tokorozawa Station)
and 1-minute walk (in front
of west exit)
The structure is a seminar
building of Waseda University
in Tōkyō.

🏙 MIYASHIRO-CHŌ

**Municipal Kasahara
Elementary School
1983**
*Miyashiro Chōritsu
Kasahara Shō-gakkō*
Architect Team Zoo–Atelier Zo
Address 1-105, Monma,
Miyashiro-chō, Minami
Saitama-gun, Saitama Pref.
Transport Train—Tōbu
Isezaki line or Subway—
Hibiya line to Tōbu Dōbutsu
Kōen Station and 8-minute
walk (3-minute walk from
Miyashiro Municipal Center)
The school is a group of
pitched and tiled roof pavilion-
type buildings designed with a
strong allusion to vernacular
architecture.

🏙 MIYASHIRO-CHŌ

Miyashiro Municipal Center
1980
Shinshūkan
Architect Team Zoo–Atelier Zo
Address 1-1, Kasahara,
Miyashiro-chō, Minami
Saitama-gun, Saitama Pref.
Transport Train—Tōbu Ise-
zaki line or Subway—Hibiya
line to Tōbu Dōbutsu Kōen
Station and 5-minute walk

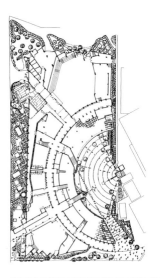

Strongly ritualistic in inspiration, and strangely
archaic in appearance, the Miyashiro Municipal
Center can be interpreted as a ruinous landscape or
a place of worship. The unfinished reinforced concrete structure—now largely covered by grape-
vines—surrounds a semicircular stepped courtyard
plaza, which, like a small amphitheater, is used for
various outdoor community events. Arched colon-
nades, multistory, top-lit corridors, narrow passages, and long ramps are all designed so as to
evoke a mysterious "medieval" atmosphere. Like
practically all of Team Zoo—Atelier Zo's work, the
Municipal Center is shaped with a "down to earth"
approach that is more intuitive and phenomenolog-
ical than abstract or rigidly rational, while not
devoid of a certain primitivism.

Saitama Prefectural Museum of Modern Art
1982

Saitama Kenritsu Gindai Bijutsukan
Architect Kisho Kurokawa
Address 30-1, Tokiwa 9-chōme, Urawa, Saitama Pref.
Transport Train—JR Keihin-Tōhoku line to Kita-Urawa Station: west exit and 3-minute walk

Leaving behind his explicitly technology-oriented Metabolist architecture, Kurokawa in the late 1970s began to explore alternate modes of generating meaning in architecture. One of the issues on which he concentrated was the realm of in-between and, more specifically, the ambiguity of spatial transitions. The Saitama Prefectural Museum of Modern Art exemplifies such preoccupations by way of its "eroding" corner (the semi-enclosed space of the entrance court), the long stairway between two parts of the building, and the multi-story interior courtyard under a skylight. Ambiguous spatial definitions are reinforced here by a range of luxurious and reflective materials—undulating glass, highly polished stone, and aluminum—that impart a vague, illusive feeling.

Saitama Civic Center
1966

Saitama Kaikan
Architect Kunio Maekawa
Address 1-4, Takasago-chō 3-chōme, Urawa, Saitama Pref.
Transport Train—JR Keihin Tōhoku line to Urawa Station: west exit and 5-minute walk

Kazama House
1987

Architect Takefumi Aida
Address 17-18, Ryōke 2-chōme, Kawaguchi, Saitama Pref.
Transport Train—JR Keihin-Tōhoku line to Kawaguchi Station: and bus to Motogō Chūgakkō stop and 3-minute walk to south (the house is near Jisshō-ji Temple across a graveyard)
Visitation Private residence; seen only from the outside.

Representing Aida's new "architecture of fluctuation," the house is composed of a system of parallel white walls that "pile up" and create sequentially layered outside and inside spaces. (See also page 26: fig. 33)

Saitō Memorial Hall of Shibaura Institute of Technology 1990

Shibaura Kō-Dai Saitō Kinenkan
Architect Takefumi Aida
Address 307, Tameigahara, Fukasaku, Ōmiya, Saitama Pref.
Transport Train—JR Utsunomiya line to Higashi-Ōmiya Station and Campus shuttle bus or 6 minutes by taxi
Visitation 10:00–17:00 (closed Sundays)

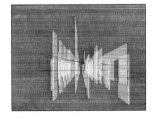

One of Aida's most recent designs, the Saitō Memorial Hall continues an architectural paradigm that, initiated in the mid-1980s, is forwarded by the significant use of primarily two-dimensional elements: concrete walls, screens, etc. In this case the parallel field of walls is deliberately interrupted by the long, wedge-shaped, although "broken" horizontal volume of the guest room section, which cuts diagonally across the flow of layered spaces both inside and out. In Aida's design, particularly noteworthy is the fragmentary arrangement of the walls and other elements that articulate the boundaries of the building as a system of thin layers. Constituting the essence of what Aida calls the "architecture of fluctuation," these layers visually overlap in various, shifting configurations and, so doing, filter the surrounding light and scenery in an intricate way. Interior spaces, centered around the long-stretching, top-lit, entrance hall with gallery levels and connecting bridges, are likewise shaped with multiple series of penetrating wall planes. The two-story structure provides several facilities for both students and faculty; on the first floor are the lobby and foyer, an auditorium with a small stage, and two exhibition spaces, while on the second, conference rooms, some offices, and a guest room are accommodated.

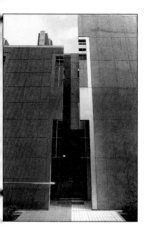

Gymnasium 2 of Shibaura Institute of Technology
1985

Shibaura Kō-Dai Daini Taiikukan
Architect Hiromi Fujii
Address 307, Tameigahara, Fukasaku, Ōmiya, Saitama Pref.
Transport Train—JR Utsunomiya line to Higashi-Ōmiya Station and Campus shuttle bus or 6 minutes by taxi (1-minute walk from Saitō Memorial Hall)
Visitation 10:00–17:00 (closed Sundays)

One of Fujii's largest works, the two-story gymnasium is an impressive "study" in surface manipulations and the "breaking down" of walls or boundaries, particularly behind the relatively solid facades.

市 ŌMIYA

Saitama Prefectural Museum
1971

Saitama Kenritsu Hakubutsukan
Architect Kunio Maekawa
Address 219, Takahana-chō 4-chōme, Ōmiya, Saitama Pref.
Transport Train—JR Keihin Tōhoku line or JR Jōetsu Shinkansen line or JR Takasaki line to Ōmiya Station: east exit and 10 minutes by taxi

市 KUMAGAYA

Risshō University Kumagaya Campus
1968

Risshō Daigaku Kumagaya Kōsha
Architect Fumihiko Maki
Address 1700, Magichi, Kumagaya, Saitama Pref.
Transport From Ueno Station in Tōkyō: Train—JR Takasaki line to Kami-Kumagaya and 25-minute walk (2.5 miles/ 4 kilometers) or 8 minutes by taxi

村 TOKIGAWA-MURA

Musashi-Kyūryō Country Clubhouse
1987

Architect Arata Isozaki
Address 2042, Tokigawa-mura, Hiki-gun, Saitama Pref.
Transport From Ikebukuro Station in Tōkyō: Train—Tōbu Tōjō line to Musashi-Ranzan Station and 25 minutes by taxi
Visitation Open daily, tel: (0493) 65-3711

市 KŌNOSU

Marutake Dolls Company Building
1976

Marutake Ningyō Kaisha
Architect Hiromi Fujii
Address 1-8, Ningyō 2-chōme, Kōnosu, Saitama Pref.
Transport Train—JR Takasaki line to Kōnosu Station: east exit and 10-minute walk

Composed of twelve, equal size, reinforced concrete cubes with various window articulations, the three-story building represents Fujii's highly conceptual architecture in progress.

🏯 HITACHI

Hitachi Civic Center 1990

Hitachi Shimin Kaikan
Architect Sakakura Associates
Address 21-1, Saiwai-chō 1-chōme, Hitachi, Ibaraki Pref.
Transport From Ueno Station in Tōkyō: Train—JR Jōban line to Hitachi Station: west exit and 2-minute walk (south from the Station)

Partly a reinterpretation of Johan Otto von Spreckelsen's Grande Arche of La Défense in Paris (1989), partly a resurrection of Isozaki, Tange, and others' Metabolist vision of a city in the air, the Hitachi Civic Center is a highly unusual structure, striking in both its bold engineering and stunning formal articulation. Standing at the southern edge of the sloping Hitachi Station plaza, the building, like a kind of proscenium, opens a huge window to the sky and the city behind, with urban areas to be developed later. Suspended above this vacuous gap is a large, stainless-steel-clad globe that accommodates the multipurpose auditorium with its service facilities. This glittering spherical volume can be seen from just about every part of the city, including from the glass-roofed entrance hall beneath it.

Santa Chiara Chapel 1974

Ibaraki Kiristōkyō Tandai Santa Chiara Kan
Architect Seiichi Shirai
Address 4048, Kuji-chō, Hitachi, Ibaraki Pref.
Transport From Ueno Station in Tōkyō: Train—JR Jōban line to Omika Station (2 stops before Hitachi Station): west exit and 5 minutes by taxi

Pachinko Parlor Kinbasha 1993

Architect Kazuyo Sejima
Address 13-3, Kashima 1-chōme, Hitachi, Ibaraki Pref.
Transport From Ueno Station in Tōkyō: Train—JR Jōban line to Hitachi Station: west exit and 9-minute walk west
Visitation Open daily, tel: (0294) 23-4122

The small building is a highly successful study in creating interpenetrating, illusive spaces, most of which are defined by reflective glass, mirrors, and highly polished metallic surfaces.

Art Tower Mito 1990

Mito Geijutsūkan
Architect Arata Isozaki
Address 6-8, Goken-chō
1-chōme, Mito, Ibaraki Pref.
Transport From Ueno Station
in Tōkyō: Train—JR Jōban
line to Mito Station: north
exit: Bus terminal—bus to
Izumichō-Itchōme stop and
3-minute walk
Visitation 9:30–18:00 (closed
Mondays; closed Tuesday if
Monday is a national holi-
day), tel: (0292) 27-8111

The large-scale complex features various cultural
facilities: concert and conference halls, a theater, a
modern-art gallery, restaurants, multiple entrance
halls and lobbies, and an observation tower, all
arranged around a public plaza. In accordance with
Isozaki's explorations of neoclassical architecture in
the last decade, the low-profile wings are designed
in a heavy, historicist style replete with large cylindrical, pyramidal, and rectangular volumes, rusticated stone or mosaic tiled surfaces, and protruding
cornices and pilasters. As opposed to this small
urban enclave, the 330-foot-/100-meter-high
tower, commemorating Mito's centennial, is a high-
tech, futuristic construct. The titanium-clad structure surges upward with tremendous force; it is
made of regular quadrilaterals 31.5 feet/9.6 meters
to a side, twisted in a triple spiral configuration, so
as to embody the structure of DNA. With such radically contrasting elements, Isozaki's project sym-
bolizes the rather schizophrenic times and urban
culture in which it has been conceived.

🛉 KOGA

Koga Sports Forum
1991

Koga Gorufu Spōtsu Fōramu
Architect Kunihiko
Hayakawa
Address 10-1, Nishimachi,
Koga, Ibaraki Pref.
Transport From Ueno Station
in Tōkyō: Train—JR Tōhoku
line or Utsunomiya line to
Koga Station; and 10 minutes
by taxi to Koga Riverside
Club (near Suzume Jinja
Shrine)
Visitation Open daily,
tel: (0280) 22-4000

Stretching along the west bank of the Watarase
River, the Koga Sports Forum is a recreation center
with an audio-visual library of sports information,
a golf clubhouse, and a multipurpose arena. The
rear facade, facing a golf course along the river, is a
slightly curving, large, aluminum-panel-clad wall
and an intricately perforated screen. The front
facade, facing a parking lot, is articulated so as to
better reveal the fragmentary spatial composition
behind. A long, pedestrian ramp that—not unlike
the one at Le Corbusier's Carpenter Center at
Harvard University (1963)—runs through the fabric of the building on the third floor. The two-story
entrance hall, continuing in the space of the
library, features a long, suspended bridge and
several audio-visual booths. Structural elements,
like those in constructivist architecture, play
important roles in shaping the building's dynamic
appearance.

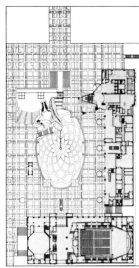

The Tsukuba Center Building was designed and built as the cultural and urban center of the new Tsukuba Science City, which has been developed since the mid-1960s. The large complex includes the eleven-story Dai-ichi Hotel, a concert hall, a conference center, a shopping mall, community facilities, and, importantly, a sunken plaza. In Isozaki's highly mannerist scheme this plaza is actually an "inverted" interpretation of Michelangelo's sixteenth-century piazza on the Capitoline Hill in Rome. A loose agglomerate of historicist and other stylistic allusions also imbue most other parts of the building. This project introduced a new stage in Isozaki's architecture, inasmuch as from the early 1980s, a more explicitly neoclassical postmodernism began to dominate many of his works. The Tsukuba Center Building is also the first significant representative of a design attitude in contemporary Japanese architecture that not only criticizes the typically heterogeneous and chaotic urban landscape, but also acknowledges it as a source of creativity.

Tsukuba Center Building, 1983
Architect Arata Isozaki
Address 1-1364 Tsukuba City, Ibaraki Pref.
Transport Train—JR Jōban line to Tsuchiura Station and bus bound for Tsukuba Center; or from Tōkyō Station in Tōkyō: bus to Tsukuba Center (2 hours) and 3-minute walk

Tsukuba South Parking Building, 1994
Architect Toyo Ito
Address 1344-6, Takezono 9-chōme, Tsukuba, Ibaraki Pref.
Transport Train—JR Jōban line to Tsuchiura Station and bus bound for Tsukuba Center; or from Tōkyō Station in Tōkyō: bus to Tsukuba Center (2 hours) and 10-minute walk

Tsukuba University Central Building for the Schools of Art and Physical Education, 1974

Tsukuba Daigaku Taiiku Geijutsu Senmongaku-gun Chūō-to

Architect Fumihiko Maki
Address Tsukuba Science City, Ibaraki Pref.
Transport Train—JR Jōban line to Tsuchiura Station and bus bound for Tsukuba Center; or from Tōkyō Station: bus to Tsukuba Center (2 hours) and 14-minute walk or 5 minutes by taxi

Due to the short construction time involved and the limited financial resources available, Maki designed the Tsukuba University Central Building largely with prefabricated elements that could be easily and quickly assembled. The structural system is a steel skeleton to which story-high panels—made of glass blocks set in steel frames—were welded. This construction creates translucent volumes that appear not only impressively light or "ephemeral," but also, in Maki's words, as ranges of "a small glassy mountain." The central entrance to the building is shaped as a pedestrian thoroughfare, a gateway to the campus. The multistory, top-lit hall above the entryway is therefore a semi-open space, highlighted by a freestanding stairway and a system of traversing bridges.

The gigantic complex—with an exhibition hall more than 1770 feet/540 meters in length, a multipurpose event hall with 9000 seats, and a full-function international conference center—is Maki's largest completed project to date. The enormous size posed several serious challenges. However, Maki, with his bold yet elegant design solution, was able to meet these challenges in a highly successful manner. The structural solution, which is as unique as it is attractive, bespeaks an engineering bravura, while the related curvilinear shapes and surfaces covered by stainless-steel plates manage to "diminish" the dimensions to a more human scale. In fact, in certain weather or rather light conditions, the complex can appear as phenomenal as a glittering mirage and as light as some clouds in the sky.

Nippon Convention Center, 1990

Makuhari Messe
Architect Fumihiko Maki
Address 2-1, Nakase, Chiba, Chiba Pref.
Transport From Tōkyō Station in Tōkyō: Train—JR Keiyō line to Kaihin Makuhari Station and 6-minute walk toward south

Memorial Auditorium of Chiba University 1963

Chiba Daigaku Kōdō
Architect Fumihiko Maki
Address Chiba University,
313 Inohana-chō, Chiba,
Chiba Pref.
Transport Train—JR Sōbu
line to Chiba Station and
30-minute walk or 10 min-
utes by taxi

One of Maki's earliest projects, the exposed reinforced concrete building, with its four vertical stair-
and-elevator shafts at the corners, and with its
slanting structural frames and volume, displays
some of the features that characterize Metabolist
architecture, such as Kikutake's Izumo Shrine
Office Building (see page 256). Even at this early
stage of his career, Maki is interested in investigat-
ing the modes of mediation between outside urban
and inside architectural spaces. There is a notice-
able free-flowing quality of the spatial matrix, and
this, rather than the structural solution, is what
makes this auditorium a notable work.

Chiba Prefectural Cultural Center 1967

Chiba-ken Bunka Kaikan
Architect Masato Otaka
Address 11-2, Ichiba-machi,
Chiba, Chiba Pref.
Transport Train—JR Sōbu
line to Chiba Station and
5 minutes by taxi (2-minute
walk from Chiba Prefectural
Central Library)

Chiba Prefectural Central Library 1968

Chiba Kenritsu Chūō Toshokan
Architect Masato Otaka
Address 11-1, Ichiba-machi,
Chiba, Chiba Pref.
Transport Train—JR Sōbu
line to Chiba Station and
5 minutes by taxi (2-minute
walk from Chiba Prefectural
Cultural Center)

Chiba Port Tower 1986

Architect Nikken Sekkei
Company
Address 1-10, Chūō-ku,
Chiba, Chiba Pref.
Transport Train—JR Sōbu
line to Chiba Station: south
exit and 5 minutes by taxi to
port; or from JR Tōkyō
Station in Tōkyō: Train—JR
Keiyō line to Chibaminato
Station and 8-minute walk to
southwest
The tessellated glass-plate-
covered 400-foot-/125-meter-
high tower is practically identical in its solution and in its
impressive appearance to the
more recent Fukuoka Tower,
also designed by Nikken
Sekkei Company (see page
288).

🏛 SAKURA

Sakura City Hall
1971
Sakura Shichōsha
Architect Kisho Kurokawa
Address 97, Kairinji-chō, Sakura, Chiba Pref.
Transport From Ueno Station in Tōkyō: Train—Keisei Densetsu line to Keisei-Sakura Station and 6-minute walk

Preceeding Kurokawa's well-known Nakagin Capsule Tower of 1972 in Tōkyō (see page 83), the Sakura City Hall betrays some indirect relationship to the latter building, insofar as the structural/ formal arrangement of the prefabricated, hollowed concrete panels seems to add up to a cluster of uniform spatial units that represent the idea of capsule architecture. The vertical shafts of reinforced concrete house the vertical circulation: elevators and stairways, while the horizontal, separate volume accommodates the large conference hall.

🏛 INZAI-MACHI

Takenaka Research and Development Institute (R-90)
1993
Takenaka Gijutsu Kenkyū-jō
Architect Takenaka Corporation
Address 5, Otsuka 1-chōme, Inzai-machi, Inba-gun, Chiba Pref.
Transport From Tōkyō: Subway—Tōei Asakusa line to Chiba New Town Terminal and 8-minute walk to northeast
Visitation Seen only from outside
The large and spectacular complex is the high-tech research center of Takenaka Corporation, one of Japan's five largest construction companies.

🏛 ONJUKU-CHŌ

Onjuku Town Hall
1993
Onjuku Yakuba
Architect Michael Graves (U.S.)
Address 1522, Suga, Onjuku-chō, Izumi-gun, Chiba Pref.
Transport From Tōkyō Station in Tōkyō: Train—JR Sotobō line to Onjuku Station: west exit and 10-minute walk up the hill

🏛 MATSUDO

Gotō Museum
1990
Gotō Bijutsukan
Architect David Chipperfield (U.K.)
Address 7-21, Shin-Matsudo, Matsudo, Chiba Pref.
Transport From Tōkyō: Subway—Chiyoda line to Shin-Matsudo Station: north exit and 10-minute walk

TŌKYŌ Map 1

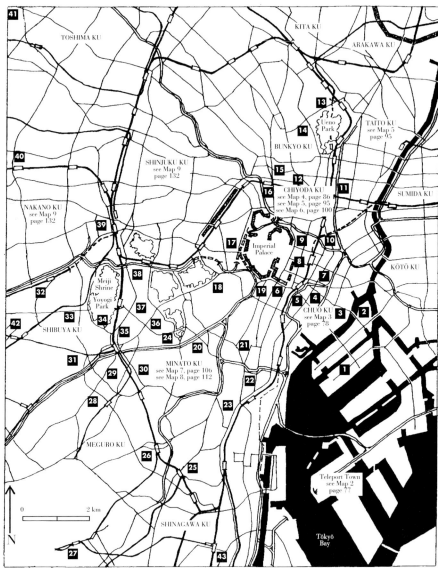

1 Harumi	**16** Jimbochō	**31** Shibuya
2 Tsukuda	**17** Kōjimachi	**32** Uehara
3 Tsukiji	**18** Akasaka	**33** Tomigaya
4 Ginza	**19** Kasumigaseki	**34** Yoyogi Park
5 Yurakuchō	**20** Roppongi	**35** Omotesandō
6 Hibiya	**21** Azabudai	**36** Aoyama-dōri
7 Kyōbashi	**22** Shiba	**37** Jingumae
8 Marunouchi	**23** Mita	**38** Sendagaya
9 Ōtemachi	**24** Azabu	**39** Shinjuku
10 Nihonbashi	**25** Gotanda	**40** Nakano
11 Akihabara	**26** Meguro	**41** Nerima
12 Ochanomizu	**27** Ōokayama	**42** Setagaya
13 Ueno	**28** Nakameguro	**43** Heiwajima
14 Hongō	**29** Daikanyama	
15 Korakuen	**30** Ebisu	

TŌKYŌ Map 2
Teleport Town Area

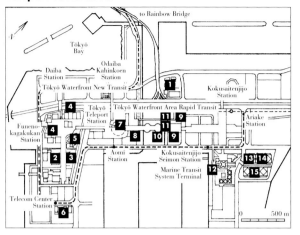

1 Ariake Clean Center
Inter City
2 World City Pavilion
3 Future City Pavilion
4 Corporate Pavilions
5 Oikos Park
6 Telecom Center
Gate City
7 Media Station
Art City
8 Event Hall

9 Citizens' Square, Green Plaza
10 Water Square
11 Multi-purpose Utility
Conduits, Water Supply
**Tōkyō International
Exhibition Center and
Congress Tower**
12 Theme Pavilion
13 Environment Exhibition
14 Cities of Japan Pavilion
15 Urban Industry Pavilion

都 TŌKYŌ
Teleport Town Area

World City Exposition Tōkyō '96, Urban Frontier 1996

Organizer: Tōkyō Metropolitan Government and Tōkyō Frontier Association
Address Daiba, Aomi, Ariake-kita, and Ariake-minami areas, Tōkyō Teleport Town, Kōtō-ku, Tōkyō (see Map 2)
Transport From JR Shinbashi Station: Train—Tōkyō Waterfront New Transit System to Ariake Terminal or other stations before it; or from JR and Subway Yurakuchō line Shinkiba Station: Train—Tōkyō Waterfront Area Rapid Transit System to Tōkyō Teleport Terminal; or from Hinode Pier of Tōkyō Port: Ferry—Marine Transit System to Tōkyō Teleport and/or Tōkyō International Convention Center
Visitation 24 March–13 October 1996

Telecom Center 1996

Architect Nippon Sogo Architectural Office and Helmuth Obata Kassabaum (U.S.)
Address Tōkyō Teleport Town, Aomi, Kōtō-ku, Tōkyō (see Map 2)
Transport From JR Shinbashi Station: Train—Tōkyō Waterfront New Transit System to Telecom Center (in front of station)
The center is a 325-foot-/99-meter-high building shaped as a huge gateway. Under the interconnecting upper part a multistory atrium serves the public. Equipped with a parabolic antenna and a satellite communications ground station, the Telecom Center is an advanced "intelligent" office building.

Ariake Clean Center 1996

Architect Katsuhiro Kobayashi (with Takenaka Corporation)
Address Tōkyō Teleport Town, Ariake-kita, Kōtō-ku, Tōkyō (see Map 2)
Transport From JR Shinbashi Station: Train—Tōkyō Waterfront New Transit System to Odaiba Kaihinkōen Station and 10-minute walk
The facility disposes garbage and sewage generated within Tōkyō Teleport Town. The heat generated by burning the garbage is used to run a regional air-conditioning system. Water purified by the sewage treatment equipment is reused. The center also features restaurants, tennis courts, a gym, a swimming pool, and a park.

Tōkyō International Exhibition Center and Congress Tower 1996

Architect Sato Architectural Office
Address Tōkyō Teleport Town, 12, Ariake 3-chōme, Kōtō-ku, Tōkyō (see Map 2)
Transport From JR Shinbashi Station: Train—Tōkyō Waterfront New Transit System to Kokusaitenjijo Seimon Station; or Marine Transit System to Exhibition Center Terminal
The exhibition complex for international industrial and cultural events covers twenty acres. The east display block consists of six units, the west four exhibition halls and an atrium. The Congress Tower is shaped as a system of four inverted pyramids supported by four huge vertical shafts.

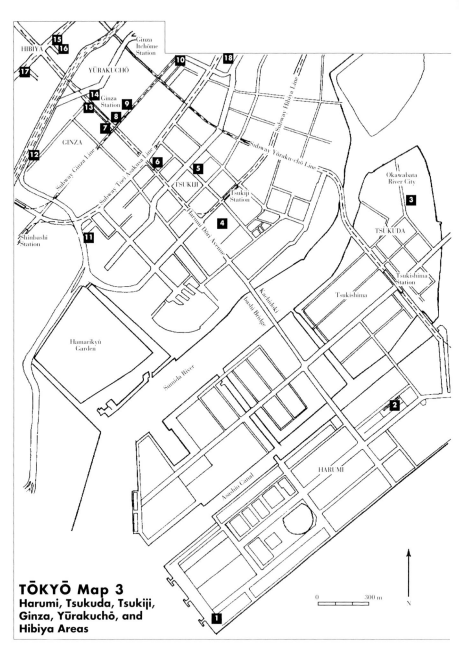

TŌKYŌ Map 3
Harumi, Tsukuda, Tsukiji, Ginza, Yūrakuchō, and Hibiya Areas

The large complex is built on reclaimed land facing Tōkyō Bay in the direction of the newly built Rainbow Bridge. Takeyama's design articulates two major parts: a long, stretching, sloping base with wide, open, public stairways leading to several observation terraces, and a multistory glass-walled structure—featuring the main lounge, a large reception hall, and a restaurant—at the top of this base. The latter is wrapped by a white-painted steel "cage" whose modular grid converges at the top to form a pyramidal roof. Underneath this "enclosing" structure the actual rooftop is arranged as an observation deck of stepped platforms filled with stairs, ramps, and bridges, and covered by four umbrella-like Teflon fiber domes. Not unlike some curious parachutes floating in the air, these translucent domes, when exposed to the sun, glow against the blue of the sky. Illuminated in the evening, the building provides a different experience, which seems to surpass even the earlier ones. Appearing as both a large house ("land mark") and a lighthouse ("water mark"), the terminal signifies land and sea equally well and makes a spectacular place for both arrival and departure. Takeyama is currently working on an extension of the complex at a nearby site.

Tōkyō International Port Terminal 1991

Harumi Kyakusen Tāmināru
Architect Minoru Takeyama
Address 7-1, Harumi 5-chōme, Chūō-ku, Tōkyō (see Map 3)
Transport Subway—Yūrakuchō line to Tsukishima Station and 6 minutes by taxi

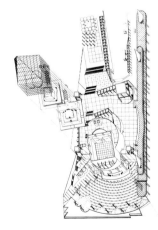

Harumi Apartments, block 15
1958

Nihon Jūtaku Kōdan Harumi Kōsō Apāto Dai Jū-gō-ban
Architect Kunio Maekawa
Address 6, Harumi 1-chōme, Chūō-ku, Tōkyō (see Map 3)
Transport Subway—Yūra-kuchō line to Tsukishima Station and 5 minutes by taxi (north of Reimei-bashi Bridge)

都 TŌKYŌ
Tsukuda Area

Egg of Winds (Okawabata River City 21, Town Gate B) 1991

Architect Toyo Ito
Address 2, Tsukuda 2-chōme, Chūō-ku, Tōkyō (see Map 3)
Transport Subway—Yūraku-chō line to Tsukishima Station and 10-minute walk to north
This huge, egg-shaped structure, made of thin, perforated metallic panels, floats above one of the main gates to the Okawabata River City Housing. Within this semi-transparent, lacy structure, a multiplicity of media devices, large TV screens, and liquid crystal projectors, come alive in the evening and emit audio-visual information for homebound residents. (See page 28: fig. 37.)

The ten-story apartment block is an early, relatively little-known, but important representative of Maekawa's postwar architecture. With its massive, reinforced concrete superstructure—whose enormous beams at every third floor provide an anti-seismic framework—and in-between secondary structures, the building is a forerunner of many Metabolist designs produced in the 1960s. It is also one of the first high-rise public housing complexes in Japan that was commissioned after the war to alleviate the severe shortages of shelter as economically as possible. Accordingly, the apartment units are uniformly small; with two tiny rooms—a living room/dining room/kitchen and a bathroom—their floor area is limited to 322 square feet/30 square meters. The rooms, like those in traditional Japanese architecture, are multi-functional and are outfitted with tatami floor mats. Moreover the apartments have balconies on both sides of each floor, an arrangement similar to the wooden-board veranda around the perimeter of old residences.

An unusual mixture of various Asian styles, including Islamic, Hindu, and Saracen, this Buddhist temple embodies a design intention of the 1930s to reconnect the course of contemporary Japanese architecture with its roots. The designer Chuta Ito—a leading architectural historian and ideologist before the war—tried to express stylistically the origin of Buddhism in India. Because he considered copying old Japanese wooden temples in reinforced concrete to be illogical, the large, two-story, stone-faced, symmetrical structure does not have any direct formal or structural reference to local architectural traditions. The central section of the building features a wide, open stairway leading to the main entrance on the second floor.

Tsukiji Honganji Temple
1935
Architect Chuta Ito
Address 15, Tsukiji 3-chōme, Chūō-ku, Tōkyō (see Map 3)
Transport Subway—Hibiya line to Tsukiji Station and 2-minute walk

Dentsu Advertising Company Building
1967
Dentsu Honsha Biru
Architect Kenzo Tange
Address 11, Tsukiji 1-chōme, Chūō-ku, Tōkyō (see Map 3)
Transport Subway—Hibiya line or Tōei Asakusa line to Higashi-Ginza Station and 7-minute walk (10-minute walk from Tsukiji Honganji Temple)

The fifteen-story building, with a central core system, employs a massive reinforced concrete structure and precast stone covers on the walls. The space under its lofty pilotis has been formed into a glass-enclosed lobby.

都 TŌKYŌ
Ginza Area

Kabuki Theater
1924

Kabuki Geki-jō
Architect Shinichirō Okada
Address 12, Ginza 4-chōme,
Chūō-ku, Tōkyō (see Map 3)
Transport Subway—Hibiya
line or Tōei Asakusa line to
Higashi-Ginza Station (the
theater is in front of the exit
of the station)

One of the prime representatives of prewar, nationalistic architecture (*teikan-yoshiki* style), the concrete structure of the Kabuki Theater imitates the features, particularly the roof, of traditional wooden architecture. The theater is a four-story symmetrical building that faces Harumi-dōri Avenue. Since it is now tightly situated between large structures, only its front facade can be seen properly. Even so, the main features of the architecture remain unobscured; they include the heavy, cylindrical columns and rectangular beams that protrude from the embellished wall surfaces, the decorative balconies on both sides, the curving forms of the tiled roof over the central main entrance, and, of course, the overpowering structure of the interconnected pair of hip and gabled roofs above the entire building.

San-Ai Dream Center
1963

Mitsubishi Dream Center
Architect Nikken Sekkei
Company
Address 7, Ginza 4-chōme,
Chūō-ku, Tōkyō (see Map 3)
Transport Subway—Ginza line
or Hibiya line to Ginza Station
(on the southwest corner of
Ginza intersection)

An early example of the now popular, so-called "media show" buildings, the San-Ai Dream Center is turned into a shaft of light in the evening when the radially arranged interior light fixtures are lit. Every other cantilevered floor recedes from the elevation to provide higher interiors with larger glass surfaces. The design bears a strong resemblance to Frank Lloyd Wright's Johnson Wax Factory Research Tower in Racine, Wisconsin (1948).

Wakō Department Store, Ginza
1931
Wakō Depāto
Architect Hitoshi (Jin) Watanabe
Address 5, Ginza 4-chōme, Chūō-ku, Tōkyō (see Map 3)
Transport Subway—Ginza line or Hibiya line to Ginza Station (on the northwest corner of Ginza intersection—across from San-Ai Dream Center)

Yamano Gakki Ginza Building
1991
Architect Takenaka Corporation
Address 5, Ginza 4-chōme, Chūō-ku, Tōkyō (see Map 3)
Transport Subway—Ginza line or Hibiya line to Ginza Station and 2-minute walk (building is two buildings away from the Wakō Department Store on the west side of Chūō-dōri Avenue)

Ginza Theater Hotel
1987
Ginza Gekijō Hotēru
Architect Kiyonori Kikutake
Address 11-2, Ginza 1-chōme, Chūō-ku, Tōkyō (see Map 3)
Transport Subway—Yūrakuchō line to Ginza Itchōme Station and 3-minute walk (The large, bladelike building, along the elevated expressway, is perpendicular to Chūō-dōri Avenue)

Nakagin Capsule Tower, 1972
Nakagin Kyapuseru Tāwā
Architect Kisho Kurokawa
Address 16-10, Ginza 8-chōme, Chūō-ku, Tōkyō (see Map 3)
Transport Train—JR Yamanote line or Keihin-Tōhoku line to Shinbashi Station and 6-minute walk; or Subway—Ginza line or Tōei Asakusa line to Shinbashi Station and 5-minute walk

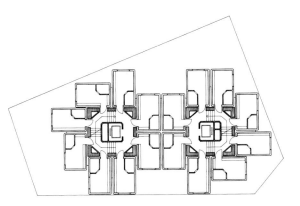

Regarded as the epitome of Metabolist architecture in Japan, the Nakagin Capsule Tower is designed with 144 prefabricated residential capsules that are bolted to two vertical reinforced concrete shafts. These stair and elevator shafts thus carry the entire weight of the assemblage. The capsules, whose size and basic construction is identical to those of standard shipping containers, provide in a minimal but flexibly arranged space a broad variety of comfort to their single owners or residents. In each unit there is a built-in bathroom, kitchenette, working area with a desk and chair, bed, stereo, TV, and air conditioning. The tower was meant to be a prototype of residences for a mobile urban society whose members could easily transport their custom-made residential capsules from place to place and "dock" them on readily available vertical "port" structures. Such interchangeability, provided by advanced industrial technology and prefabrication, was one of the goals of many architects in the 1960s.

Shizuoka Press and Broadcasting Offices 1967

Shizuoka Shinbun and *Hōsō Tōkyō Shiten*
Architect Kenzo Tange
Address 3, Ginza 8-chōme, Chūō-ku, Tōkyō (see Map 3)
Transport Train—JR Yamanote line or Keihin-Tōhoku line to Shinbashi Station; or Subway—Ginza line or Tōei Asakusa line to Shinbashi Station and 5-minute walk

Sony Building 1966

Sony Biru
Architect Yoshinobu Ashihara
Address 1, Ginza 5-chōme, Chūō-ku, Tōkyō (see Map 3)
Transport Train—JR Yamanote line or Keihin Tōhoku line to Yūrakuchō Station and 3-minute walk; or Subway—Yūrakuchō line to Yūrakuchō Station and 3-minute walk; or Ginza line, Hibiya line, or Marunouchi line to Ginza Station and 1-minute walk

Ginza Sukiyabashi Police Box 1982

Ginza Sukiyabashi Koban
Architect Kazumasa Yamashita
Address 4, Ginza 4-chōme, Chūō-ku, Tōkyō (see Map 3)
Transport Train—JR Yamanote line or Keihin Tōhoku line to Yūrakuchō Station and 3-minute walk; or Subway—Yūrakuchō line to Yūrakuchō Station and 3-minute walk; or Ginza line or Hibiya line or Marunouchi line to Ginza Station and 1-minute walk (on the corner diagonally opposite from Sony Building)

Patterned along the same idea that shaped its "predecessor," Tange's Yamanashi Press and Broadcasting Center in Kōfu (1966) (see page 161), this much smaller office tower is supported by only one cylindrical, vertical, service shaft. Offices and other spatial units are cantilevered in a "random" manner out of this central shaft finished in dark, oxidized, cast aluminum plates. Standing on a sharply angled triangular site, the building, like some exclamation mark, has become a powerful urban symbol of the East Ginza area. Well maintained, this tower remains one of Tange's most impressive works in Tōkyō.

Daiichi Life Insurance Building 1938

Daiichi Seimeikan
Architect Hitoshi (Jin) Watanabe
Address 9, Yūrakuchō 1-chōme, Chiyoda-ku, Tōkyō (see Map 3)
Transport Subway—Chiyoda line, Tōei Mita line, or Hibiya line to Hibiya Station and 1-minute walk (on east side of Hibiya-dōri Avenue)

Like the Tōkyō Imperial Museum in Ueno (1937) (see page 97), this building is the result of a competition in which Watanabe's design was chosen over that of Kunio Maekawa. The granite-clad, seven-story, reinforced concrete building became the fourth largest structure in Japan in terms of floor space at the time of its completion. Its architecture, unlike that of the museum, represents a rational design in the so-called "stripped classicism" often favored by the regimes of international fascism. Despite its original ideological affiliation, the building displays important qualities that are acknowledged by many today as contributions to the cause of modernism. Watanabe's building served as the general headquarters of the American forces and General MacArthur after World War II. Today there is a high-rise addition, the Yūrakuchō 1-chōme Building (1994), designed by the American architect Kevin Roche.

Yūrakuchō 1-chōme Building, 1994

Architect Kevin Roche (U.S.)
Address 13, Yūrakuchō 1-chōme, Chiyoda-ku, Tōkyō (see Map 3)
Transport Subway—Chiyoda line, Tōei Mita line, or Hibiya line to Hibiya Station and 3-minute walk (behind Daiichi Life Insurance Building)

Nissei Hibiya Building (Theater), 1963

Nihon Seimei Hibiya Biru
Architect Togo Murano
Address 12, Yūrakuchō 1-chōme, Chiyoda-ku, Tōkyō (see Map 3)
Transport Subway—Hibiya line, Tōei Mita line, or Chiyoda line to Hibiya Station and 2-minute walk (on east side of Hibiya-dōri Avenue)

都 **TŌKYŌ**
Kyōbashi Area

Kanematsu Building 1994

Architect Shimizu Corporation
Address 14-1, Kyōbashi 2-chōme, Chūō-ku, Tōkyō (see Map 3)
Transport Subway—Tōei Asakusa line to Takarachō Station and few steps (on east side of Shōwa-dōri Avenue)

The Kanematsu Building is supported by four large corner shafts and a connecting megastructure. It provides one of the most elegant entrance spaces and lobbies—made with extensive glass surfaces—in recent office buildings in Tōkyō.

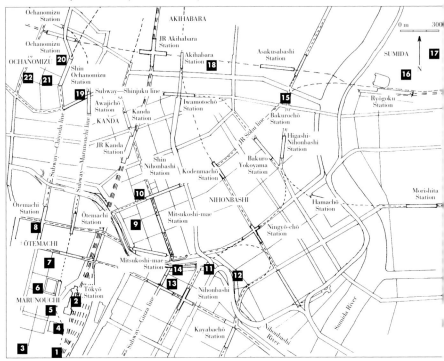

1 Tōkyō International Forum, page 86
2 Tōkyō Station, page 87
3 Meiji Life Insurance Building, page 87
4 Tōkyō Central Post Office, page 88
5 Marunouchi Building, page 88
6 Kaijō Building, page 88
7 Industrial Bank of Japan, page 89
8 Sanwa Bank, page 89
9 Bank of Japan, page 90
10 Morigō Shōten Office

Building (now Kinsan Building), page 90
11 Edobashi Soko Building (now Mitsubishi Soko Honsha Building), page 91
12 Canal Tower, page 91
13 Shirokiya (now Tōkyū) Department Store, page 91
14 Nihonbashi Nomura Building (now Nomura Shōken Building), page 91
15 Higashi Nihonbashi Police Box, page 91
16 Edo-Tōkyō Museum.

page 92
17 YKK Research Center, page 92
18 Koizumi Lighting Theater and IZM Office and Showroom, page 93
19 Metrotour—Edoken Head Office Building, page 94
20 Nikolai Orthodox Cathedral, page 94
21 Mitsui (Taishō) Insurance Company Building, page 94
22 Ochanomizu Square Building, page 94

 **TŌKYŌ**
Marunouchi Area

Tōkyō International Forum
1996
Tōkyō Kokusai Fōramu
Architect Rafael Vinoly (U.S.)
Address Marunouchi 3-chōme, Chiyoda-ku, Tōkyō (see Map 4)

Transport Train—JR Yamanote or Keihin Tōhoku line to Yūrakuchō Station and 1-minute walk; or Subway—Yūrakuchō line to Yūrakuchō Station and 1-minute walk (2-minute walk from Meiji Life Insurance Building or Tōkyō Central Post Office)

he brick-faced building of the old Tōkyō Station—
ow part of a much larger facility than when it was
uilt some eighty years ago—still serves as a pas-
·nger terminal and also provides the west entrance
f the station from the Marunouchi area. Although
ot the most prominent work of Tatsuno, this pop-
lar landmark in Tōkyō, rendered in a "free-style
assicism," further extended the already broad
)ectrum that characterized Japanese architecture
y the end of the Meiji Era. More specifically, the
ong-stretching, three-story, symmetrical building,
atterned after P. J. H. Cuypers's highly pictur-
sque Central Station in Amsterdam (1889),
isplays some of the features of late-nineteenth-
·ntury Dutch eclecticism. Badly damaged during
ie war, the station had to be reconstructed, but
art of the upper structure, including the two
omes over the north and south wings, were not
·built. On the other hand, in front of the west ele-
ation, an extensive canopy was added. Despite all
ie alterations, however, the Tōkyō Station today
ill retains much of Tatsuno's original design,
icluding decorative red brick walls and steeply
itched Mansard roofs with windows.

**Tōkyō Station
1914**
Tōkyō Eki
Architect Kingo Tatsuno
Address Marunouchi
1-chōme, Chiyoda-ku, Tōkyō
(see Map 4)
Transport Any train or sub-
way to Tōkyō Station: west
(Marunouchi) exit

**Meiji Life Insurance
Building
1934**
Meiji Seimeikan
Architect Shinichirō Okada
Address 1, Marunouchi
2-chōme, Chiyoda-ku, Tōkyō
(see Map 4)
Transport Subway—Chiyoda
line to Nijūbashi-Mae Station
and 1-minute walk (on east
side of Hibiya-dōri Avenue)

都 TŌKYŌ
Marunouchi Area

Tōkyō Central Post Office
1931

Tōkyō Chūō Yūbinkyoku
Architect Tetsuro Yoshida
Address 7, Marunouchi
2-chōme, Chiyoda-ku, Tōkyō
(see Map 4)
Transport From Tōkyō Station: west exit and 1-minute
walk (2-minute walk from the
Tōkyō International Forum;
building is on the south side
of station plaza)

One of the few remaining eminent examples of the
rationalist modern architecture of prewar Japan,
Yoshida's Tōkyō Central Post Office is a masterpiece in functional design. The building is laid out
along a simple but systematic structural framework, which is evident on the curving north main
facade. Large infill windows are set within this
reinforced concrete skeleton. At the south side of
the building is a 413-foot/126-meter loading platform, whose straightforward articulation is interrupted only by the huge clock that fills an entire
bay, and the linear cornice above the fourth floor.
In addition to the rational design of the structure,
Yoshida outfitted the building with advanced heating, ventilation, and fire-prevention systems, and
with a 4000-foot/1200-meter conveyor apparatus.

Marunouchi Building
1923
Marunouchi Biru
Architect Mitsubishi Goshi
Company
Address 4, Marunouchi
2-chōme, Chiyoda-ku, Tōkyō
(see Map 4)
Transport From Tōkyō Station: west exit and 2-minute
walk (few steps across the
road from the Tōkyō Central
Post Office; building is on the
southwest corner of the station plaza)
The Marunouchi Building was
designed according to the
principles of rationalism and
functionalism.

Kaijō Building
1974
Tōkyō Kaijō Biru Honkan
Architect Kunio Maekawa
Address 2, Marunouchi
1-chōme, Chiyoda-ku, Tōkyō
(see Map 4)
Transport Subway—Chiyoda
line to Nijūbashimae Station
and 3-minute walk or Tōei
Mita line to Ōtemachi Station
and 3-minute walk; Train—
JR Yamanote line to Tōkyō
Station: west exit and
4-minute walk, 2 blocks west
The red brick panel-covered
high-rise building is the head
quarters of the Marine and
Fire Insurance Company.

Industrial Bank of Japan 1974

Nihon Kōgyō Ginkō
Architect Togo Murano
Address 3-3, Marunouchi
1-chōme, Chiyoda-ku, Tōkyō
(see Map 4)
Transport Subway—Chiyoda
line or Tōzai line to Ōtemachi
Station and 2-minute walk on
Eitai-dōri Avenue (2-minute
walk from Kaijō Building,
toward north)

With a peculiarly sharp edge as its north elevation, the building, faced in dark brown granite, cuts into the space of the busy Eitai-dōri Avenue. This triangular section houses air-conditioning, ventilation, and all other mechanical equipment and machinery. Murano's design shows the influence of Eero Saarinen's CBS Building in New York (1964) in the shaping of the slightly raised, triangular profile of the vertical wall segments, also covered with highly polished stone. With this project, the highly versatile Murano brought his architecture close to Seiichi Shirai's design paradigm of the bizarre.

**Sanwa Bank
1973**

Sanwa Ginkō Tōkyō Biru
Architect Nikken Sekkei
Company
Address 1-1, Ōtemachi
1-chōme, Chiyoda-ku, Tōkyō
(see Map 4)

Transport Subway—Chiyoda
line to Ōtemachi Station and
1-minute walk; or Tōzai line
or Marunouchi line to Ōtemachi Station and 2-minute
walk (5-minute walk from the
Industrial Bank of Japan)
This high-rise building

includes an innovative structural design, facade articulation with deeply recessed fenestration, and fluidity of first
floor lobby space. (See page
19: fig. 16)

Bank of Japan
1896

Nihon Ginkō Honten
Architect Kingo Tatsuno
Address 1, Nihonbashi-
Hongoku-chō 2-chōme,
Chūō-ku, Tōkyō (see Map 4)
Transport Subway—Ginza
line to Mitsukoshi-mae
Station and 2-minute walk; or
Hanzōmon line to Mitsuko
shi-mae Station and 1-minute
walk

Morigō Shōten
Office Building
(now Kinsan Building)
1931

Architect Togo Murano
Address 1-21, Nihonbashi-
Muromachi 4-chōme, Chūō-
ku, Tōkyō (see Map 4)
Transport Subway—Ginza
line to Mitsukoshi-mae
Station and 2-minute walk; or
Hanzōmon line to Mitsukoshi-
mae Station and 3-minute
walk to north; or from JR
Higashi-Nihonbashi Station, a
few steps (along the north
side of Edo-dōri Avenue)

Perhaps the largest and most outstanding work of Tatsuno, the Bank of Japan is among the most prominent representatives of Meiji Era architecture. Like many of his contemporaries upon receiving a major commission, Tatsuno spent a year abroad, mainly in London, to study the bank architecture of the West. In fact, he designed most of the building there. Therefore it is not surprising that the bank fully reflects the contemporary eclectic style that prevailed in Europe. While such Western-ization was an explicit goal of the Japanese at that time, Tatsuno's design far surpassed in monumentality as well as detailing anything that had been built in Japan. Even after its completion, only a few projects, such as Tokuma Katayama's Akasaka Detached Palace (1909) (see page 105), were able to match the qualities of this bank. The complex, which was enlarged later on, had been designed, in the Beaux-Arts tradition, with a square plan and patterned after the courtyard-type palace architecture of France. The three-story, neo-Renaissance-style building was constructed with brick structural walls, reinforced with iron bands, and covered entirely with stone. It was one of the first buildings to use a steel frame in the first floor and roof structures and steel-sash windows. Tatsuno's design still serves as part of the Bank of Japan Headquarters.

Edobashi Soko Building (now Mitsubishi Soko Honsha Building) 1930

Architect Mitsubishi Soko Company
Address 1-19, Nihonbashi 1-chōme, Chūō-ku, Tōkyō (see Map 4)
Transport Subway—Asakusa line to Nihonbashi stop and 1-minute walk (on east side of Shōwa-dōri Avenue at Edobashi Bridge and 2-minute walk from Nomura Building)

The five-story structure is an urban warehouse and office building, a type that was first developed in the United States. It is located along the Nihon-bashi River and, perhaps for this reason, its design evokes the image of a ship. This is particularly pronounced in the rooftop "tower," which looks like a ship's bridge. Moreover, the architecture calls to mind the features of one of the most prominent works by the Japanese Secession Group, Kikuji Ishimoto's now demolished Asahi Newspaper Building (1927) in Tōkyō.

Canal Tower, 1990
Architect Minoru Takeyama
Address 9-3, Koami-chō, Nihonbashi, Chūō-ku, Tōkyō (see Map 4)
Transport Subway—Asakusa line to Nihonbashi stop and 1-minute walk (1-minute walk from Edobashi Soko Building)
The tower is a small, multi-story, infill office building.

Shirokiya (now Tōkyū) Department Store, 1931 facade redesigned, 1957
Tōkyū Depāto
Architect Kikuji Ishimoto; new facade: Junzo Sakakura
Address 4, Nihonbashi 1-chōme, Chūō-ku, Tōkyō (see Map 4)
Transport Subway—Ginza line or Tōzai line to Nihon-bashi Station and few steps
The facade of the original building was drastically redesigned by Junzo Saka-kura in 1957; therefore it does not resemble Ishimoto's design, which was inspired partly by Erich Mendelsohn's early expressionist works. (See page 14, fig. 4)

Nihonbashi Nomura Building (now Nomura Shōken Building) 1930
Nomura Shōken Biru
Architect Takeo Yasui
Address 1-9, Nihonbashi 1-chōme, Chūō-ku, Tōkyō (see Map 4)
Transport Subway—Hanzō-mon line to Mitsukoshi-mae stop and 2-minute walk across Nihonbashi bridge; or Ginza line or Tōzai line to Nihonbashi stop and 1-min-ute walk to north (on east side of Chūō-dōri Avenue)
The highly eclectic structure is one of the office buildings of Nomura Securities Company.

Higashi Nihonbashi Police Box 1992
Higashi Nihonbashi Hashutsu-jō
Architect Atsushi Kitagawara
Address 1, Bakuro-chō 2-chōme, Higashi Nihon-bashi, Chūō-ku, Tōkyō (see Map 4)
Transport Subway—Shinjuku line to Bakuro Yokoyama Station and 5-minute walk on Edo-dōri Avenue; or Train—JR Sōbu line to Bakuro Station and 2-minute walk
Located on a triangular cen-ter island at a major intersec-tion, the small building is wrapped with an oval, three-story screen.

Edo-Tōkyō Museum 1992

Edo-Tōkyō Hakubutsukan
Architect Kiyonori Kikutake
Address 4-1. Yokoami
1-chōme, Sumida-ku, Tōkyō
(see Map 4)
Transport Train—JR Sōbu
line to Ryōgoku Station: west
exit and 3-minute walk
Visitation 10:00–18:00;
Friday 10:00–19:00 (closed
Mondays)

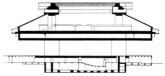

The enormous volume of the Edo-Tōkyō Museum, whose shape suggests the form of traditional Japanese roofs, is elevated on and fully supported by four huge shafts. These tall shafts, enclosing vertical circulation and other service facilities, provide for a covered, urban-scale plaza—a futuristic space under the "roof." The concept of this monumental "megastructure" is derived from such Metabolist projects as Kenzo Tange's Yamanashi Press and Broadcasting Center in Kōfu (1966) (see page 161) and his space frame of the Theme Pavilion at the Ōsaka Expo '70 (see page 19, fig. 15). Therefore, by extension, the museum also calls to mind the numerous visionary urban projects with the idea of a city in the air that the architects in the Metabolism group proposed in the 1960s.

YKK Research Center 1993

Architect Fumihiko Maki
Address 22. Kamezawa
3-chōme, Sumida-ku, Tōkyō
(see Map 4)
Transport Train—JR Sōbu
line to Ryōgoku Station: west
exit and 15-minute walk
(15-minute walk from Edo-
Tōkyō Museum)
Visitation 9:00–17:00 on
working days

Asahi Beer Super Dry Hall, 1989

Asahi Biru Azumabashi Hōru
Architect Philippe Starck
(France) (with Makoto
Nozawa and GETT)
Address 25, Azuma-bashi
1-chōme, Sumida-ku, Tōkyō
Transport Subway—Ginza
line or Tōei Asakusa line to
Asakusa Station and 10-
minute walk across Sumida
River on Azuma-bashi Bridge

Located in a densely built, traditional, working-class area of Tōkyō, Hasegawa's building, shaped and finished largely with metallic materials, perforated aluminum, and layers of translucent screens, intends to create a metaphysical townscape of the Sumida district. Around a small inner plaza, three volumes are arranged. The southwest volume accommodates assembly and communication spaces, a hall, and a planetarium; that in the southeast features an information center and a library; while the third volume has study rooms, offices, and, on the top floor, counseling rooms for children. The three parts are connected by bridges.

Sumida Cultural Center, 1994
Sumida Bunka Gakushū Center
Architect Itsuko Hasegawa
Address 38, Higashi-Mukōjima 2-chōme, Sumida-ku, Tōkyō
Transport From Asakusa: Train—Tōbu-Isseki line to Hikifune Station and 4-minute walk to north; or to Higashi-Mukōjima Station and 4-minute walk to south (near the train line and Meiji-dōri Avenue)

都 TŌKYŌ
Akihabara Area

Koizumi Lighting Theater and IZM Office and Showroom 1990
Koizumi IZM Biru

Architect Peter Eisenman (U.S.) (with Kojiro Kitayama)
Address 12, Kanda-Sakuma-chō 3-chōme, Chiyoda-ku, Tōkyō (see Map 4)
Transport Subway—Hibiya line to Akihabara Station and 10-minute walk to east

Metrotour, Edoken Head Office Building
1990

Edoken Tōkyō Honsha-ya
Architect Atsushi Kitagawara
Address 1-1, Kanda-Awaji-chō 1-chōme, Chiyoda-ku, Tōkyō (see Map 4)
Transport Subway—Shinjuku line to Ogawamachi Station; or Marunouchi line to Awajichō Station, A5 exit and 1-minute walk (on north side of Yasukuni-dōri Avenue in front of Subway exit)

Standing on a corner site, the dark, Belgian-glass-plate-covered office tower is wrapped around on each floor by a system of lacy, metallic catwalks for maintenance. In certain light conditions, this system renders the building almost immaterial, a phenomenon of vibrant luminance.

Nikolai Orthodox Cathedral
1891

Nihon Harisutosu Nikorai-dō
Architect Josiah Conder (U.K.)
Address 1-3, Kanda-Surugadai 4-chōme, Chiyoda-ku, Tōkyō (see Map 4)
Transport Train—JR Chūō or Sōbu line to Ochanomizu Station; east exit and 3-minute walk to southeast; or Subway—Chiyoda line to Shin-Ochanomizu Station and few steps across the road

Mitsui (Taishō) Insurance Company Building
1984

Mitsui-Taishō Kaijō Honsha Biru
Architect Nikken Sekkei Company
Address 9, Kanda-Surugadai 3-chōme, Chiyoda-ku, Tōkyō (see Map 4)
Transport Train—JR Chūō or Sōbu line to Ochanomizu Station; east exit and 4-minute walk south; or Subway—Chiyoda line to Shin-Ochanomizu Station and 1-minute walk west

Ochanomizu Square Building
1987

Shufunotomo-sha Biru
Architect Arata Isozaki
Address 6-9, Kanda-Surugadai 1-chōme, Chiyoda-ku, Tōkyō (see Map 4)
Transport Train—JR Chūō or Sōbu line to Ochanomizu Station; west exit and 2-minute walk to south (on east side of avenue)
The building has been conceived with explicit allusions to a postmodernist classicism.

TŌKYŌ Map 5
Ochanomizu, Ueno, Hongō, and Kōrakuen Areas

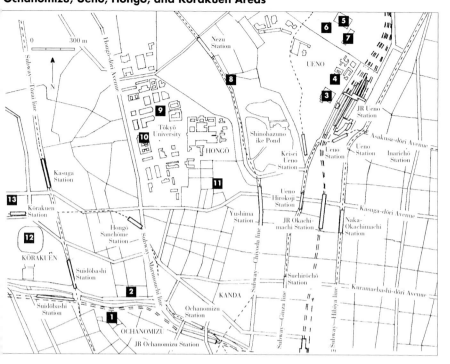

1 Athene Française, page 95
2 Century Tower, page 95
3 Tōkyō Metropolitan Festival Hall, page 96
4 National Museum of Western Art, Ueno, page 96
5 Tōkyō Imperial Museum, Ueno (now Tōkyō National Museum), page 97
6 Hyōkeikan, page 97
7 Tōkyō National Museum and Gallery, page 97
8 Ueno Green (Bonsai) Club, page 97
9 Yasuda Hall of Tōkyō University, page 98
10 Tōkyō University Library, page 98
11 Iwasaki Mansion, page 98
12 Tōkyō Dome, Big Egg, page 98
13 Tōkyō War Dead Memorial Park, page 98

都 TŌKYŌ
Ochanomizu Area

Athene Française
1962
Architect Takamasa Yoshizaka
Address 11, Kanda-Surugadai 2-chōme, Chiyoda-ku, Tōkyō (see Map 5)
Transport Train—JR Chūō or Sōbu line to Ochanomizu Station; west exit and 6-minute walk to west
The building houses a French and English language school. Located amidst a district of many educational facilities, the building surpasses most in both its functional arrangement and elegant articulation.

Century Tower
1991
Architect Norman Foster (U.K.) (with Obayashi Corporation)
Address 2-9, Hongō 2-chōme, Bunkyō-ku, Tōkyō (see Map 5)
Transport Subway—Marunouchi line to Ochanomizu Station and 5-minute walk to west; or Train—JR Chūō or Sōbu line to Ochanomizu Station: west exit and 7-minute walk, across Ochano-mizu-bashi Bridge and then to west on north side of Sotobori-dōri Avenue

Tōkyō Metropolitan Festival Hall
1961

Tōkyō Bunka Kaikan
Architect Kunio Maekawa
Address 5-45, Ueno Park, Taitō-ku, Tōkyō (see Map 5)
Transport Subway—Ginza line or any train to Ueno Station: west exit and 1-minute walk (in front of west exit to Ueno Park)

The large cultural complex, which includes a theater, auditorium, and exhibition space, is one of Maekawa's most outstanding designs. Following his similar intentions in the Kyōto Hall a year earlier, Maekawa combined the features of modern and traditional Japanese architectures, thereby creating a building that befits both the past and present of Tōkyō. The post-and-beam reinforced concrete structure supports an extensive roof with curving eaves. This exposed concrete roof provides a unifying element that visually holds together the various forms and spaces defined by the functional units. A stone podium set within a shallow pool on the northern, outdoor terrace is reminiscent of the ramparts and moats of medieval European castles, while the spatial quality of the lobby and foyer is evocative of traditional Japanese interiors.

National Museum of Western Art in Ueno
1959

Kokuritsu Seiyō Bijutsukan
Architect Le Corbusier (Switzerland) (with K. Maekawa, J. Sakakura, and T. Yoshizaka)
Address 7-7, Ueno Park, Taitō-ku, Tōkyō (see Map 5)
Transport Subway—Ginza line or any train to Ueno Station: west exit and 2-minute walk (museum is north of Tōkyō Metropolitan Festival Hall)
Visitation 9:30–17:00 (closed Mondays)

Tōkyō Imperial Museum in Ueno (now Tōkyō National Museum), 1937

Tōkyō Kokuritsu Hakubutsukan
Architect Hitoshi Watanabe
Address 13, Ueno Park, Taitō-ku, Tōkyō (see Map 5)
Transport Subway—Ginza line; or any train to Ueno Station: west exit and 10-minute walk (in the northern part of the Ueno Park)
Visitation 9:30–17:00 (closed Mondays)

The Tōkyō Imperial Museum in Ueno is noted in the history of prewar Japanese architecture as being the foremost representative of the Imperial Crown style (*teikan yoshiki*). In the mid-1930s the increasingly chauvinistic, ruling military circles not only favored but in fact demanded that major buildings be designed in a "Japanese taste." Therefore, the jury for the museum's architectural competition rejected entries like that of Kunio Maekawa conceived in the modern International Style, despite their merits. Watanabe, responding to the requirements of the architectural competition, designed a massive and fully symmetrical building. The shape and material of the monumental, tiled roofs were patterned after similar structures of traditional temple and shrine architecture. The horizontally stretching volume of Watanabe's museum is laid out with a square plan that surrounds two courtyards. The entrance portico, also covered by a heavy roof, leads to a high-ceilinged lobby and a grandiose stairway to the second-floor main galleries. In regard to their natural lighting and spatial articulation, these upper-level galleries are more successful than those on the first floor. (See also page 14, fig. 3)

Hyōkeikan 1909

Architect Tokuma Katayama
Address 13, Ueno Park, Taitō-ku, Tōkyō (see Map 5)
Transport Subway—Ginza line or any train to Ueno Station: west exit and 10-minute walk (west of the Tōkyō Imperial Museum in Ueno)
The Hyōkeikan displays a design sensibility to stylistic articulations similar to that of Katayama's Akasaka Detached Palace. Both were conceived in a French neo-baroque idiom. (See page 13, fig. 2)

Tōkyō National Museum and Gallery 1968

Tōkyō Kokuritsu Hakubutsukan: Tōyōkan
Architect Yoshiro Taniguchi
Address 13, Ueno Park, Taitō-ku, Tōkyō (see Map 5)
Transport Subway—Ginza line or any train to Ueno Station: west exit and 8-minute walk (east of the Tōkyō Imperial Museum in Ueno)
The large building is an attractive representative of Japanese modern architecture shaped with a sensibility toward traditional solutions.

Ueno Green (Bonsai) Club 1993

Architect Shin Takamatsu
Address 3-42, Ueno Park, Taitō-ku, Tōkyō (see Map 5)
Transport Subway—Ginza line or any train to Ueno Station: west exit and 15-minute walk; or Subway—Chiyoda line to Nezu Station and 2-minute walk to south; building is west of Ueno Zoo, slightly east of Shinobazu-dōri Avenue
Covered with aluminum panels, the building's articulation and volume is similar to Fumihiko Maki's Tepia Science Pavilion (1989) in Tōkyō.

都 TŌKYŌ
Hongō Area

Yasuda Hall of Tōkyō University
1925
Tōkyō Daigaku Yasuda Kinenkan
Tōkyō University Library
1928
Tōkyō Daigaku Toshokan
Architect Yoshikazu Uchida (with Hideto Kishida)
Address Hongō 7-chōme, Bunkyō-ku, Tōkyō (see Map 5)
Transport Subway—Marunouchi line to Hongō-San-chōme Station and 8-minute walk to north on Hongō-dōri Avenue to Tōkyō University (Tō-Dai) campus.

Iwasaki Mansion
1896
Kyū Iwasaki-tei
Architect Josiah Conder (U.K.)
Address 10, Yūshima 4-chōme, Bunkyō-ku, Tōkyō (see Map 5)
Transport Subway—Chiyoda line to Yūshima Station and 6 minutes by taxi (within the compound of the Supreme Court Legal Study Center)
Visitation 10:00–11:00, 13:00–15:00 by appointment only, tel: 3813-2101
The mansion is one of the very few extant works designed by Conder.

都 TŌKYŌ
Kōrakuen Area

Tōkyō Dome, Big Egg
1988
Architect Nikken Sekkei Company and Takenaka Corporation
Address 1, Kōraku 1-chōme, Bunkyō-ku, Tōkyō (see Map 5)
Transport Train—JR Sōbu line to Suidōbashi Station and 5-minute walk north; or Subway—Tōei line to Suidōbashi Station and 5-minute walk; or Subway—Marunouchi line to Kōrakuen Station and 2-minute walk
The stadium features a cable-reinforced air membrane roof structure that is glowing white, hence the name of the dome.

都 TŌKYŌ
Kōrakuen Area

Tōkyō War Dead Memorial Park
1988
Tōkyō-to Senbotsusha Reinen
Architect Takefumi Aida
Address 14-4, Kasuga 1-chōme, Bunkyō-ku, Tōkyō (see Map 5)
Transport Subway—Marunouchi line to Kōrakuen Station and 8-minute walk east of Chūō University; enter from Kasuga-dōri Avenue
Visitation 10:00–17:00 (closed Sundays)

The Tōkyō War Dead Memorial Park, both a peace park and a monument built in honor of the 160,000 Japanese who died in Tōkyō during World War II, is one of Aida's most successful recent projects, and exposes his new "architecture of fluctuation." The complex is comprised mainly of freestanding, reinforced concrete walls and gatelike passages arranged along two axes so as to interpenetrate and conflict. Reflective surfaces, light and shadows, partial and fragmented views, and the sight and sound of water complement the architectural scheme and viewer's experience. Together they inscribe a unique path, the thin and elusive borderline between inside and outside, architecture and nature, permanence and transitoriness.

都 TŌKYŌ
Mejirodai Area

Saint Mary's Cathedral 1964

Tōkyō Katedorāru— Sei-Maria Taiseidō

Architect Kenzo Tange
Address 16-5, Sekiguchi 3-chōme, Bunkyō-ku, Tōkyō
Transport Train—JR Yamanote line to Mejiro Station: north exit and 5 minutes by bus to Sekiguchi and 2-minute walk to east; or Subway—Yūrakuchō line to Edogawa-bashi Station and 8-minute walk to northwest (on north side of Mejiro-dōri Avenue)

Tange's building replaced its predecessor, which was destroyed in 1945. The new Saint Mary's Cathedral has been laid out along a cruciform, which is inscribed in the soaring interior by the intersecting lines of two long skylights. The symmetrical building is engendered by four reinforced concrete shells of hyperbolic-paraboloids, curving geometric surfaces that can be defined entirely by straight lines. This unique feature is emphasized by the folds of the exterior corrugated aluminum plates. The majestic structural forms of the cathedral are perceived from the outside with the sun bouncing back from the reflective metallic surfaces, and, from the inside, through a mysterious dimness created by the steeply tapering spaces leading to the narrow skylights overhead. The cathedral most certainly qualifies as one of the most outstanding achievements of both Tange's and twentieth-century Japanese architecture.

都 TŌKYŌ
Ōtsuka Area

Sky House, 1958
Kikutake Tei
Architect Kiyonori Kikutake
Address 11-15, Ōtsuka 1-chōme, Bunkyō-ku, Tōkyō
Transport Subway— Yūrakuchō line to Gokokuji Station and 8-minute walk uphill (east of Otowa-dōri Avenue)

Visitation Private residence; seen only from the outside. This small building, revolutionary in its time, is elevated over a steep site by means of four reinforced concrete wall-columns. The pilotis space, however, has since been enclosed with glass walls. (See page 17, fig. 10)

TŌKYŌ Map 6
Imperial Palace, Jimbōchō, Kōjimachi, and Akasaka Areas

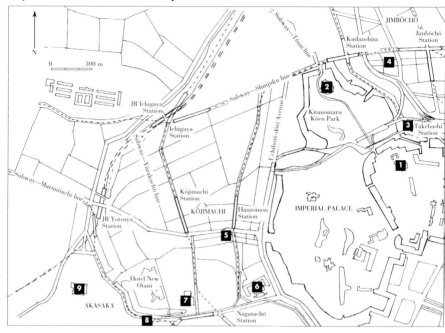

TŌKYŌ
Imperial Palace Area

Imperial Music Hall
1966

Gakudō or *Tōka Ongaku-dō*
Architect Kenji Imai
Address Kōkyō Higashi Gyōen (Imperial Palace East Garden), Chiyoda-ku, Tōkyō (see Map 6)
Transport Subway—Tōzai line to Takebashi Station and 5-minute walk

Nippon Budōkan
1964

Architect Mamoru Yamada
Address Kitanomaru Kōen Park, Chiyoda-ku, Tōkyō (see Map 6)
Transport Subway—Shinjuku line or Tōzai line to Kudanshita Station and 5-minute walk (10-minute walk from Palaceside Building, or 3-minute walk from Soldiers' Hall) The huge octagonal structure—designed with a traditional roof—is a multipurpose facility to accommodate martial arts and other sports events and concerts.

都 TŌKYŌ
Imperial Palace Area

Palaceside Building 1966

Paresusaido Biru

Architect Nikken Sekkei Company

Address 1, Hitotsubashi 1-chōme, Chiyoda-ku, Tōkyō (see Map 6)

Transport Subway—Tōzai line to Takebashi Station and few steps (5-minute walk from Imperial Music Hall)

At the time of its completion the Palaceside Building was one of the largest commercial complexes in Tōkyō. Today it houses the offices of Reader's Digest and those of the Mainichi Newspaper and all its service facilities. At street level there is a two-story shopping arcade linked to the surrounding urban streets, making this building one of the first multiuse urban complexes in Japan. Its two cylindrical shafts, reminiscent of numerous Metabolist designs, enclose stairways and elevators along with their lobbies. Particularly noteworthy is the mode in which the elevations are articulated with delicately designed metallic louvers, drainpipes, and spandrels. Such craftsmanship lends this impressive building an aesthetic quality that is akin to that of traditional solutions.

都 TŌKYŌ
Jimbōchō Area

Soldiers' Hall 1934

Kudan Kaikan

Architect Ryūji Kawamoto (with Chuta Ito)

Address 6, Kanda-Jimbō-chō 1-chōme, Chiyoda-ku, Tōkyō (see Map 6)

Transport Subway—Shinjuku line or Tōzai line to Kudan-shita Station and 2-minute walk (3-minute walk from Nippon Budōkan, or 10-minute walk from Palaceside Building)

Another eminent example of the Imperial Crown Style, Soldiers' Hall is outfitted with a system of large roofs reminiscent of traditional religious architecture. Designed with the assistance of the architectural theoretician Chuta Ito, who served as an advisor, the building features a mixture of stylistic elements that have been assembled from various sources including classicism, as seen in the vertically grouped windows among pilasters, and Wright's Prairie Style, represented by various detailings and by the asymmetrical massing.

Wacoal Kōjimachi Building
1984

Architect Kisho Kurokawa
Address 1-2, Kōjimachi 1-chōme, Chiyoda-ku, Tōkyō (see Map 6)
Transport Subway—Hanzō-mon line to Hanzōmon Station and 10-minute walk

Shaped with elements of various origin—sleek high-tech materials, popular motifs, and traditional Japanese details—the Wacoal Kōjimachi Building is one of the first representatives of a design philosophy that Kurokawa calls "symbiosis in architecture." The aluminum-panel-clad building with crystal glass fenestration is capped with the vaulted spaces of the reception room and the roof garden. The large circular window here is inspired by a contemporary astrological chart devised by Shunzo Yoshio, while the *fusuma* sliding doors and the garden reveal their origin in Japanese design. On the other hand, much of the exterior is highly futuristic in appearance; note, for example, the flying-saucer-like canopies and corner ventilation outlets.

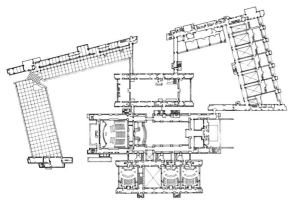

Supreme Court Building, 1974
Saikō Saiban-shō
Architect Shinichi Okada
Address 4-2, Hayabusa-chō, Chiyoda-ku, Tōkyō (see Map 6)
Transport Subway—Hanzōmon line to Hanzōmon Station and 6-minute walk; or Marunouchi line or Chiyoda line to Kokkaigijidō-mae Station and 10-minute walk to the intersection of Uchibori-dōri and Aoyama-dōri avenues

Standing at a busy intersection and facing the Imperial Palace compound, the Supreme Court Building displays a monumental, volumetric architecture. Its gigantic rectangular blocks, faced with rough, gray granite slabs, bring to mind the forms of both ancient Egyptian and modern Brutalist structures. Okada, who studied at Yale University and worked for Skidmore, Owings and Merrill in the United States, seems to have been strongly influenced by his masters, Paul Rudolph and Louis Kahn. Using Kahn's terminology, Okada described his design for the Supreme Court Building as a combination of large "served" and small "serving" spaces, wherein the latter, in the form of a double-walled system of "space walls," surround and define the former, including various court rooms, the entrance hall, and other large public spaces. The extensive complex is arranged around two major and several minor courtyards.

Akasaka Prince Hotel 1982
Architect Kenzo Tange
Address 1-2, Kioi-chō, Chiyoda-ku, Tōkyō (see Map 6)
Transport Subway—Hanzōmon line to Nagatachō Station and 2-minute walk; or Ginza line or Marunouchi line to Akasakamitsuke Station and 5-minute walk
The hotel is a high-rise building with a zigzagging V-shaped volume.

Imanishi Motoakasaka 1992

Architect Shin Takamatsu
Address 1–6, Motoakasaka
1-chōme, Minato-ku, Tōkyō
(see Map 6)
Transport Subway—Ginza line
or Marunouchi line to Akasakamitsuke Station and
3-minute walk (behind the
twin towers of Kajima
Building)

Sandwiched between two structures, the Imanishi Motoakasaka is a small and meticulously symmetrical retail and office building, whose narrow and only facade facing south is dominated by an uncanny design, highly polished metallic and stone materials, excessive detailings, and, above all, pervading dark colors. This concave facade also reveals a cylindrical glass volume that, as a buried column, bulges from its background. The seven-story building also features a basement, which is accessible directly from the street level through a small sunken courtyard with plants in front of the main entrance. Flanking this outside entrance are two large and sharply pointed glass cones that are skylights over the subterranean spaces. The most important feature is the elaborate facade that acts, almost literally, as a mask. Alternatively, its design can impart the image of a huge piece of jewelry, a surreal or virtual "object of desire." The "simple" glass cones, on the other hand, foretell the atrium space of the Kunibiki Messe (1993) (see page 255). This project is one of the best representatives of Takamatsu's highly manneristic architecture in Tōkyō.

The Akasaka Detached Palace, which is both the largest structure and most outstanding achievement of Meiji Era (1868–1912) architecture, was designed as a residence for the crown prince Yoshihito, who later became Emperor Taishō (1912–26). Nevertheless, the prince never occupied what he considered to be overly luxurious premises, and the huge complex is used today to accommodate foreign dignitaries visiting Japan. Katayama designed the palace with an explicit reference to French palaces; therefore, the neo-baroque building is often called the "Japanese Versailles." In addition to the exterior grandeur, the richness of interior ornamentation is practically unparalleled in any building in Japan; the design thus represents an exceptional accomplishment in the course of Westernization of Japanese architecture. The stone-faced structure is constructed of reinforced brick using several thousand tons of iron. The palace was renovated in 1974 under the supervision of Togo Murano.

Akasaka Detached Palace 1909

Akasaka Rikyū
Architect Tokuma Katayama
Address Moto-Akasaka 2-chōme, Minato-ku, Tōkyō (see Map 6)
Transport Train—JR Sōbu line or Chūō line to Yotsuya Station; or Subway—Marunouchi line to Yotsuya Station and 3-minute walk to south
Visitation Seen only from outside the iron gates

TŌKYŌ Map 7
Akasaka, Kasumigaseki, Roppongi, Azabu-dai, Shiba, Mita, and Azabu Areas

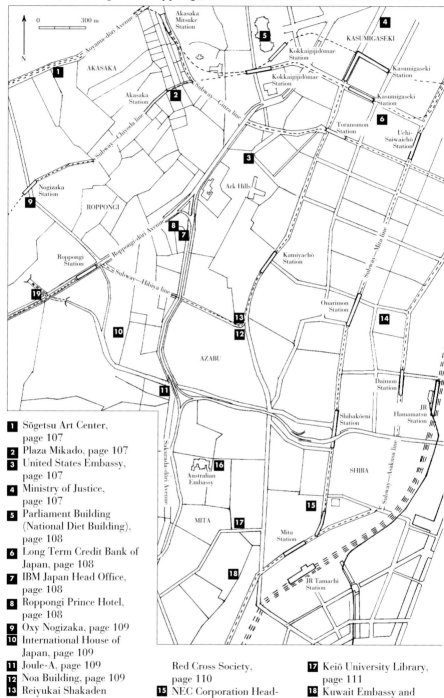

Sōgetsu Art Center
1977
Sōgetsu Kaikan
Architect Kenzo Tange
Address 2-21, Akasaka
7-chōme, Minato-ku, Tōkyō
(see Map 7)
Transport Subway—Ginza
line or Hanzōmon line to
Akasakaitchōme Station and
5-minute walk along south
side of Aoyama-dōri Avenue
to east
The *L*-shaped, twelve-story
building is the headquarters
of the Sogetsu Ikebana
School, but it also accommodates Tange's own architectural offices. The spectacular
lobby was designed by the
sculptor Isamu Noguchi.

Plaza Mikado
1990
Architect Edward Suzuki
Address 14-5, Akasaka
2-chōme, Minato-ku, Tōkyō
(see Map 7)
Transport Subway—Chiyoda
line to Akasaka Station and
2-minute walk to southeast
The plaza is a mixed-use commercial facility. The seven-
story building with shops and
restaurants is defined by the
extensive use of frosted glass
screens and walls.

United States Embassy
1976
Amerika Taishikan
Architect Cesar Pelli (U.S.)
Address 10-5, Akasaka
1-chōme, Minato-ku, Tōkyō
(see Map 7)
Transport Subway—Ginza
line to Toranomon Station
and 8-minute walk

Ministry of Justice
1895
Hōmushō Chōsha
Architect Ende and Böckmann
Partnership (Hermann Ende
and Wilhelm Böckmann)
(Germany)
Address 1, Kasumigaseki
1-chōme, Chiyoda-ku, Tōkyō
(see Map 7)
Transport Subway—Yūraku-
chō line to Sakuradamon Sta-
tion and 2-minute walk; or
Chiyoda line, Marunouchi line,
or Hibiya line to Kasumigaseki
Station and 1-minute walk

Of the two projects the Ende and Böckmann firm designed in Tōkyō, only the
Ministry of Justice remains today; the Supreme Court Building (1896) was
demolished in the 1970s. The building was designed in German neo-Renaissance style with French Second Empire mansard roofs. For earthquake protection, the red brick and stone ornamented structure was laid out with a low,
three-story, horizontally expanding volume. The design made use of an early
version of a "floating foundation," a system also employed by Frank Lloyd
Wright in his Imperial Hotel (1923) (see page 173) in a more advanced form.
Both buildings survived the devastating 1923 Kantō earthquake largely
because of this new type of foundation. To alleviate the horizontality of the
otherwise fairly rational design, Ende and Böckmann articulated the facades
with as many vertical elements as possible: porticoes, loggias, pilasters, etc.
The construction was supervised by the Japanese architect Kozo Kawai.

Parliament Building (National Diet Building)
1936
Kokkai Gijidō
Architect Ministry of Finance Architecture Department
Address 7, Nagata-chō 1-chōme, Chiyoda-ku, Tōkyō (see Map 7)
Transport Subway—Marunouchi line or Chiyoda line to Kokkaigijidō-mae Station and 1-minute walk

The completion of the Parliament Building was preceded by several years of debate about the form it should take. The design competition for the building was held in 1918. Though the winning project was to serve as the basis for the building, the effective design and working documents carried out by the Ministry of Finance Architecture Department deviated completely from this project. In its realized form the building, which took fifteen years to complete, assumed a style that drew from European—but also Asian, particularly Egyptian—models to satisfy the growing imperative for an architecture conceived in an Asian spirit. The building represents an overall technical/technological skill rather than an outstanding architectural achievement in prewar Japanese design.

都 TŌKYŌ
Kasumigaseki Area

Long Term Credit Bank of Japan, 1993
Tōkyō Chōkiteki Shintaku Ginkō
Architect Nikken Sekkei Co.
Address 2-2, Uchisaiwai-chō 2-chōme, Chiyoda-ku, Tōkyō (see Map 7)
Transport Subway—Tōei Mita line to Uchisaiwai-chō Station and 1-minute walk

都 TŌKYŌ
Roppongi Area

IBM Japan Head Office 1971
IBM Honsha Biru
Architect Nikken Sekkei Company
Address 2-12, Roppongi 3-chōme, Minato-ku, Tōkyō (see Map 7)
Transport Subway—Hibiya line to Roppongi Station and 10-minute walk

Roppongi Prince Hotel 1984
Architect Kisho Kurokawa
Address 2-7, Roppongi 3-chōme, Minato-ku, Tōkyō (see Map 7)
Transport Subway—Hibiya line to Roppongi Station and 10-minute walk (next to Nikken Sekkei's IBM Japan Head Office)

Oxy Nogizaka, 1987

Architect Kiyoshi Sei Takeyama

Address 2-8, Roppongi 7-chōme, Minato-ku, Tōkyō (see Map 7)

Transport Subway—Chiyoda line to Nogizaka Station and 2-minute walk south on west side of Gaien-Higashi-dōri Avenue

It is a multistory office and commercial complex, dominated by an exposed reinforced concrete curving wall structure. The Lucchino Pub on the first basement level has been designed by the interior designer Shirō Kuramata.

International House of Japan, 1955

Kokusai Bunka Kaikan

Architect Kunio Maekawa with Junzo Sakakura and Junzo Yoshimura

Address 11-6, Roppongi 5-chōme, Minato-ku, Tōkyō (see Map 7)

Transport Subway—Hibiya line to Roppongi Station and 12-minute walk (10-minute walk from Joule-A)

Visitation Open daily, tel: (03) 3470-4611

The house is a lodging complex for foreigners, and is surrounded by a large, attractive Japanese garden.

Joule-A, 1990

Architect Edward Suzuki

Address 10, Azabu-Jūban 1-chōme, Minato-ku, Tōkyō (see Map 7)

Transport Subway—Hibiya line to Roppongi Station and 20-minute walk (10-minute walk from International House of Japan)

The building is a mixed-use commercial complex.

Seiichi Shirai, who studied history and philosophy with Karl Jaspers in Berlin, Germany, was a self-trained architect. Evidence of his European and individualistic training is manifested in many of his unique works. Yet, above all, Shirai's architecture, shaped by his powerfully mannerist approach to design, is evocative of the bizarre. His Noa Building and the Shinwa Bank Buildings in Sasebo (1967–75) (see page 291) are the best examples of this. A showroom and office tower, the Noa juxtaposes two disjunctive, curving volumes and forms, rendered in two incongruous materials with two primary colors and two different surface treatments. Here a rusticated, red brick lower section acts as a podium for a tall, oval block finished in smooth blackened bronze plates alternating with slim, flush-mounted windows. They impart an image that is akin to a temple of some unknown cult. To heighten the effect, an oversized arched gate leads to a rather dark, almost cryptic entry space that continues in other dimly lit but smaller spaces. While Shirai's works are unique in their intensity, their bizarre mannerism is not completely unparalleled in Japanese architecture. Shirai influenced many of his contemporaries and many younger-generation architects including Arata Isozaki, Shin Takamatsu, and Atsushi Kitagawara.

都 TŌKYŌ
Azabudai Area

Noa Building 1974

Noa Biru

Architect Seiichi Shirai

Address 3, Azabudai 2-chōme, Minato-ku, Tōkyō (see Map 7)

Transport Subway—Hibiya line to Kamiyachō Station and 5-minute walk to the intersection to the south

都 TŌKYŌ
Azabudai Area

Reiyukai Shakaden Buddhist Temple 1975

Architect Takenaka Corporation
Address 7, Azabudai 1-chōme, Minato-ku, Tōkyō (see Map 7)
Transport Subway—Hibiya line to Kamiyachō Station and 3-minute walk south (2 minutes from Noa Building, or 1 minute from the intersection)

Headquarters of a new Buddhist sect, the dark granite-covered temple matches in intensity Seiichi Shirai's bizarre architecture. Although its strange form may incorporate the motif of traditional temple roofs, the overall impression is more of a huge black coffin or mortuary. The design no doubt evokes the feeling of a heavy volume, but, because this volume is placed on pilotis, it also seems to float above the ground. The enormous, reinforced concrete and steel structure features several levels both above and underground. The main worship hall with extensive galleries seats 5000 people, and is approachable through a wide, open-air stairway leading directly from the plaza in front of the temple to the second floor. A large meditation space called the place of "inner journey" is located on the first floor, while a smaller multi-purpose auditorium with a stage is on the first basement level.

都 TŌKYŌ
Shiba Area

Japan Headquarters of the Red Cross Society 1977

Nihon Sekijūji Honsha
Architect Kisho Kurokawa
Address 1-5, Shiba daimon 1-chōme, Minato-ku, Tōkyō (see Map 7)
Transport Subway—Tōei Mita line to Onarimon Station and 3-minute walk to east

NEC Corporation Headquarters 1990

Nippon Denki Honsha Biru
Architect Nikken Sekkei Company
Address 7-1, Shiba 5-chōme, Minato-ku, Tōkyō (see Map 7)
Transport Train—JR Yamanote line or JR Keihin-Tōhoku line to Tamachi Station and 6-minute walk; or Subway—Tōei Mita line or Tōei Asakusa line to Mita Station and 2-minute walk to north

Mitsui Club Tsunamachi, 1913

Mitsui Kurabu
Architect Josiah Conder (U.K.)
Address 3, Mita 2-chōme, Minato-ku, Tōkyō (see Map 7)
Transport Train—JR Yamanote line or Keihin-Tōhoku line to Tamachi Station and 18-minute walk; or Subway—Tōei Asakusa line or Tōei Mita line to Mita Station and 15-minute walk (next to the Australian Embassy)
Visitation Private club; seen only from the outside

Conder was one of the first and most influential foreign architects invited by the Meiji government to assist in the design and construction of numerous buildings and in the education of Western-type architects in Japan. He completed many important projects, but only a few remain today. One of them is this small private club commissioned and formerly owned by the Mitsui family, and now owned by their corporation. The architecture reflects the prevailing trend in the contemporary United Kingdom; it is conceived in a neo-Renaissance style with some baroque elements. The front and rear elevations are fairly different; the former is rather "closed" and formal, while the latter is informal and open to a garden with a system of porches on both floors. The interior is equally impressive and is used for receptions. The building was renovated in 1929 and is in remarkably good condition.

Keiō University Library 1981
Keiō Daigaku Toshokan
Architect Fumihiko Maki
Address 15-45, Mita 2-chōme, Minato-ku, Tōkyō (see Map 7)
Transport Train—JR Yamanote line or JR Keihin-Tōhoku line to Tamachi Station: north exit and 10-minute walk; or Subway—Tōei Asakusa line or Tōei Mita line to Mita Station and 6-minute walk

Kuwait Embassy and Chancery Building 1970
Kuwēito Taishikan
Architect Kenzo Tange
Address 13-12, Mita 4-chōme, Minato-ku, Tōkyō (see Map 7)
Transport Train—JR Yamanote line to Tamachi Station: west exit and 6 minutes by taxi Tange's building well exemplifies some of the attributes of Metabolist architecture (see page 17, fig. 12).

UNHEX NANI NANI 1989
Architect Philippe Starck (France)
Address 9-23, Shiroganedai 4-chōme, Minato-ku, Tōkyō
Transport Subway—Tōei Asakusa line to Takanawadai Station and 15-minute walk to northwest, then across Meguro-dōri Avenue; or Train—JR Yamanote line to Meguro Station: east exit and 6-minute walk east (along north side of Meguro-dōri Avenue)

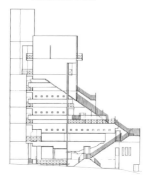

Azabu Edge
1987
Architect Ryōji Suzuki
Address 1-1, Nishi-Azabu
1-chōme, Minato-ku, Tōkyō
(see Map 7)
Transport Subway—Hibiya
line to Roppongi Station and
5-minute walk to west on
Roppongi-dōri Avenue
(165 feet/50 meters north
from avenue)

This multistory building has rental spaces for a variety of restaurants and offices. Located on a wedge-shaped site, the Azabu Edge is dominated by a wide rooftop stairway from which, as a grandstand, one can get an expansive view of the Aoyama area of Tōkyō. The reinforced concrete structure is intercepted with bands of windows and other slits. In one section this structure is "broken off"; the "ruined" wall seems to be suspended from above. One of the most talented contemporary avant-garde architects, Suzuki has developed an "archaeological" mode of design in which he admittedly aims at "excavating" elements, fragments, or "fossil specimens" that are buried deep in the history of early modern architecture as well as in the collective memory of the city and its citizens. The hauntingly powerful agglomerate and/or ruinous forms of the Azabu Edge are the result of such operations.

TŌKYŌ Map 8
Azabu, Daikanyama, Ebisu, Shibuya, Yoyogi Park, and Omotesandō Areas

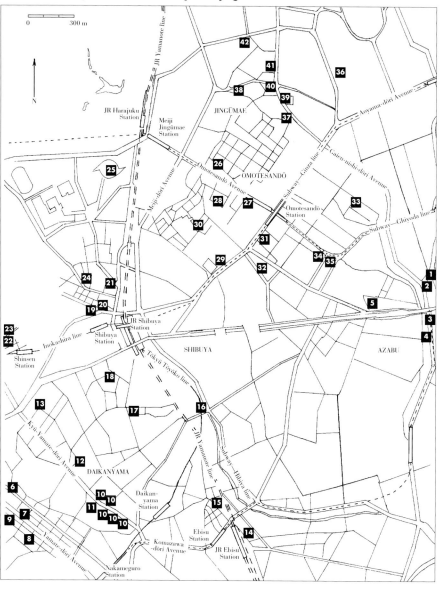

都 TŌKYŌ
Azabu Area

Scala Building
1992

Architect Atsushi Kitagawara
Address 14-17, Nishi-Azabu
1-chōme, Minato-ku, Tōkyō
(see Map 8)
Transport Subway—Hibiya
line to Roppongi Station and
15-minute walk or 5 minutes
by taxi; or Chiyoda line to
Nogizaka Station and
10-minute walk (Scala is next
to Angelo Tarlazzi Building to
the north)

Scala is a six-story office and commercial building
topped with an additional semicylindrical wall.
A series of shifting glass screen walls, like a scale,
surge upward in front of the black shield of the
cylindrical wall. The screens wrap around and
define an attractive entrance lobby at the corner.
As the structure is situated on a very small site, its
proportions give the impression of a slender tower,
the shape of the numerous "pencil buildings" in
Tōkyō. Enhanced by the vivid color scheme of the
exterior surfaces—yellow and black on the solid
walls, and green on the curtain walls—the design,
although much higher than the adjacent Tarlazzi
Building, engages its neighbor in a friendly dialog.

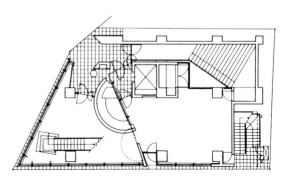

TŌKYŌ
Azabu Area

Angelo Tarlazzi Building
1987

Architect Hajime Yatsuka
Address 6-14, Nishi-Azabu
1-chōme, Minato-ku, Tōkyō
(see Map 8)
Transport Subway—Hibiya
line to Roppongi Station and
15-minute walk or 5 minutes
by taxi; or Chiyoda line to
Nogizaka Station and
10-minute walk (on east side
of Gaien-Nishi-dōri Avenue
north from Roppongi-dōri
Avenue)

The small, colorful building was built as a boutique of the Paris-based fashion designer Angelo Tarlazzi, although it is used today as an architectural office. In this refreshing architectural composition every element—the rear wall covered in dark oxidized aluminum plate, the unfinished concrete front facade, the red roof units, and the bright yellow external stairway—is rendered as an "autonomous" entity, independent from the whole, which thus appears to be rather fragmentary. The vocabulary Yatsuka used here is clearly from the inventory of modern architecture. With this project he has introduced a line of design that aims at the "acceleration of the Modern." But he also understands that such acceleration cannot be accomplished without restructuring the old official doctrine of modernism. Therefore his strategy is a form of "deconstruction" to release modernism's untapped potentials from its binding dogmas.

Kono-Shente (interior) 1991
Architect Coop Himmelblau
Atelier (Austria)
Address Nakajima Building
B1 F, 17-15, Nishi-Azabu
3-chōme, Minato-ku, Tōkyō
(see Map 8)
Transport Subway—Hibiya
line to Roppongi Station and
15-minute walk (5-minute
walk from The Wall and
The Tower)
The bar is the only design by
Coop Himmelblau in Japan.

The Wall Restaurant and Bar, 1988
The Tower, 1991
Architect Nigel Coates and
Branson Coates Architects
(U.K.)
Address 2, Nishi-Azabu
4-chōme, Minato-ku, Tōkyō
(see Map 8)
Transport Subway—Hibiya
line to Roppongi Station and
15-minute walk (on west side
of Gaien-Nishi-dōri Avenue
south from Roppongi-dōri
Avenue)

Fuji Film Company Headquarters, 1969
Fuji Firumu Tōkyō Honsha
Architect Yoshinobu Ashihara
Address 26-30, Nishi-Azabu
2-chōme, Minato-ku, Tōkyō
(see Map 8)
Transport Subway—Hibiya
line to Roppongi Station and
20-minute walk west along
the north side of Roppongi-
dōri Avenue (15-minute walk
from Azabu Edge Building or
6-minute walk from Angelo
Tarlazzi Building)

都 TŌKYŌ
Gotanda Area

Pola Home Offices
1971

Pōra Gotanda Biru
Architect Nikken Sekkei
Company
Address 2-3, Nishi-gotanda
2-chōme, Shinagawa-ku,
Tōkyō
Transport Train—JR Yama-
note line to Gotanda Station:
south exit and 5-minute walk
along the west side of
Yamanote line to north

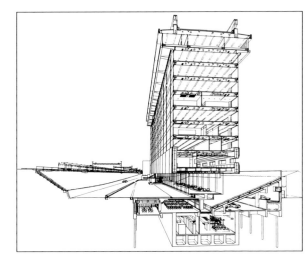

This remarkable "early" project by Nikken Sekkei
Company attests to a high quality synthesis
between structural design and architectural/spatial
articulation. Story-high girders span between two
vertical circulation cores to allow the lobby to hang
free from intermediary columnar support. Shaped
with a cantilevered and "floating" floor and enclosed by floor-to-ceiling glass panes on two sides,
the lobby seems to expand beyond its physical lim-
its and to be defined by the train embankment to
the east and by the equally sloping, planted roof of
the carport to the west. The reflective gray glass
ceiling inside and the shallow pool of water outside
further enhance the illusive effect imparting the
experience of the truly phenomenal.

Tōkyō Design Center
1992

Architect Mario Bellini (Italy)
(with Obayashi Corporation)
Address 25-19, Gotanda 5-
chōme, Shinagawa-ku, Tōkyō
Transport Train—JR Yamanote line to Gotanda Station:
east exit and 2-minute walk
(on north side of Sakurada-
dōri Avenue)

**Meguro Gajō-en
Hotel
1991**
Architect Nikken Sekkei
Company
Address 8-1, Shimo-meguro
1-chōme, Meguro-ku, Tōkyō
Transport Train—JR Yama-
note line to Meguro Station:
west exit and 5-minute walk
to west, down the hill toward
Meguro-gawa River

**Saint Anselm Meguro
Church
1956**
Sei Anserumu Meguro Kyōkai
Architect Antonin Raymond
(U.S.)
Address 6-22, Kami Ōsaki 4-
chōme, Shinagawa-ku, Tōkyō
Transport Train—JR Yama-
note line to Meguro Station:
south exit and 2-minute walk
to south

House F, 1987
Architect Kazunari Sakamoto
Address 9-4, Koyama 7-
chōme, Shinagawa-ku, Tōkyō
Transport Train—JR Yama-
note line to Meguro Station;
change train for Tōkyū-
Mekama line to Senzoku
Station and 5-minute walk
Visitation Private residence;
seen only from the outside.
See page 29, fig. 38.

Tōkyō Institute of Technology Centennial Hall 1987

Tō-Kō-Dai Kinenkan
Architect Kazuo Shinohara
Address 12-1, Ōokayama
2-chōme, Meguro-ku, Tōkyō
Transport Train—Tōkyū-
Ōimachi line or Tōkyū-
Mekama line to Ōokayama
Station: south exit and
1-minute walk (in front of the
station, within TIT campus,
near the main gate)

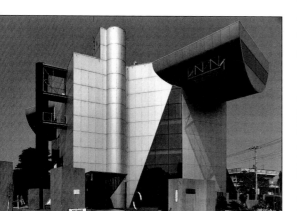

The Tōkyō Institute of Technology (TIT) Centennial Hall has been designed according to Shinohara's acceptance of the peculiar qualities of the Japanese city—qualities he previously rejected or, at best, toward which he had displayed a genuine disinterest. From the mid-1980s, he has begun to acknowledge, although not necessarily endorse, the chaotic urban conditions as a potential source of creativity within his designs, pursuing his new concept of "progressive anarchy." The Centennial Hall is articulated with a design vocabulary that does not seem to formulate a coherent statement in itself, yet makes sense in its urban context. Indeed, its many "accidental" forms are largely the result of a design sensibility that is capable of deciphering the unpredictable nexus of urban relationships and events. The four-story structure is a faculty center and alumni hall of Tōkyō Institute of Technology, with exhibition galleries, conference rooms, and—within the fourth-floor, horizontally laid, cylindrical volume—a restaurant and bar. This most unconventional architectural form, with some allusions to a crashed plane fuselage, is designed with a broken axis to visually connect the railroad station in front of the campus gate with the center plaza of the campus, and, on clear days, with Mount Fuji in the far distance. In accordance with the profile of TIT, the hall has been shaped so as to make a powerful expression of contemporary high technology.

都 TŌKYŌ
Tamagawa Area

House in Higashi-Tamagawa 1, 1973
House in Higashi-Tamagawa 2, 1983

Architect Kazuo Shinohara
Address 6, Higashi-Tamagawa 1-chōme, Setagaya-ku, Tōkyō
Transport Train—Tōkyū-Mekama line to Okusawa Station and 10-minute walk to southwest (the two houses are side by side on a street corner)
Visitation Private residences; seen only from the outside

The two small houses, now connected to each other, were built ten years apart. The more recent structure on the street corner is the residence and small private clinic of a physician, while the one behind is the house of the doctor's parents. Representing two stages in Shinohara's design career, the two houses show interesting differences. The first, completed in 1973, is built entirely of exposed reinforced concrete and, with practically no openings toward the outside, is a strongly inward-oriented, protective structure. The second building, although even more puzzling in its formal disposition than the previous one, is more open to its vicinity through various windows positioned almost randomly in the elevations. The facades are articulated with smooth stainless steel surfaces in addition to unfinished concrete and reflective glass. The pitched roof section of this building houses the residential quarters, while the slanting volume, cantilevered at forty-five degrees, contains the study and library within a unique spatial arrangement.

都 TŌKYŌ
Naka-Meguro Area

Chiyoda Life Insurance Building
1966

Chiyoda Seimei Honsha Biru
Architect Togo Murano
Address 19-85, Kami-meguro 2-chōme, Meguro-ku, Tōkyō
Transport Train—Tōkyū-Tōyoko line or Subway—Hibiya line to Naka-meguro Station and 6-minute walk (on west side of Komazawa-dōri Avenue)
The extensive, *U*-shaped complex is within a large landscaped garden.

Melrose
1984

Architect Tadao Ando
Address 18-1, Aobadai 2-chōme, Meguro-ku, Tōkyō (see Map 8)
Transport Train—Tōkyū-Tōyoko line or Subway—Hibiya line to Naka-meguro Station: south exit and 15-minute walk (2-minute walk from Tanabe Agency Building)
Melrose is a multistory office and showroom complex for a fashion design company; it has a curving glass facade.

Tanabe Agency Building
1984

Architect Kazuhiro Ishii
Address 21-4, Aobadai 2-chōme, Meguro-ku, Tōkyō (see Map 8)
Transport Train—Tōkyū-Tōyoko line or Subway—Hibiya line to Naka-meguro Station: south exit and 10-minute walk (on east side of Yamate-dōri Avenue)
This two-story building, with its "heavy," metallic-plate-covered structure, was designed as a scaled-down version of a sturdy bridge.

T Building in Nakameguro, 1991

Nakameguro T Biru
Architect Toyo Ito
Address 17-16, Higashiyama 1-chōme, Meguro-ku, Tōkyō (see Map 8)
Transport Train—Tōkyū-Tōyoko line or Subway—Hibiya line to Naka-meguro Station and 8-minute walk north on Yamate-dōri Avenue (on a corner site 500 feet/150 meters west from avenue)
Visitation 9:00–17:00 work days, tel: (03) 3719-3722

Toyo Ito's recent architecture can be classified into two groups: the first is designed with extensive, softly curving, light roof structures; the second is dominated by a crisp, orthogonal geometry, and simple, glass, boxlike volumes. The T Building belongs to the second group. The light, steel-frame structure of this small office building accommodates a three-story glass screen, which wraps around it on three sides. This glass skin, with its applied milk-white stripes of film, affords good views while providing some privacy and sun protection for the occupants. Behind this translucent/transparent sheet of glass the multistory entrance hall unfolds with an impressive spatial quality brought about by the straightforward but elegant simplicity of the steel structural elements, glass block surfaces, and punched metallic screens, as well as the light color scheme. Suspended in this ethereal realm are containerlike toilet booths, a glazed elevator shaft, and the thin decks of galleries on two floors. Ito's building, shaped with certain qualities of industrial structures, represents a new type of office space that is responsive to the exterior and the natural world.

Toy Block House 7 1983

Architect Takefumi Aida
Address 9-17, Higashiyama 2-chōme, Meguro-ku, Tōkyō (see Map 8)
Transport Train—Tōkyū-Tōyoko line or Subway—Hibiya line to Naka-meguro Station: south exit and 8-minute walk from station (or 2-minute walk from T Building)
Visitation Private residence, seen only from the outside.

The house was designed with the idea of cutting up a large box (represented by the dark gray walls) filled with toy blocks (painted white), and shifting the fragments. The resulting interstices were developed into the rooms, and the gaps between them into windows.

Hillside Terrace Apartments
Phase 1, 1969
Phase 2, 1973
Phase 3, 1976
Phase 5, 1987
Phase 6, 1992

Daikanyama Shūgō Jūkyō
Architect Fumihiko Maki
Address 18, 29-8, Sarugaku-chō, Shibuya-ku, Tōkyō (see Map 8)
Transport Train—Tōkyū-Tōyoko line to Daikanyama Station and 5-minute walk to north (on both sides of Kyū-Yamate-dōri Avenue)

The mixed-use, three- to four-story, residential buildings, housing apartments, rental offices, studios, small shops, and cafes are arranged around a system of attractively interconnecting and intimate courtyards that are, in effect, small public plazas. Accordingly, the buildings that surround and define these open spaces assume a porous fabric wherein the loose volumes are penetrated by various entries, walkways, and passages. Linked as they are to the surrounding urban areas, they are able to successfully mediate between the busy stree and the quieter residential and park zones behind. The low-profile urban development has been designed by Maki in several stages over the past three decades. The several phases of design provide an excellent account of the development of Maki's architecture, which has been articulated in response to the Japanese urban context. A modernist at heart and a decided rationalist in his early work, Maki has gradually enriched his design vocabulary, which now sensitively addresses not only the physical/formal but also the cultural/-phenomenal or the more intangible aspects of place-making. The initial blocks of the Hillside Terrace Apartments were rather volumetric, while the more recent phases have become more flexible compositions of collaged layers in which lighter elements and materials, including various frames. metallic screens, and glass and reflective tile surfaces, play important roles.

Royal Danish Embassy
1979
Zainichi Denmāku Taishikan
Architect Fumihiko Maki
Address 29-6, Sarugaku-chō, Shibuya-ku, Tōkyō (see Map 8)
Transport Train—Tōkyū-Tōyoko line to Daikanyama Station and 6-minute walk next to Hillside Terrace Apartments Phase 3 on west side of Kyū-Yamate-dōri Avenue)

Bigi Atelier
1983
Architect Tadao Ando
Address 9-6, Hachiyama-chō, Shibuya-ku, Tōkyō (see Map 8)
Transport Train—Tōkyū-Tōyoko line to Daikanyama Station and 18-minute walk (north from Kyū-Yamate-dōri Avenue, behind the Baptist church)
It is a studio and production building for the Bigi company.

Atelier Yoshie Inaba (Bigi 3), 1985
Architect Tadao Ando
Address 16-1, Nanpeidai-chō, Shibuya-ku, Tōkyō (see Map 8)
Transport Train—Tōkyū-Tōyoko line to Daikanyama Station and 15-minute walk (north from Kyū-Yamate-dōri Avenue)
The building is a design studio and office complex for a fashion design company.

都 TŌKYŌ
Ebisu Area

Studio Ebis
1981
Architect Makoto Suzuki
Address 9-2, Ebisu 1-chōme, Shibuya-ku, Tōkyō (see Map 8)
Transport Train—JR Yamanote line to Ebisu Station; or Subway—Chiyoda line to Ebisu Station and 2-minute walk to the east under railroad bridge
A small, multistory building of exposed reinforced concrete wall structure with several open voids in the volume.

Octagon
1989
Architect Shin Takamatsu
Address 3-6, Ebisu-nishi 1-chōme, Shibuya-ku, Tōkyō (see Map 8)
Transport Train—JR Yamanote line to Ebisu Station and 5-minute walk; or Subway—Hibiya line to Ebisu Station and 5-minute walk toward north
The building boasts an octagonal tower covered with stone and shaped in the typical Takamatsu manner.

都 TŌKYŌ
Shibuya Area

Shibuya Higashi T Building
1989
Architect Kisho Kurokawa
Address 28-1, Higashi 1-chōme, Shibuya-ku, Tōkyō (see Map 8)
Transport From Shibuya Station: 10-minute walk to southeast on Meiji-dōri Avenue
This slim infill building is distinguished by a tall, triangular slit in the street facade and a "floating" roof shaped as an inverted arch.

都 TŌKYŌ
Shibuya Area

Aoyama Technical College
1990
Aoyama Seizu Senmon Gakkō chiban-kan
Architect Makoto Sei Watanabe
Address 7-9, Uguisudani-chō, Shibuya-ku, Tōkyō (see Map 8)
Transport From Shibuya Station: 15-minute walk to southwest (8-minute walk from Hillport Hotel); building is near Sakuragaoka Yūbinkyoku (Post Office)

Hillport Hotel
1982
Architect Hiroshi Hara
Address 23-19, Sakuragaoka-chō, Shibuya-ku, Tōkyō (see Map 8)
Transport From Shibuya Station: 10-minute walk, first to south under elevated expressway, then west uphill
Facing north, the seven-story, symmetrical building features regressing layers of facade walls covered by a light gray glass mosaic. An attractive lobby is on the first floor.

109 Building
1978
Tōkyū or Ichi-Maru-Kyū Biru
Architect Minoru Takeyama
Address 29-1, Dogenzaka 2-chōme, Shibuya-ku, Tōkyō (see Map 8)
Transport From Shibuya Station: Hachiko (northwest) exit and 7-minute walk west
Takeyama's large, commercial building, with a cylindrical volume at the corner, occupies the west edge of the busy Shibuya Station plaza. (See illustration on page 11)

都 TŌKYŌ
Shibuya Area

Re/m Building
1988

Architect Akira Komiyama
Address 23-11, Udagawa-chō, Shibuya-ku, Tōkyō (see Map 8)
Transport From Shibuya Station: Hachiko exit and 5-minute walk northwest

The Re/m Building is located within the highly popular Shibuya area. Komiyama's design, geared to young customers who frequent the district, has a certain populist appeal to it, yet any excessiveness is kept in check by an almost modernist vocabulary. The Re/m nonetheless is expressive of action, insofar as its architecture is dominated by dynamic elements: the elevator shaft at the rounded corner; the emergency stairway, service stairs, and bridges over the rooftop; and a system of slanting structural bars painted red.

Humax Pavilion
1992

Architect Hiroyuki Wakabayashi
Address 20-15, Udagawa-chō, Shibuya-ku, Tōkyō (see Map 8)
Transport From Shibuya Station: Hachiko exit and 8-minute walk (on south side of Kōen-dōri Avenue)
A multistory commercial complex with shops, a restaurant, and a movie theater on top.

Ueda Shōkai Guest House
1992

Architect Hiroshi Hara
Address 19-1, Shinsen-chō, Shibuya-ku, Tōkyō (see Map 8)
Transport From Shibuya Station: Train—Keiō Inokashira line to Shinsen Station and 4-minute walk to northwest
Visitation 9:30–17:00 work days

Shōtō Museum
1980

Shibuya Kuritsu Shōtō Bijutsukan
Architect Seiichi Shirai
Address 14-14, Shōtō 2-chōme, Shibuya-ku, Tōkyō (see Map 8)
Transport From Shibuya Station: Train—Keiō Inokashira line to Shinsen Station and 5-minute walk to north (3-minute walk from Ueda Shōkai Guest House)

Rise Cinema Complex, 1986

Architect Atsushi Kitagawara
Address 27-6, Udagawa-chō, Shibuya-ku, Tōkyō (see Map 8)
Transport From Shibuya Station: Hachiko exit and 12-minute walk to northwest (building is at the upper end of Spanish Slope [*Spain-zaka*])

Rise's strongly surrealistic forms—reminiscent of the work of the Austrian architect Hans Hollein—have been designed to match the highly theatrical quality of the urban landscape in this entertainment district of Tōkyō. In fact, the building itself adds up to a stage set in the urban theater of Shibuya: the undulating roofs with "collapsing" forms are covered with folded drapery, molded in cast aluminum; other surfaces are defined by steel or wire mesh screens; and the entrance is signified by a cluster of disordered, obelisklike, black pillars. The interior of Rise is equally "unreal" and as entertaining as the exterior. Thus the cinema project of this art-oriented architect is a good representative of an architecture that is influenced by contemporary media culture.

都 TŌKYŌ
Komaba Area

Japan Folk Craft Museum, addition 1982

Nihon Mingeikan Shinkan
Architect Kazumasa Yamashita
Address 3-33, Komaba 4-chōme, Meguro-ku, Tōkyō
Transport From Shibuya Station: Train—Keiō Inokashira line to Komaba Tōdai-mae Station and 5-minute walk; or 7-minute walk from Earthtecture Sub-1

都 TŌKYŌ
Uehara Area

Tōkyō Club 1992

Architect Edward Suzuki
Address 35-3, Nishihara 1-chōme, Shibuya-ku, Tōkyō
Transport Subway—Chiyoda line or Train—Odakyū line to Yoyogiuehara Station: north exit and 20-minute walk to north; or Train—Keiō line to Hatagaya Station: south exit and 6-minute walk east

House on a Curved Road, 1978

Architect Kazuo Shinohara
Address 18-11, Uehara 3-chōme, Shibuya-ku, Tōkyō
Transport Subway—Chiyoda line or Train—Odakyū line to Yoyogiuehara Station: east exit and 8-minute walk
Visitation Private residence; seen only from the outside. See page 24, fig. 27.

House in Uehara
1976

Architect Kazuo Shinohara
Address 46-2, Uehara
2-chōme, Shibuya-ku, Tōkyō
Transport Subway—Chiyoda
line or Train—Odakyū line to
Yoyogiuehara Station: east
exit and 8-minute walk
Visitation Private residence:
seen only from the outside.

Shinohara's architecture displays a profound disinterest in its urban environment. It closes the interior from the exterior as much as possible, and has only a few, uniquely shaped windows. The design concentrates on the qualities of the inside spaces and aims at a new form of urban habitat. One of Shinohara's primary considerations of the house was its structural solution. To cantilever a section of the house over the carport, he used an oversized, reinforced concrete frame, whose columns are outfitted with huge, diagonal brackets. These brackets are exposed as part of the exterior facade, but also appear as freestanding elements within the interior, where, with their brutish power, they evoke the space and experience of the "savage jungle." The house remains one of the best representatives of Shinohara's abstract architecture of the 1970s.

Earthtecture Sub-1
1990

Architect Shin Takamatsu
Address 30-4, Uehara
2-chōme, Shibuya-ku, Tōkyō
Transport Subway—Chiyoda
line or Train—Odakyū line to
Higashi-Kitazawa Station and
12-minute walk to east (on
north side of the road)

The uniquely designed, small coffee shop and office building is an underground facility with four basement levels, and only three large, sharply angled, curving, glass skylights above the street.

Toy Block House 10
1984

Architect Takefumi Aida
Address 19, Kamiyama-chō,
Shibuya-ku, Tōkyō
Transport Subway—Chiyoda
line to Yoyogi-Kōen-Mae
Station; or Train—Odakyū
line to Yoyogi Hachiman
Station and 10-minute walk
or 5 minutes by taxi (near
New Zealand Embassy)
Visitation Private residence;
seen only from the outside.

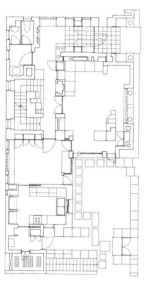

In the early 1980s Aida designed a series of small residences in which he explored a new approach to architecture. His method resembled the way children build structures out of toy blocks. In his toy block houses, among which number 10 is perhaps the most successful, Aida reduced every building component to its simplest geometrical solid: rectangle, prism, cylinder, or sphere. Having established a kit of more or less standardized components, he then combined them to shape his own projects. Needless to say, these strategies were merely formal operations and did not involve actually producing or prefabricating the units themselves. Rather, they provided Aida with an architectural vocabulary, with which he aimed at generating new meanings. Influenced by both the Italian master Aldo Rossi's similar intentions with a new urban typology (the "analogous city"), and by the preoccupations of postmodern architecture in general, Aida—as exemplified by his Toy Block House 10—has produced a playful architecture.

House in Tomigaya
1987

Green Way Tomigaya—
T House
Architect Itsuko Hasegawa
Address 24-2, Tomigaya
1-chōme, Shibuya-ku, Tōkyō
Transport From Shibuya
Station: Train—Keiō Inoka-
hira line to Shinsen Station
and 15-minute walk or 5
minutes by taxi; or 8-minute
walk from Earthtecture Sub-1

STM Building
1991

Architect Itsuko Hasegawa
Address 8-3, Tomigaya
2-chōme, Shibuya-ku, Tōkyō
Transport Subway—Chiyoda
line to Yoyogi Kōen Station
and 7 minute walk south on
Yamate-dōri Avenue; or
train—Odakyū line to
Yoyogihachiman Station and
6-minute walk south on west
side of Yamate-dōri Avenue

Olympic Gymnasia 1964

Kokuritsu Yanai Sōgō Kyōgijō
Architect Kenzo Tange
Address 1, Jinnan 2-chōme, Shibuya-ku, Tōkyō (see Map 8)
Transport Train—JR Yamanote line to Harajuku Station or Subway—Chiyoda line to Meijijingūmae Station and 5-minute walk to southwest

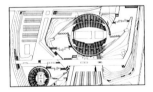

Tange's masterpiece consists of two structures: the large 15,000 capacity hall for swimming and diving pools and the small 4,000 capacity hall for ball games. The two are connected by a platform that houses service facilities below ground, while accommodating a public plaza and promenade above. Tange sculpted both structures in a similar manner, with curvilinear lines and forms and suspension structures whose magnificent shapes are second to none among such structures. The roofs of the halls are suspended from massive reinforced concrete pylons (two in the large hall and one in the small one) by means of steel cables and other high-tension elements. Both design and construction testify to the highly developed industrial society and available technology in Japan in the early 1960s. At the same time, the gracefully curving lines of the buildings make an implicit reference to the silhouettes of Buddhist temple roofs. Tange's outstanding achievement with the gymnasia resides in the fact that he was able to synthesize the qualities of both traditional and modern architectures, thereby linking together the past, present, and even the future in a manner that is timeless. The Olympic Gymnasia have justly become a symbol in Tōkyō and a landmark in contemporary Japanese and world architectures.

Aoyama Apartments 1926

Architect Dojunkai Housing Corporation
Address 12, Jingūmae 4-chōme, Harajuku, Shibuya-ku, Tōkyō (see Map 8)
Transport Subway—Ginza line, Hanzōmon line, or Chiyoda line to Omotesandō Station and 3-minute walk on north side of Omotesandō-dōri Avenue)
This group of three- and four-story apartment blocks displays the unique impact of international modernism on housing in prewar Japan.

Hanae Mori Building 1978

Architect Kenzo Tange
Address 34-1, Kita-Aoyama 3-chōme, Minato-ku, Tōkyō (see Map 8)
Transport Subway—Ginza line, Hanzōmon line, or Chiyoda line to Omotesandō Station and 3-minute walk (on south side of Omotesandō-dōri Avenue)
The prismatic glass building is an omnirental facility featuring the studio and offices of the fashion designer Hanae Mori.

LP House 1, 1981
LP House 2, 1984

Architect Akira Komiyama
Address 6-17, Jingūmae 5-chōme, Shibuya-ku, Tōkyō (see Map 8)
Transport Train—JR Yamanote line to Harajuku Station and 12-minute walk; or Subway—Ginza line, Hanzōmon line, or Chiyoda line to Omotesandō Station and 5-minute walk

都 TŌKYŌ
Aoyama-dōri Area

United Nations University, Phase 2 1992

Kokuren Daigaku
Architect Kenzo Tange
Address 52, Jingūmae 5-chōme, Shibuya-ku, Tōkyō (see Map 8)
Transport Subway—Ginza line, Hanzōmon line, or Chiyoda line to Omotesandō Station and 6-minute walk along north side of Aoyama-dōri Avenue

Metroca Apartment Building 1989

Metorosa Apāto Biru
Architect Atsushi Kitagawara
Address 40-10, Jingūmae 5-chōme, Shibuya-ku, Tōkyō (see Map 8)
Transport Subway—Ginza line, Hanzōmon line, or Chiyoda line to Omotesandō Station and 15-minute walk
Visitation Private residences; seen only from the outside. Kitagawara's explicitly manneristic but highly successful design is articulated around a two-story sunken courtyard as a metaphoric "urban plaza." (See page 31, fig. 46)

Tange's United Nations University is articulated with a heavy, volumetric architecture. It reveals its strong classical inspiration in both its stepped pyramidal overall form and its detailing.. The unique shape of the building is the outcome of a rigid pyramidal" structural frame combined with a superstructure of inverted *Y* braces at every third level. This solution made possible the elimination of interior columns, and served the designer well when arranging the two large conference halls on the third and sixth floors in the "center" of the pyramid. The building is the headquarters of the United nations' only educational institution, which carries out research and training on global issues.

Spiral Building
1985

Architect Fumihiko Maki
Address 6-23, Minami-
Aoyama 5-chōme, Minato-ku,
Tōkyō (see Map 8)
Transport Subway—Ginza
line, Hanzōmon line, or
Chiyoda line to Omotesandō
Station (in front of subway
exit B-1 along the south side
of Aoyama-dōri Avenue)

Old Yamada House
(now coffee shop)
1959

Kyū Yamada Tei
Architect Mamoru Yamada
Address 11-20, Minami-
Aoyama 5-chōme, Minato-ku,
Tōkyō (see Map 8)
Transport Subway—Ginza
line, Hanzōmon line, or
Chiyoda line to Omotesandō
Station (7-minute walk from
Spiral Building, first west
toward Shibuya, then south
along a small side street of
Aoyama-dōri Avenue)

Ambiente Showroom
1991

Architect Aldo Rossi (Italy)
(with Morris Adjmi [U.S.])
Address 11-1, Minami-
Aoyama 4-chōme, Minato-ku,
Tōkyō (see Map 8)
Transport Subway—Ginza
line, Hanzōmon line, or
Chiyoda line to Omotesandō
Station, A-4 exit and 10
minute walk (first south, then
east, then, after Aoyama-
kaikan Hotel, south again)

The large, multistory, cultural complex owned by
the Wacoal Company—producers of women's fashion apparel—is an infill building that displays only
one facade to the busy urban street. This elevation
is a largely fragmentary composition of sophisticated elements, surfaces, and images that are collaged
together in a rather unusual yet attractive manner.
Maki's design is rendered in highly polished aluminum, glass, and other high-tech materials and
structures, with references to classical Western,
traditional Japanese, and, more importantly, high-
modernist architecture; it represents a new standard in regard to both architectural sensibility and
the quality of public spaces. Appropriate to its
name, the facade seems to spiral upward, as does
the long, ceremonial ramp that connects the first-
floor lobby, cafe, and gallery with the mezzanine
floor shops within the top-lit atrium space.

The From 1st Building, with its brick architecture, is reminiscent of some British architecture popular in the 1960s. It is one of the most successful early mixed-use urban complexes; on six floors Yamashita arranged numerous shops, cafes, restaurants, a beauty salon, small offices, and unique, apartment-type design studios, plus parking on two underground levels. The two-story internal public plaza provides intimacy, repose, and relief from the bustling outside world. The close proximity of From 1st and Collezione provides a rare opportunity to directly compare two urban complexes that, although similar in function, are different in architectural interpretation, while each being successful in its own right. While both are designed with internal courtyards, From 1st has been conceived in a spirit different from Ando's architecture forwarded in unfinished reinforced concrete structures.

From 1st Building
1976

Architect Kazumasa Yamashita
Address 3-10, Minami-Aoyama 5-chōme, Minato-ku, Tōkyō (see Map 8)
Transport Subway—Ginza line or Hanzōmon line or Chiyoda line to Omotesandō Station A-5 exit and 5-minute walk (south from Aoyama-dōri Avenue, next to Collezione)

Collezione
1990

Architect Tadao Ando
Address 1-13, Minami-Aoyama 6-chōme, Minato-ku, Tōkyō (see Map 8)
Transport Subway—Ginza line, Hanzōmon line, or Chiyoda line to Omotesandō Station A-5 exit and 5-minute walk (south from Aoyama-dōri Avenue, next to From 1st Building)

One of the latest additions to Ando's small urban commercial complexes, the Collezione—not unlike its predecessors—is designed with an interior public courtyard that connects the several basement levels with the ones above. This mixed-use building is characterized by intricate entryways, passages, and various stairways linking the outside streets on three sides with the court inside to provide an urban experience. As always in Ando's designs, the introduction of natural light and shadows into the realm of architecture evokes a poetic dimension that is seldom matched in intensity today.

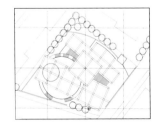

Tepia Science Pavilion, 1989

Architect Fumihiko Maki
Address 8-44, Kita-Aoyama
2-chōme, Minato-ku, Tōkyō
(see Map 8)
Transport Subway—Ginza
line or Hanzōmon line to
Gaienmae Station and
8-minute walk to north

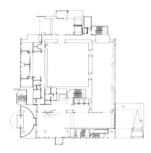

Watari-Um Gallery and Shop Complex, 1990

Architect Mario Botta
(Switzerland)
Address 7-6, Jingūmae
3-chōme, Shibuya-ku, Tōkyō
(see Map 8)
Transport Subway—Ginza
line or Hanzōmon line to
Gaienmae Station and
12-minute walk north on west
side of Gaien-Nishi-dōri
Avenue

United Arrows Harajuku Main Shop, 1992

Architect Ricardo Bofill
(Spain)
Address 28-9, Jingūmae
3-chōme, Harajuku, Shibuya-
ku, Tōkyō (see Map 8)
Transport Train—JR
Yamanote line to Harajuku
Station and 10-minute walk
(5-minute walk from 4th
Building)

The Tepia Science Pavilion, with such facilities as exhibition and conference halls, a video library, meeting rooms, a cafeteria, and various service functions, is dedicated to the promotion of science and technology. In accordance with its purpose, the building itself is a testimony to architectural and constructional technology, with a high level of contemporary craftsmanship. Continuing the legacy of Modern architecture, the building has been designed with a rectangular geometry—save for a semicircular glass block wall on the first floor—with thin wall planes and delicate surfaces, including perforated metallic screens. Both the materials and the spatial articulation contribute to a phenomenal "lightness" of the architecture—a quality that characterizes many other recent designs by Maki. Beyond the overall composition, however, it is the increasingly sophisticated detailing that makes this building an outstanding representative of late-twentieth-century urban, public architecture in Japan.

Located on an exceptionally tight urban site, not much larger than 100 square feet/9.3 square meters, this small residence is arranged on six floors. Assuming the form of a slim tower of reinforced concrete, the house, with its vertically interconnected rooms, unfolds along an intricately designed but, by all means, narrow stairway. From the basement to the top floor are the living room and den; a car port; an entrance, kitchen and dining room; a bathroom; a master bedroom; and a child's room. While this architect's residence may be an extreme example of confined building, the lack of available inner-city sites and exorbitant land prices in metropolitan areas of Japan in the past decades have forced many owners and architects to follow a similar path. Azuma's design is certainly one of the most innovative among them, while also foreshadowing a trend of internalized buildings that later became known as "defensive architecture."

都 TŌKYŌ
Jingūmae Area

Azuma House, 1967
Architect Takamitsu Azuma
Address 39, Jingūmae 3-chōme, Shibuya-ku, Tōkyō (see Map 8)
Transport Subway—Ginza line or Hanzōmon line to Gaienmae Station and 8-minute walk on east side of Gaien-Nishi-dōri Avenue (1-minute walk from Watari-Um Gallery)
Visitation Private residence; seen only from the outside.

4th Building, 1986
Architect Akira Komiyama
Address 35-16, Jingūmae 3-chōme, Shibuya-ku, Tōkyō (see Map 8)
Transport Train—JR Yamanote line to Harajuku Station and 15-minute walk; or Subway—Chiyoda line to Meiji-Jingūmae Station and 12-minute walk (5-minute walk from Azuma House or 5-minute walk from United Arrows Harajuku Main Shop)

Terrazza, 1991
Architect Kiyoshi Sei Takeyama
Address 8-2, Jingūmae 2-chōme, Shibuya-ku, Tōkyō (see Map 8)
Transport Train—JR Sōbu line to Sendagaya Station and 10-minute walk south on west side of Gaien-Nishi-dōri Avenue; or Subway—Ginza line or Hanzōmon line to Gaienmae Station and 15-minute walk north on west side of Gaien-Nishi-dōri Avenue (3-minute walk from Azuma House) (see page 31, fig. 47)

Manin Building, 1986
Architect Makoto Suzuki
Address 22-12, Jingūmae 2-chōme, Shibuya-ku, Tōkyō (see Map 8)
Transport Train—JR Sōbu line to Sendagaya Station and 10-minute walk (8-minute walk from 4th Building)

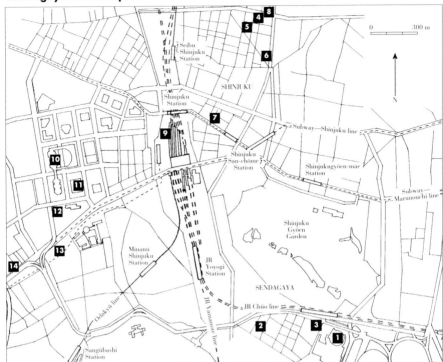

0   300 m

Seibu
Shinjuku
Station

SHINJUKU

Shinjuku
Station

Subway—Shinjuku line

Shinjuku
San-chōme
Station

Shinjukugyōen-mae
Station

Subway—
Marunouchi line

Shinjuku
Gyōen
Garden

Minami
Shinjuku
Station

JR
Yoyogi
Station

SENDAGAYA

Odakyū line

JR Yamanote line

JR Chūo line

Sangūbashi
Station

1. Tōkyō Metropolitan Gymnasium, page 132
2. Hamlet Residential Complex, page 134
3. Tsuda Hall, page 134
4. Ichiban-kan Building, page 135
5. Niban-kan Building, page 135
6. Kabuki-chō Tower, page 135
7. Kinokunya Building, page 135
8. Sky Building 3, page 136
9. Shinjuku Station Building, page 136
10. New Tōkyō City Hall, page 136
11. Shinjuku NS Building, page 137
12. Shinjuku Park Towers, page 137
13. Dai-Tōkyō Fire and Marine Insurance Shinjuku Building, page 137
14. NTT Headquarters Building, page 137

都 TŌKYŌ
Sendagaya Area

Tōkyō Metropolitan Gymnasia
1990

Tōkyō Taiikukan
Architect Fumihiko Maki
Address 17-1, Sendagaya 1-chōme, Shibuya-ku, Tōkyō (see Map 9)
Transport Train—JR Sōbu line to Sendagaya Station and 1-minute walk (across from Tsuda Hall, in front of the station)

Completed twenty-six years after Tange's Olympic Gymnasia (see page 126), Maki's scheme shows an interesting contrast to its earlier counterpart, while matching it in architectural achievements. The main arena seats 10,000 while the swimming pool arena seats 900, and there are additional structures for a training hall, large entrance hall, and administration building. The whole complex, which also includes an open-air practice field with a running track, is connected under a slightly elevated urban plaza. In Maki's design, every element is shaped differently to form a loose, collaged composition in which the unity of the whole is challenged by the individuality of its constituent parts. This large urban complex addresses the heterogeneous quality of Tōkyō, while not compromising the structural requirements involved. In fact, Maki has been able to second the spectacular achievements represented by his Fujisawa Municipal Gymnasia (1984) (see page 154); here on an even larger scale he has repeated the unique structural design of the large arena using only curvilinear elements, girders, and frames, whose articulation greatly contributes to the arresting appearance of the structure. Like its predecessor in Fujisawa, the Tōkyō Metropolitan Gymnasia is also covered with stainless steel sheets whereby the entire volume is able to radiate a certain lightness and floating quality.

Hamlet Residential Complex
1988

Architect Riken Yamamoto
Address 20-8, Sendagaya
4-chōme, Shibuya-ku, Tōkyō
(see Map 9)
Transport Train—JR Sōbu
line to Sendagaya Station and
10-minute walk to west
(across from the National Noh
Theater, along a narrow road)
Visitation Private residence;
seen only from the outside.

Tsuda Hall
1988

Architect Fumihiko Maki
Address 18-24, Sendagaya
1-chōme, Shibuya-ku, Tōkyō
(see Map 9)
Transport Train—JR Sōbu
line to Sendagaya Station and
1-minute walk (across from
Tōkyō Metropolitan Gymna-
sia, in front of the station)
The building is a cultural center with a large concert hall.

The small complex is comprised of four residences
for an extended family. The four-story building is
laid out in an *L* shape to enclose a courtyard to the
south. The narrow site, which extends far from the
street, is besieged by high-rise office blocks and
other buildings at close range. Yamamoto's goal
was to alleviate the tight condition while protecting
the privacy of the inhabitants. Translucent Teflon-
fiber "tents," stretched above the rooftops, numerous terraces, open-air bridges, and courtyards,
shield much of the residences from the intrusions of
the surrounding city. The four residences are
designed as independent units, yet with some com-
monly shared spaces. The Hamlet is constructed of
light steel frames over concrete substructures.

都 TŌKYŌ
Shinjuku East Area

Ichiban-kan Building, 1969
Niban-kan Building, 1970

Architect Minoru Takeyama
Address 16 and 21, Kabu-kichō 2-chōme, Shinjuku-ku, Tōkyō (see Map 9)
Transport Train—JR Yamanote line to Shinjuku Station: east or north exit and 12-minute walk; or Train—JR Yamanote line to Shinō-kubo Station and 8-minute walk (Niban-kan is 65 feet/20 meters south from Ichiban-kan on the opposite side of the same street)

Two unusually designed omnirental buildings, the Ichiban-kan (left) and Niban-kan (right) are located in Kabuki-chō, the entertainment and nightlife district of Shinjuku, not far from each other. Following an architectural paradigm that was emerging in the early 1970s, Takeyama responded to the highly festive, if often garish, character of the urban milieu almost to the point of celebrating it rather than concentrating on structural systems, industrial technology, and rational design (the attributes of contemporary Metabolist architecture). As a result, the buildings became early representatives of an openly populist mode of design, yet they did so without falling victim to a trivial commercialism. The reinforced concrete volumes are shaped with a dynamic, although abstract, geometry and are extensively painted with primary colors. The Niban-kan, which was featured as the frontispiece of Charles Jencks's *Language of Post-Modern Architecture* (London: Academy Editions, 1977), has in fact been repainted several times with various patterns.

Kabuki-chō Tower 1993
Architect Richard Rogers (U.K.)
Address 1-5, Kabuki-chō 2-chōme, Shinjuku-ku, Tōkyō (see Map 9)
Transport Train—JR Yamanote line to Shinjuku Station: east or north exit and 12-minute walk; or Subway—Shinjuku line or Marunouchi line to Shinjuku-san-chōme Station and 8-minute walk northward or 7-minute walk east from Ichiban-kan Building (along east side of a very narrow street)

Kinokunya Building 1964
Kinokunya Biru
Architect Kunio Maekawa
Address 17, Shinjuku 3-chōme, Shinjuku-ku, Tōkyō (see Map 9)
Transport From JR Shinjuku Station: east or north exit and 5-minute walk (on the north side of Shinjuku-dōri Avenue) The building is a multistory bookshop.

都 TŌKYŌ
Shinjuku East Area

Sky Building 3
1970
Dai San Sukai Biru
Architect Yōji Watanabe
Address 1-10, Ōkubo
1-chōme, Shinjuku-ku, Tōkyō
(see Map 9)
Transport Train—JR Yamanote line to Shin-Ōkubō Station and 12-minute walk; or
3-minute walk from Ichiban-
kan Building (on the north
side of Shokuan-dōri Avenue)

Mochida Building
1979
Architect Hiromi Fujii
Address 4-24, Nishi-Waseda
2-chōme, Shinjuku-ku, Tōkyō
Transport Subway—Tōzai
line to Waseda Station and
10-minute walk to west on
south side of Waseda-dōri
Avenue
The five-story, sharply angled
structure is a small office
building.

都 TŌKYŌ
Shinjuku West Area

Shinjuku Station
Building, West Plaza,
and Parking
1964
Shinjuku Eki Nishi-guchi
Biru and *Hiroba*
Architect Junzo Sakakura
Address 1, Nishi-Shinjuku
1-chōme, Shinjuku-ku, Tōkyō
(see Map 9)
Transport From JR Shinjuku
Station: west exit and few
steps

都 TŌKYŌ
Shinjuku West Area

New Tōkyō
City Hall
1991
Tōkyō Shin Tōchōsha
Architect Kenzo Tange
Address 8-1, Nishi-Shinjuku
2-chōme, Shinjuku-ku, Tōkyō
(see Map 9)
Transport From JR Shinjuku
Station: west exit and
10-minute walk to west

Replacing Tange's Old Tōkyō City Hall (1957) (see page 16, fig. 9) in the
Marunouchi area, the New Tōkyō City Hall shifted the administrative center of
Tōkyō to the rapidly developing, high-rise district of west Shinjuku. The central building with two towers is the second highest structure (797 feet/243
meters) in Japan to date. Designed in a postmodernist paradigm, the overall
symmetrical scheme unmistakably calls to mind the historic architectural
model of European, particularly French, cathedrals, the spiritual centers of
Western medieval cities. This model has been questioned by many, both critics
and citizens, as an appropriate expression of twentieth-century Japan and
Japanese urbanism, whose kaleidoscopic texture typically defies the emergence
of dominant urban centers. The overly monumental structure, almost an entire
city in itself, includes just about every function and facility that contemporary
urban life can provide, save for residences: offices, conference and cultural
centers, sports facilities, galleries, and assembly hall. Moreover, the extensive
horizontal wings that bridge across a major avenue at two places surround a
vast and rather formal, even sterile, urban plaza.

Shinjuku NS Building 1982

Architect Nikken Sekkei Company
Address 4-1, Nishi-Shinjuku 2-chōme, Shinjuku-ku, Tōkyō (see Map 9)
Transport From JR Shinjuku Station: west exit and 10-minute walk (next to the New Tōkyō City Hall to the south)

The thirty-story structure is representative of contemporary "corporate urbanism." The multipurpose building, most of which is rental offices, features a wide variety of public facilities: shops, exhibition halls, and information center on the lower levels; restaurants and pubs on the two uppermost floors. All these are arranged around a central atrium, whose space, soaring through the entire 430-foot/130-meter height of the building, is covered with a large skylight built with a story-high steel space frame. This 130-by-200-foot/40-by-60-meter atrium provides an indoor plaza, which is accessible from the adjacent streets, on the first floor. Glass-walled corridors on each floor face onto the atrium. Visitors can experience the atrium from glass-covered lounges sitting atop elevator shafts that rise part way up the atrium, or from a bridge that crosses the space at the twenty-ninth floor.

Shinjuku Park Towers 1994

Architect Kenzo Tange
Address 3-7, Nishi-Shinjuku 2-chōme, Shinjuku-ku, Tōkyō (see Map 9)
Transport From JR Shinjuku Station: west exit and 12-minute walk to west (the three, interconnected, high-rise office towers with sharply cut and staggered rooflines are south of New Tōkyō City Hall)

Dai-Tōkyō Fire and Marine Insurance Shinjuku Building 1989

Dai-Tōkyō Kaijō Shinjuku Biru
Architect Fumihiko Maki
Address 3-25, Yoyogi 3-chōme, Shibuya-ku, Tōkyō (see Map 9)
Transport From JR Shinjuku Station: south exit and 12-minute walk west (on south side of Kōshū Kaidō Avenue)

NTT Headquarters Building, 1995

Architect Cesar Pelli (U.S.)
Address 18, Nishi-Shinjuku 3-chōme, Shinjuku-ku, Tōkyō (see Map 9)
Transport From JR Shinjuku Station: west exit and 15-minute walk; or Train—Odakyū line to Sangūbashi Station and 8-minute walk north then across Kōshū Kaidō Avenue (6-minute walk from Shinjuku NS Building)

Nakano Sun Plaza
1973

*Zenkoku Dōrō Seishōnen
Kaikan—Sunpurāza*
Architect Nikken Sekkei
Company
Address 1-1, Nakano
4-chōme, Nakano-ku, Tōkyō
Transport Train—JR Chūō
line to Nakano Station: north
exit and 3-minute walk

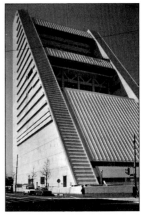

The building is a multipurpose cultural center used primarily by various youth
organizations. The tall structure boasts a unique triangular shape that has
been derived from functional considerations. Nikken Sekkei arranged the
numerous facilities within so that the less-frequented spaces are on the upper
floors while those accommodating large crowds occupy the lower floors. This
way, in case of emergency, the building can be evacuated quickly. Accordingly,
the hotel is in the topmost section, followed by classrooms, meeting halls, and
restaurants, accompanied by several terraces. The first and mezzanine levels
are occupied by the entrance hall, a 2,500-seat auditorium/theater, and related
services, while underground are a swimming pool, bowling alleys, gymnasia,
and parking. Vertical circulation and mechanical shafts are located in two corners of the building and are articulated with solid wall surfaces. These large
service cores, like those in many buildings inspired by the principles of Metabolist architecture, also function as the means of vertical support; huge horizontal structural systems hang between them to provide for large-span spaces.

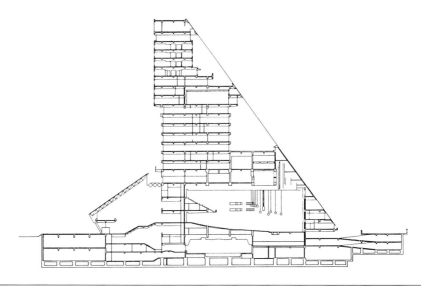

N.C. Housing
1984

N.C. House

Architect Itsuko Hasegawa
Address 53-23, Chūō
2-chōme, Nakano-ku, Tōkyō
Transport Subway—Marunouchi line to Nakanosakaue
Station and 8-minute walk to
northwest
Visitation Private residences;
seen only from the outside.

The three-story residential building, comprised of twelve small apartments, is located in a congested urban area of Tōkyō. Responding to the restrictive site conditions and applicable building codes, while trying to use all available space in order to reduce costs, Hasegawa designed the building in a straightforward manner, with no obvious preconceptions concerning the overall formal articulation. The result is an unusually bold composition in which every form and element stands out as an autonomous part; the building displays elevations that are not only all different, but also seem to be incongruous. The design of N.C. Housing is dominated by the application of unfinished reinforced concrete structures and perforated aluminum surfaces that define the boundaries of walls of the corridors on the street side and loggias to the rear. These loggias and some of the rooms on the top floor are capped by pyramidal aluminum roofs, which, along with the other metallic surfaces, reflect light on sunny days with a brilliant intensity. These small pitched roofs also denote the roofscape of clustered small "houses" and, so, the image of prototypical residential architecture, as in a miniature urban enclave.

House in Nerima
1986

Architect Itsuko Hasegawa
Address 18-35, Hayamiya
1-chōme, Nerima-ku, Tōkyō
Transport Subway—Yūrakuchō line to Hikawadai
Station and 10-minute walk
to west
Visitation Private residence;
seen only from the outside.

Hasegawa's designs are shaped by her interpretation of "architecture as second nature." In this line
of design she intends to resensitize architecture
toward nature, which has been squeezed out from
the city by the rapid and, all too often, reckless
urban developments in Japan. Her strategy is two-
pronged. On the one hand it involves the reincorpo-
ration of natural phenomena into the realm of
architecture; on the other hand it aims to shape the
built environment so as to endow it with certain
qualities, like the suppleness of nature.

Accommodating two residences—one for a poet
and his wife, another for their adult daughter—the
House in Nerima consists of two sections. In between them is a common entry court, which is partially filled with open-air stairways connecting the
two residences. Above these stairs and over the
rooftop terrace a light, corrugated metal, softly
undulating roof provides additional connection.
Moreover, this airy upper realm features a small
porch that, extending beyond the sloping surface of
the roof, serves as a moon-viewing platform.
Various perforated aluminum screens help define
these "open" spaces so that they can be both
exposed to the outside world of nature and protected from the intrusions of the city.

Kōunji Buddhist Temple 1991

Architect Ryōji Suzuki
Address 12-22, Kinuta
7-chōme, Setagaya-ku, Tōkyō
Transport From Shinjuku
Station: Train—Odakyū line
to Seijō-gakuenmae Station
and 10-minute walk to
southeast

One of Suzuki's largest projects to date, the Kōunji Buddhist Temple combines elements of traditional and contemporary architectures in an abstract manner. The scheme is dominated by a large, tiled roof in the form of those on historic Buddhist temples, but whose wooden roofing is supported by a steel frame structure. Moreover, since environmental considerations prompted the designer to sink the complex into the ground, only this roof emerges above the street level, creating an unexpected appearance. The temple is designed with a sunken courtyard in front; reminiscent of the enclosed courtyards of ancient Buddhist compounds, it features a uniquely curving open stairway, terraces, and an overhead bridge. The extensive system of various rooms below grade level and under the large central worship hall of the temple itself is lit by narrow skylights arranged above what the designer calls "gaps" formed in between the structural and/or volumetric entities. Suzuki's design is thus derivative of the dense Japanese urban fabric, wherein myriads of gaps and voids add up to an extensive and intricate network.

**Pastina Restaurant
1989**
Architect Toyo Ito
Address 9-9, Kinuta
1-chōme, Setagaya-ku, Tōkyō
Transport From Shinjuku
Station: Train—Odakyū line
to Seijō-gakuenmae Station
and bus bound for Shibuya
Station to NHK Gijutsu-
Kenkyū-shō-Mae stop and
1-minute walk; or from
Shibuya Station: Subway—
Hanzōmon or Shin-Tama-
gawa line to Yōga Station and
5 minutes by taxi (on the
south side of Setagaya-dōri
Avenue, next to Honda
Showroom)

**Honda Showroom
1986**
Architect Toyo Ito
Address 9-9, Kinuta
1-chōme, Setagaya-ku, Tōkyō
Transport From Shinjuku
Station: Train—Odakyū line
to Seijō-gakuenmae Station
and bus bound for Shibuya
Station to NHK Gijutsu-
Kenkyū-shō-Mae stop and
1-minute walk; or from
Shibuya Station: Subway—
Hanzōmon or Shin-Tama-
gawa line to Yōga Station and
5 minutes by taxi (on the
south side of Setagaya-dōri
Avenue, next to Pastina
Restaurant)

**Yōga Promenade
1986**
Yōga Promenādo
Architect Team Zoo—
Atelier Zo
Address Yōga 4, Kami-yōga
5-chōme, Setagaya-ku, Tōkyō
Transport Subway—Hanzōmon or Shin-Tamagawa line
to Yōga Station and 5-minute
walk to west from the station
on the way to the Setagaya
Art Museum

都 TŌKYŌ
Setagaya-ku Area

House at a Bus Stop in Seijō, 1981
House at a Cross-road in Seijō, 1983
Seijō House In-between, 1988

Architect Kunihiko Hayakawa
Address 11-9, Seijō 2-chōme, Setagaya-ku, Tōkyō
Transport From Shinjuku Station: Train—Odakyū line to Seijō-gakuenmae Station: south exit and 6-minute walk
Visitation Private residences: seen only from the outside.

Setagaya Art Museum 1985
Setagaya Bijutsukan
Architect Shozo Uchi
Address 1-2, Kinuta-kōen, Setagaya-ku, Tōkyō
Transport Subway—Hanzō-mon or Shin-Tamagawa line to Yōga Station and 15-minute walk to Kinuta-kōen Park to the west

Yōga A-Flat 1993
Architect Kunihiko Hayakawa
Address 1-17, Kami-yōga 3-chōme, Setagaya-ku, Tōkyō
Transport Subway—Hanzō-mon or Shin-Tamagawa line to Yōga Station and 10-minute walk to north
It is an apartment/office complex, designed around an attractive courtyard plaza.

In about eight years, Hayakawa designed three residences side by side in this suburb of Tōkyō. Responding to the same condition of a busy street intersection in front, the three houses display a similar design scheme. In designing the small buildings, one of the primary goals of the architect was to provide protection to the residents from the noise and pollution of the road. Hayakawa introduced various ways of articulating the frontal zones of the reinforced concrete buildings with a system of layered walls. These walls, with carefully modulated openings and intricate spaces in between them, create a buffer zone to filter out unwanted environmental intrusions while not shutting off entirely the interiors in this direction. On the other side, toward their backyards or gardens, all three houses are more open than in front.

Housing in Daita
1990

Architect Yasumitsu
Matsunaga
Address 9-11, Daita
6-chōme, Setagaya-ku, Tōkyō
Transport Train—Keiō
Inokashira line or Odakyū
line to Shimokitazawa Station
and 10-minute walk (near
Seitoku-gakuen High School
at a T intersection of small,
residential roads)
Visitation Private residences;
seen only from the outside.

Located on a corner site, this compound of five small residences and their courtyards is enclosed by story-high walls. The majority of the rooms, arranged on two floors, therefore look over intimate private yards rather than the adjacent streets. In this attractive urban housing, wherein solid volumes alternate with enclosed voids, the roofs over each unit emerge as important compositional elements. They form an interconnected fabric of multilateral domes, which, not unlike similar structures in Islamic architecture, are shaped after models of the cosmic world. While acknowledging the differences between ancient and modern cosmic views, attributable to the tremendous scientific and technological progress since the earlier models, Matsunaga's scheme admittedly makes an implicit reference to both of them. Yet, it does this in a way that also expresses the idea and image of prototypical primitive huts.

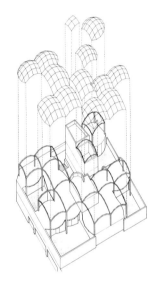

都 TŌKYŌ
Kita-ku Area

**Maruichi Company
Building
1991**

Architect Akira Komiyama
Address 21-12, Horifune
3-chōme, Kita-ku, Tōkyō
Transport Subway—Chiyoda
line to Machiya Station;
change to Train—Arakawa
line to Kajiwara Station and
5-minute walk to north

都 TŌKYŌ
Ayase Area

**Tōkyō Budōkan
1989**

Architect Kijo Rokkaku
Address 20, Ayase 3-chōme,
Adachi-ku, Tōkyō
Transport Train—Jōban line
to Ayase Station and
10-minute walk to north
The large complex with an
unusual roof structure features several sports facilities.

Yamatō International Building, 1987

Yamatō Intānashonāru Biru
Architect Hiroshi Hara
Address 1-1, Heiwa-jima
5-chōme, Ōta-ku, Tōkyō
Transport Train—JR Yamanote line to Hamamatsu
Station, change to Tōkyō
Monorail to Ryūtsu Center
Station and 10-minute walk
west across Expressway 1, or
from JR Shinagawa Station:
Train—Keihin-Kyūkō line to
Heiwa-jima Station and
15-minute walk to the east

In this newly developing area of the metropolis, Hara's design is meant to act as a core of further urbanization. Therefore, the Yamatō International Building, headquarters of a fashion design company, is shaped with an image of urban scenery. Various layers of the elevation can be interpreted as rows of buildings in a hillside town; there are roof elements and semi-open gazebos that seem to cascade from the upper levels onto a lower deck. This deck, which is a kind of podium filling the entire site, is designed so as to interconnect with the surrounding urban realm; its height matches and, so, seems to counter the powerful structure of the nearby elevated highway. This two-story rectangular section, with storage and service spaces within, encloses a small urban plaza, which is open to the sky as well as to both the park and the street through large, gatelike openings. The top of this structure provides a roof terrace, another "public plaza" from where numerous pedestrian paths, including the bridge of the "sky circuit," depart and run through the building both inside and out. The delicately carved and crafted facades are covered with highly polished aluminum panels, which, along with the flush-mounted, etched glass surfaces, reflect the changing weather. Altogether this spectacular work appears as the mirage of what Hiroshi Watanabe appropriately called a "high-tech Shangri-la."

**Nunotani Building
1992**
Architect Peter Eisenman
Architects (U.S.)
Address 21, Chūō 1-chōme,
Edogawa-ku, Tōkyō
Transport Train—JR Sōbu
line to Shin-Koiwa Station
and 12-minute walk to south-
east on Heiwabashi-dōri
Avenue, then northeast on
Chiba-kaidō Avenue

**Tōkyō Sea Life Park
1990**
*Tōkyō-to Kasai Rinkai
Suizokukan*
Architect Yoshio Taniguchi
Address 2-3, Rinkai-chō 6-
chōme, Edogawa-ku, Tōkyō
Transport From JR Tōkyō
Station: Train—JR Keiyō line
to Kasai Rinkai-ken Station
and 8-minute walk south

市 **TAMA**

Nagayama Amusement Center 1993
Nagayama Humax Pavilion
Architect Toyo Ito
Address 3-4, Nagayama
1-chōme, Tama, Tōkyō Pref.
Transport From Shinjuku
Station: Train—Keiō
Sagamihara line or Odakyū
Tama line to Nagayama
Station and 1-minute walk
north (in front of the station)
Visitation Guests only, no
photography is allowed inside

The project is a comprehensive commercial complex featuring restaurants, banquet halls, a large
public bath, a sauna, bowling alleys, and many
other activities; there is also a separate restaurant
building near the train station. The futuristic,
seven-story, main building is finished with metallic
materials and, not unlike Ito's Yatsushiro Municipal
Museum (K.A.P) (1991) (see page 295), is designed with two horizontal, flattened oval volumes
on top (for the bowling alleys and meeting rooms)
and triangular vaulted roofs (over the public bath,
and banquet hall). While the interior of the complex is articulated like the exterior, although with
more applied color, the garage space has been
turned into a gigantic mechanical jungle. The
building is connected to the station of the private
Keiō and Odakyu railroad lines by a pedestrian
deck leading to both the restaurant block and the
main entrance of the complex.

⌂ HACHIŌJI

Tōkyō University of Art and Design 1993

Tōkyō Zōkei Daigaku
Architect Arata Isozaki
Address 1575, Utsunuki-chō, Hachiōji, Tōkyō Pref.
Transport From Shinjuku Station: Train—JR Chūō line to Hachiōji Station, change to JR Yokohama line to Aihara Station; or from Shinjuku Station: Train—Keiō Sagamihara line to Hashimoto Terminal, change to JR Yokohama line to Aihara Station (one stop): east exit and 5 minutes by the university's shuttle bus
Visitation Open daily, tel: (0426) 61-4401

Located in a hilly suburban area of Tōkyō, the campus is laid out along a decentralized plan in order to preserve the natural environment. There are three groups of buildings connected by green areas and a service road. The main complex, which provides a large, arched entrance to the campus, surrounds a trapezoidal and sloping courtyard. Above the entranceway is the administration building topped with the cylindrical glass volume of the lounge. Within the two wings of the main complex, Isozaki arranged a series of classrooms, small lecture halls, and a library. At the far end of the courtyard the museum connects the two wings; it was built according to Seiichi Shirai's early designs, and exhibits the work of the Italian sculptor Giacomo Manzù. These main facilities are complemented by a studio group to the north, which includes a cylindrical dining hall and cafeteria. Further down the road, an atelier group is divided into two sections: one for painting and the other for sculpture.

⌂ CHŌFU

Ichigoya 1988

Ichigoya Honkan
Architect Shin Takamatsu
Address 19-2, Kokuryō-chō 2-chōme, Chōfu, Tōkyō Pref.
Transport From Shinjuku Station: Train—Keiō line to Kokuryō Station: north exit and 3-minute walk
Ichigoya is an extensive commercial and office complex.

⌂ KODAIRA

Musashino Art University Building 10, 1981

Musashino Bijutsu Daigaku Jūgō-kan
Architect Minoru Takeyama
Address 736, Ogawa-chō 1-chōme, Kodaira, Tōkyō Pref.
Transport From Shinjuku Station: Train—JR Chūō line to Kokubunji Station: change to Train—to Seibu Kokubunji line to Takanodai Station and 10-minute walk to west (just over .5 mile/.8 kilometer)

Y's Court Nakahara 1991
Architect Yasumitsu Matsunaga
Address 876-1, Kami-odanaka, Nakahara-ku, Kawasaki, Kanagawa Pref.
Transport From Yokohama Station in Yokohama or Shibuya Station in Tōkyō: Train—Tōkyū-Tōyoko line to Musashi-Kosugi Station: change to Train—Nanbu line to Musashi-Nakahara and 10-minute walk toward north
Visitation Private dormitory; seen only from the outside.

The Y's Court Nakahara has been designed as a new type of dormitory for company workers. Since Japan is experiencing a growing labor shortage, more and more companies try to attract young employees by offering them dormitory accommodations that resemble hotels rather than simple lodgings. Accordingly, Matsunaga's project includes various facilities that had not been part of such buildings in the past. On the lower levels there are a dining hall, lounge, cafeteria, bath, swimming pool, and exercise rooms for common use; the rooftop, under a uniquely shaped tubular steel structure, can be used for other recreational purposes. The rooftop terrace features a canopy with an intricate steel frame. Elegantly outfitted, the single rooms approximate the size and layout of small studio apartments. All have small balconies and are designed so as to provide visual privacy from neighboring rooms. More interesting, however, is the inclusion and shaping of a multistory-high interior courtyard. This space, with a section of a pointed spearhead, is defined by segmented walls, curving in both horizontal and vertical directions. Tiny windows, in three rows on each floor, connect this atrium/court with the surrounding corridors and, along with numerous small skylights, provide mysterious lighting that lends the space a certain "cosmic" dimension.

Kawasaki City Museum 1988
Kawasaki Shimin Hakubutsukan
Architect Kiyonori Kikutake
Address 3049-1, Todoroki, Nakahara-ku, Kawasaki, Kanagawa Pref.
Transport Train—JR Nanbu line to Musashi-Nakahara Station: or Train—Tōkyū-Tōyoko line to Shin-Maruko Station and 8 minutes by taxi

🏯 KAWASAKI

Communicate Saloon "PIA"
1992
Architect George Kunihiro
Address 16-1, Ekimae Honchō, Kawasaki-ku, Kawasaki, Kanagawa Pref.
Transport Train—JR Tōkaidō line or Keihin Tōhoku line to Kawasaki Station; or Keihin Kyūkō line to Keikyū Kawasaki Station and 1-minute walk (the building is in between the two stations)

Cubic Forest House (now Masayoshi Nakamura Museum)
1971
Nakamura Masayoshi Bijutsukan
Architect Kazuo Shinohara
Address 2-8, Hosoyama 7-chōme, Aso-ku, Kawasaki, Kanagawa Pref.
Transport From Shinjuku Station: Train—Odakyū Odawara line to Yomiuri Land Mae Station and Bus bound for Keiō Yomiuri Land Station to Hosoyama stop and 5-minute walk to northwest; or from Shinjuku Station in Tōkyō: Train—Keiō line to Keiō Yomiuri Land Station and Bus bound for Teraodai-danchi to Hosoyama stop and 5-minute walk northwest
Visitation Wednesday–Sunday: 11:00–17:00; also open on Mondays and Tuesdays, when these days are national holidays; closed in summer and winter for long periods; tel. (044) 953-4936

🏯 YOKOHAMA

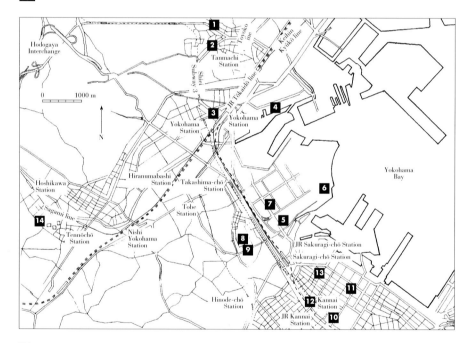

1. Rotunda Building, page 149
2. Gazebo Building, page 150
3. Tower of Winds, page 150
4. Alte Yokohama, page 150
5. Landmark Tower, page 150
6. Pacifico Yokohama, page 150
7. Yokohama Art Museum, page 150
8. Kanagawa Concert Hall and Library, page 150
9. Kanagawa Prefectural Youth Center, page 151
10. Yokohama City Hall, page 151
11. Open-port Memorial Hall, page 151
12. Marutan Building, page 151
13. Kanagawa Prefectural Museum, page 151
14. Yokohama Galleria, page 153

市 YOKOHAMA

Rotunda Building 1987

Architect Riken Yamamoto
Address 28-2, Matsumoto
4-chōme, Kanagawa-ku,
Yokohama, Kanagawa Pref.
(see map)
Transport From Shibuya
Station in Tōkyō or Yoko-
hama Station in Yokohama:
Train—Tōkyū-Tōyoko line
to Tanmachi Station and
8-minute walk west on north
side of Road 1 (or 6-minute
walk from Gazebo)
Visitation Above the third
floor, the building houses only
private residences, which can
be seen only from the outside.

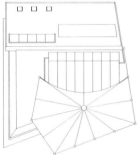

In the mid-1980s Yamamoto began to receive commissions for buildings other than single-family residences. Prompted by this shift, and responding to the quickly changing city, he initiated a new approach to architecture. The Gazebo and Rotunda buildings are the first in the line of increasingly larger projects. Both are mixed-use urban complexes in which some commercial facilities (shops, boutiques, and offices) fill the lower levels, while residences, including the owners', fill the upper stories. This functional "separation" has been rein-forced by articulating the two sections in entirely different ways. The lower parts are relatively solid, boxy volumes, whereas the upper realms include ample, open, roof terraces, platforms, stairways, and bridges, under softly curv-ing, light canopies. In the five-story Rotunda Building, this canopy, comprising the "rotunda" itself, is made of a translucent Teflon-fiber tent, stretched over a light steel frame and supported by ten steel-pipe columns. Yamamoto's design, which is derivative of his interpretation of the "city as topography," intends to both fill a gap in the fabric of the existing city and devise a new kind of archi-tecture above this layer. In so doing, he assures that the residential units, while actively engaging their natural as well as man-made environment, remain aloof from the hodgepodge of this busy semi-industrial suburb of Yokohama.

Toy Block House 2
1979
Architect Takefumi Aida
Address 5-7, Aobadai
2-chōme, Midori-ku, Yoko-
hama, Kanagawa Pref.
Transport From Shibuya
Station in Tōkyō: Subway—
Tōkyū Shin-Tamagawa line
to Aobadai Station and
2-minute walk
Visitation Private residence;
seen only from the outside.

Aobadai Tōkyū
Department Store
1993
Architect Jean-Michel
Wilmotte (France)
Address 1-1, Aobadai
2-chōme, Midori-ku, Yoko-
hama, Kanagawa Pref.
Transport From Shibuya
Station in Tōkyō: Subway—
Tōkyū Shin-Tamagawa line
to Aobadai Station and
2-minute walk (in front of the
south exit of the station)

Gazebo Building
1986
Architect Riken Yamamoto
Address 15-5, Izumi-chō,
Kanagawa-ku, Yokohama,
Kanagawa Pref. (see map)
Transport From Shibuya
Station in Tōkyō or Yoko-
hama Station in Yokohama:
Train—Tōkyū-Tōyoko line
to Tanmachi Station and
6-minute walk west
Visitation Above the second
floor, the building houses only
private residences, which can
be seen only from the outside.

Tower of Winds
1986
Yokohama Kaze no To
Architect Toyo Ito
Address Nishi-ku, Yokohama,
Kanagawa Pref. (see map)
Transport Any train to
Yokohama Station: in front of
west exit, in the center of
Yokohama station square
With the help of thousands of
flickering electric lights, the
Tower displays in the night
the changing direction and
velocity of wind, the noise
level of the surrounding
urban square, and, as a clock,
the passing of time.

Alte Yokohama
1992
Architect Michael Graves
(U.S.)
Address Ōno-chō, Kanagawa-ku, Yokohama,
Kanagawa Pref. (see map)
Transport Any train to Yokohama Station: east exit and
8-minute walk to northeast
The symmetrical structure is
a high-rise office building on
an extensive, three-story,
square base, similar to that of
Michael Graves's Portland
Building (1982), a seminal
example of American post-
modern architecture.

Landmark Tower
1993
Architect Hugh Stubbins
(U.S.) (with Mitsubishi Real
Estate Architectural Office)
Address 2, Minatomirai 2-
chōme, Nishi-ku, Yokohama,
Kanagawa Pref. (see map)
Transport Train—Keihin-
Tōhoku line or Tōkyū-
Tōyoko line to Sakuragi-chō
Station and 5-minute walk
north, toward the sea
Visitation "Sky Garden"
observation deck open 10:00–
22:00 (July–September),
10:00–21:00 (October–June)
The 970-feet/296-meter
tower is the highest building
in Japan.

Pacifico Yokohama
1991
Architect Nikken Sekkei
Company
Address 1, Minatomirai 1-
chōme, Nishi-ku, Yokohama,
Kanagawa Pref. (see map)
Transport Train—Keihin
Tōhoku line or Tōkyū-Tōyo-
ko line to Sakuragi-chō
Station and 12-minute walk
(7-minute walk from
Landmark Tower)
The complex is a hotel and
convention center with a wide
variety of facilities, including
extensive exhibition halls.

Yokohama Art Museum
1989
Yokohama Bijutsukan
Architect Kenzo Tange
Address 4, Minatomirai 3-
chōme, Nishi-ku, Yokohama,
Kanagawa Pref. (see map)
Transport Train—Keihin
Tōhoku line or Tōkyū-
Tōyoko line to Sakuragi-chō
Station and 10-minute walk
(5-minute walk from
Landmark Tower)
The symmetrical composition
of horizontal volumes is
accentuated with a semi-
cylindrical tower in its center.

Kanagawa Concert Hall
and Library, 1954
*Kanagawa Kenritsu
Ongakudō* and *Toshokan*
Architect Kunio Maekawa
Address Momijigaoka, Nishi-
ku, Yokohama, Kanagawa
Pref. (see map)
Transport Train—Keihin-
Tōhoku line or Tōkyū-
Tōyoko line to Sakuragi-chō
Station and 10-minute walk
(first 5 minutes north along
the train line then 5 minutes
west uphill—next to the
Kanagawa Prefectural Youth
Center)

Kanagawa Prefectural Youth Center, 1962

Kanagawa-ken Seishōnen Sentā

Architect Kunio Maekawa
Address Momijigaoka, Nishi-ku, Yokohama, Kanagawa Pref. (see map)
Transport Train—Keihin Tōhoku line or Tōkyū-Tōyoko line to Sakuragi-chō Station and 10-minute walk (first 5 minute north along the train line then 5 minute west uphill)

This project is a cultural center providing a wide variety of facilities such as an auditorium, a conference hall, discussion and study rooms, a library, and a planetarium. A representatives of what Robin Boyd termed the "New Japan Style," Maekawa's Kanagawa Prefectural Youth Center is built of exposed reinforced concrete in robust sculptural forms. Maekawa implemented much of the vocabulary from his Tōkyō Metropolitan Festival Hall (1961) (see page 16) in this work (post and beam skeleton, curving eaves and balconies, etc.), yet here there are powerful, solid concrete walls that alternate with deeply recessed windows and loggias. Located next to his Kanagawa Concert Hall and Library (1954), the Youth Center well exemplifies the shift in Maekawa's architectural articulation, similar to that in Tange's work of the same period.

Yokohama City Hall, 1959

Yokohama Shichōsha
Architect Togo Murano
Address 1-1, Minato-chō, Naka-ku, Yokohama, Kanagawa Pref. (see map)
Transport Train—JR Negishi line or Subway to Kannai Station: north exit and a few steps

Marutan Building, 1991

Architect Arata Isozaki
Address 4-54, Onoe-chō, Naka-ku, Yokohama, Kanagawa Pref. (see map)
Transport Train—JR Negishi line or Subway to Kannai Station: north exit and 4-minute walk to northwest (2-minute walk from Yokohama City Hall)
Visitation Open daily, tel: (045) 651-0123

Open-port Memorial Hall, 1917

Kaikō Kinenkan
Architect Shichigorō Yamada and Shirō Sato
Address 1-6, Hon-chō, Naka-ku, Yokohama, Kanagawa Pref. (see map)
Transport Train—JR Negishi line to Kannai Station: north exit and 5-minute walk north

Kanagawa Prefectural Museum, 1904

Kanagawa Kenritsu Hakubutsukan
Architect Yorinaka Tsumagi
Address 5-60, Minami-Naka-dōri, Naka-ku, Yokohama, Kanagawa Pref. (see map)
Transport From Sakuragichō Station: Train—JR Negishi line or Subway to Kannai Station: north exit and 5-minute walk to north

Ryokuen-toshi Inter-junction City 1992–94

Architect Riken Yamamoto
Address 1-6, Ryokuen 4-chōme, Izumi-ku, Yokohama, Kanagawa Pref.
Transport From Yokohama Station: Train—Sagami (Sōtetsu) line to Ryokuen-toshi Station (on both sides of station and along both sides of the main road crossing under the elevated station)

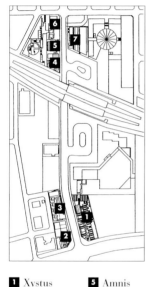

1 Xystus
2 Loggia
3 Obelisk
4 G.F.
5 Amnis
6 Prado
7 Arcus

This large project by Yamamoto, surpassing in size even his Hotakubo Public Housing (K.A.P.) in Kumamoto (1991) (see page 301), is built in several stages. Developed largely by the private Sagami railroad company serving this suburban area of Yokohama, the Inter-junction City—with individual buildings named Xystus (shown in these photographs), Arcus, G.F. (all 1992), Obelisk, Loggia, Amnis (all 1993), and Prado (1994)—is located on both the east and west sides of the Ryokuen-toshi Station. The project is comprised mainly of housing but also features numerous commercial and cultural facilities, shops, boutiques, and a post office. This large work continues the line of Yamamoto's innovative designs for mixed-use projects exploring the possible relationships between private and public realms, and, so, aiming at a more interconnected and interactive life in the city. The buildings are constructed of reinforced concrete with exposed concrete block walls and of light, metallic balconies, stairways, and bridges and vaulted roofs. The lower sections, which accommodate shops accessible from the street, comprise a "podium" for an upper public plaza with restaurants and cafes and, above them, the residential units in several groups on several floors. These "podia" are joined by a system of thoroughfares of various forms: stairways, passages and bridges. Covered with corrugated steel and translucent acrylic canopies but otherwise open to the outside, the semi-public spaces and extensive terraces and balconies provide intimate areas for residents and other users.

5 YOKOHAMA

Sōtetsu Cultural Center 1990
Sōtetsu Bunka Sentā
Architect Hiroshi Hara
Address 3-28, Ryokuen 1-chōme, Izumi-ku, Yokohama, Kanagawa Pref.
Transport From Yokohama Station: Train—Sagami (Sōtetsu) line to Ryokuen-toshi Station east exit and 10-minute walk uphill on the left (east of Xystus in Ryokuen-toshi Inter-junction City)

Yokohama Galleria 1989
Architect Mario Bellini (Italy) (with YBP Architects Office)
Address 134, Kōbe-chō, Hodogaya-ku, Yokohama, Kanagawa Pref. (see map)
Transport From Yokohama Station: Train—Sagami (Sōtetsu) line to Tennōji Station and 6-minute walk to west (across Yokohama Business Park)

市 KAMAKURA

Kamakura Prefectural Museum of Modern Art, 1951 addition, 1966
Kanagawa Kenritsu Kamakura Gindai Bijutsukan
Architect Junzo Sakakura
Address 1-53, Yukinoshita 2-chōme, Kamakura, Kanagawa Pref.
Transport Train—JR Yokosuka line to Kamakura Station and 10-minute walk (near the Tsurugaoka Hachiman Shrine)

The Kamakura Prefectural Museum of Modern Art, along with Antonin Raymond's Reader's Digest Building in Tōkyō of the same year, is one of the first prominent buildings completed after World War II. The original structure was extended with an addition, also by Sakakura, in 1966. The entire museum is located within the compound of the famous Tsurugaoka Hachiman Shrine and is surrounded by a park. Facing a small pond to the south, the two wings of the museum were designed so as to "step" into the water that separates them. A covered bridge connects the two across the inlet of the pond; this bridge also looks over a few sculptures placed in the water. The first building is essentially a rectangular windowless volume, covered by asbestos panels and elevated on pilotis by slim steel columns, while the addition displays its interiors through two-story glass walls set in structural steel frames. Therefore, they respectively reveal the influence of Le Corbusier and Mies van der Rohe, while articulating a design sensibility that has always shaped traditional Japanese architecture, particularly its elegant but intimate relationship with nature.

市 FUJISAWA

Fujisawa Municipal Gymnasia, 1984

Fujisawa-shi Akibadai Bunka Taiikukan
Architect Fumihiko Maki
Address 3172, Endo, Fujisawa, Kanagawa Pref.
Transport From Shinjuku Station in Tōkyō: Train—Odakyū Enoshima line to Shōnandai Station: west exit and bus bound for Keiō Daigaku to Taiikukan stop, or 8 minutes by taxi

Maki's architecture changed course in the early 1980s. The first representative of this change is the Fujisawa Municipal Gymnasia, a large complex comparable in size and curvilinear articulation to Tange's Olympic Gymnasia in Tōkyō (see page 126). Like Tange's, Maki's scheme articulates the program in two distinct parts: a large arena and a smaller training hall. The gymnasia of both projects are connected with a low-profile entrance hall, lobbies, and other common facilities. Moreover, they are constructed of an exposed reinforced concrete lower section with a steel roof structure spanning the arenas. However, the similarity between Tange's and Maki's designs ends here. The Fujisawa Municipal Gymnasia is covered by thin stainless steel plates that lend a futuristic appearance to the complex. The design deviates from articulating the composition as a unified formal entity. The whole is consistently challenged by its multifarious parts: the fragmented surfaces of the roofs, the divergent patterns of seam lines, and the contradictory elevations, rooflines, silhouettes, and details. As one walks around the complex, these parts suggest the images of spaceship, UFO, zeppelin, a mask, a helmet, even a turtle or a bug. Such motifs—which alternatively refer to the futuristic and the traditional, the technological and the biological—purposely open up a range of readings of Maki's architecture. To this end Maki has mobilized the potentials of both the tectonic (advanced structure and technologies) and the scenographic (ambiguous surfaces, silhouettes, and imagery) aspects of architecture in a manner in which the enveloping skin of the building is largely freed from the constrains of the supporting structure.

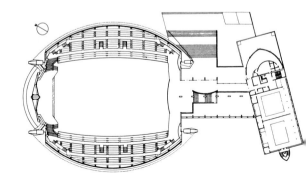

🏛 FUJISAWA

Shōnandai Cultural Center
1991

Shōnandai Bunka Sentā
Architect Itsuko Hasegawa
Address 8, Shōnandai
1-chōme, Fujisawa, Kanagawa
Pref.
Transport From Shinjuku
Station in Tōkyō: Train—
Odakyū Enoshima line to
Shōnandai Station; or Train—
JR Tōkaidō line to Fujisawa
Station, change to Odakyū
Enoshima line to Shōnandai
Station: east exit and 5-minute
walk to east

Occupying two city blocks in this satellite town of Tōkyō, the Shōnandai
Cultural Center is an urban-scale project, and the largest work to date by
Hasegawa. The center features a children's museum, workshops, galleries,
rehearsal rooms for various performances, a civic theater in the large globe, a
space theater in the small globe, an open-air theater, and an intricate outdoor
promenade on top of the buildings. These facilities are arranged as a small
urban community around a public plaza and playground, the roof of underground spaces, exhibition halls, and parking garage. The plaza is highlighted
by a stream of water, a pool, small bridges, artificial trees of metallic screens
and a unique clock that performs an audio-visual show on every hour. In addition to the spherical forms, Hasegawa designed numerous tiny pyramidlike
roofs and canopies wrapped in stainless steel or highly polished aluminum. The
image created by the complex is both futuristic and vernacular, even "natural," insofar as Hasegawa redefines "architecture as second nature." She alludes
not only to natural forms or the evocation of natural elements, but also to the
provision of ample space and opportunity for natural phenomena to interact
with the realm of architecture. With its supple and fragmentary qualities, the
Shōnandai Cultural Center continues the heterogeneous, collagelike texture of
the surrounding city, yet, by way of both the "primitivism" of the vernacular
and the application of technological details, it also substantially redefines the
same environment. The project thus is the outcome of a paradoxical design
strategy, in which the forces of both simulation and dissimulation act together.

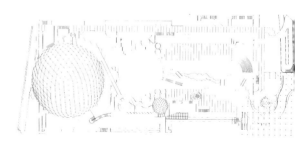

🏛 FUJISAWA

Keiō University Shōnan-Fujisawa Campus
1992
Keiō Daigaku Fujisawa Shōnan Kyampasu
Architect Fumihiko Maki
Address 5322, Endo, Fujisawa, Kanagawa Pref.
Transport From Shinjuku Station in Tōkyō: Train—Odakyū Enoshima line to Shōnandai Station; or Train—JR Tōkaidō line to Fujisawa Station, change to Odakyū Enoshima line to Shōnandai Station, west exit and bus to Keiō Daigaku
The extensive campus features many buildings all designed by Maki.

Keiō Shōnan-Fujisawa Junior-Senior High School, 1992
Keiō Shōnan-Fujisawa Chūgakkō and Kōtō Gakkō
Architect Yoshio Taniguchi
Address 5466, Endo, Fujisawa, Kanagawa Pref.
Transport From Shinjuku Station in Tōkyō: Train—Odakyū Enoshima line to Shōnandai Station; or Train—JR Tōkaidō line to Fujisawa Station, change to Odakyū Enoshima line to Shōnandai Station, west exit and bus to Keiō Daigaku (the high school is southwest of the university campus)
See page 28, fig. 35.

🏛 CHIGASAKI

Pacific Hotel
1966
Architect Kiyonori Kikutake
Address 4-60, Higashikaigan-Minami 6-chōme, Chigasaki, Kanagawa Pref.
Transport Train—JR Tōkaidō line to Chigasaki Station and 12-minute walk toward the seashore to the south

🏛 HIRATSUKA

House with Fifty-four Windows
1975
Sōya Clinic
Architect Kazuhiro Ishii
Address 33-24, Hanamizudai, Hiratsuka, Kanagawa Pref.
Transport Train—JR Tōkaidō line to Hiratsuka Station and 10 minutes by taxi

Ishii's design for this medical clinic and residence is an exercise in the visual language of architecture. In the 1970s the emphasis in Japanese architecture shifted from the technological and structural to the possibilities of architectural languages and meaning. Architects became interested in the variety of expressions that could be generated by details and architectural references in the locality of prevailing urban conditions. Here Ishii selected the window as the theme of his design. Within a simple, rational, structural framework of a cubical grid he provided some fifty-four variations on the idea of "window," revisiting as well as expanding both its Western and Japanese definitions. Ishii's colorful design is both a serious and daring act and a lighthearted joke, pun, or even a satire.

Hirano Dental Clinic
1973
Hirano Haisha Kurinikku
Architect Kazumasa Yamashita
Address 1-33, Matsukaze-chō, Hiratsuka, Kanagawa Pref.
Transport Train—JR Tōkaidō line to Hiratsuka Station and 6-minute walk

CHŪBU AND HOKURIKU REGIONS

Chūbu makes up the middle section of the main Honshū Island, and includes the mountainous regions of Yamanashi, Nagano, Shizuoka, Aichi, and Gifu prefectures. The area is rich in both urban developments and natural attractions. The former are represented by such large cities as Nagoya (2.1 million), Toyota City (.47 million), Hamamatsu (.53 million), Shizuoka (.47 million), Nagano, and Kōfu, and the latter by the beautiful high ranges of the Japan Alps with their deep river valleys and gorges; by Mount Fuji, Japan's tallest mountain (12,388 feet/3,776 meters); and by the Izu peninsula, with its variegated seacoast.

Many outstanding works of well-known architects, such as Kenzo Tange, Kazuo Shinohara, Arata Isozaki, Hiroshi Hara, Toyo Ito, and Kisho Kurokawa, provide excellent examples of contemporary design in Chūbu. Projects include both the latest achievements—Ito's Shimosuwa Municipal Museum (1993) and Hara's Iida City Museum (1988)—and earlier landmarks—Isozaki's Kamioka Town Hall (1978) and Tange's Yamanashi Press and Broadcasting Center in Kōfu (1966)—of Japanese postwar architecture.

Furthermore, the region has many excellent representatives of prewar, traditional architecture and urbanism. Meiji-mura is a large, open-air village museum that displays a substantial collection of well-preserved buildings from the mid-nineteenth to early-twentieth century. Among the many structures, Frank Lloyd Wright's Imperial Hotel (1923) emerges as the most famous one, which, after being demolished in Tōkyō in 1965, was partially reconstructed here in 1980.

The Chūbu region also boasts numerous traditional urban areas, small towns, and other settlements, many of which, like those along the Kiso River valley in Nagano Prefecture—Narai-juku, Tsumago-juku, etc.—are located among the mountains. Takayama in the Hida region of Gifu Prefecture is a famous Edo Era (1603–1868) merchant town, in which several intact and well-maintained old districts give an excellent picture of the urban culture and architecture of previous ages. Shirakawa, also in Gifu Prefecture, is an old hamlet with numerous large and magnificent farmhouses of high-pitched, thatched roofs, and sturdy, multistory wooden structures.

Nagano City features Zenkō-ji (1707), the most important Buddhist temple complex in the region. Matsumoto's medieval castle (1597), with its double donjons, is not only one of the largest and most beautiful castles in the country, but is also among the twelve such original structures that have survived almost unscathed the vicissitudes of Japan's turbulent history. The other surviving and famous castle in Chūbu, the Inuyama Castle (1601), north of Nagoya, is the only one in the country today that is still privately owned by the descendants of its Edo Era castellans, the Naruse family.

The climate in the Chūbu Region is by and large identical to that of Kantō. In the mountains the winters are cold and have plenty of snow, while the summers are cooler than those in the coastal areas. The rainy season in June and early July brings substantial precipitation. Around the seashore south of the mountains, the wet months are followed by a hot and muggy summer; the winter is mild and relatively dry.

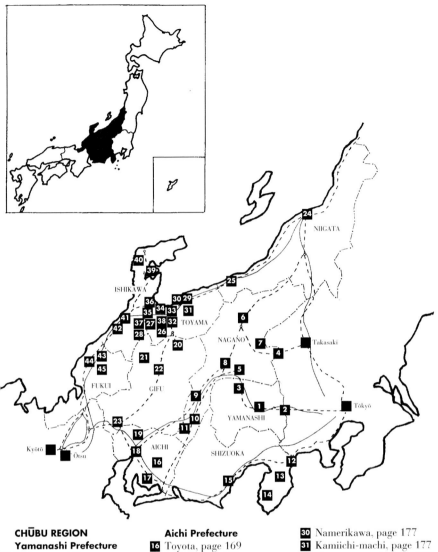

Located north of the Kantō and Chūbu regions, Hokuriku is a long and relatively narrow area along the coast of the Japan Sea. This region covers the northern ranges of the Japan Alps and the plains beyond, plus the Noto Peninsula; it offers plenty of untouched nature, good agricultural land, remote rural and lively urban areas, and many touristic attractions. There are also several places that played significant roles in Japanese history and culture: Eihei-ji (1244) is the largest Sōtō Zen monastery and Maruoka Castle (1576) is the oldest among the twelve extant castle keeps in the country (both sites are in Fukui Prefecture).

In Kanazawa, one of the most important medieval castle towns—although the castle itself is now gone, with only the huge stone ramparts and two magnificent gates standing—many districts of old, but well-preserved, wooden townhouses remain. Kanazawa is not only a charming traditional town; it is also a thriving contemporary city, which today plays as important a role in Japanese culture as it did in its heyday during the Edo Period (1603–1868). Additional, though smaller, urban communities with similar qualities include Takaoka, Toyama, Fukui, and Komatsu. Niigata, to the east along the sea coast, is the largest industrial city and most important port in the region.

Contemporary architectural developments that began to gain momentum during the economic boom of the 1980s are represented by the works of such prominent figures as Kisho Kurokawa, Arata Isozaki, Fumihiko Maki, and, more recently, Shōei Yoh, Itsuko Hasegawa, and Kiko Mozuna. Some of these projects are among the most outstanding ones produced by their architects. The YKK Guest House, for example, is one of Maki's best designs from the early 1980s, while the Noto Monzen Family Inn and the Notojima Glass Art Museum are perhaps Mozuna's most astonishing works to date. In all three cases the architectural experience is enhanced by the building's spectacular natural setting, as are Isozaki's small projects in Toga-mura, located in a tiny, isolated hamlet with some old farmhouses that are scattered in a valley high among the breathtaking mountains of Toyama Prefecture.

Toyama Prefecture, following the lead of Kumamoto's Kumamoto Art Polis (K.A.P.) Project, initiated its own Machi-no-Kao Project. Launched in the late 1980s with the help of Arata Isozaki as commissioner, the Machi-no-Kao is a sort of urban beautification program, and, therefore, is much smaller in both scale and actual architectural programming than its Kumamoto counterpart. The invited designers, all of whom are foreigners, have completed bus stops, rest pavilions, observation platforms, and the like in various urban locations in the prefecture, and many of their works are remarkable pieces of architecture.

Seasonal changes prevail in this region, with long and cold winters in the mountains and hot and humid summers elsewhere. The six-week rainy season begins late in May.

Yamanashi Press and Broadcasting Center, 1966 addition, 1974

Yamanashi Bunka Kaikan
Architect Kenzo Tange
Address 6-10, Kitaguchi 2-chōme, Kōfu, Yamanashi Pref.
Transport From Shinjuku Station in Tōkyō: Train—JR Chūō Main line to Kōfu Station: north exit and 5-minute walk

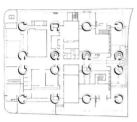

One of the most notable works of Tange, the Yamanashi Press and Broadcasting Center comes close to realizing a visionary urban scheme produced by the architects of the Metabolism Group in the early 1960s. The center recollects particularly well Isozaki's projects for a Joint Core System and City in the Air (see page 20, figs. 18 and 19), which he designed while working in Tange's URTEC studio. Therefore, Tange's design can be interpreted as both a large building and a small city elevated above the ground. The entire complex, housing a broadcasting company, a newspaper facility, and a commercial printing office, is supported solely by sixteen cylindrical shafts. These reinforced concrete shafts accommodate stairways, elevators, ducts, and service spaces. The floor structures, like bridges, span between these shafts so as to leave many voids within the volume. The center was enlarged in 1974 by partially filling these voids and also by adding floors above the existing structure. Even in its enlarged form, the building retains many open cavities in its volume; nevertheless, it seems to be rather monumental and dominant in its urban fabric.

町 UENOHARA-CHŌ

Lake Sagami Country Clubhouse 1989

Architect Arata Isozaki
Address 5000 Yuzurihara, Uenohara-chō, Kitatodome-gun, Yamanashi Pref.
Transport From Shinjuku Station in Tōkyō: Train—JR Chūō Main line to Uenohara Station and 15 minutes by taxi
Visitation Tel: (0554) 67-2221

町 KOBUCHIZAWA-CHŌ

Risonare Vivre Club Kobuchizawa 1992

Risonare Vivre Club, Ongaku-no-mori
Architect Mario Bellini (Italy) (with Takeda Associate Architects)
Address 129-1, Tsuboide, Kobuchizawa-chō, Kitakoma-gun, Yamanashi Pref.
Transport From Shinjuku Station in Tōkyō: Train—JR Chūō Main line to Kobuchizawa and 5 minutes by taxi.

⊞ KARUIZAWA

Tasaki Art Museum 1986

Tasaki Bijutsukan
Architect Hiroshi Hara
Address 2141-279, Naga-kurayokobuki, Karuizawa, Nagano Pref.
Transport Train—JR Jōetsu or Shinkansen Jōetsu line to Takasaki Station; change to JR Shinetsu line to Naka-Karuizawa Station and 12-minute walk first west then, at supermarket, north
Visitation 9:30–17:00, closed in winter

The Tasaki Art Museum, located in the outskirts of this mountain resort town, houses the permanent exhibition of the painter Hirosuke Tasaki. In addition to galleries, there are offices, a reception room, and a cafeteria, all arranged around a small courtyard surrounded by zigzagging, story-high, frameless glass walls. Natural light is therefore the main source of lighting. The spatial definition is rendered ambiguous by the use of etched glass, polished and matte stone, white pebbles, and softly curving forms. Used in both the interior and exterior, they provide interesting and unexpected reflections and various optical effects to blur the boundary between the two. Nature and architecture blend in an inseparable way. The undulating roofs are covered with highly polished aluminum plates, evoking the image of white clouds floating in the sky.

⊞ SANADA-MACHI ⊞ NAGANO

Hotel D
1977
Architect Toyo Ito
Address Sugadaira, Sanada-machi, Nagano Pref.
Transport Train—JR Jōetsu or Shinkansen Jōetsu line to Takasaki Station, change to JR Shinetsu line to Ueda Station; bus to Sugadaira Kōgen stop and 20-minute walk south (along Road 406)

Kaii Higashiyama Gallery (Shinano Art Museum)
1989
Nagano-ken Shinano Bijutsu-kan Higashiyama Kaii-kan
Architect Yoshio Taniguchi
Address Within Shiroyama Kōen Park (near the castle), Nagano, Nagano Pref.
Transport Train—JR Chūō Main line or Shinonoi line to Nagano Station, change to Nagano Dentetsu line to Zenkōjishita Station and 10-minute walk

The curving, narrow, 330-foot-/100-meter-long site of the Shimosuwa Municipal Museum parallels the shore line of Suwa-ko Lake, which is to the south. The volume of the two exhibition spaces (one displays the local folklore, the other the memorabilia of the poet Akahiko Shimagi, who was born in the city) follows this site line, while the small storage rooms on the north side of the galleries are housed in a boxy volume. The design is dominated by the arched, double bent form of the exhibition building, whose shape is made by steel frames set ten feet/three meters apart, which create an arc in both section and elevation adding up to a continuously and softly curving surface. From afar the museum resembles a ship turned upside down, floating on the lake, or a huge wave emerging from the water. To emphasize the dynamics and floating quality of this shell structure, its surface is covered by a .1-inch-/3-millimeter-thick aluminum membrane; when it bounces back the changing daylight or the lights of the night, the building is turned into a glowing arch. The completion of the museum commemorated the city's centenary.

Shimosuwa Municipal Museum 1993

Shimosuwa Chōritsu Hakubutsukan
Architect Toyo Ito
Address 10616-111, Kosui-bata, Shimosuwa-machi, Suwa-gun, Nagano Pref.
Transport From Shinjuku Station in Tōkyō: Train—JR Chūō Main line to Shimosuwa Station and 5 minutes by taxi or 20-minute walk
Visitation 9:30–18:00 (closed Tuesdays, the day after a national holiday, and from 28 December–4 January): tel: (0266) 27-1627

Kaichi Primary School
1876

Kaichi Gakkō or Nagano-ken Kyōiku Shiryōkan
Architect Kiyoshige (Seijō) Tateishi
Address 4-2, Kaichi 2-chōme, Matsumoto, Nagano Pref.
Transport From JR Matsumoto Station: east exit and 10 minutes by bus or 25-minute walk (10-minute walk north from Matsumoto Castle)
Visitation 8:30–16:30 daily from April through November (closed Sundays and national holidays); tel: (0263) 32-5725
The building is an Important National Cultural Property.

The well-maintained building is a masterpiece of early Meiji Era architecture; it shows an interesting blending of Western and Japanese influences. It was designed and built by the master carpenter Tateishi, who lived in Matsumoto. In order to investigate the new Western styles already popular in Tōkyō by that time, he traveled to the capital. He then adopted a Western plan and elements of Western styles in this school, but, having no training in corresponding Western building techniques, he employed the traditional Japanese construction method used in storehouse-like structures (*kura*). The wooden building is heavily plastered inside and out, including the "cornerstones" and "stone" base. The school is decorated with an octagonal tower and a Chinese gable roof over the porch, which features two angels. After serving as an elementary school for almost ninety years on the bank of the Metoba-gawa River, the building was relocated to its present site in 1963, because of frequent flooding of the river. In 1965 it was converted into a museum displaying the furniture, textbooks, documents, and other memorabilia that served modern education in Japan more than a century ago.

The Ukiyoe Museum, housing one of Japan's best wood block print (*ukiyoe*) collections, is located in the western outskirts of Matsumoto, amidst wide fields and rice paddies. The building is laid out in an *L* shape with simple rectangular volumes intersecting at a 130-degree angle. Its exterior is constructed of exposed reinforced concrete alternating with flush-mounted glass. The main elevations are composed of 26-foot/8-meter squares, which are articulated by the geometric shapes of the structural concrete and non-structural glass surfaces, dividing the areas diagonally, along a quarter-circle ring, etc. The concrete wall elements, as if defying the laws of gravity, seem to float within the light and reflective zones of glass. The abstract shaping of the elevations could be achieved only by resolving very difficult structural problems; in order to balance the wall planes, the roof supports the walls as much as the walls support the roof, in this way forming an unusual "unit construction." In addition to the surrounding unique wall surfaces, the two-story lobby features a steel, spiral stairway and all the pipes and ducts of air conditioning and heating that are exposed in the otherwise simple space. The *ukiyoe* collection is displayed in a windowless gallery on the first floor; a storage room occupies the second floor. In pursuing the theoretical issues of "discreteness" and "surfaceness" in this building, Shinohara was able to conceive a design with qualities similar to those of *ukiyoe* itself.

Ukiyoe Museum 1982

Nihon Ukiyoe Hakubutsukan
Architect Kazuo Shinohara
Address 2206-1, Shimadachi, Matsumoto, Nagano Pref.
Transport From JR Matsumoto Station: Train—Matsumoto Dentetsu line to Oniwa Station: north exit and 6 minutes by taxi or 15-minute walk
Visitation 10:00–17:00 (closed Mondays)

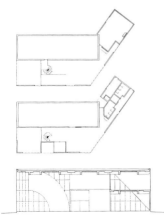

🏛 IIDA

Iida City Museum 1988

Iida Shiritsu Hakubutsukan
Architect Hiroshi Hara
Address 2, Ōtemachi, Iida,
Nagano Pref.
Transport From Nagoya
Station in Nagoya: Highway
bus to Iida City bus terminal
and 2-minute walk to east; or
from JR Iida Station:
8-minute walk to east
Visitation 10:00–17:00
(closed Mondays)

This cultural complex occupies the former site of the Nagahime Castle, and adjoins an old shrine on a steep hill facing south. The building includes an art gallery, a museum of regional natural history, exhibition rooms, an auditorium, and a planetarium. The site is designed as a park, together with the restored ruins of the castle. Hara's museum continues this park insofar as it features numerous rooftop terraces, gazebos, and public promenades and stairways from where one can enjoy the breathtaking scenery of the Japan Alps. Echoing the ranges of the surrounding mountains, Hara designed the sloping and reflective stainless steel roofs in both softly undulating forms and rugged pyramidal shapes. Inside the 260-foot-/80-meter-long lobby the "natural" scenery continues: numerous concrete columns with steel trusses evoke the image of a forest. As do most other designs of Hara's recent "architecture of modality," this project blends the man-made and technological with the natural, the inside with the outside, and the real with the illusive by blurring the boundaries between them.

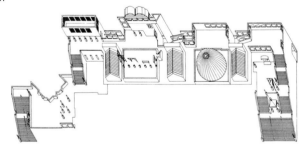

Up in the mountains of the Izu Peninsula, this small, private gallery is located on a steep site among residential buildings. The design articulates its two basic functions: a storage and display space for large paintings and sculpture within a reinforced concrete volume, and an adjoining exhibition space in a light, metallic shell. To emphasize the lightness and openness of this part, Ito has provided an independent vaulted canopy over its entrance and a patio. Perforated aluminum screens and intricate natural lighting sets a continuity from the gallery to the patio to nature.

Ueda Art Gallery 1991

Gyararī Ueda Yugawara
Architect Toyo Ito
Address 766, Miyaue, Yugawara, Shizuoka Pref.
Transport From JR Yugawara Station: 6 minutes by taxi; or from JR Atami Station: 15 minutes by taxi

町 SHŪZENJI-CHŌ

Japan Cycle Sports Center 1971
Nippon Cykuru Spōtsu Sentā
Architect Nikken Sekkei Company

Address Ono, Shūzenji-chō, Tagata-gun, Shizuoka Pref.
Transport Train—JR Tōkaidō Shinkansen to Mishima Station: change to Train—Izuhakōne line to Shūzenji Station and Tōkai bus to Nippon Cycle Sports Center

Located in a spectacular natural environment amidst hills and mountains, the cycling course takes advantage of the terrain. The spectators' grandstand features a unique, extensively cantilevered suspension structure.

Chōhachi Art Museum, 1986

Chōhachi Bijutsukan
Architect Osamu Ishiyama
Address 23, Matsuzaki, Matsuzaki-chō, Shizuoka Pref.
Transport From JR Atami Station: Train—Izukyūkō line to Shimoda Terminal: bus to Matsuzaki-chō and 3 minute walk along Road 136
Visitation 9:00–17:00 (year round, every day): tel: (0558) 42-2540

The Chōhachi Art Museum is dedicated to the work of Irie Chōhachi, the most renowned and respected Japanese plasterer, who pursued his profession on the level of high art in the late Edo and early Meiji eras, that is, in the mid-nineteenth century. Honoring the memory of Chōhachi, who lived in Matsuzaki-chō, some 2000 plasterers came from all over Japan to help build the main section of the museum. The complex is comprised of four parts: the art museum, folk-craft museum, outdoor theater, and a plaza that connects them. The two buildings have contrasting designs; the art museum is the result of craftsmanship, displaying traditional skills, while the adjacent structure was built by machines in steel, glass, and concrete. Two steel towers standing on the elevated plaza in front of the folk craft museum also denote contemporary technology. Set against the greenery of a steep hill, and bordering on the main coastal road, the various parts of this complex appear as a curious stage set.

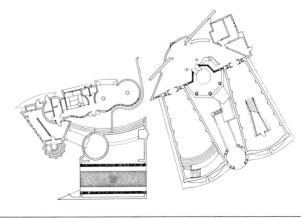

Kaba House (Toyota Motors Labor Union Hall) 1992

Toyota Jidōsha Rōdō Kumiai Kaikan
Architect Kōji Yagi
Address 5-1, Maruyama-chō 10-chōme, Toyota, Aichi Pref.
Transport From Nagoya Station in Nagoya: Train—Meitetsu Nagoya line to Naka-Okazaki, change to Aichi-kanjō line to Mikawa Station and 8-minute walk to north

Yagi's largest and most remarkable work to date, the Kaba House is the head-quarters of various labor unions within the Toyota Motors Company. In addition to numerous offices, the large complex houses many cultural and recreational facilities: gymnasia, baths, pools, restaurant, lounge, and a 100-seat multipurpose auditorium on the top, fifth floor. The diversity of the program has resulted in the diversity of architectural articulation; the Kaba House is a composite of different forms and structures as well as materials. Yet these elements, while claiming their independence, support an entity with a sense of an open-ended whole. Therefore, every vantage point suggests another image or reading of the building. The structure is comprised of two main volumes—a three-story mass on the west and a five-story one on the east. In between them Yagi arranged a multistory atrium under the curving vaults of a glass roof. Filled with light and highlighted by colorful interior elements, this atrium, the centerpiece of the design, is both a dramatic and a pleasantly attractive space.

市 **TOYOTA**

市 **NISHIO**

Shokyodō Museum for Wood Block Prints 1979

Shokyodō Bijutsukan
Architect Hiroshi Hara
Address 13, Higashiyama, Wakabayashi-Higashi-chō, Toyota, Aichi Pref.
Transport From Nagoya or Toyota Station: Train—Meitetsu Mikawa line to Wakabayashi Station: south exit and 15-minute walk (near Wakabayashi Higashi Shōgakkō Elementary School)
Visitation Open only for specific exhibitions; tel: (0562) 52-3150

Toyota Kuragaike Commemorative Hall 1974

Toyota Kuragaike Kinenkan
Architect Fumihiko Maki
Address 250, Ikeda-chō-Minami, Toyota, Aichi Pref.
Transport From Toyota or Shin-Toyota Station: 15 minutes by taxi (5 miles/8 kilometers west)
The horizontally stretching complex blends into its encircling hilly landscape. With its angular volumes and large glass surfaces, it takes advantage of the surrounding views.

Orphe 1987

Architect Shin Takamatsu
Address 9, Gosuke, Choda-chō, Nishio, Aichi Pref.
Transport From Nagoya Station: Train—Meitetsu line to Shin-Anjo Station, change to Meitetsu-Nishio line to Nishio Station: east exit and 6-minute walk to east (on north side of road)
Visitation Open daily, tel: (0563) 56-2222
Mixed-use commercial and office building.

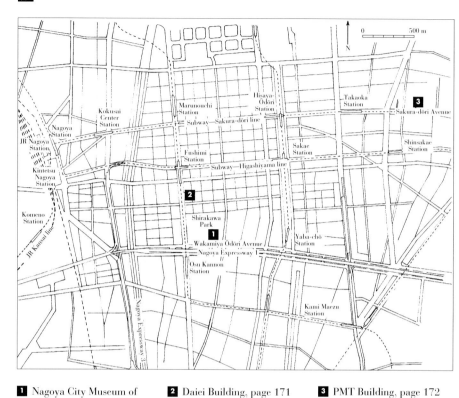

1 Nagoya City Museum of Modern Art, page 171

2 Daiei Building, page 171

3 PMT Building, page 172

市 NAGOYA

Toyota Memorial Hall, Nagoya University, 1960

Architect Fumihiko Maki
Address Nagoya University, Furo-chō, Chigusa-ku, Nagoya, Aichi Pref. (see map)
Transport From Nagoya Station: Subway—Higashiyama line to Motoyama Station: bus for Nagoya Daigaku (third stop) and 2-minute walk

The first completed building by Maki, the Toyota Memorial Hall houses a lecture hall and conference room. It features extensive semi-enclosed spaces under a large roof and within a reinforced concrete structural frame. This intermediary space between outside and inside can be used as a place for outdoor activities or as a small plaza.

市 NAGOYA

Nagoya City Museum of Modern Art, 1987

Nagoya-shi Bijutsukan
Architect Kisho Kurokawa
Address 17-25, Sakae
2-chōme, Naka-ku, Nagoya,
Aichi Pref. (see map)
Transport From Nagoya
Station: Subway—Higashi-
yama line to Fushimi Station:
Exit 5 and 6-minute walk
(inside Shirakawa Kōen Park)
Visitation 9:30–17:00; Friday
9:30–20:00 (closed Mondays
and 29 December–3 January),
tel: (052) 212-0001

As the Nagoya City Museum of Modern Art is situated in an attractively wooded urban park,
Kurokawa intended to keep its height low so as not
to exceed that of the trees. Therefore, in order to
accommodate its extensive program, the two-story
building is complemented by a basement that looks
over a sunken sculpture garden. Kurokawa's
scheme defines two wings that intersect at a sharp
angle while wrapping around this garden. The larger volume includes most of the exhibition rooms
and galleries and is lit through extensive skylights.
The slimmer but longer section contains a space-
frame pergola (which defines the axis of approach
from the north), the entrance, and a multistory
lobby. The lobby has a large, curving glass wall
and is crossed by two bridges connecting the two
wings. Contrasting with the surrounding greenery,
the architecture of the museum is dominated by
shades of white in its materials: tile, aluminum,
and stone. The design incorporates details, elements, and motifs that have their origin in both
traditional Japanese and contemporary, modern
architectures. The blending of the two is particularly attractive on the south side, where a Japanese
garden with a pond is intercepted by the alu-
minum- and stone-clad elements of the building.
Within the freestanding "structural" frame of the
south facade, one can also discover a stainless steel,
although broken, Shintō *torii* gate signifying the
passage through the frame.

Daiei Building 1973

Architect Paul Rudolph (U.S.)
Address 9-5, Sakae 2-chōme,
Naka-ku, Nagoya, Aichi Pref.
(see map)
Transport From Nagoya
Station: Subway—Higashi-
yama line to Fushimi Station:
Exit 5 and 4-minute walk

PMT Building
1978

Architect Toyo Ito
Address 1-1, Ishigamido-chō,
Higashi-ku, Nagoya, Aichi
Pref. (see map)
Transport From Nagoya
Station: Subway—Higashi-
yama line to Shinsakaemachi
Station and 10-minute walk;
or Subway—Sakura-dōri line
to Takaoka Station and
10-minute walk (on the north
side of Sakura-dōri Avenue)
Visitation Open daily,
tel: (052) 935-9551

This small office and showroom building of a printing company signaled the beginning of an important new stage in Ito's architecture. Until the mid-
1970s he designed most of his projects with
inward-oriented spaces enclosed in concrete volumes, with almost no communication with their
disordered urban environment. Recognizing the
limitations of such "defensive architecture," Ito
reorganized his strategy by "masking" the PMT
Building with a light and independent facade. The
building is composed of a modernist space within
an "empty" structural frame, which is then covered
by an undulating, paper-thin aluminum facade
that, almost like a soft flag in the wind, is "waved"
in front of the tectonic frame. Ito admits that by
devising a "silent sign" amidst the flood of commercial icons in the city, he wished to attain "a certain superficiality of expression in order to reveal
the nature of void hidden beneath" such signs.

Imperial Hotel, 1923
reconstructed, 1980

Teikoku Hotēru
Architect Frank Lloyd Wright
(U.S.)
Address 1, Uchiyama, Inuya-
ma, Aichi Pref. (within the
Meiji-mura Village Museum)
Transport From Meitetsu Bus
Terminal near Nagoya Station
in Nagoya: highway bus to
Meiji-mura (50 minutes); or
from Inuyama Station: bus
(20 minutes)
Visitation 10:00–16:00 daily
year round
See also page 15, fig. 6

Designed by Frank Lloyd Wright and completed in
1923, the original Imperial Hotel occupied a large
site in Hibiya across from the Imperial Palace compound in Tōkyō. Another American architect, the
Czech-born Antonin Raymond, assisted in this
project. The three-story building with a *U*-shaped
plan spread extensively to better resist the frequent
earthquakes in Japan. Moreover, Wright utilized a
new monolithic concrete foundation system, which
could "float" on the soft soil of the reclaimed land
in case of seismic movement. Both design decisions
proved Wright correct; the building survived the
devastating Great Kantō Earthquake that shook
Tōkyō and its vicinity on 1 September 1923, the
opening day of the hotel. The building was, however, demolished in 1965 to give way to a high-rise
hotel. The central section of Wright's structure,
including the main entrance, lobby, and adjoining
spaces, was nevertheless saved and, after fifteen
years of reconstructive work costing $25 million,
rebuilt in Meiji-mura. The shallow pool in front of
the hotel was also rebuilt, yet today, instead of
reflecting the urban landscape of Tōkyō, it mirrors
the rolling hills surrounding Meiji-mura.

**Meiji-mura—Village
Museum of Meiji and
Taishō Eras (1868–1926)**
Address 1, Uchiyama,
Inuyama, Aichi Pref.
Transport From Meitetsu Bus
Terminal near Nagoya Station
in Nagoya: highway bus to
Meiji-mura (50 minutes); or
from Inuyama Station: bus
(20 minutes)
Visitation 10:00–16:00
(1 November–28/29 Febru-
ary); 10:00–17:00 (1 March–
31 October) (open daily year
round), tel: (0568) 67-0314

Kamioka Town Hall, 1978

Kamioka-chō Yakuba
Architect Arata Isozaki
Address 378, Ōaza-Higashi, Kamioka-chō, Yoshiki-gun, Gifu Pref.
Transport Train—JR Takayama line to Takayama Station; east exit and bus to Kamioka (1.5 hours)

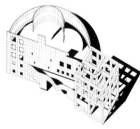

市 HAJIMA

Hajima City Hall 1959

Hajima Shichōsha
Architect Junzo Sakakura
Address 55, Takehana-chō, Hajima, Gifu Pref.
Transport Train—JR Tōkaidō main line or Shinkansen to Gifu-Hajima Station and 7 minutes by taxi (1 mile/ 1.6 kilometers)
The building is a good example of the numerous city halls, built around the late 1950s and early 1960s, that represented the "New Japan Style" with their reinforced concrete post-and-beam construction and exposed surfaces.

The Kamioka Town Hall concluded a very important and perhaps most creative period in Isozaki's design career. In his projects produced in the 1970s, either the cube or the cylinder played a leading role in generating architectural form. This building was the first to combine these two geometric systems. The smaller four-story volume is a perfect cube, finished with stone plates around square windows, while the larger, five-story one is dominated by various concentric cylindrical forms in polished aluminum panels with curving glass-block surfaces. The axis shifts between the two buildings, breaking the unity of the whole. As a result of this rotational shift, there are several in-between zones that are disfigured into sensuously undulating forms and that seem to depart the tectonic body of the main volumes. Among the numerous architectural quotations Isozaki used, the most conspicuous is the semicircular colonnade on the first floor of the three-story reception hall, and in the two-story council chamber on the third floor; both spaces are reminiscent of Palladio's Teatro Olimpico in Vicenza (1580). From outside, the hall appears as a shiny, futurist construct, and it is often likened to a spaceship or to a UFO that is ready to take over this small mining town huddled among ranges of high mountains.

Tanimura Art Museum
1983

Tanimura Bijutsukan
Architect Togo Murano
Address 1-13, Miyakogazaki
2-chōme, Itoigawa, Niigata
Pref.
Transport Train—JR Hokuriku line to Itoigawa Station
and 7 minutes by taxi
Visitation 9:00–17:00 (closed
28 December–4 January);
tel: (0255) 52-9277

Perhaps the last mas-
terpiece of Murano,
who was already in his
nineties at the build-
ing's completion, the
small museum across a
courtyard features
cavelike and "mysteri-
ous" interiors highlight-
ed by intricate lighting.
There are some ten
Buddha statues exhibit-
ed in the museum.

村 **TOGA-MURA**

**Toga Sanbō Theater and
Amphitheater
1982**
Toga Sanbō Gekijō
**Toga-mura
Library/Studio
1987**
Toga-mura Toshokan
Architect Arata Isozaki
Address Nakamura, Toga-
mura, Higashi-Tonami-gun,
Toyama Pref.
Transport Train—JR Taka
yama line to Etchū-Yatsuo
Station and bus (1.5 hours) to
Gatcho-guchi stop (bus only
thrice a day)
Visitation For information or
tickets, tel: (0763) 68-2214
or -2356

町 **SHŌGAWA-
MACHI**

**Observation and Rest
Pavilion
1993**
*Shōgawa-machi Funado Kōen
Gēto to Tembō Kyūkeijō*
Architect Carlos Villanueva
(Spain)
Address 86-1, Ogawara,
Kaneya, Shōgawa-machi,
Higashi-Tonami-gun,
Toyama Pref.
Transport From Takaoka
City: Train—JR Jōhana line
to Tonami Station and bus to
Shōgawa-machi (Pavilion is
the gate to Funado Kōen
Park)

町 **INAMI-MACHI**

**Museum for
Woodcarving
1993**
Inami Chō oku Sōgō Kaikan
Architect Peter Salter (U.K.)
(with K. Tohata Architects)
Address 733, Kitagawa,
Inami-machi, Higashi-
Tonami-gun, Toyama Pref.
Transport From Takaoka
City: Train—JR Jōhana line
to Fukuno-machi Station and
bus or taxi to Inami

🕌 KUROBE

YKK Guest House 1983

Maezawa Garden House
Architect Fumihiko Maki
Address 3-418,
Maesawadani, Kurobe,
Toyama Pref.
Transport Train—JR Hoku-
riku line to Kurobe Station
and 15 minutes by taxi

One of the few designs by Maki that is not located in an urban area, the YKK Guest House occupies a site within a pastoral landscape at the entrance of a widening river valley. The building is reminiscent of a large country villa with pitched roofs; however, despite its setting, it also displays many urban qualities. The complex provides short-term accommodations for foreign visitors of the YKK Company, whose training facility is in nearby Kurobe. Responding to the "geometry" of the site, the two rectangular sections of the building come together at a slight angle; their axes intersect at a point marked by a small gazebo in front of the house. Maki's design features many sophisticated details that use both Scarpa-esque motifs and Japanese design elements. The most appealing part of the building is the two-story great hall, which is articulated with a stairway shaft wrapped in translucent glass, uniquely designed glass wall surfaces, and a structural concrete skeleton whose intersecting posts and beams—not unlike their traditional counterparts in old farm houses—are exposed in the space.

🏙 NAMERIKAWA

Observation Platform Namerikawa
1992

Hamanasu Kōen Tembōji
Architect Tom Heneghan and Inga Dagfinnsdottir (U.K.)
Address 405, Nakagawahara, Namerikawa, Toyama Pref.
Transport Train—JR Hokuriku line to Namerikawa Station and taxi to Hamanasu Kōen park (structure is within the park)
Located along the coast of Namerikawa, this structure was built to view the seashore, the water, and the horizon.

🏙 KAMIICHI- MACHI

Observation and Rest Pavilion
1993

Kamiichi-machi Babashima Tembō Kyūkei-jō
Architect Peter Salter (U.K.) (with Tamura Architects)
Address Iori, Kamiichi-machi, Naka-shinkawa-gun, Toyama Pref.
Transport From Namerikawa or Toyama: Train—Toyama-chihō line to Kamiichi Station and taxi
The pavilion is located on the edge of a river in a mountainous landscape.

🏙 TATEYAMA- MACHI

Tateyama Museum of Regional History, Tenji-kan and Yuhō-kan Halls
1991

Toyama-ken Tateyama Hakubutsu-kan
Architect Arata Isozaki
Address 93-1, Ashikuraji, Tateyama-machi, Nakashinkawa-gun, Toyama Pref.
Transport From Toyama Station: Train—Tateyama line to Chigaki Station and local bus to Ōyama Jinja-mae stop
Visitation 9:30–17:00 (closed Mondays); tel: (0764) 81-1216

🏙 TOYAMA

Kōshi Kaikan
1986

Architect Kisho Kurokawa
Address 3-1, Chitōse 1-chōme, Toyama, Toyama Pref.
Transport Train—JR Hokuriku line to Toyama Station; south exit and 7-minute walk to east (on south side of main road in front of station)
Visitation Open daily, tel: (0764) 41-2255

Toyama Shimin Plaza
1989

Architect Fumihiko Maki
Address 6-14, Ōtemachi, Toyama, Toyama Pref.
Transport Train—JR Hokuriku line to Toyama Station and 15-minute walk or 5 minutes by taxi (along Ōtedōri Avenue Mall behind Toyama Castle)
Visitation Open daily, tel: (0764) 93-1313

🏙 KOSUGI- MACHI

Kosugi Bus Terminal
1992

Kosugi Eki Nishi-guchi Hiroba Basu Hatchakujō
Architect Ron Herron (U.K.) (with Fukumi Architects)
Address 2595-1, Mitsuge, Kosugi-machi, Izumi-gun, Toyama Pref.
Transport Train—JR Hokuriku line to Kosugi Station; south exit and few steps (the pink-canopy-covered, long bus terminal is in front of the station)

Galaxy 92
1993

Taikōzan-Land Furusatō Palace
Prospecta 92
1993

Taikōzan-Land Tembō-tō
Architect Shōei Yoh
Address 4774-6, Taikōzan-land, Kurokawa, Kosugi-machi, Izumi-gun, Toyama Pref.

Transport Train—JR Hokuriku line to Kosugi Station and 10 minutes by taxi to Taikōzan-land (the two buildings are a 5-minute walk from each other)
Visitation 9:00–17:00 (closed Tuesdays and 29 December–3 January); tel: (0766) 56-6116

ŌSHIMA-MACHI

Picture Book Museum in Ōshima
1994
Ōshima-machi Ehonkan
Architect Itsuko Hasegawa
Address 50, Tottori, Ōshima-machi, Izumi-gun, Toyama Pref.
Transport Train—JR Hokuriku line to Takaoka Station and 10 minutes by taxi; or JR Hokuriku line to Echū-Daimon Station and 5 minutes by taxi (next to Ōshima Chūō Kōen Park)

Divided House Monument, Ōshima
1993
Toki-no-kan
Architect Gordon Benson and Alan Forsyth (U.K.)
Address Chūō Kōen, Ōshima-machi, Izumi-gun, Toyama Pref.
Transport Train—JR Hokuriku line to Takaoka Station and 10 minutes by taxi or JR Hokuriku line to Echū-Daimon Station and 5 minutes by taxi (inside Ōshima Chūō Kōen Park)

DAIMON-MACHI

Daimon Bus Station
1993
Daimon-machi Basu Machiai-jō
Architect Ron Herron (U.K.) (with Yoshida Architects)
Address 167-10, Nagawari, Daimon-Aza, Daimon-machi, Izumi-gun, Toyama Pref.
Transport Train—JR Hokuriku line to Echū-Daimon Station
As Daimon-machi is well-known for kite making, the station has a fabric canopy not unlike that of a kite.

HIMI-SHI

Elementary School in Busshōji-mura
1993
Busshōji Shōgakkō
Architect Itsuko Hasegawa
Address 1927, Busshōji-mura, Himi-shi, Toyama Pref.
Transport Train—JR Hokuriku line to Takaoka Station and 15 minutes by taxi

TAKAOKA

Station Pavilion, Takaoka
1993
Takaoka-eki Minami-guchi Hiroba-no Seibi
Architect Enric Miralles (Spain) (with Total Architecture of Toyama)
Address Eki-minami 5-chōme, Takaoka, Toyama Pref.
Transport Train—JR Hokuriku line to Takaoka Station: south exit and few steps (in front of south exit)

Located on an attractive hillside, the classrooms of Hasegawa's design follow the curving ridge line of the terrain, thus taking advantage of the views and topography of the natural landscape. The radially arranged reinforced concrete structural system allows for a covered porch in front of the classrooms. The space of the two-story public hall behind is equally curving and is lit by a series of skylights. The soft colors and playful patterns of interior details match the world of children. The shell-like roof above is covered by thin metallic plates. Complementing the classroom building is the rectangular volume of the school gym.

Notojima Glass Art Museum
1991

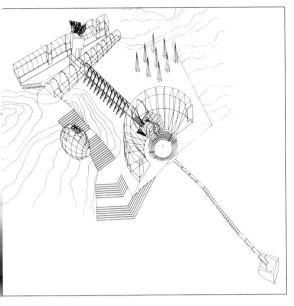

Ishikawa Notojima Gurāsu Bijutsukan
Architect Kiko (Monta) Mozuna
Address 125-10. Koda, Notojima-chō. Kashima-gun, Ishikawa Pref.
Transport From JR Kanazawa Station: Train—Nanao line to Wakura-Onsen Station and Bus—Notojima Kōtsu line to Notojima (30 minutes)
Visitation 9:00–17:00 **(**April–November); 9:00–1630 (December– March) (closed third Tuesday of every month and 29 December–4 January); tel: (0767) 84-1175

Located on a steep slope of Notojima Island with a spectacular view of the Japan Sea, the Notojima Glass Art Museum is designed so as to form a "city of glass." The configuration of the numerous buildings, structures, and objects on display reflects Mozuna's respect for the principles of ancient geomancy, traditional design of dry gardens, and neo-Orientalism (*wakonyosai*). Many traditional concepts are forwarded in modern, even futuristic, interpretations, such as fractal geometry and high-tech materials (stainless steel, aluminum, and, of course, glass). Every element in the complex, from exhibition spaces to connecting bridges, has been arranged so as to utilize and display as many expressive qualities of glass as possible. For example, a circular window in the centrally located lounge is made of liquid crystal glass. When approached, its translucent surface turns—with the help of photocells and electronic systems—to transparent, revealing an outside pool and, beyond, the sea.

Noto Monzen Family Inn
1991
Noto Monzen Famiri-in Byū-Sunsetto
Architect Kiko (Monta) Mozuna
Address 29-58, Aza-Sendai, Monzen-chō, Keshi-gun, Ishikawa Pref.
Transport From JR Kanazawa Station: Train—Nanao line to Namizu Station—Bus bound for Monzen to Minami-Kuroshima (30 minutes) and 10-minute walk uphill

Comprised of numerous individual elements designed in different forms, the complex is located on a sloping site, about .3 mile/.5 kilometer up the coastal main road, with a spectacular view of the Sea of Japan. As the head temple of Sōtō Zen Buddhism used to be located in the town of Monzen, there is a plan to develop a Mandala Village on this site. The Noto Monzen Family Inn is a guest house that would serve as the gate to this future village. On the west side of the compound is a Western-style garden with the zigzagging main approach to the inn. Adjoining to this approach are two towers with the administrative offices; next to them a restaurant takes the shape of the wing of a bird, while the entrance to the housing is in a spherical volume. On the east, the residential rental units and common baths, both in clusters, evoke the image of a small "village" within a Japanese-style pond garden. All are loosely arranged on the two sides of a long, arched, semi-covered, pedestrian deck, set on pilotis above the terrain. While there are numerous attractive qualities in every part of the design, it is the pedestrian deck that steals the show. This curving, futuristic promenade is made of arched steel frames and a blackened wooden shell, and is roofed with metallic plates. Its east side opens widely toward the residential units, while on the west there is a long, low-profile, horizontal slit that allows visitors to enjoy the spectacle of the setting sun for which this area of the Noto Peninsula is famous; the Japanese name of the complex includes the term "Sunset View Inn."

市 KANAZAWA

Ishikawa Cultural Center
1977
Kenkō Bunka Sentā or
Ishikawa Kōseinenkin Kaikan
Architect Kisho Kurokawa
Address 17-1, Ishibiki-chō
4-chōme, Kanazawa,
Ishikawa Pref.
Transport Train—JR Hoku-
riku line to Kanazawa Station
and 15 minutes by bus to
Kōseinenkin Kaikan or taxi
(2.5 miles/4 kilometers)

市 KOMATSU

Honjin Memorial Museum of Art
1990
*Komatsu Shiritsu Honjin
Kinen Bijutsukan*
Architect Kisho Kurokawa
Address 19, Marunouchi
Kōen-chō, Komatsu, Ishikawa
Pref.
Transport Train—JR Hoku-
riku line to Komatsu Station
and 15-minute walk or taxi
(near Komatsu City Hall or
Shiyakushō)

KANSAI (OR KINKI) REGION

Cradle of the Japanese nation and culture, the region is centered around such ancient cities as the previous capitals of Naniwa (now Ōsaka) (645–667), Nara (710–784), and Kyōto (794–1868). The importance of the Kansai Region today is better understandable in light of the fact that Kyōto remained the capital of Japan, and the seat of the emperor, until the middle of the nineteenth century, when Tōkyō (previously Edo)—after being the administrative center of the country for more than two and one-half centuries (1603–1868) under the Tokugawa Shōgunate—took over the role of the capital. Symbolizing the origins of both the country and the imperial family, Ise Grand Shrine (founded circa AD third century), the most revered center of Shintō religion, is also located here, within Mie Prefecture.

Today Ōsaka (2.5 million) is the second largest city and metropolitan area (16 million) in the country, while Kyōto (1.4 million) remains a major urban center and, together with Nara, one of the most visited historic attractions in Japan. (All three of these cities are located within separate prefectures that bear their name.) Other significant cities in the region include Kōbe, Himeji, and Wakayama. Many cities, like Ōsaka Himeji, have developed out of medieval strongholds, and are also known for their extensive castle compounds. Himeji Castle (1609) is the largest and most magnificent in Japan, and also one of the twelve such structures that have survived in their original state. Ōsaka Castle (1583), a massive, wooden structure, burned down in 1868 and was replaced with a reinforced concrete replica in 1931.

The Ise Grand Shrine maintains its role as the most venerable religious place in the country, with millions of pilgrims visiting the site annually. It continues the unique ritual of completely rebuilding the entire compound every twenty years. The latest, that is, the sixty-first, reconstruction took place in 1993. Ise is only one of the innumerable historic monuments that populate the Kansai Region, most of which are found in or around Kyōto or Nara. Here the high concentration of Buddhist temples and monasteries, Shintō shrines, imperial villas, teahouses and gardens, and old urban districts and townhouses (*machiya*), including many of the most famous ones in the country, make escaping the past impossible. To mention but a few, Nara has the Hōryū-ji (AD 607), Yakushi-ji (AD 718), and Tōdai-ji (AD 752) temples and the Kasuga Shrine (AD 709), while Kyōto has the Katsura Imperial Villa (seventeenth

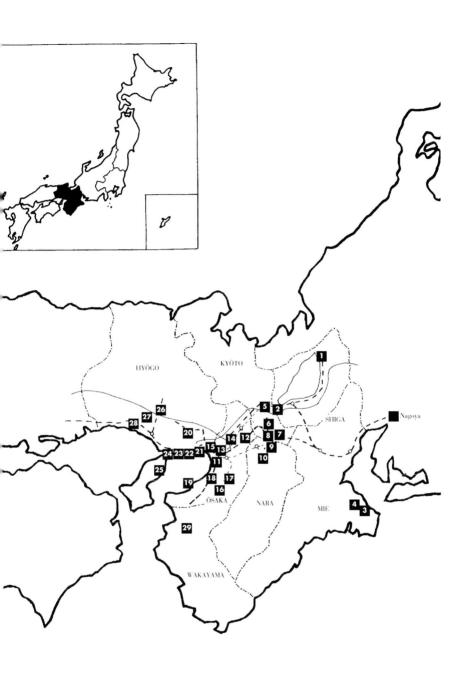

century), the rock garden of Ryōan-ji (circa 1499), and the Buddhist temple compounds of Ginkaku-ji (1383), Tō-ji (AD 794), Kiyōmizu-dera (1633), Daitoku-ji (1319), and many others, most of which feature Japan's most exquisite landscape and stroll gardens, for which Kyōto is also famous.

Yet in Kansai today, architectural and urban developments seem to be as intensive and significant as in the past, while not really lagging behind—either in quantity or quality—the similar developments in the Kantō area. The two regions, represented by Ōsaka and Tōkyō, have always been undeclared rivals in this respect. The 1964 Olympic Games were hosted by Tōkyō, and not much later the grandiose show of the 1970 Expo was staged by Ōsaka, both events having an undeniably significant impact on the modernization and progress of their respective cities. The design and realization of the Ōsaka Expo, similar to those of the 1964 Olympic Games in Tōkyō, involved Japan's most talented architects, with Kenzo Tange as the chief planner and organizer (Tange also designed the world-famous Olympic Gymnasia in Tōkyō).

The dynamics of urbanism in Osaka, Kōbe, and beyond, just as much as in Tōkyō, Yokohama, and their vicinity, is also well demonstrated by the mushrooming of new urban districts, new towns, and major and exceptional complexes. In recent years Kansai too has witnessed the creation of several artificial islands, including the large Port Island and Rokkō Island, that provide reclaimed land for further urban developments within the Ōsaka Bay. One of the latest of such huge projects is the New Kansai International Airport, south of Ōsaka, designed by the Italian Renzo Piano and now close to completion.

Although the number of foreign architects working in Kansai is growing, mirroring the general tendency in Japan, the vast majority of the work is carried out, for quite obvious reasons, by Japanese designers. And indeed there are many who were or are active in this region, and have produced a long list of outstanding projects; they include Kingo Tatsuno, Tokuma Katayama, Tetsuro Yoshida, Togo Murano, the Nikken Sekkei Company, Kunio Maekawa, Kenzo Tange, Sachio Otani, Kisho Kurokawa, Hiroshi Hara, Arata Isozaki, Itsuko Hasegawa, and, most importantly, Shin Takamatsu and Tadao Ando.

Based in this region, both Takamatsu and Ando have completed the majority of their best works here. Moreover, both of them have been as much influenced by the local urban culture of Kyōto and Ōsaka respectively, where they live and work, as they have left a profound impact on the architecture of these two cities. This is so to the extent that, although their works now can be found in many other parts of the country and even abroad, their names have become inseparably associated with Kyōto and Ōsaka. Yet, if there is any one architect today whose designs best denote contemporary architecture in the Kansai Region, that person has to be Tadao Ando.

A village-run resort lodge for visiting groups of school children, company employees, and local citizens, the Yogo Forestry Cultural Center is located outside residential areas, deep in the mountains, near a ski slope, and is surrounded by a thick forest. The meticulously symmetrical small building is constructed primarily of wood, with reinforced concrete used in certain parts. The main section is covered by a pitched shingle roof with a unique skylight on it, while semicircular and cylindrical volumes, containing the dining hall and large, Japanese common baths, feature dome structures covered by stainless steel plates. The rectangular, central, two-story section, accommodating all *tatami* rooms for the visitors, and the dining hall with an inside gallery, are shaped with wooden columns and wooden roofing whose intricate structural system is exposed to the spaces below. Moreover, on both sides of the building the exterior balconies are designed with an attractive wooden skeleton. The Yogo Forestry Cultural Center is one of Watanabe's works in which he successfully explores new possibilities for wooden architecture and craftsmanship combined with novel curvilinear forms.

Yogo Forestry Cultural Center 1990

Yogo Shinrin Bunka Koryū Sentā

Architect Toyokazu Watanabe

Address Koaza Kitano-no-kusa, Ōaza Nakanogo, Yogo-chō, Ika-gun, Shiga Pref.

Transport Train—JR Hokuriku line to Yogo Station and 10 minutes by taxi

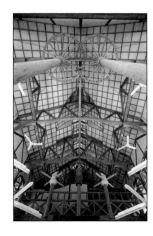

Links
1989
Architect Shin Takamatsu
Address 19-10, Nishinoshō, Ōtsu, Shiga Pref.
Transport From JR Zeze Station or Keihan-Zeze Station: north exit and 10-minute walk (on the south side of Kusatsu-dōri Avenue along the lake shore)
Visitation Open daily during working hours. tel: (0775) 24-7777

Ōtsu Prince Hotel
1989
Architect Kenzo Tange
Address 7-7, Nionohama 4-chōme, Ōtsu, Shiga Pref.
Transport From JR Zeze Station or Keihan-Zeze Station: north exit and 10-minute walk (the tower of the hotel is at the lake shore).

Seibu Department Store
1976
Seibu Ōtsu Shopping Center
Architect Kiyonori Kikutake
Address 3-1, Nionohama 2-chōme, Ōtsu, Shiga Pref.
Transport From JR Zeze Station or Keihan-Zeze Station: north exit and 6-minute walk (on the north side of Kusatsu-dōri Avenue)

The six-story commercial building is symmetrical, save for the emergency stairway in front of the west elevation. Like many of Takamatsu's works from the late 1980s and early 1990s, including the Orphe in Nishio (1987) (see page 169) and Ichigoya in Chōfu (1988) (see page 146), this design reveals a strong influence of classicism disguised and/or represented by numerous high-tech, even futuristic, details. The reinforced concrete structure on the first three floors features a huge entranceway flanked by the outside stairways. The upper three floors include aluminum-clad pilasters, a colonnade with repetitive fenestration, and large overhanging eaves whose slanting underside is finished in highly polished metallic plates. Inside the spaces are even more illusory and sleek, and as much futuristic as "classical." At the same time, as a result of Takamatsu's curious and long-standing design sensibility, Links is also imbued with an inexplicably "disturbing" or sinister quality.

Built within the compound of the Nippon Electric Glass Company factory, Isozaki's building, featuring a restaurant, a meeting room, lockers, and a gymnasium, is shaped so as to fit into its industrial environment. It displays horizontally striped elevations and the generous use of structural steel elements, tension rods, and a large variety of high-tech glass products, manufactured by the company. The interiors are also articulated with elements of industrial design and popular art. For example, the elegantly slim and light colored steel structure is complemented by painted details in the dining room.

NEG Employee Service Facilities 1980

NEG Ōtsu Kōjō
Architect Arata Isozaki
Address 7-1, Seiran 2-chōme, Ōtsu, Shiga Pref.
Transport Train—JR Biwakō line to Ishiyama Station and 10-minute walk to northwest; or Keihan Ishizaka line to Kuritsu Station and 2-minute walk to northeast
Visitation Tel: (0775) 37-1700

 TOBA

Sea Folk Museum 1992
Umi no Hakubutsu-kan
Architect Hiroshi Naito
Address 1731-68, Ogitsu, Uramura-chō, Toba, Mie Pref.
Transport From Ōsaka or Nagoya: Train—Kintetsu line to Toba Station and bus or 20 minutes by taxi

Shima Art Museum 1993
Shima Bijutsukan
Architect Hiroshi Naito
Address 1772, Daikichi, Uramura-chō, Toba, Mie Pref.
Transport From Ōsaka or Nagoya: Train—Kintetsu line to Toba Station and bus to Shima Bijutsukan

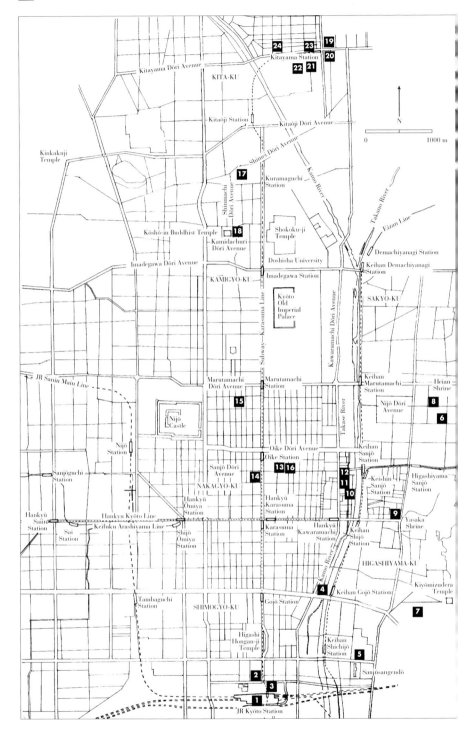

市 KYOTO

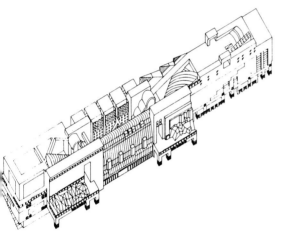

JR Kyōto Station
1997
Kyōto Eki
Architect Hiroshi Hara
Address Shimogyō-ku, Kyōto
City (see map)
Transport Any train (JR,
Kintetsu, etc.) to Kyōto
Station

When completed, the huge complex of the station,
department store, hotel, cultural center, and shopping center, currently under construction, will be
Hara's largest and, perhaps, most spectacular
building. Hara received the commission upon winning an international competition in 1990. Hara's
scheme features what he calls a "geographical concourse," which, covered by a large glass canopy,
implies the traditional Japanese aesthetic device of
the "borderless boundary." Acting also as a gateway to the city, this 1,540-foot-/470-meter-long,
88.5-feet-/27-meter-wide, 197-foot-/60-meter-
high concourse/atrium allows the passengers and
visitors to encounter the sky of Kyōto.

卐 KYŌTO

Kyōto Tower and Hotel
1964
Architect Mamoru Yamada
Address Karasuma Shichijō,
Shimogyō-ku, Kyōto City
(see map)
Transport In front of JR
Kyōto Station, north exit

Renaissance Building
1986
Architect Minoru Takeyama
Address 849, Shiokōji-chō,
Higashi-Tōindōri, Shimogyō-
ku, Kyōto City (see map)
Transport From JR Kyōto
Station: north exit and
2-minute walk to east side of
station plaza
It is a large cultural and com-
mercial building.

Koboku Lighting
Showroom
1978
Architect Shin Takamatsu
Address 771, Nishihashizume
chō, Gojō-agaru, Tera-machi,
Shimogyō-ku, Kyōto City
(see map)
Transport From Kyōto Station
north exit and Bus 2 or 5 to
Kawaramachi Gojō stop and
2-minute walk; or Train—
Keihan line to Gojō Station an
3-minute walk to west
Visitation Open daily,
tel: (075) 341-9271

Kyōto National Museum
1895
Kyōto Kokuritsu Hakubutsukan
Architect Tokuma Katayama
Address 527, Chaya-chō,
Higashiyama-ku, Kyōto City
(see map)
Transport From Kyōto
Station: north exit and Bus
18, 206, or 208 to Higashi-
yama-Shichijō stop and
1-minute walk to west; or
Train—Keihan line to Shichi-
jō Station and 8-minute walk
to east
The building is an Important
National Cultural Property.

Constructed one year after Katayama's Nara National Museum (see page 202), this larger structure stands in a picturesque setting at the foot of the Higashiyama Mountains of Kyōto, near the famous Sanjūsangendō Temple (1266). The impressive French Renaissance-style building, representing mid-Meiji Era, West-inspired architecture, stretches in the north-south direction in an extensive garden with fountains. The central and end sections of the symmetrical complex are crowned with the high and softly curving volumes of the tiled roofs, topped with ornamental forged iron railings. A large, decorative front gate lies to the west, while two small ticket office buildings occupy the north and south end. The museum has a reinforced brick structure richly embellished by the color scheme of its stone and brick surfaces.

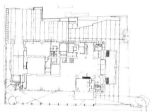

The Kyōto National Museum of Modern Art is a rectangular, four-story building that looks over the small Biwakosōsui Canal to the south. The building has relatively few windows, the majority of which are located in front on the first floor to establish a direct relationship with the outdoor patio. The system of joints connecting the fenestration and the stone and aluminum plates inscribes a network of squares in every elevation. Yet Maki's gridiron pattern does not remain a visually "negative" or abstract device, as in the works of Hiromi Fujii, Arata Isozaki, and other contemporaries. It is actually a symbolic device, and so a positive statement, insofar as it makes an implicit reference to Kyōto's original city structure, laid out along the grid plan of the T'ang Dynasty capital, Chang'an.

Service and/or emergency stairwells, located in the corners of the volume, are wrapped in intricate layers of glass walls and capped with small pyramidal roofs; they emerge as vertical shafts of light in the evening. The upper floor and the large entrance atrium are lit from above through a skylight whose flat triangular forms add to the shape of the building. The design of the museum culminates in this impressive atrium with its large, ceremonial stairway and sophisticated soft lighting. Numerous other details—which include the Scarpa-esque articulation of the corner stairs, the fashioning of the first-floor cafeteria, and the surface treatment of and openings through the exhibition walls—highlight the interiors.

Kyōto National Museum of Modern Art 1986

Kyōto Kokuritsu Gindai Bijutsukan
Architect Fumihiko Maki
Address 9, Okazaki, Enshōji-chō, Sakyō-ku, Kyōto City (see map)
Transport From Keihan Sanjō Station: streetcar—Keihan Keishin line to Higashiyama Sanjō stop and 8-minute walk to northwest; or from JR Kyōto Station: north exit and Bus 5 to Jingūmichi stop and 5-minute walk to north (inside Okazaki Kōen Park, beside the large red torii gate of Heian Shrine)

Gallery Kiyōmizu 1989

Architect Kan Izue
Address 6-540-7, Gojōbashi-higashi, Higashiyama-ku, Kyōto City (see map)
Transport From JR Kyōto Station: north exit and Bus 18 or 206 to Gojōzaka stop and 5-minute uphill; or Train—Keihan line to Keihan-Gojō Station and 5 minutes by taxi

✈ KYŌTO

Kyōto Hall
1960
Kyōto Kaikan
Architect Kunio Maekawa
Address 13, Okazaki,
Saishōji-chō, Sakyō-ku,
Kyōto City (see map)
Transport From JR Kyōto
Station: north exit and Bus 5
to Heian Jingū stop and
1-minute walk (4-minute
walk north from Kyōto
National Museum of Modern
Art)

Completed just one year before Maekawa's Tōkyō Metropolitan Festival Hall
(see page 96), the Kyōto Hall displays many features similar to its counterpart
in Tōkyō: reinforced concrete post-and-beam construction, large protruding
eaves with curving surfaces, and horizontally stretching volumes. In addition it
includes on the first floor a system of pilotis that defines a passage to the courtyard plaza within the U-shaped complex. The public character of this open
space is further underscored by an extensive concourse on the second-floor terraces. Inside the building there is a large multipurpose auditorium for 2,500
visitors, and a smaller theater for 1,300, as well as various conference halls. In
order not to compete with the architecture of this ancient capital, and, more
specifically, that of the nearby Heian Shrine, Maekawa's large design displays
a sensible restraint in both forms and materials (selected also for their colors),
concrete, black tile, and off-red brick pavement.

Marutō Building 4
1987
Architect Shin Takamatsu
Address Higashi-Ōji Nishi-
iru, Gion, Tominaga-chō,
Higashiyama-ku, Kyōto City
(see map)
Transport From Kyōto
Station: north exit and Bus 18
or 206 to Yasaka Jinga
(shrine) stop and 2-minute
walk; or Train—Keihan line
to Shijō Station and
10-minute walk east toward
Yasaka Shrine

Pontochō-no-Ochaya
(Yoshida House)
1982
Architect Shin Takamatsu
Address Pontochō, Sanjō-
Sagaru, Nakagyō-ku, Kyōto
City (see map)
Transport Train—Keihan line
to Keihan Sanjō Terminal and
4-5-minute walk; or Hankyū
line to Kawaramachi Terminal and 8-minute walk (on the
west side of Pontochō lane)
It is a very small teahouse,
with a dark, highly polished,
stone facade.

Cella
1991
Marutō Nishi-Kiyamachi Biru
Architect Shin Takamatsu
Address 69-2, 72, Daikoku-
chō, Sanjō-Sagaru, Kawaramachi, Nakagyō-ku, Kyōto
City (see map)
Transport Train—Keihan lin
to Keihan Sanjō Terminal an
5-minute walk; or Hankyū
line to Kawaramachi Terminal and 10-minute walk; or
from JR Kyōto Station: north
exit and Bus 4, 5, 14, or 17 te
Kawaramachi Sanjō stop and
5-minute walk north along
the west side of Kiyamachi-
dōri Avenue (2-minute walk
south from Time's 1 and 2)

Time's 1, 1984
Time's 2, 1991

Architect Tadao Ando
Address 92, Nakajima-chō, Kawaramachi-higashi-iru, Sanjō-dōri, Nakagyō-ku, Kyōto City (see map)
Transport Train—Keihan line to Keihan Sanjō Terminal and 5-minute walk; or Hankyū line to Kawaramachi Terminal and 10-minute walk; or from JR Kyōto Station: north exit and bus to Kawaramachi Sanjō stop and 10-minute walk (on the west side of Kiyamachi-dōri Avenue at Sanjō-Ōhashi Bridge)

One of Ando's most remarkable small urban projects, the Time's complex is located within a popular urban district made up of generally low-profile, few-story commercial buildings, restaurants, shops, and nightclubs with some residential units. This busy area finds some relief in its surprisingly clear Takase-gawa River, lined with large trees. The layered scheme of the Time's design was developed to take full advantage of this condition, incorporating the benefits of the water, while filtering out the congestion, noise, and other disturbing qualities of the city. The building can be approached from its river side through an open stairway descending to a curving deck at the water level and by a narrow bridge running parallel with the river. This bridge connects directly to the Sanjō-Ōhashi Bridge that crosses the shallow river. Outdoor stairways, passages, and a tiny courtyard add to the spatial experience and generate a sense of intimacy. The concrete and concrete-block structure combines with the steel elements of the bridge and the light, stainless-steel-covered metallic roof structures. The elongated three-story first phase of the building is roofed by a shallow vault, while the vertical and taller square shaft of the second phase is covered by a dome.

Nakagyō Post Office 1903
Nakakyō Yūbinkyoku
Architect Shirō Mitsuhashi
Address Higashino-Tōin Kita-Higashi Kaku, Sanjō-dōri, Nakagyō-ku, Kyōto City (see map)
Transport Subway—Karasuma line to Ōike Station and 5-minute walk: 1 block south on Karasuma-dōri Avenue and 1 block east on Sanjō-dōri Avenue (west of the Heian Museum)

Daiichi Kangyō Bank 1907
Daiichi Kangyō Ginkō
Architect Kingo Tatsuno (with Kasai Office)
Address Sanjō, Minami-Nishi Kaku, Karasuma-dōri, Nakagyō-ku, Kyōto City (see map)
Transport Subway—Karasuma line to Ōike Station and 2-minute walk south on Karasuma-dōri Avenue; (on southwest corner of Sanjō-dōri Avenue; 1-minute walk from Nakagyō Post Office)

Face House 1973
Kaō no Ie
Architect Kazumasa Yamashita
Address Nijō Aguru, Koromonotana-dōri, Nakagyō-ku, Kyōto City (see map)
Transport Subway—Karasuma line to Marutamachi stop and 3-minute walk: first west on Marutamachi-dōri Avenue, then south on Koromonotana-dōri, the third side street

Heian Museum (now Museum of Kyōto), 1907
Heian or *Kyōto Bunka Hakubutsukan*
Architect Kingo Tatsuno and Uheiji Nagano
Address Takakura Kita-Nishi Kaku Sanjō-dōri, Nakagyō-ku, Kyōto City (see map)
Transport From Kyōto Station: Subway—Karasuma line to Ōike Station and 5-minute walk: 1 block south on Karasuma-dōri Avenue and 1 block east on Sanjō-dōri Avenue (east of the Nakagyō Post Office)
The building is an Important National Cultural Property.

Nakagawa Photo Gallery, 1993
Architect Toru Murakami
Address 14, Koyama, Nakamizo-chō, Kita-ku, Kyōto City (see map)
Transport Subway—Karasuma line to Kuramaguchi Station and 6-minute walk first north then west on the south side of Shimei-dōri Avenue

Standing on a corner, this small, red-brick-faced, two-story museum was originally built as the Kyōto Branch Office of the Bank of Japan. Designed in the typically eclectic style of Western neo-classicism with certain Baroque elements, the museum is another representative of Meiji Era architecture, which used European models as the most appropriate for the many new types of public facilities in Japan. Here the main, south facade facing Sanjō-dōri Avenue reveals a tripartite and symmetrical arrangement, centered on the entrance, which is emphasized with a heavy, stone frame and arched canopy. Additional features are the rhythmical pilasters and the decorative roof elements.

Origin 1, 1981
Origin 2, 1982
Origin 3, 1986

Hinaya Honsha-ya
Architect Shin Takamatsu
Address Shinmachi-dōri,
Kamidachuri-agaru, Kamigyō-
ku, Kyōto City (see map)
Transport Subway—Karasuma
line to Imadegawa Station and
8-minute walk to Shinmachi-
dōri Avenue

Origin is a relatively early project of Takamatsu, yet it remains one of his most successful. The complex was commissioned and is owned by a small company, the Hinaya, that designs and produces the traditional Japanese dress, the *kimono*, and its decorative sash, the *obi*. Completed in three stages, the buildings extend in the east-west direction on a narrow site between two small roads. The three structures—of which only the first and third can be seen from the two streets—have been rendered in different architectural languages.

Origin 1 (above left) reveals primarily its east facade, which is shaped with uncanny forms of curving lines and surfaces. It is covered with highly polished, reddish brown granite panels, which are dotted by numerous copper rivets. The most unusual feature of this elevation is its entrance. It is carved into the stone surface as a huge vertical slit topped with a large oval window. The overall image is an uneasy one, and may appear to be that of a prehistoric monster or a mythical creature with a Cyclopean eye. Origin 2 is an exposed reinforced concrete, semicircular structure added to the rear of Origin 1.

Origin 3 (above right), at the opposite end of the site, displays more mechanical references and is much more aggressive in its articulation. The number of metallic elements here has increased, and include sharply angled skylights and large "porthole" windows. A sunken, stepped courtyard, an octagonal tower, and a horizontal volume comprise this part of the compound. The tower emerges as some tragic monument wrapped in black granite and embellished with metallic, bladelike skylights and a deep-red dome. The Origin complex signals the beginning of a conscious design methodology in which, in Takamatsu's words, "function follows form."

🏛 KYŌTO

Syntax
1990

Ashihara Kyōei Biru—
Syntax Biru
Architect Shin Takamatsu
Address Minami-shiba-chō,
Shimogamo, Sakyō-ku, Kyōto
City (see map)
Transport Subway—Kara-
suma line to Kitayama
Station and 1-minute walk
east on north side of Kita-
yama-dōri Avenue

The uniquely shaped structure concludes as well as highlights a line of design in Takamatsu's work, which began with Origin 1, then continued in such outstanding projects as Origin 3 (1986), Kirin Plaza, Ōsaka (1987) (see page 212), and Solaris in Amagasaki (1990) (see page 224). Syntax is located on Kitayama-dōri Avenue, in the rapidly developing northern part of Kyōto, where Takamatsu has completed several other projects, including the noted Week Building (1986). Like most buildings on the road, the four-story Syntax with two basement levels features commercial facilities, shops, boutiques, and restaurants. Takamatsu's design articulates a narrow and symmetrical volume perpendicular to the road, with large open stairways on the rooftops leading to two cantilevered structures. The steep stairways are interrupted by two rows of curving and sharply angled skylights, which, together with the outstretched cantilevers, give the building the image of the bridge of a ship. Covered with a variety of polished dark stones, aluminum panels, and metallic elements, Syntax emerges from its urban context as a surrealistic vision.

Kitayama Ining '23
1987
Architect Shin Takamatsu
Address Maehagi-chō,
Shimogamo, Sakyō-ku, Kyōto
City (see map)
Transport Subway—Kara-
suma line to Kitayama Sta-
tion and 1-minute walk east
(on south side of Kitayama-
dōri Avenue, across from
Syntax)

Kyōto Symphony Hall
1995
Kyōto-shi Konsāto Hōru
Architect Arata Isozaki
Address Hanki-chō,
Shimogamo, Sakyō-ku, Kyōto
City (see map)
Transport Subway—Kara-
suma line to Kitayama Station
and few steps (east of botani-
cal garden on south side of
Kitayama-dōri Avenue)

Garden of Fine Arts
1994
Architect Tadao Ando
Address Hanki-chō,
Shimogamo, Sakyō-ku, Kyōto
City (see map)
Transport Subway—Kara-
suma line to Kitayama
Station and 5-minute walk
It is an open-air garden and
structure with both Western
and Japanese pieces.

B-Lock Kitayama
1990
Architect Tadao Ando
Address Iwagagakiuchi-chō, Kamigamo, Kita-ku, Kyōto City (see map)
Transport Subway—Karasuma line to Kitayama Station and 4-minute walk to west on north side of Kitayama-dōri Avenue
This two-story commercial building has a curving facade.

Week Building
1986
Architect Shin Takamatsu
Address Sakurai-chō, Kamigamo, Kita-ku, Kyōto City (see map)
Transport Subway—Karasuma line to Kitayama Station and 6-minute walk west on north side of Kitayama-dōri Avenue
(See page 30, fig. 41)

TAK Building
1991
Architect David Chipperfield (U.K.)
Address 3, Ichijōji, Tsukuda-chō, Sakyō-ku, Kyōto City
Transport From Demachi-yanagi Station Train—Eizan line to Chayama Station and 15-minute walk northeast or 5 minutes by taxi

Kyōto International Conference Hall
1966
addition, 1973
Kokuritsu Kyōto Kokusai Kaikan
Architect Sachio Otani
Address Takaragaike, Sakyō-ku, Kyōto City
Transport Subway—Karasuma line to Kitaōji Station and Bus 4 to Takaragaike

The Kyōto International Conference Hall is situated on the north shores of Takaragaike Pond north of Kyōto. Stretching horizontally, the building, when seen from the pond, resembles a mysterious pleasure boat floating on the water. The huge complex, which was extended in 1973 by Otani, is built with prefabricated reinforced concrete frames and panels in a hexagonal structural system. Consequently there are practically no vertical columns or walls; all slant like the structures of a pitched roof. The analogy is not accidental; Otani, like many designers in the Metabolism group, used the image of traditional Japanese roofs to make reference to the building's setting in historic Kyōto. Indeed, his composition is evocative of the forms of the Ise Shrine, whose roofs feature decorative finials (*chigi*). Set in an attractive landscape and garden at the edge of the water, the gracefully "aging" building is an outstanding example of establishing a successful relationship between architecture and nature.

Santō Industry Headquarters 1991

Santō Sangyō Biru
Architect Atsushi Kitagawara
Address 4, Takehana,
Takenokaidō-chō,
Yamashina-ku, Kyōto City
Transport From JR or Keihan
Kyōzu line Yamashina
Station; south exit and
8-minute walk (on north side
of Take-no-kaidō Road)

The small building along a major highway in the eastern part of Kyōto is an office and showroom building of Santō Industries, producer of home appliances. Because of the busy road in front, the three-story reinforced concrete structure with one basement level opens to an interior courtyard. This phenomenal space is the focal point of Kitagawara's design; while it is defined on two sides by the *L*-shaped interior of the building, on the other two sides it is wrapped in a screen of translucent frosted glass panels. Supported by a steel frame behind, the panels on this frame are arranged so as to leave open gaps between the quadrilateral units. This screen provides both privacy and the possibility of the inside space to breathe, to let air and light in. Since the court is open also to the sky, rain and snow can penetrate the space and fall onto the steeply sloping floor of the court, planted with vegetation. Floating above this slanting surface are a black marble bridge with a stainless steel canopy suspended over it and a uniquely shaped stairway with both open structures, including a "floating" terrace, and closed forms, covered with blue, metallic plates. Evoking the spirit of the tiny "pocket gardens" (*tsubo-niwa*) in traditional Kyōto residences, Kitagawara's courtyard attains a spectacular quality.

Maruzen Bakery Yamashina 1992

Architect Kazuyuki Negishi
Address 3-3, Takehana,
Nishinokuchi-chō,
Yamashina-ku, Kyōto City
Transport From JR or Keihan
Kyōzu line Yamanashi Station; south exit and 9-minute
walk (on south side of Take-no-kaidō Road)

Pharaoh (Asano Dental Clinic) 1984

Asano Haisha Kurinikku
Architect Shin Takamatsu
Address 11, Minami-karato-chō, Kamitoba, Minami-ku,
Kyōto City
Transport From Kyōto
Station: Train—Kintetsu
Kyōto line to Jūjō Station and
5-minute walk; or Subway—
Karasuma line to Jūjō Station
and 8-10-minute walk
Visitation Private clinic for
patients only; seen only from
the outside.

Following the influence of Seiichi Shirai's mannerist works of architecture, Takamatsu, in the early
1980s, became fascinated by the power, dynamics,
and form of the primitive machine, and the
achievements of early machine-age engineering.
The first expression of this fascination in
Takamatsu's designs is the Ark, a building that
most likely reminds the observer of a strange loco-
motive. While this metaphor is reinforced by the
Ark's close proximity to a railroad station, on closer
analysis, the image cannot be precisely associated
with any type of machinery, and so it is rather an
unidentifiable mechanism. A large, horizontal,
silver-painted, cylindrical form laid over a rectangular concrete volume comprises the basic composition. This cylinder is "closed" at both ends by
enormous "lids." Ten metallic lanterns act as skylights that bring light into the small gallery space
inside. The doctor's residence and clinic are situated below this gallery. This unusual architecture
appears even more mysterious in the evening when
the lights within the skylights are lit.

Ark (Nishina Dental Clinic) 1983

Nishina Haisha Kurinikku
Architect Shin Takamatsu
Address 10-4, Tango,
Momoyama-chō, Fushimi-ku,
Kyōto City
Transport Train—Keihan Uji
line to Momoyama Minami
Station and 1-minute walk; or
JR Nara line to Momoyama
Station and 5 minutes by taxi
to Keihan Momoyama
Minami Station
Visitation Private clinic for
patients only; seen only from
the outside.

Zassō Forest Kindergarten 1977

Zassō-no-mori Gakuen
Architect Kijo Rokkaku
Address 55, Kokuzō-dani, Tanabe-chō, Tsuzuki-gun, Kyōto Pref.
Transport From Kyōbashi Station in Ōsaka: Train—JR Katamachi line to Ōsumi Station and 5 minutes by taxi; or from Kyōto Station: Train—Kintetsu Kyōto line to Shin-Tanabe Station and 12 minutes by taxi

Located in a wooded, hilly landscape south of Kyōto, the Zassō Forest Kindergarten is surrounded by nature. Rokkaku's design is a unique response to this environment in its efforts to introduce the manifestations of nature to children. The building features seven towers of different heights and a glass pyramidal structure that covers the indoor play area. While nature can be closely observed from any part of the compound, it is first of all the towers and the play area that dramatize one of nature's invisible manifestations: the wind; these towers are equipped with wind sculptures, and the playground with a special propellerlike windmill. Designed by the well-known sculptor Susumu Shingu, the seven stretched Teflon-fiber surfaces on revolving mechanisms, like weathervanes, indicate the movement and direction of wind, while they appear as some large musical notes cast against the forest and the sky. The movement of the three-blade "propeller" atop the play area is transmitted by a system of axles and joints into the well-lit space, where the revolving motion can be harnessed by children plugging various toys into special outlets in the wall and the floor. These toys, including a small suspended airplane in the middle of the space, then come alive and move when breeze arises in the forest.

École Music School
1990
Jeugia Kabushiki Kaisha
Architect Shin Takamatsu
Address 3, Kabuto-Dai
6-chōme, Kizu-chō, Shoraku-
gun, Kyōto Pref.
Transport From Kyōto
Station: Train—Kintetsu
Kyōto line to Takanohara
Station and 8 minutes by taxi;
or from Kyōbashi Station in
Ōsaka: Train—JR Katamachi
line to Hōsone Station and
8 minutes by taxi
Visitation Open daily during
working hours; tel: (07747)
3-0615

This project, although contemporary with Takamatsu's Syntax and Solaris (see pages 196 and 224), represents the early stage of a new direction in his architecture. The composition of the building is explicitly asymmetrical, and is comprised of simpler, less agitated, less detailed volumes than those in the other cases. The majority of the structure is covered by polished aluminum plates, while stone and concrete appear in some areas, especially in the interior. A spiral stairway inside is marked as well as lit by a large skylight shaped as a lantern over a towerlike shaft, a design element almost identical to the elevator tower of Takamatsu's Solaris, built in the same year. The interior is further embellished by sophisticated, often high-tech elements. For instance, several series of tiny red diode lights are embedded in the stone floors and stair steps of the lobby, which blink slowly and mysteriously to indicate directions inside. Also there is a story-high, vertical, rectangular block of glass that is lit from inside and glows as an immaterial volume of light. The complex includes several classrooms, a performance hall, offices, and showrooms of the Jeugia Company, the owner of the school. The building is part of a newly developed urban area south of Kyōto.

町 YAMASHIRO-CHŌ

**Minami Yamashiro
Cultural Center
1990**
*Yamanami Hōru-Minami
Yamashiro Bunka Kaikan*
Architect Kisho Kurokawa
Address Kita-kawara Aza,
Minami-Yamashiro mura,
Yamashiro-chō, Sagaru gun,
Kyōto Pref.

Transport From Kyōbashi
Station in Ōsaka: Train—JR
Katamachi line to Kizu Station,
change to JR Nara line; or from
Kyōto Station: Train—JR Nara
line to Tanakura Station and
10 minutes by taxi
Visitation Open daily during
working hours; tel: (07439)
3-0560

🏛 NARA

■ Nara National Museum,
page 202
■ Nara City Museum of
Photography, page 203
■ Nara Hotel, page 203

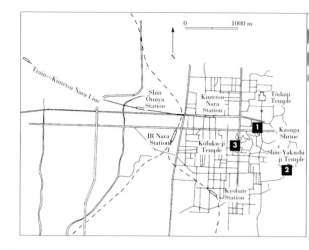

Nara National Museum 1894

Nara Kokuritsu Hakubutsukan
Architect Tokuma Katayama
Address 50, Noborioji, Nara,
Nara Pref. (see map)
Transport From Kintetsu
Nara Terminal: 8-minute
walk to east on Noborioji-dōri
Avenue to Nara Park
Visitation 9:00–16:30 (closed
Mondays and 26 December–3
January), tel: (0742) 22-7771

Nara National Museum addition, 1972

Nara Kokuritsu Hakubutsukan
Architect Junzo Yoshimura
Address 50, Noborioji, Nara,
Nara Pref. (see map)
Transport From Kintetsu
Nara Terminal: 8-minute
walk to east on Noborioji-dōri
Avenue to Nara Park (east of
Nara National Museum)

Tokuma Katayama was one in the first group of architects trained by Josiah Conder in Western-style education at the Tōkyō Imperial University. Others among the first graduates were Kingo Tatsuno and Yorinaka Tsumagi; all three of these architects subsequently became very well-known designers, completing innumerable important public buildings in the latter part of the Meiji Era. The Nara National Museum in Nara is the first of two major museums Katayama designed for the ancient capitals of Nara and Kyōto (1895). The neoclassical, Second Empire-style building of reinforced brick structure is articulated with rusticated stucco walls and pilasters. Its Corinthian columns support an arched pediment above the entrance portico; this motif is reminiscent to that at the Louvre in Paris.

NARA

Nara City Museum of Photography
1992

Nara-shi Shashin Bijutsukan
Architect Kisho Kurokawa
Address 600-1, Takahata-chō, Nara, Nara Pref. (see map)
Transport From Kintetsu Nara Terminal: Bus 1, 2, 5, or 6 to Waruishichō stop and 10-minute walk to east (Museum is west of Shin-Yakushiji-Temple)
Visitation 9:30–17:00 (closed Mondays and 27 December–3 January), tel: (0742) 22-9811

Kurokawa designed this small museum on a slightly sloping site, west of the famous Shin-Yakushiji Temple. Inlaid in the terrain, the majority of the facility (including all the exhibition rooms) is arranged underground and overlooks a sunken garden. Above ground the visitor encounters only the lobby and a reflective pool and terraces over the underground sections. The lobby, with a small cafe at its rear, is approached from the west via a flight of stairs. This space is entirely defined by large, story-high, glass walls without any mullions, and is covered by an extensive roof with large overhangs supported by interior columns. The roof, finished with heavy tiles, recollects the similar structures of ancient Buddhist temples that populate the area and Nara in general. The ceiling, although revealing the form of the pitched roof above, is shaped with highly polished aluminum surfaces and curving details around the columns and the recessed electric lights. Internal partitions are provided by translucent fabric screens stretched between the ceiling and floor by means of thin steel cables and stainless steel fittings. As a result of this design, the "heavy" roof appears to be floating above the lobby, whose space in turn is rendered phenomenally fluid, elusive, and almost ethereal. For this project—which houses the photographs of the late photographer Taikichi Irie, a native of Nara—Kurokawa won the annual prize of the Japan Art Academy for 1992.

 NARA

Nara Hotel
1909

Architect Kingo Tatsuno and Yasushi Kataoka
Address 1096, Takahata-chō, Nara, Nara Pref. (see map)
Transport From Kintetsu Nara Terminal: 16-minute walk to south of Araike Pond

YAMATŌ-KŌRIYAMA

Mikakuto Candy Factory
1983

Mikakuto Nara Kōjō
Architect Minoru Takeyama
Address 137-5, Imakokufu, Yamatōkōriyama, Nara Pref.
Transport Train—JR Kansai main line to Yamatō-Koizumi Station and 5 minutes by taxi

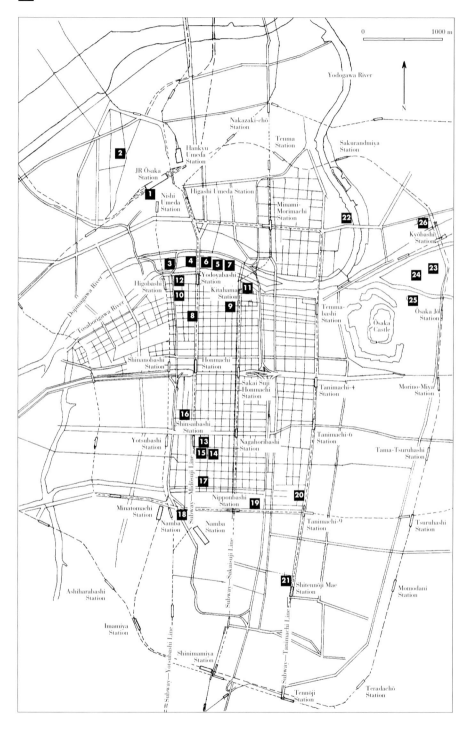

0   1000 m

Yodogawa River

Nakazaki-chō Station

Tenma Station

Sakuranōmiya Station

Hankyu Umeda Station

JR Ōsaka Station

1 Nishi Umeda Station

Higashi Umeda Station

Minami-Morimachi Station

22

26 Kyōbashi Station

2

3 **4** **6** **5** **7**

Yodoyabashi Station

12

Higobashi Station

10

Kitahama Station

11

23

24

8

Dojimagawa River

Tosaborigawa River

9

25

Temma-bashi Station

Ōsaka Castle

Ōsaka Jō Station

Shinmabashi Station

Honmachi Station

Sakai Suji Honmachi Station

Tanimachi-4 Station

Morino-Miya Station

16

Shinsaibashi Station

Yotsubashi Station

13

15 **14**

Nagahoribashi Station

Tanimachi-6 Station

Tama-Tsuruhashi Station

17

20

Nipponbashi Station

19

Minatomachi Station

18

Namba Station

Namba Station

Tanimachi-9 Station

Tsuruhashi Station

Ashiharabashi Station

21 Shitennōji Mae Station

Momodani Station

Imamiya Station

Subway—Yotsubashi Line

Subway—Midosuji Line

Subway—Sakaisuji Line

Subway—Tanimachi Line

Shinimamiya Station

Tennōji Station

Teradachō Station

市 ŌSAKA

Ōsaka Central Post Office 1939

Ōsaka Chūō Yūbinkyoku
Architect Tetsuro Yoshida
Address 2-4, Umeda 3-chōme, Kita-ku, Ōsaka City (see map)
Transport From JR Ōsaka Station: south exit and 2-minute walk to west side of station plaza

Like Yoshida's previous major project, the Tōkyō Central Post Office (1931) (see page 88), this building is an outstanding example, perhaps the last one, of prewar Japanese modern architecture. As the increasingly chauvinistic and militaristic political circles discouraged—in effect, prohibited—the pursuit of international modernism in Japan, particularly in prominent public and cultural facilities, modern architecture in the 1930s was restricted to utilitarian structures. Within the Architecture Department of the Ministry of Telecommunications a small group of talented designers emerged as flag-bearers of a straightforward, functional architecture. The Ōsaka Central Post Office is the work of the leading figure in the group, Tetsuro Yoshida. He designed the building with a simple structural skeleton and large glass wall/window surfaces among the grayish brick covered frames, which seem to diminish the height of the building and, with the emphasized eaves, give a look of solidity. Completed some eight years later than its counterpart in Tōkyō, the Ōsaka Central Post Office is much more advanced in terms of functional planning and organization. Public entrances face the large urban square in front of Ōsaka Station, while all the service ramps for loading and unloading face a street behind.

Umeda Sky Building 1993

Shin-Umeda City
Architect Hiroshi Hara
Address 1-20, Ōyodonaka
1-chōme, Kita-ku, Ōsaka City
(see map)
Transport Any train or subway line to Ōsaka Station or
Umeda Station: north or
northeast exit and 10-minute
walk

Part of the new Shin-Umeda City urban development, the 567-foot/173-meter Umeda Sky Building
is located northwest of Ōsaka Station. Hara's original scheme for the large complex had to be reduced
somewhat for financial reasons, and it is now comprised of three vertical blocks. The architectural
designs for one of these blocks, occupied by the
Westin Hotel, were prepared by the hotel corporation itself. Hara was responsible for only the two
remaining larger ones. In his arrangement, however, these two blocks—thirty-eight stories each—
while emerging as independent forms 177 feet/
54 meters apart, are interconnected by a huge multistory structure on the top floors, providing what
Hara calls a "Mid-air Garden."

As an urban enclave, featuring offices and shops, plus conference, sports, cultural, and other public facilities, the design brings to mind the somewhat similar urban schemes of the Metabolists, particularly Isozaki's "City in the Air"
(1961) (see page 20, fig. 19). The large bridge structure with a square plan
opens to both above and below through a circular sky window. Softly curving
and undulating forms articulate a series of small, metallic roofs that, not unlike
some clouds in the sky, make the Garden seem to almost float in the sky.
Additional features of this futuristic project include an attractive sunken garden and a ground-level plaza under the "urban roof" that defines a huge, open
atrium filled with bridges and freestanding elevator shafts, and is illuminated
in the evening with a spectacular light show.

The Umeda Sky Building, which is the result of advanced structural engineering, nevertheless equally emphasizes the importance of surfaces, finishing
materials, and formal articulation. With these, Hara has significantly counter-
balanced and softened the monumental volumes of the building. Reflective
mirror glass surfaces alternate with transparent ones, while flush-mounted,
polished aluminum plates cover the upper regions and the roof garden.

**Dentsu Advertising
Company
1960**
Dentsu Ōsaka Shiten
Architect Kenzo Tange
Address 3-1, Nakanoshima
2-chōme, Kita-ku, Ōsaka City
(see map)
Transport Subway—Yotsubashi line to Higobashi Station and 3-minute walk north
across Higobashi Bridge then
to east (third building from
Yotsubashi-suji Avenue, next
to the elevated expressway)

**Bank of Japan,
Ōsaka Branch
1903**
Nihon Ginkō Ōsaka Shiten
Architect Kingo Tatsuno
Address 1-45, Nakanoshima
2-chōme, Kita-ku, Ōsaka City
(see map)
Transport Subway—Midōsuji
line to Yodoyabashi Station
and 2-minute walk to north
on west side of Midōsuji
Avenue
(See page 13, fig. 1)

**Bank of Japan,
Ōsaka Branch
addition, 1980**
Nihon Ginkō Ōsaka Shiten
Architect Nikken Sekkei
Company
Address 1-45, Nakanoshima
2-chōme, Kita-ku, Ōsaka City
(see map)
Transport Subway—Midōsuji
line to Yodoyabashi Station
and 2-minute walk to north
on west side of Midōsuji
Avenue

Ōsaka Library
1904
*Ōsaka Furitsu Nakanoshima
Toshokan*
Architect Sumitomo Eizen
Design Office
Address 2-1, Nakanoshima
1-chōme, Kita-ku, Ōsaka City
(see map)
Transport Subway—Midōsuji
line to Yodoyabashi Station
and 4-minute walk to east on
Nakanoshima (behind Ōsaka
City Hall)
The Ōsaka Library is an
Important National Cultural
Property.

The Ōsaka Library is an example of Western
eclecticism in Japan. It is practically the first work
of the Sumitomo Eizen Design Office, the Architecture Department of Sumitomo Conglomerate
(*zaibatsu*), established in 1900. The explicitly
classical design features a symmetrical composition with a central section and two flanking wings.
A broad, outdoor, ceremonial stairway leads to the
main entrance and the impressive lobby under a
large dome. This central space of the two-story,
stone-faced, brick structure is designed with classical details of both stone and wood. Upon its
completion the library was donated by the
Sumitomo family to Ōsaka Prefecture. The building was extended on its two sides by Yutaka
Hidaka and Eikichi Hasebe, two leading designers
in Sumitomo Eizen, in 1922.

Ōsaka City Hall
1986
Ōsaka Shichōsha
Architect Nikken Sekkei
Company
Address 3-20, Nakanoshima
1-chōme, Kita-ku, Ōsaka City
(see map)
Transport Subway—Midōsuji
line to Yodoyabashi Station
and 2-minute walk north on
east side of Midōsuji Avenue

Nakanoshima Central Auditorium 1918

Ōsaka-shi Chūō Kōkaidō
Architect Shinichirō Okada; Kingo Tatsuno and Yasushi Kataoka
Address 1-27, Nakanoshima 1-chōme, Kita-ku, Ōsaka City (see map)
Transport Subway—Midōsuji line to Yodoyabashi Station and 8-minute walk (behind the Ōsaka Library)

Facing east, the Nakanoshima Central Auditorium has a commanding view of Nakanoshima Island, which features an extensive park with recreational facilities. The complex was commissioned and financed by Einosuke Iwamoto, a stock market speculator, and designed by Shinichirō Okada, whose proposal was selected in a 1912 architectural competition. Okada's original scheme had to be modified and the changes in design were made by Tatsuno and Kataoka, who collaborated in giving the building its final form. It manifests an eclectic style in which Renaissance motifs dominate. At its completion the auditorium represented a cultural facility that was far superior to its contemporaries in both size and quality.

Ōsaka Gas Building 1933

Ōsaka Gasu Biru
Architect Takeo Yasui
Address 1-2, Hirano-chō 4-chōme, Chūō-ku, Ōsaka City (see map)
Transport Subway—Midōsuji line to Yodoyabashi Station and 5-minute walk to south (on southwest corner of Midōsuji Avenue)

Artemis 1992

Imanishi Koraibashi Biru
Architect Shin Takamatsu
Address 5-2, Koraibashi 2-chōme, Chūō-ku, Ōsaka City (see map)
Transport Subway—Midōsuji line to Yodoyabashi Station and 8-10-minute walk to east Artemis is a small commercial and office building.

🏯 ŌSAKA

Hilis
1988
Imanishi Hirisu Biru
Architect Shin Takamatsu
Address 16-1, Imabashi
4-chōme, Chūō-ku, Ōsaka
City (see map)
Transport Subway—Midōsuji
line to Yodoyabashi Station
and 6-minute walk south on
Midōsuji Avenue then west on
Imabashi Street (on southwest
street corner)
Hilis is a small commercial
and office building.

Ōsaka Stock Exchange
1935
Ōsaka Shōken Torihikijō
Architect Eikichi Hasebe and
Kenzo Takegoshi Design
Office
Address 8-6, Kitahama
1-chōme, Chūō-ku, Ōsaka
City (see map)
Transport Subway—Sakaisuji
line to Kitahama Station and
few steps; or Train—Keihan
main line to Kitahama Station
and few steps (on the corner
of Sakaisuji Avenue)

Sumitomo Bank
1926
Sumitomo Biru
Architect Sumitomo Eizen
Design Office
Address 6-5, Kitahama
4-chōme, Chūō-ku, Ōsaka
City (see map)
Transport Subway—Midōsuji
line to Yodoyabashi Station
and 2-minute walk to west; or
Yotsubashi line to Higobashi
Station and 3-minute walk to
east along south bank of
Tosabori River

In 1900 Sumitomo *zaibatsu* decided to enter the banking business. In order to house its bank headquarters, which would also serve as the center of all its operations, the company concluded that a new, major building was necessary. The building in both size and quality had to represent the national stature of the quickly expanding Sumitomo. To this end Sumitomo established its own in-house architectural department led by two young graduates of Tōkyō Imperial University, Kenzo Takegoshi and Eikichi Hasebe. Upon being hired, they were sent to Europe for one year in order to study the architecture of similar buildings. To gain practical experience before starting the work on the bank building, the department was commissioned by Sumitomo to design various smaller structures, including the Ōsaka Library (1904) and several residences for members of the Sumitomo family. All this reveals the utmost importance of the new building. The northern part, facing the river, was completed in 1926 and the rest in 1931. The seven-story complex is organized around two internal light courts providing illumination to the first floor of the banking hall. This hall is richly decorated in the style of classical architecture. On the other hand, the exterior is surprisingly plain, a manifest sign of a rational, quasi-modernist design. The stone-faced elevations are broken by stylistic elements only around the three major entrances, which are flanked by pairs of Ionic columns with decorative architraves carrying the insignia of Sumitomo.

Sony Tower
1976

Architect Kisho Kurokawa
Address 2-10, Shinsaibashi-suji 1-chōme, Chūō-ku, Ōsaka City (see map)
Transport Subway—Midōsuji line to Shinsaibashi Station and 1-minute walk

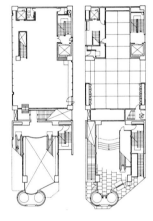

The Sony Tower, a showroom complex for the display of various Sony products, stands at the intersection of a major, multilane, urban avenue and the famous Shinsaibashi-suji shopping arcade, a long pedestrian shopping street (*shōtengai*). This unique urban "monument," with an overall form and details that are as precisely designed as a Sony Walkman, marks an important turning point in Kurokawa's architecture. Although it does feature elements of his earlier Metabolist designs, namely the capsules he used in the Nakagin Capsule Tower in Tōkyō (1972) (see page 83), the Sony Tower is much more than a mechanical device of prefabricated structures. It foreshadowed the qualities of an architecture of the electronic age of information and communication. In effect, the building is almost entirely generated by movement; the elevations are dominated by the slanting forms of escalators and the vertical shafts of elevators. These shafts, as opposed to those in Metabolist works of the 1960s, are made of transparent glass, as are the elevator cars themselves. The capsule units, attached to the side of the tower, are wrapped in stainless steel, whose glittering surfaces add to the overall high-tech image of the design. The experience is heightened in the evening when, through the transparent skin, all the movement inside appears as light.

Galleria Akka
1988
Architect Tadao Ando
Address 16-20, Higashi-
Shinsaibashi 1-chōme, Chūō-
ku, Ōsaka City (see map)
Transport Subway—Midōsuji
line to Shinsaibashi and
8-minute walk (on east side
of narrow road, which is the
second to the east from
Shinsaibashi-suji shopping
arcade)

Sōgō Department Store
1935
Sōgō Depāto
Architect Togo Murano
Address 8-3, Shinsaibashi-
suji 1-chōme, Chūō-ku,
Ōsaka City (see map)
Transport Subway—Midōsuji
line to Shinsaibashi Station
and 1-minute walk south on
east side of Midōsuji Avenue
(between Midōsuji Avenue
and Shinsaibashi-suji shopping arcade)
(See page 14, fig. 5)

Organic Building Ōsaka
1993
Architect Gaetano Pesce
(Italy)
Address 7-21, Minami-
Funaba 4-chōme, Chūō-ku,
Ōsaka City (see map)
Transport Subway—Midōsuji
line to Shinsaibashi Station
and 10-minute walk to north
then west

Among the growing number of small urban commercial complexes by Ando, the Galleria Akka, in
the busiest part of downtown Ōsaka, is perhaps the
most remarkable. Situated on a long, narrow,
twenty-six-foot-/eight-meter-wide site perpendicular to the small street in front, the building is
designed, like most of Ando's architecture, with an
interior courtyard that runs through the four floors
above ground and two under. Shaped by a curving
concrete wall and accessible from the street level
via several flights of stairs, this court provides light
for most of the small shops and, in conjunction
with the movable vaulted glass roof, a gallery on
the top floor. This multistory space is designed to
be a quiet public place in contrast to the busy street
outside. While rather blank outside, the building
comes alive inside, thus redefining the surrounding
cityscape within the realm of architecture.

Kirin Plaza
1987

Architect Shin Takamatsu
Address 7-2, Sōemon-chō,
Chūō-ku, Ōsaka City
(see map)
Transport Subway—Midōsuji
line to Namba Station and
10-minute walk; or Sennichi-
mae line to Namba Station; or
Train—Kintetsu Nara line to
Namba Station and 5-minute
walk, first to north then to
east after Dotombori Bridge
to Ebisubashi Bridge

Kirin Plaza is surrounded by an urban area flooded by commercial signs, neon lights, colors, and forms. Takamatsu's design both acknowledges its popular environment and counters it in its own way. In so doing, the building, while obviously paradoxical in many of its attributes, is able to make a very signifi-cant architectural statement in the locality of Dotombori, and, further, in the contemporary Japanese urban conditions in general. The eight-story building is a cultural and entertainment center, with bars, restaurants, an art gallery, and a multipurpose auditorium, and is owned by Japan's most popular beer com-pany, Kirin. Designed with a square plan, the building is shaped with biaxial symmetry. The almost windowless volume is covered with black, highly pol-ished and matte granite with stainless steel details, whose scale ranges from the minuscule to the large. Each elevation is articulated with an overscaled gate and, more importantly, a giant lighting device. These four shafts of light are as tall, if not taller, than the main structure itself. This curious urban monument becomes even more startling in the night when its shafts glow and when its glittering surfaces reflect the flickering lights of the surrounding urban land-scape. The Kirin Plaza remains one of Takamatsu's most outstanding works.

New Kabuki Theater
1958

Ōsaka Shin-Kabukiza
Architect Togo Murano
Address 3, Namba 4-chōme, Chūō-ku, Ōsaka City
(see map)
Transport Subway—Yotsu-bashi line or Sennichimae line to Namba Station and 5-minute walk to south; or Subway—Midōsuji line to Namba Station and few steps (on west side of Midōsuji Avenue)

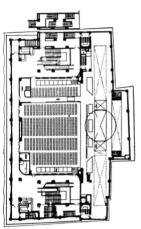

The New Kabuki Theater is perhaps Murano's most exuberant design. As a tribute to the traditional theater of Kabuki, it imitates traditional roof motifs in a most explicit way. Murano used four layers of undulating eaves (*kara hafu*) above the first floor arcade and large gabled eaves (*chidori hafu*) over the entire building. All are finished with copper roofing, whose patinated, dark color contrasts with the white painted walls and balustrades and the white marble columns of the first floor. The 2,000-seat theater is decorated with brilliantly painted ceilings of red, gold, and green, which echo the colors of the stage. In the foyer the floor is carpeted, the walls are painted, and the columns are covered with white marble. The theater is located in the Namba area of Ōsaka, where there are many other theaters and cinemas.

National Bunraku Theater
1983

Kokuritsu Bunraku Gekijō
Architect Kisho Kurokawa
Address 12-10 Nihonbashi 1-chōme, Chūō-ku, Ōsaka City (see map)
Transport Subway—Sennichi-mae line or Sakai-suji line to Nihonbashi Station; or Train—Kintetsu Namba line to Nihonbashi Station and 5-minute walk to east (on north side of Sennichi-mae Avenue)

Le Baron Vert
1992

Architect Philippe Starck (France)
Address 5-1, 5-11, Tanimachi 9-chōme, Chūō-ku, Ōsaka City (see map)
Transport Subway—Tanimachi line or Sennichi-mae line to Tanimachi 9-chōme Station and 5-minute walk to north (on west side of Tanimachi-suji Avenue)
The commercial/office building is "covered" with plants.

Rikyū Housing
1990

Parē Royāru Yuhigaoka Rikyū
Architect Shin Takamatsu
Address 2-29, 31, Yuhigaoka-chō, Tennōji-ku, Ōsaka City (see map)
Transport Subway—Tanimachi line to Shitennōji-mae Station and 2-minute walk (165 feet/50 meters west from Tanimachi-suji Avenue)
The building is a mixed-use residential and office complex.

🏛 ŌSAKA

Raika Headquarters 1989

Raika Honsha Biru
Architect Tadao Ando
Address 1-6, Nankō-kita, Suminoe-ku, Ōsaka City
Transport Subway—Chūō line to Ōsaka-kō Terminal and Raika Bus for Intex and Raika (15 minutes)

Santory Museum-Tempōzan 1994

Architect Tadao Ando
Address 5-1, Kaigan-dōri 1-chōme, Minato-ku, Ōsaka City
Transport Subway—Chūō line to Ōsaka-kō Terminal and 4-minute walk

Tempōzan Harbor Village 1990

Tempōzan Hābā Bireji
Architect Cambridge Seven Associates (U.S.)
Address 1, Kaigan-dōri 1-chōme, Minato-ku, Ōsaka City
Transport Subway—Chūō line to Ōsaka-kō Terminal and 5-minute walk (buildings, plaza, and aquarium are along Kaigan-dōri Avenue)

Headquarters of the Raika fashion design company, the complex is one of Ando's largest projects. It is located on reclaimed land, and is part of an extensive urban development project at the shores of Ōsaka port. Raika Headquarters is comprised of two volumes, which are interconnected with an overhead bridge. The larger one is centered around the multistory cylindrical space of the entrance hall/atrium, an interior courtyard, but also features within its extensive structural matrix a system of outside courtyards on the upper floors. Particularly noteworthy is the entrance sequence among layers of concentric translucent glass and glass block walls wrapping around the second-floor atrium, which has a diameter of 131 feet/40 meters. One uses a system of ramps or stairways to emerge and further ascend in the dramatic atrium space, where light penetrates through the curving and glittering surfaces of glass-block walls extending to the seven-story-high ceiling. The smaller volume, surrounded by a plaza, houses public spaces such as shops, an exhibition hall, training facilities, and galleries on its upper levels. Like most other parts of the complex, it is covered by a stainless-steel-plated, vaulted roof. Raika is Ando's first design that explores the cylinder as a new type of space.

Both the Dormitory and the Sempukan were designed and supervised by the English engineer James T. Waters who, like many other foreign experts, had been invited to Japan to help build the infrastructure for the new, Western-type, Japanese economy in the early Meiji Era. Both structures, whose architecture is heavily indebted to the influence of contemporary Western neo-classicism, are kept in their original form. The Sempukan, constructed of reinforced brick and faced with white plaster, was built as the reception building and guest house of the Ōsaka Mint Bureau in the pavilion style, with Tuscan stone columns at the balcony representing the contemporary colonial style. The Dormitory—used today as a youth art gallery—represents a more direct, and somewhat heavier, interpretation of Roman classicism. The symmetrical building is finished in stone, and features a six-column portico in front of the entrance, which is approached through a wide stairway. The two buildings are among Waters's few remaining works.

Ōsaka Mint: Dormitory and Sempukan
1871
Kyū-Zōhei Ryō Genkan and *Sempukan*
Architect Thomas James Waters (U.K.)
Address 1-58, Temmabashi 1-chōme, Kita-ku, Ōsaka City (see map)
Transport Subway—Tanimachi line to Minami-Morimachi Station and 15-minute walk east to Sakuranomiya-bashi Bridge, or Tanimachi line to Temmabashi Station and 15-minute walk across Temmabashi Bridge, then to the northeast along the river beyond Sakuranomiya-bashi Bridge
The buildings are Important National Cultural Properties.

Tōkiō Marine Plaza
1990
Ōsaka Tōkyō Kaijō Biru
Architect Kajima Corporation
Address 2-53, Shiromi 2-chōme, Chūō-ku, Ōsaka City (see map)
Transport Train—JR Loop line to Kyōbashi Station and 8-minute walk south on the elevated promenade (within Ōsaka Business Park)

Twin 21 Office Towers
1986
National or *Matsushita Tsuwin-21*
Architect Nikken Sekkei Company
Address 1-61, Shiromi 2-chōme, Chūō-ku, Ōsaka City (see map)
Transport Train—JR Loop line to Kyōbashi Station and 10-minute walk south on the elevated and covered promenade (within Ōsaka Business Park)
The towers, joined by a large, glass-roofed atrium, include the headquarters of the electronic industrial giant, the National Company.

🏯 ŌSAKA

Ōsaka-jō Hall
1983
Architect Nikken Sekkei
Company
Address 3-1, Ōsakajō, Chūō-
ku, Ōsaka City (see map)
Transport Train—JR Loop
line to Ōsakajō-Kōen Station
and 5-minute walk
Ōsaka-jō Hall is a multipurpose cultural and sports arena
with an impressively large
roof structure.

International Friendship
Pavilion of Expo '90
1990
Aqua Hall of Expo '90
1990
Kokusai Hana to Midori no
Hakurankai
Architect Arata Isozaki
Address Tsurumi Nature
Park, Tsurumi-ku, Ōsaka City
Transport Train—JR Loop
line or Keihan line to Kyō-
bashi Station and Subway—
Tsurumi-Ryokuchi line to
Tsurumi-Ryokuchi Station
and 5-minute walk to park
(the two buildings are within
the Tsurumi Nature Park)

Garden of Fine Arts
1990
Architect Tadao Ando
Address Tsurumi Nature
Park, Tsurumi-ku, Ōsaka City
Transport Train—JR Loop
line or Keihan line to Kyōbashi Station and Subway—
Tsurumi-Ryokuchi line to
Tsurumi-Ryokuchi Station
and 8-minute walk to park
(the building is within the
Tsurumi Nature Park)
The project is an open-air
exhibition of art with forty-
five, 41.3-foot/12.5-meter-
high, freestanding pillars in a
pool of water.

K2 Office Building
1990
Kei-tsū Biru
Architect Kazuo Shinohara
Address 9-7, Higashinoda-
chō 2-chōme, Miyakojima-ku,
Ōsaka City (see map)
Transport Train—JR Loop
line to Kyōbashi Station or
Keihan line to Keihan
Kyōbashi Station and
3-minute walk to west

Located between two urban streets near Kyōbashi
Station, the K2 was designed to address difficult
site conditions: the curving profile of the smaller
street to the south and a subway line crossing
below the northwest corner. These conditions made
the construction of the foundations, as well as the
entire structural design, a very complex task. The
two sides of the building are supported by two
basically different structural frames, which are
clearly revealed in the articulation of the elevations
along the two roads. "Intercepted" by an existing
building at the southwest corner, the K2 breaks
down to an incidental and fragmentary composition, which nonetheless expresses well both the circumstances of its own conception and the prevailing urban conditions in Japan.

Hoshida Common City Housing 1991

Komon City Hoshida Jūtaku
Architect Kazunari Sakamoto
Address 5332-7, Hoshida, Nishi 4-chōme, Katano, Ōsaka Pref.

Transport From JR Kyōbashi Station in Ōsaka: Train—JR Gakuentoshi line to Higashi-Neyagawa Station and 5 minute taxi or 15-minute walk first east then south uphill

A selected number of architects were given the commission to design parts of a new residential urban development not far from the city of Ōsaka. Sakamoto's scheme with 112 houses is one of the most innovative in recent multiunit residential developments. All the residences are independent, two-story houses with small backyards. There are two types of houses, differing in size and form, that are built together in various configurations. The units are steel frame, reinforced concrete structures with corrugated metallic sheets on most walls. Curving, lightweight metallic roofs over steel frames seem to float above the well-lit spaces of the living areas below. Between the rows of houses Sakamoto arranged both small vehicular roads and an extensive system of pedestrian promenades that are lined with a stream of flowing water on the sloping terrain. Areas between the buildings are attractively landscaped; residential units have windows focused onto this system of small interconnected parks. A strong sense of community is fostered by including a small community center in the scheme. Open terraces, a waterfall, and other facilities, sit under Teflon-fiber tent structures stretched over a vaulted metallic frame. With its straightforward but sensitive articulation of private and public spaces, the interrelationship between inside and outside, and the employed materials and structures, Sakamoto's architecture represents what may be called a new industrial vernacular.

Hoshida Common City Community Center 1991

Komon City Hoshida Jūmin Shisetsu
Architect Hiroaki Kimura
Address 5332-7 Hoshida, Nishi 4-chōme, Katano, Ōsaka Pref.

Transport From JR Kyōbashi Station in Ōsaka: Train—JR Gakuentoshi line to Higashi-Neyagawa Station and 5 minutes by taxi or 15-minute walk east then south uphill

Landmark Tower of Ōsaka Expo '70 1970

Nihon Bankoku Hakurankai Tāwā

Architect Kiyonori Kikutake
Address 10, Banpaku-Kinen-Kōen (Expo '70 Memorial Park), Senri, Suita, Ōsaka Pref.
Transport From Umeda Station in Ōsaka City: Subway—Midōsuji-line to Senri-chūō Station; or Train—Hankyū Senriyama line to Yamada Station and Monorail to Banpaku-Kinen-Kōen Station and 5-minute walk
Visitation 10:00–17:00 (closed Wednesdays, or Thursday if Wednesday is a national holiday)

The 1970 World Exposition in Ōsaka was one of the largest and most ambitious in the world; it featured the most innovative, most future-oriented structures. Most Metabolist architects—including Kenzo Tange, who was responsible for the general site planning and the design of the gigantic space frame of the Theme Pavilion (see page 19, fig. 15)—participated in the project by designing various facilities. These were all dismantled after the fair, except for the space frame and Kikutake's Landmark Tower. In 1978 Tange's huge steel-frame structure was demolished as well, leaving only the tower standing today. Its structure, similar to that of Tange's project, was assembled from steel pipes with special joints. The unique feature of Kikutake's scheme, beyond its structural solution, is its system of observation decks shaped as multilateral geodesic domes that, like capsules, are clipped to the frame of the main structure, in a way that recollects the British Archigram group's proposal for the tower of the Montreal Expo 1967. Revealing a high level of industrialization and advanced technology, the tower remains as an outstanding monument that faithfully represents the spirit of Japanese architecture in the 1960s.

Seven years after the Ōsaka Expo '70 closed its gates and its facilities were pulled down, Kurokawa completed the National Ethnological Museum within the original compound of the Expo. The elapse of eight years witnessed a change in Kurokawa's architecture. He shifted the focus of his designs from the expression of changeability based on the primary use of industrial technologies toward the expression of a multiplicity of meanings. He developed an architectural language that could evoke both traditional and contemporary modes of use or understanding. Toward this end Kurokawa began to explore the ambiguous qualities of in-between spaces, forms, and even colors. The two- and three-story museum is designed with a system of large quadrilateral units each with a square courtyard while a central court with abstract, stepped, geometric forms and a shallow pool composes what Kurokawa has called "a relic of the Future." These courtyards are intended as in-between realms, while the selected materials (concrete, aluminum panels, ceramic tiles, and stone) take on various shades of gray, an in-between color. The building continues a new line of design first represented by Kurokawa's Sony Tower in Ōsaka (1976) (see page 210), while cylindrical, vertical circulation shafts, and audio-visual booths shaped like capsules are remnants of his previous Metabolist architecture. Since its completion, the museum has been extended four times by Kurokawa himself between 1978 and 1989.

National Ethnological Museum, 1977

Kokuritsu Minzoku-gaku Hakubutsukan
Architect Kisho Kurokawa
Address 10-1, Banpaku-Kinen-Kōen (Expo '70 Memorial Park), Senri, Suita, Ōsaka Pref.
Transport From Umeda Station in Ōsaka City: Subway—Midōsuji-line (Kita-Ōsaka Kyūkō line) to Senri-chūō Terminal and monorail to Banpaku-Kinen-Kōen Station and 15-minute walk north; or Subway—Sakaisuji line (Hankyū Senriyama line) to Yamada Station and monorail to Banpaku-Kinen-Kōen Station and 15-minute walk north
Visitation 10:00–17:00 (closed Wednesdays and December 28–January 4)

National Museum of International Fine Arts 1970

Kokuritsu Kokusai Bijutsukan
Architect Kiyoshi Kawasaki
Address 10-4, Banpaku-Kinen-Kōen (Expo '70 Memorial Park), Senri, Suita, Ōsaka Pref.
Transport Subway—Sakaisuji line (Hankyū Senriyama line) to Yamada Station and monorail to Banpaku-Kinen-Kōen Station and 12-minute walk

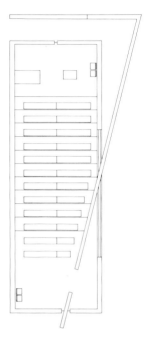

Church with Light
1989
Hikari-no Kyōkai
Architect Tadao Ando
Address 3-50, Kitakasu-
gaoka 4-chōme, Ibaraki,
Ōsaka Pref.
Transport From JR Ibaraki
Station: Bus 2 (bound for
Kasugaoka Kōen) to
Kasugaoka Kōen Terminal
and 2-minute walk

⛩ TOYONAKA

Senri New Town Center
1970
Senri Chūō Chiku Sentā Biru
Architect Fumihiko Maki
Address 2-1, Higashi-chō
1-chōme, Shinsenri,
Toyonaka, Ōsaka Pref.
Transport Subway—Midōsuji
line (Kita-Ōsaka Kyūkō line)
to Senri-Chūō Station and
1-minute walk
(See page 19, fig. 14)

One of Ando's smallest projects, the Church with Light is comparable to his Azuma House in Sumiyoshi, Ōsaka (1976) in both its use of structural concrete and its powerful simplicity. The building is essentially an elongated, windowless, cubical volume containing only one space. The rectangular spatial geometry, however, is interrupted by an independent, skewed wall that, by cutting across one of the corners of the box, inscribes an entry space and, by wrapping partially around another corner, a tiny, semi-enclosed courtyard outside. The floor and the plain benches—both of rough wooden planks—slope down from the entrance toward the altar. The cavelike interior is rather dark. This darkness is intercepted by the dramatic introduction of a limited amount of natural light, much of which pierces through two narrow slits that form a large cross of light in the wall behind the altar. The Church with Light is one of a growing number of religious edifices Ando has designed. The series of these buildings includes his Chapel on Mount Rokko (1986) (see page 228), Church on the Water (1988) (see page 47), and Water Temple (1991)(see page 232).

郡 MINAMI-KAWACHI-GUN
Chikatsu-Asuka Historical Museum
1994
Ōsaka Furitsu Chikatsu-Asuka Hakubutsukan
Architect Tadao Ando
Address 299, Taishi-Higashi-yama, Kannan-chō, Minami-Kawachi-gun, Ōsaka Pref.
Transport From Abenobashi Station (near Tennōji Station) in Ōsaka City: Train—Kintetsu Minami-Ōsaka line to Furuichi Station, change to Kintetsu Nagano line to Kishi Station and 20 minutes by bus bound for Hannan Neopolis Terminal and 10-minute walk
Visitation 10:00–17:00 (closed Mondays); tel: (0721) 93-8321

The purpose of the museum is to introduce the culture of the Tumuli (*Kofun*) Period of Japan (AD 300–538). In this southern part of Ōsaka Prefecture—the site of the museum and the cradle of Japanese civilization—there are more than 200 burial mounds, including four imperial ones. The museum therefore serves as a place wherein unearthed objects are exhibited, and from where a large number of the mounds scattered in the area can be observed. Ando's design features an extensive system of stairs as the rooftop of the building. This makes the huge, reinforced concrete structure seem to emerge from the terrain; in fact, the building is meant to be a man-made hill that blends with and highlights its natural, wooded environment. Topped with an additional observation tower, and punctuated by a square-shaped, large light court, the stepped roof is designed so as to be the center of various outdoor activities: festivals, performances, and lectures. Many of the interior spaces are buried in the ground, creating the atmosphere of being inside a large and dark *kofun*. The museum is one of Ando's recent designs that uses earth as an architectural element.

市 TONDABAYASHI

PL Institute Kindergarten
1974
PL Gakuen Yōchien
Architect Takefumi Aida
Address Kamiyama-chō 1-chōme, Ebitani, Tondabayashi, Ōsaka Pref.
Transport From Abenobashi Station (near Tennōji Station) in Ōsaka City: Train—Kintetsu Minami-Ōsaka line to Furuichi Station, change to Kintetsu Nagano line to Tondabayashi Station and 10 minutes by taxi

Ōsaka Prefectural Sports Center
1972

Ōsaka-fu Rinkai Spōtsu Sentā
Architect Fumihiko Maki
Address 6-1, Takashina-hama-chō, Takaishi, Ōsaka Pref.
Transport From Namba Station in Ōsaka: Train—Nankai line to Takashina-hama Station (change train at Hagoromo Station) and 8-minute walk to west

The huge complex, located in a satellite town south of Ōsaka, features an Olympic-size swimming pool, a gymnasium, and training halls. Maki's design was elaborated in response to two sharply different urban developments that border on the site. The taller, more monumental volumes of the center face a large-scale industrial area across a canal to the west, while the smaller spaces of the entrance hall, administrative offices, and training gymnasia match the low-profile, more intimate residential areas to the east. Moreover, the entirely prefabricated and locally assembled structure was articulated so as to mediate between the two zones; the exposed structural steel recollects the quality of industrial installations while the gently curving shapes of the cylindrical posts and large roof panels is reminiscent of the architecture of traditional settlements. The applied color scheme of dark grayish brown and off-white is equally ambiguous in its references. Laid out along a 430-foot/129-meter, two-story lobby—an interior public promenade—and around the spaces of open terraces, Maki's extensive and highly successful scheme is in itself allusive to a small urban formation.

🏯 TAJIRI-CHŌ

Kansai International Airport
1994
Shin Kansai Kokusai Kūkō
Architect Renzo Piano (Italy)
Address Shin Kansai Kokusai Kūkō, Tajiri-chō, Kita-Sennan, Ōsaka Pref.
Transport From Ōsaka Station, Shin-Ōsaka Station, and other locations in Ōsaka City: Airport bus or airport limousine; or From Shin-Ōsaka, Ōsaka, and Tennōji stations in Ōsaka City: Train—special JR airport express trains

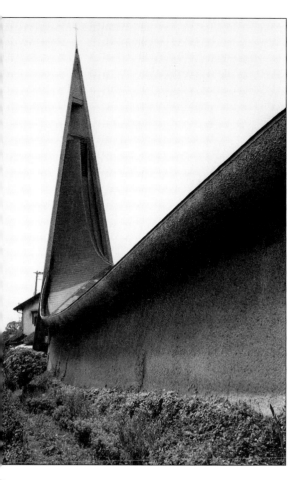

Takarazuka Catholic Church 1967

Takarazuka Katorikku Kyōkai

Architect Togo Murano
Address 7-7, Minami-guchi 1-chōme, Takarazuka, Hyōgo Pref.
Transport From Hanshin Imazu Station or Hankyū Nishinomiya Station: Train—Hankyū Imazu line to Takarazuka-Minamiguchi Station and 2-minute walk

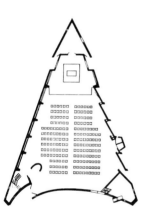

This unique design by Murano is defined by expressively curving lines and surfaces, revealing unmistakable references to Erich Mendelsohn's architecture. The reinforced concrete building, finished in roughened white mortar, is arranged in a triangular plan that looks like an arrowhead. In one corner, a 75-foot-/23-meter-high spire, continuing the undulating, wavelike form of the copper-clad roof, sweeps up into a sharply pointed peak with a cross on top. This wedge-shaped spire is hollowed inside and channels light down on the sacristy and altar from a skylight high above. The interior is equally dominated by the powerfully curving ceiling and the triangular space, the experience of which is compounded by the intricate and soft light introduced through a limited number of carefully positioned openings.

Takarazuka City Hall 1980

Takarazuka Shichōsha
Architect Togo Murano
Address 1, Toyo-chō 1-chōme, Takarazuka, Hyōgo Pref.
Transport From Hanshin Imazu Station or Hankyū Nishinomiya Station: Train—Hankyū Imazu line to Sakasegawa Station and bus to Takarazuka Shichōsha (building is on the west bank of Mukogawa River)

Solaris
1990

Taketsu Sorārisu Biru
Architect Shin Takamatsu
Address 8-24, Minami
Mukonosō 1-chōme,
Amagasaki, Hyōgo Pref.
Transport From Hankyū
Umeda Station in Ōsaka City:
Train—Hankyū Kōbe line to
Mukonosō Station: south exit
and 2-minute walk

Cōna Village Housing
1990

Kōna Bireji
Architect Itsuko Hasegawa
Address 1-17, Tsunematsu,
Amagasaki, Hyōgo Pref.
Transport From Hankyū
Umeda Station in Ōsaka City:
Train—Hankyū Kōbe line to
Mukonosō Station: north exit
and 10 minutes by taxi or
18 minute by bus bound for
Cōna Village

Located on a 65.5-feet-/20-meter-wide and 130-feet-/40-meter-deep site, this small, four-story commercial complex of shops, boutiques, restaurants, and bars is one of Takamatsu's bizarre "urban monuments" in the vein of his Kirin Plaza in Ōsaka (1987) (see page 212). The primary intention here was to design a structure to contrast with its rather non-descript, unchallenging surroundings. The excessively embellished and meticulously chiseled building displays qualities and images that are as "desirable" as those of a piece of precious jewelry. A spirelike elevator tower is separate from the main building, and its top serves as a skylight or lantern. Highly polished, reflective, black stone surfaces alternate with stainless steel and other metallic elements and "irresistible" details as well as uniquely designed and positioned lighting devices to engender an unusual piece of architecture and a world that is as seductive as it is uncanny. Takamatsu explains that "Solaris is the name of the mysterious planet created by Stanislaw Lem, a space in which obedient times and pleasant realities are completely irrelevant." (*JA Library 1: Shin Takamatsu* [Spring 1993]: 48.) The second- and third-floor interiors were designed by the French designer Jean-Michael Wilmotte.

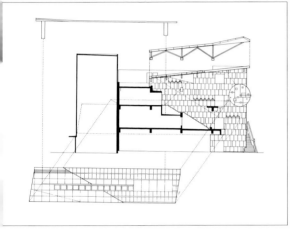

Wing
1991
Sōgō Wing
Architect Hajime Yatsuka
Address 6-12, Minami
Koshiki-Iwa, Nishinomiya,
Hyōgo Pref.
Transport From Hankyū
Umeda Station in Ōsaka City:
Train—Hankyū Kōbe line to
Shukugawa Station, change
train to Hankyū Koyo line to
Kurakuen Station and
4-minute walk to west

Ōtemae Art Center
1992
Ōtemae Āto Sentā
Architect Tadao Ando
Address 8-12, Gōmen-chō,
Nishinomiya, Hyōgo Pref.
Transport From Hankyū
Umeda Station in Ōsaka City:
Train—Hankyū Kōbe line to
Shukugawa Station: south
exit and 6-minute walk to
southwest (building is along
south side of JR line)
Visitation 9:30–16:00 (closed
Saturdays and Sundays);
tel: (0798) 32-5016

The three-story building is approached by a long
and ceremonial open stairway that, splitting the
volume of the structure into two, continues into a
wedge-shaped crevice. This atrium space is crossed
by small bridges and covered by a flying, winglike,
double canopy. As one descends the stairs from the
atrium, a spectacular view opens toward both the
city and the nearby mountains behind. The extensive, partially enclosed void carved into the building and acting as a theatrical urban stage attracts
passersby who observe the movement of shoppers.
Yatsuka designed the Wing as a fragmentary composition wherein just about every element, often
rendered only as signs, claims an autonomous quality. Exterior surfaces are rendered in red, Indian
sand-stone, aluminum panels, and other high-quality materials that are collaged to create a new kind
of urban building.

市 **ASHIYA**

Yamamura House
(now Yodogawa Steel
Company Guest House)
1924
Architect Frank Lloyd Wright
(U.S.) (with Arata Endo)
Address 173, Yamate-chō,
Ashiya, Hyōgo Pref.
Transport From Hankyū
Umeda Station in Ōsaka City:
Train—Hankyū Kōbe line to
Ashiyagawa Station: north
exit and 12-minute walk
north uphill along Ashiya-
gawa River
Visitation Sundays and
national holidays only
The building is an Important
National Cultural Property.

市 KŌBE

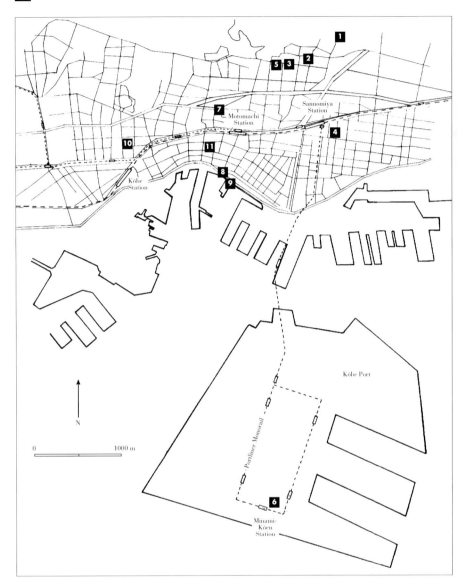

Editor's note: this book went to press shortly after the devastating earthquake of January 1995; sites in and around Kōbe should be checked before visiting.

Rokkō Housing 1 1983
Rokkō Housing 2 1993

Architect Tadao Ando
Address 14-12, Shinohara, Kitamachi 3-chōme, Nada-ku, Kōbe, Hyōgo Pref.
Transport From Hankyū Umeda Station in Ōsaka City: Train—Hankyū Kōbe line to Rokkō Station and 12-minute walk uphill
Visitation Private residences; seen only from the outside.

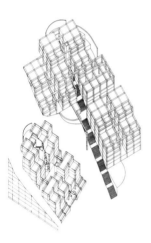

After designing numerous and much-acclaimed small, private residences, Ando completed his first apartment complex in 1983. Rokkō Housing 1 (on the left in photo), located on the steep southern slope of Mount Rokkō, contains twenty two-story apartments, occupied primarily by foreigners. These apartments are lined up along a system of exterior stairways that follow the slope of the site and divide the complex into a western and eastern section. Midway up the stairs, a small paved inner courtyard (a trademark of Ando) introduces a division between northern and southern parts. In this way the arrangement emphasizes the importance of public places among the four groups of private residences, lending a certain urban quality to the scheme. Taking advantage of the stepped disposition of the residential units, the lower sections provide large terraces for the higher ones; small bridges connect the apartments and their terraces. Using the same dynamics of the site, Rokkō Housing 2 of 1993 (on the right in photo) expands the intentions of the first complex to integrate architecture into nature. Although still steep, the available land is somewhat more generous than that of the first stage, allowing for a looser arrangement. As opposed to the previous scheme, which was structured along a matrix of solid, load-bearing walls, the new development is dominated by concrete post-and-beam frames with infill walls. Much of the frame is left open to articulate outdoor spaces. The residential units, arranged in stepped formation, follow a longer stairway than that of their predecessor and are complemented by an underground cable-car/elevator to facilitate access. Again, heightened attention has been paid to the inclusion and shaping of public zones as small plazas within the overall scheme. A third and even larger phase, Rokko Housing 3, has already been designed by Ando to be built after Rokko Housing 2 is completed.

Chapel on Mount Rokkō, 1986

Rokkō no Kyōkai
Architect Tadao Ando
Address 1878, Nishitani-yama, Rokkōdai-chō, Nada-ku, Kōbe, Hyōgo Pref. (within the compound of Rokkō Oriental Hotel)
Transport From Hankyū Umeda Station in Ōsaka City: Train—Hankyū Kōbe line to Rokkō Station: bus to cable car, take cable car up and 5 minutes by bus or 15-minute walk to east to Rokkō Oriental Hotel

Ando's scheme is comprised of four distinct elements: a 130-foot/40-meter colonnade enclosed with frosted glass walls and roof, the boxy volume of the chapel itself, a bell tower, and a freestanding wall that wraps partially around a sloping green courtyard. The glass colonnade, open at both of its ends, is part of the intricate entrance sequence to the chapel. Walking along this light-filled passage, the visitor views the landscape as it unfolds—not unlike in a high-powered telescope—through the end opening of the tube. Continuing through the space, one discovers the entrance to the chapel to the right. Upon entering, the vista is focused internally and, through a large opening with a cross in it, on the interior of the courtyard. This modulation of the entry sequence recollects similar experiences in traditional Japanese religious compounds. The simple interior space of the chapel is highlighted with the introduction of sharp streaks of light penetrating through a few narrow slits in the concrete walls.

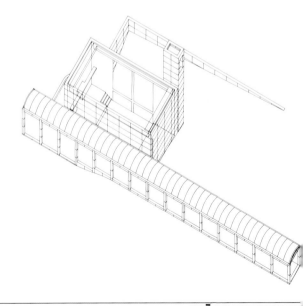

Orchid Court Condominiums
1991
Ōkiddo Kōtō Daiichi-ki
Architect Charles Moore (U.S.)
Address 25, Nishi-Okamoto 2-chōme, Higashi-Nada-ku, Kōbe, Hyōgo Pref.
Transport From JR Ōsaka Station in Ōsaka City: Train —JR Tōkaidō line to Sumiyoshi Station: north exit and 5-minute walk east (between the railroad and Miyamoto-dōri Avenue to the north)

Ōhara Ikebana School
1962
Ōhara-ryu Iemoto Kaikan-Geijutsū Sanko-kan
Architect Kiyosi Seike
Address 14, Sumiyoshi-Yamate 4-chōme, Higashi Nada-ku, Kōbe, Hyōgo Pref.
Transport From Hankyū Umeda Station in Ōsaka City: Train—Hankyū Kōbe line to Mikage Station: north exit and 5-minute walk to north

Rin's Gallery
1981
Architect Tadao Ando
Address 7, Kitano-chō 2-chōme, Chūō-ku, Kōbe, Hyōgo Pref. (see map)
Transport Train—JR Tōkaidō line or Hankyū Kōbe line to Sannomiya Station: north exit and Subway to Shin-Kōbe Station (first stop) and 8-minute walk west

Kitano Foreign Houses of Meiji Era
1868–1912
Architect various foreign architects
Address Kitano-chō 2-, 3-, and 4-chōme, Yamamoto-dōri, Chūō-ku, Kōbe, Hyōgo Pref. (see map)
Transport Train—JR Tōkaidō line or Hankyū Kōbe line to Sannomiya Station: north exit and 20 minute walk north uphill or 8 minutes by taxi

Kitano Alley
1977
Architect Tadao Ando
Address 9, Yamamoto-dōri 2-chōme, Chūō-ku, Kōbe, Hyōgo Pref. (see map)
Transport From Sannomiya Station: north exit and 18-minute walk northwest uphill to Yamamoto-dōri Avenue, or 5 minutes by taxi (8-minute walk from Rin's Gallery)

Helios, 1990
Imanishi Kensetsu
Heriosu Biru
Architect Shin Takamatsu
Address 6-12, Onoe-dōri, Chūō-ku, Kōbe, Hyōgo Pref. (see map)
Transport Train—JR Tōkaidō line or Hankyū Kōbe line to Sannomiya Station: south exit and 2-minute walk

Rose Garden
1977
Architect Tadao Ando
Address 8-15, Yamamoto-dōri 2-chōme, Chūō-ku, Kōbe, Hyōgo Pref. (see map)
Transport Train—JR Tōkaidō line or Hankyū Kōbe line to Sannomiya Station: north exit and 18-minute walk north-west uphill to Yamamoto-dōri Avenue, or 5 minutes by taxi (one-half-minute walk from Kitano Alley)

An early, small, commercial complex by Ando, Rose Garden is located among old, Western-style residences, many of which were built in this area in the Meiji Era (1868–1912). For this reason, the four-story structure is finished with dark, reddish-brown brick, while it is covered by pitched and gabled steel roofs. Between two sections of the building Ando arranged an interior public court from which the majority of the shops can be approached by way of open walkways surrounding the multistory, yet intimate, space.

Jun Port Island Building
1985

Architect Tadao Ando
Address 6, Nakamachi 7-chōme, Minatojima, Chūō-ku, Kōbe, Hyōgo Pref. (see map)
Transport Train—JR Tōkaidō line or Hankyū Kōbe line to Sannomiya Station: change to portliner to Minami Kōen Station and 5-minute walk toward north

The building is located on a man-made island that is linked to Kōbe Port and the mainland by the Kōbe Ōhashi Bridge and a monorail system. The site features a landscaped area with a grassy hillock, which provides some privacy for the building. This green lawn, representing nature, penetrates the building's enclosed courtyard—within the lower, longer wing—which mediates between outside and inside spaces.

Housing the main offices, reception area, and multipurpose hall of a couturier, the structure is laid out along a grid of squares 21 feet/6.4 meters to a side to form an L-shaped composition. The large, reinforced concrete walls are complemented by the frosted glass screen of the south elevation, which can filter out infrared light. The two-story space of the second-floor foyer is defined by a curving, exposed concrete wall with a glass roof. This circular wall is wrapped around by stairs both inside and out. They lead to the entrance and provide an experience that is as dynamic as it is poetic. The top-lit and tapered space of the foyer displays an attractive show of shadow effects on both the stairs and wall surfaces when sunlight penetrates the roof.

Hyōgo Prefectural Office, south wing 1902

Hyōgo Kenchō Minami Chōsha
Architect Hanroku Yamaguchi
Address 57, Shimo-Yamate-dōri 4-chōme, Chūō-ku, Kōbe, Hyōgo Pref. (see map)
Transport Train—JR Tōkaidō line to Motomachi Station: north exit and 8-minute walk to northwest; or Subway—to Kenchōmae Station.

Kōbe Port Tower 1964

Architect Nikken Sekkei Company
Address Hatoba-chō, Chūō-ku, Kōbe, Hyōgo Pref. (see map)
Transport Train—JR Tōkaidō line to Motomachi Station: south exit and 14-minute walk south (on Meriken Pier)

Fish Dance Restaurant 1987

Architect Frank Gehry (U.S.)
Address 2-8, Hatoba-chō, Chūō-ku, Kōbe, Hyōgo Pref. (see map)
Transport Train—JR Tōkaidō line to Motomachi Station: south exit and 12-minute walk (on Meriken Pier near Kōbe Port Tower)

Kōbe Regional Courthouse 1904

Kōbe Chihō Saibanshō
Architect Kozo Kawai
Address 2-1, Tachibana-dōri 2-chōme, Chūō-ku, Kōbe, Hyōgo Pref. (see map)
Transport Train—JR Tōkaidō line to Kōbe Station: north exit and 8-minute walk to north

Kawai graduated from the engineering department of the Tōkyō Industrial College (later Imperial University) in 1883. Subsequently, he studied in Germany (1887–89) with Yorinaka Tsumagi and Yuzuru Watanabe, with whom he was also employed in the Provisional Architectural Bureau, a government agency. As a result of this experience, he designed the Kōbe Regional Courthouse in a German Renaissance style, comparable to that of the Ministry of Justice in Tōkyō (1895) (see page 107) (whose construction Kawai supervised) by the Ende-Böckmann Partnership. The roof of the Kōbe Court House was damaged during the war and had to be rebuilt. Moreover, in 1990 an additional three-story section was built on top of the original by the Ministry of Construction and the Kinki Regional Construction Bureau. Although the complex now looks rather awkward, the new part, designed with glass curtain walls, is clearly distinguished from the preserved old structure.

Daiichi Kangyō Bank Kōbe Branch (now Mitsui Bank) 1916

Mitsui Ginkō Kōbe Shiten
Architect Uheiji Nagano
Address 6-1, Motomachi-dōri 3-chōme, Chūō-ku, Kōbe, Hyōgo Pref. (see map)
Transport Train—JR Tōkaidō line to Motomachi Station: south exit and 8-minute walk (along Sakaemachi-dōri Avenue)

Water Temple, 1991
Shingon-shū Honpuku-ji
Mizu-godō
Architect Tadao Ando
Address 1392 and 1309-1
Ura, Higashiura-chō, Tsuna-
gun (Awaji Island), Hyōgo Pref.
Transport Train—JR Sanyō
line to Takatori Station and
bus to Suma-kō Port and 45
minutes by Awaji Ferry to
Ōiso-kō Port on Awaji Island
and 25-minute walk south
along main road, then west
uphill to Honpuku-ji Temple;
or 6 minutes by taxi
Visitation 9:30–17:00;
tel: (0799) 74-3624

Following the design of three Christian chapels, this building is the first religious project by Ando that is dedicated to the Buddhist faith. Built as an addition to the existing Honpukuji, a Shingon Sect Temple, it now serves as the main hall of the compound. The site is located on Awaji Island, within a hilly terrain with a sweeping view of Ōsaka Bay. However, the majority of Ando's building is placed underground, revealing only its roof above. This roof is shaped as an oval pool of water, which is filled with lotus flowers and which captures the reflection of the sky as much as the sea below. Approaching the temple, the curving path passes by an old Buddhist cemetery, then, guided by two freestanding concrete walls, an intricate entryway leads to a flight of stairs passing through the roof; the visitor can descend these stairs into the subterranean temple. The interior is articulated with a wooden post and beam structure, whose red-painted color contrasts with the exposed concrete material of interior and exterior walls. Only one corner of this space opens to the outside; here, at the end of the day, light coming through a screened opening suffuses the hall in a reddish glow. The Water Temple is one of Ando's most poetically evocative designs.

The small but colorful Okanoyama Graphic Arts Museum, designed after the completion of Isozaki's Tsukuba Center Building (1983)(see page 71), houses a collection of paintings by Tadanori Yokoo, a graphic artist who was born in Nishiwaki. The galleries in the two-story museum are arranged in a series, interrupted by two, interior, plant-filled and top-lit atria, resulting in a long narrow building capped with vaulted roofs. The two spaces for offices and a meditation room that project from both sides of the main volume do not diminish the trainlike image of the building. Such articulation gains special relevance here since the museum is located adjacent to a railroad line. Isozaki references the stairway of Michelangelo's Laurentian Library in Florence (1559) and the Egyptian pyramids in this building, indicating his interest in a historicizing, postmodernist architecture.

Okanoyama Graphic Arts Museum, 1984

Okanoyama Bijutsukan
Architect Arata Isozaki
Address 345-1, Kamihie-chō, Okanoyama, Nishiwaki, Hyōgo Pref.
Transport From JR Shin-Ōsaka Station in Ōsaka City: Highway (*Kōsoku*) Bus— Shinki bus line to Nishiwaki Bus Terminal (90 minutes) and 10 minutes by taxi ; or Train—JR Kakogawa line to Nihon Hesō Kōen Station (building is in front of station)
Visitation 10:00–17:00 (closed Mondays and national holidays), tel: (0795) 23-6223

Nishiwaki Earth Science Museum, 1992

Terra Dōme
Architect Kiko (Monta) Mozuna
Address 334-2, Kamihie-chō, Okanoyama, Nishiwaki, Hyōgo Pref.

Transport From JR Shin-Ōsaka Station in Ōsaka City: Highway (*Kōsoku*) Bus— Shinki bus line to Nishiwaki Bus Terminal (90 minutes) and 10 minutes by taxi ; or Train—JR Kakogawa line to Nihon Hesō Kōen Station and

8-minute walk uphill (6-minute walk from Isozaki's Okanoyama Graphic Arts Museum)
Visitation 10:00–17:00 (closed Mondays and 29 December–3 January), tel: (0795) 23-2772

Footwork Computer Center
1992

Architect Itsuko Hasegawa
Address 475-3, Yashiro, Yashiro-chō, Kato-gun, Hyōgo Pref.
Transport From Ōsaka Station in Ōsaka City: Bus—Chūgoku or Shinki Highway (*Kōsoku*) Bus to Takino-Yashiro Interchange and 10 minutes by taxi

Located on an artificial green hill with parking beneath, the Footwork Computer Center welcomes the visitor with a large, double-glass-walled entrance passage that mirrors the surrounding small settlement and reflects the glow of the setting sun in a spectacular way. This system of transparent yet reflective screens acts both as a "protective boundary" of the courtyard behind, and also as an independent facade, or, rather, a "mask" in front of the building that stretches far back along the south side of the site.

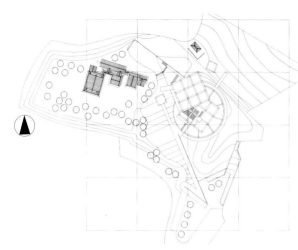

Museum of Literature, Himeji 1991

Himeji Bungakukan
Architect Tadao Ando
Address 84, Yamanoi-chō, Himeji, Hyōgo Pref.
Transport From JR Himeji Station: north exit and bus bound for Shosya Nishi Jūtaku to Ichinohashi-Bungakukan-mae and 10-minute walk to north
Visitation 10:00–17:00 (closed Mondays)

Dedicated to the work of the Japanese philosopher Tetsuro Watsuji, the Museum of Literature, Himeji exhibits material about writers primarily of this region. It is located closer to the city center of Himeji than Ando's previous two projects are, and has a commanding view of Himeji's famous medieval castle just .33 mile/500 meters to the northeast. Composed of two intersecting cubical volumes of 74 feet/22.5 meters to a side—one of which is wrapped around a large circular wall with 65.5-foot/20-meter diameter—the museum is delineated from the south by a shallow, cascading pool of water. Since the articulation of the building's geometric composition leaves ample spaces open to the outside, the visitor who walks around and within the complex can experience the presence of the water and the sight of the castle. Ando has employed, in addition to the structural concrete framework, walls, stairs, ramps, and bridges, a system of thin translucent screens onto which various photographic images are projected in the interior. These, along with the penetrating light-and-shadow effects, render the three-story gallery space not only dynamic but also poetically phenomenal.

Children's Museum Hyōgo, 1989

Hyōgo Kenritsu Kodomo no Yakata
Architect Tadao Ando
Address Sakurayama-Kohan, Himeji, Hyōgo Pref.
Transport From JR Himeji Station: north exit and bus for Kodomo no Yakata (25 minutes) and 5-minute walk
Visitation 9:30–16:30 (closed Tuesdays and last Sunday of each month), tel: (0792) 67-1153

First in a series of large-scale projects by Ando in Himeji, the Children's Museum Hyōgo is located outside urban areas, near hills, a lake, and plenty of greenery. Utilizing these ideal site conditions, the complex intends to introduce nature and natural phenomena for children to foster their artistic sensibilities. There are three major parts of the museum: the main building, a studio building, and an intermediary plaza. The main building features a library, indoor and outdoor theaters, gallery, multipurpose hall, and a restaurant. Facing directly onto the lake, the structure is shaped with ample, in-between, void spaces—walkways, a ramp, bridges, and a rooftop terrace—to absorb the environment as much as possible. There is also a surrounding system of shallow pools whose water cascades down the slope of the site. Far to the north, Ando designed a studio building where children can work on various projects without parental and material restraints. These two facilities are connected by a long walkway along a simple reinforced concrete wall that penetrates and defines the extensive site. The path is interrupted at midway by a small plaza with a "forest" of sixteen concrete columns on it. Resting at this intermediate plaza, visitors can observe the spectacular views that unfold around them.

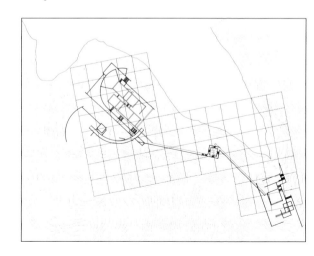

Children's Seminar House, Himeji 1992

Himeji Shiritsu Hoshinoko Yakata
Architect Tadao Ando
Address Sakurayama-Kohan, Himeji, Hyōgo Pref.
Transport From JR Himeji Station: north exit and bus bound for Kodomo no Yakata to Hoshinoko-kan stop (23 minutes) and 1-minute walk (10-minute walk from Children's Museum Hyōgo)
Visitation 9:30–16:30 (closed Tuesdays and last Sunday of each month), tel: (0792) 67-3050

The Children's Seminar House is situated in a rich natural environment, similar to that of the Children's Museum Hyōgo. Serving primarily as a lodging facility for children, the building is comprised of two volumes. The lower section has rooms for one hundred people, a restaurant, and other service facilities. The taller, towerlike block, set at forty-five degrees, includes a library, a meeting room, recreation space, and an astronomical observatory on top. Extensive stairways and a system of ramps provide both access to the building and places from which to observe the scenery. Adjacent to the structures, a cascading pool and a small, open amphitheater complement the composition. Ando's scheme, while carrying the typical elements and qualities of his highly acclaimed architecture, also displays some archaic features, alluding to the image of a fairy-tale castle, appropriate for children.

Angle 1988

Okano Shokuhin Kōjō
Architect Kunihiko Hayakawa
Address 391, Kokubunji, Mikunino-chō, Himeji, Hyōgo Pref.
Transport From JR Himeji Station: taxi to Okano Shokuhin Kōjō along Route 2; or from JR Himeji Station: Train to Gochaku Station (first stop) and 10-minute walk

This small commercial complex with buildings (restaurants, cafes, and shops) is arranged around an interwoven system of courtyard plazas. The attractive public facility, featuring reinforced concrete and colorfully painted steel structures, is part of the Okano Food Industrial Complex.

CHŪGOKU AND SHIKOKU (ISLAND) REGIONS

Occupying the southwest corner of the main Honshū Island, Chūgoku, like most other parts of the country, is primarily a mountainous region. Therefore, larger urban developments are located along the extensive south and north coastlines that face the beautiful Seto Inland Sea and Japan Sea respectively. This area has a slightly warmer climate than the regions discussed earlier: hot and humid summer, mild winter, with spring and fall remaining the most pleasant seasons. Today, among the cities of Chūgoku, which include Okayama, Kurashiki, Kure, Matsue, and Tottori, Hiroshima is the largest (1.1 million). Because of its destruction in World War II, and its current importance as an industrial and cultural center, it is also the Chūgoku Region's best known city abroad.

The region as a whole has always played a very important role in Japan's history, contributing significantly to the religious, cultural, industrial, and commercial achievements of the country. The second largest center of Shintō religion, the famous and monumental Izumo Taisha Shrine (established circa AD fifth century) is located here, in Shimane Prefecture. The celebrated Itsukushima Shrine compound (circa AD sixth century; rebuilt 1243), whose natural setting over a small bay of Miyajima Island is considered one of the most attractive sites by the Japanese, is near Hiroshima. Also in Hiroshima Prefecture, Onomichi, always an important center on the Inland Sea, is the location of many important ancient Buddhist temples, including Jōdō-ji (1192) with its famous *tahōto* pagoda.

Many of today's urban centers were famous feudal castle towns in the Edo Period (1603–1868); Matsue (1611) in Shimane Prefecture and Bitchū-Matsuyama (1684) in Okayama Prefecture still retain their original castle compounds, while in Hiroshima, Okayama, and Fukuyama, the castle donjons were destroyed in World War II, and were rebuilt. Hagi lost its castle upkeep in a fire in the late nineteenth century, yet it still boasts numerous old districts with rows of town houses along narrow streets, whose impressive Edo Era architecture reveals the atmosphere of the previous urban culture in the city. In a similar way, several well-preserved urban areas in many other smaller

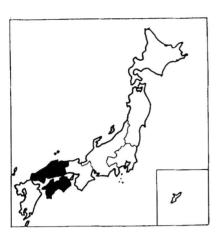

settlements, such as the merchant and market towns of Kurashiki, Takehara, Tsuwano, and Kurayoshi, also attest to the rich heritage of traditional architecture and urbanism in the region.

Contemporary architectural developments are, in general, concentrated around major urban areas. This is particularly evident in the case of the more industrialized southern coastal cities, but their counterparts in the northern part of the region have shown remarkable progress as well. The broad range of works found in Chūgoku includes more than a few outstanding examples of postwar Japanese architecture. Kenzo Tange's Hiroshima Peace Center, the first major architectural success in postwar Japan, was soon followed by other remarkable projects, even masterpieces, by both Tange and such leading architects at that time as Kiyonori Kikutake, Togo Murano, Takamasa Yoshizaka, and Shizutaro Urabe.

Later on, Kisho Kurokawa, Hiromi Fujii, and several younger-generation architects—Kazuhiro Ishii, Osamu Ishiyama, etc.—began to add to the increasing number of important contemporary architectural achievements. More recently, Ryōji Suzuki, one of the most innovative avant-garde designers, has completed two small but excellent projects on Sagi Island, near Mihara city, while Toru Murakami, who has established his practice in Hiroshima, is contributing to the architecture of the region with the growing volume of his unique, high-quality designs, primarily private residences. Furthermore, Shin Takamatsu, a native of Shimane Prefecture but now living and working in Kyōto, has extended his activities to the region by turning out public projects that are among his largest and, arguably, most innovative.

The smallest among the four main islands of Japan, Shikoku lies across the Seto Inland Sea. Because of its relative isolation, similar to that of Hokkaidō Island to the north, this region developed slower after the war than Honshū and Kyūshū islands. It used to be the area least frequented by tourists and foreign visitors. This is now changing rapidly, since the completion of the huge Seto Ōhashi Bridge system between Honshū and Shikoku at Sakaide in 1985. Today, there is direct vehicular and train connection to the rest of the country, particularly to the more industrialized areas of Honshū: Okayama, Kōbe, and Ōsaka. The situation will improve even further when a second bridge system is completed in a couple of years or so, linking Imabari on Shikoku with Onomichi and, further, Hiroshima on Honshū.

The island, apart from the extensive coastal regions, is occupied primarily by mountainous areas, although the ranges are not as high as their counterparts on Honshū or Kyūshū. The climate is generally warmer than that of the Kansai and Chūgoku regions of Honshū; summers are long and almost tropical, while winters have practically no snow. Springs and autumns are also warm. Shikoku is perhaps more exposed than most other parts of the country to typhoons that, coming from the southwest, pound the island, especially its southern shores, in late summer and early fall.

Shikoku is dominated by beautiful rural landscapes with several old villages and traditional small towns, such as Waki in Tokushima Prefecture and

Uchiko and Ōzu in Ehime Prefecture. One of the famous Shintō Shrine compounds and shrine towns (*monzen-machi*) of Japan, the Kompira-san (founded AD ninth century) in Kotohira, is located in Kagawa Prefecture. As a religious pilgrimage destination, it competes only with the famous eighty-eight-temple circuit that commemorates the great Buddhist monk and teacher, Kūkai (774–835), who was born on the island. His birthplace is marked by Zentsū-ji, a Shingon sect temple that he founded in 813 and that is the seventy-fifth one along the circuit. Remaining castles from previous feudal towns are found in Marugame (1660), Kōchi (1747), and Matsuyama (1854).

The majority of contemporary urban areas are located along the northern coastline, closest to the main island of Honshū. There are relatively fewer and smaller cities on Shikoku; they include Imabari, Niihama, Marugame, Tokushima, and the largest ones, Takamatsu and Matsuyama (population 450,000). Kōchi is the only important city in the southern part of the island. The number of outstanding postwar architectural examples is also proportionately less than in other regions, yet again the situation has been changing in recent years. The first significant projects after the war are Kenzo Tange's early but highly successful work. Born in Imabari, Ehime Prefecture, Tange designed his first buildings, the Ehime Civic Hall (1953) and Imabari City Hall and Public Hall (1958), in this area. Continuing the line of his work on the island, he completed the Kagawa Prefectural Office Building (1958) in Takamatsu, one of the masterpieces of modern Japanese architecture.

Later on, Kazuhiro Ishii's work on Naoshima Island and Itsuko Hasegawa's work in Matsuyama City added several important pieces of architecture to the slowly growing number of new projects in the region. The early 1990s have witnessed the completion of numerous exceptional projects by such outstanding architects as Tadao Ando, Hiroshi Hara, Toyo Ito, and Yoshio Taniguchi, as well as the talented young couple Akiko and Hiroshi Takahashi. These works should dispel any doubt in anybody seriously interested in the contemporary architecture of Japan, in regard to visiting Shikoku. Unquestionably, a trip here is to be amply rewarding.

市 OKAYAMA

YKK Okayama 1
1994
Architect Shin Takamatsu
Address 103-4, Nishi-ichi, Okayama, Okayama Pref.
Transport From JR Okayama Station: Train—JR Seto Ōhashi line to Bizen Nishi-ichi Station (second stop) and 10 minute walk to east (on the north side of Okayama bypass)
It is a small office building with a large glass facade.

Bank of Japan Okayama Branch Office
1922
Nihon Ginkō Okayama Shiten
Architect Uheiji Nagano
Address 6-1, Marunouchi 1-chōme, Okayama, Okayama Pref.
Transport From JR Okayama Station: Streetcar 4 stops and 2-minute walk
The bank is a two-story, stone building with four large Corinthian columns and classical pediment at the entrance.

Okayama Prefectural Art Museum, 1963
Okayama Bijutsukan
Architect Kunio Maekawa
Address 7-15, Marunouchi 2-chōme, Okayama, Okayama Pref.
Transport From JR Okayama Station: Streetcar 4 stops and 10-minute walk (three blocks to east, near the Prefectural Government Office and the Kōrakuen Gardens)
Visitation 9:30–16:30 (closed Mondays and between 28 December–2 January)

町 TAKEBE-CHŌ

Kindergarten with Fifty-four Roofs
1979
Takebe-chō Yōchien
Architect Kazuhiro Ishii
Address Ichiba, Takebe-chō, Mitsu-gun, Okayama Pref.
Transport From JR Okayama Station: Train—JR Tsuyama line to Takebe Station and 15-minute walk

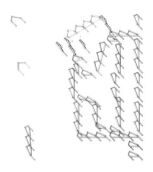

Takebe International House, 1990
Takebe-chō Kokusai Kōryūkan
Architect Osamu Ishiyama
Address 586, Sako, Takebe-Kamiaza, Takebe-chō, Ōtsu-gun, Okayama Pref.
Transport From JR Okayama Station: Train—JR Tsuyama line to Fukuwatari Station (one stop after Takebe Station) and 10 minute by taxi

Following his playful architectural study on the theme of the window in his House with Fifty-four Windows in Hiratsuka (1975) (see page 157), Ishii designed this school by using the idea of the roof. He selected one structural/formal element, a reinforced concrete frame with a gabled configuration, and incorporated it fifty-four times in his scheme. In so doing, he not only redefined the use, form, and meaning of this architectural element—that is, the roof along with its related facade—but also articulated it so as to comprise a miniature settlement, a "children's village." Providing a broad range of variations, the roof forms can signify individual buildings or rows of houses clustered around a semienclosed courtyard with playgrounds, the "urban" plaza of the "village." Ishii's playful design successfully recollects the essential attributes of vernacular architecture by which the building is surrounded, while simultaneously alluding to the imaginative world of children.

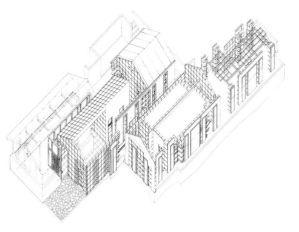

🚽 USHIMADO-CHŌ

Ushimado International Arts Festival Building 1985

Ushimado Kokusai Geijutsu-Sai Jimukyoku
Architect Hiromi Fujii
Address 496-1, Kiritani, Ushimado-chō, Oku-gun, Okayama Pref.
Transport From JR Okayama Station: south exit and bus bound for Ushimado-chō to Ushimado Terminal(2 hours) and 10 minutes by taxi

Despite its high-sounding name, the Ushimado International Arts Festival Building is a very small structure that houses only a tiny exhibition room, an office, and a snack bar/cafe, complemented by a semi-open terrace. The building boasts an exceptionally attractive site. Yet, beyond its location, the project is also a stunning piece of architecture, perhaps Fujii's finest to date. The design utilizes an old, traditional storehouse that was on the site by extending it through extruded and staggered volumes. Each volume steps out of or overlaps with the previous one while undergoing significant transformations. Along this process the material substance as well as the idea of an immutable architecture seem to erode approaching a void—that is, the empty stage of the terrace with a breathtaking view of Seto Inland Sea. In other words, Fujii, continuing his highly theoretical and rational structuralist operations that he calls "metamorphology," has repeatedly transformed the formal and spatial codes of the existing architecture to the extent that these codes are neutralized or lost, becoming only the traces of their origins. One might say that Fujii has deconstructed the old storehouse into something that is both analogous to a ruinous landscape like the Acropolis, and also evocative of an imperceptible realm of absence. This realm, less confined by the material world, is more open to the phenomenal one that surrounds it with an ineffable intensity.

Hall of Thirty-Three Meters, 1988

Architect Kazuhiro Ishii
Address 496-1, Kiritani, Ushimado-chō, Oku-gun, Okayama Pref.
Transport From JR Okayama Station: south exit and bus bound for Ushimado-chō to Ushimado Terminal (2 hours) and 10 minutes by taxi (in front of Festival Building)
The circular, wooden structure is a guest house for international visitors.

Nagi Museum of Contemporary Art 1994
Nagi-chō Gendai Bijutsukan
Architect Arata Isozaki
Address 441, Toyosawa, Nagi-chō, Okayama Pref.
Transport Train—JR Tsuyama line or JR Kishin line to Tsuyama Station and highway bus to Nagi-chō
Visitation Open daily, tel: (0868) 36-5811

Kurashiki International Hotel 1963
Kurashiki Kokusai Hotēru
Architect Shizutaro Urabe
Address 1-44, Chūō 1-chōme, Kurashiki, Okayama Pref.
Transport Train—JR Sanyō line or Shinkansen line to Kurashiki Station: south exit and 5-minute walk to southeast (along the road to Old Kurashiki City Hall)

Ōhara Art Museum, addition 1961
Ōhara Bijutsukan Shinkan
Architect Shizutaro Urabe
Address 1-5, Chūō 1-chōme, Kurashiki, Okayama Pref.
Transport Train—JR Sanyō or Shinkansen line to Kurashiki Station: south exit and 6-minute walk to southeast (near the Kurashiki International Hotel)

市 **KURASHIKI**

Kurashiki Ivy Square and Hotel 1974
Architect Shizutaro Urabe
Address 7-2, Hon-machi, Kurashiki, Okayama Pref.
Transport Train—JR Sanyō line or Shinkansen line to Kurashiki Station: south exit and 10 minutes by bus or 18-minute walk (9-minutes east of Old Kurashiki City Hall)

Shizutaro Urabe, who is a native of Kurashiki, used a Meiji Era (1868–1912) textile mill as the basis for his design of a new hotel facility. The old brick buildings have been completely remodeled, dismantling some of their parts while reorganizing others. Some of the existing structures have been removed to create two internal plazas: one, accessible through a large vaulted gate, is open to vehicles; the other, larger one is only for pedestrians. In other words, within the low-profile, pavilionlike hotel, a system of urban spaces was introduced thereby blending public and private realms in an attractive way. Much of the interior is articulated with decorative wooden structural elements, while the outside plazas are paved with tiles, brick, and stone yielded by the demolished sections. Today the walls are largely covered by ivy, giving the name to the place. The building is not only one of Urabe's most successful works, but also a fine example of a "contextual architecture" that came to the fore after the demise of the modernist design paradigm.

Kurashiki Civic Hall 1972
Kurashiki Shimin Kaikan
Architect Shizutaro Urabe
Address 17-1, Hon-machi, Kurashiki, Okayama Pref.
Transport Train—JR Sanyō line or Shinkansen line to Kurashiki Station: south exit and 10 minutes by bus or 20-minute walk (next to Kurashiki Ivy Square and Hotel)

Old Kurashiki City Hall (now Kurashiki Art Museum) 1960

Kyū Kurashiki Shichōsha
Architect Kenzo Tange
Address 6-1, Chūō 2-chōme, Kurashiki, Okayama Pref.
Transport Train—JR Sanyō line or Shinkansen line to Kurashiki Station: south exit and 8-minute walk to southeast

Following his first major internationally acclaimed work, the Hiroshima Peace Center (1955) (see page 249), Tange built numerous city halls within a government program that promoted the strengthening of public offices in Japanese cities. Tange completed his first such projects in Tōkyō and Kurayoshi (1957) (see page 253), then a year later in Takamatsu and Imabari (see pages 263 and 266). At this time Tange's work came under the influence of the ancient Japanese Jōmon Culture (10,000–300 BC), which, as the culture of lower classes, was characterized by a creative vitality and strength, yet also by a certain unrefined quality. Therefore, his works around 1960 were conceived in heavy and massive concrete forms, and with an explicit monumentality. The Old Kurashiki City Hall is an outstanding example of this type of architecture. It is dominated by huge, reinforced concrete structures and sturdy, precast concrete slabs. These slabs are attached to their frames in a way that, while emphasizing the horizontality of the structure, makes the building resemble the wooden-log-type (*azekura-zukuri*) architecture of the Shōsōin, the Imperial Repository of the Tōdaiji Temple in Nara (AD 752). Inside, the *béton-brut* expression continues, and it is clearly manifested in the articulation of the multistory lobby. The building eventually became inadequate in accommodating the expanding city government functions, and, after the completion of Shizutaro Urabe's New City Hall in 1980, it was converted into an art museum. At the same time, the surfaces were refinished with new cement mortar; this smoothed concrete diminishes the strength of Tange's design.

Kurashiki New City Hall 1980

Shin Kurashiki Shichōsha
Architect Shizutaro Urabe
Address 640, Nishi-naka-shinden, Kurashiki, Okayama Pref.
Transport Train—JR Sanyō line or Shinkansen line to Kurashiki Station: south exit and 10 minutes by bus or 15-minute walk to southeast (8-minute walk from Old Kurashiki City Hall)

Sagishima "RING" Guest House 1994

Ring; S.B.S. and YAS Company Guest House
Architect Ryōji Suzuki
Address Aza Onoura, Sunami Sugiura-chō, Mihara (Sagi Island), Hiroshima Pref.
Transport From JR Mihara Station: 10-minute walk south to the port: Ferry— Habu-Shōsen ferry to Sagi Island (25 minutes) and 5-minute walk north (along the road following the seashore)

The three-story wooden building is a small residential complex, with a public cafe and snack bar, owned by S.B.S. Company and used as a vacation lodge by the employees. The design is not only one of the latest by Suzuki, but also the most innovative, epitomizing his long evolving neo-avant-garde architecture. Particularly striking is the articulation of interior spaces as "gaps" that are dramatically yet poetically highlighted by intricate window openings and enhanced by the dynamic elements of unique stairways and bridges, along with the wooden structural system itself. When its second part is completed, the building will surround a *U*-shaped courtyard that faces the sea across the road.

Architect Ryōji Suzuki
Address 2535-11, Aza-Akaishi. Sunami Sugiura-chō, Mihara (Sagi Island), Hiroshima Pref.
Transport From JR Mihara Station: 10-minute walk to the port: Ferry—Habu-Shōsen ferry to Sagi Island (25 minutes) and 10-minute walk south, along the road following the shore
Visitation Private residence; seen only from the outside

A small private residence for a retired couple, the House at Sagi is located far from any beaten path, near the city of Mihara on the shore of a small island. The two-story structure is designed with a dense wooden framework, which is visible in most parts of the house, particularly on the second level, where it envelopes outdoor spaces, a rooftop terrace, and a balcony. The first floor is the residence of the owners, while the second level with two *tatami* rooms is reserved for guests. The plan is composed of two rectangular elements of different size, intersecting each other at forty-five degrees. A curving line is introduced in the orthogonal matrix by the upper edge of an independent facade wall along the front. The premises have ample but carefully designed openings toward the sea, which is opposite the road in front of the house. To balance the overwhelming horizontality of the water and the horizon, the wooden structural elements emphasize the vertical dimension. The applied mode of design, what Suzuki calls "experience in material," is an attempt to probe into the material reality of experience and, by way of the dynamics of movement, find the inseparable unity of the material and immaterial qualities of architecture.

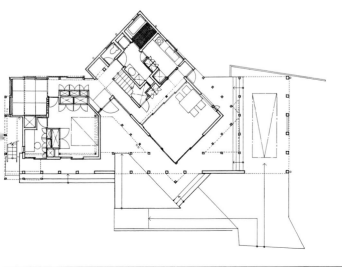

市 HIROSHIMA

1 World Peace Memorial
  Cathedral, page 248
2 Hiroshima Peace Center
  and Hiroshima Inter-
  national Conference
  Center, page 249
3 Hiroshima Art Museum,
  page 249
4 Motomachi and Chōjuen
  High-rise Apartment
  Blocks, page 250
5 Hiroshima City Museum
  of Contemporary Art,
  page 251

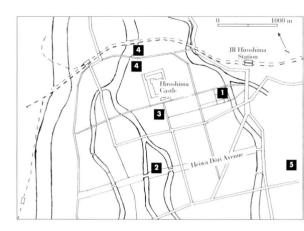

World Peace Memorial Cathedral 1953

Sekai Heiwa Kinen Seidō
Architect Togo Murano
Address 4-29, Nobori-chō,
Naka-ku, Hiroshima,
Hiroshima Pref. (see map)
Transport From JR Hiro-
shima Station: south exit and
10-minute walk

In his lengthy professional career extending from 1918 to the early 1980s,
Murano designed and completed more than 300 projects. Many of his works
are outstanding representatives of contemporary Japanese architecture. His
first major accomplishment after World War II, and one of his finest designs, is
the World Peace Memorial Cathedral. While it can be called a modern building
in general terms, there are many features or qualities of its architecture that
recollect various Western historic precedents. Comprised of two rectangular
volumes—a nave and a bell tower—this geometric composition is enhanced by
its exposed concrete post-and-beam frame with infill wall surfaces of rough
brick. The expressive mood created here is reminiscent of August Perret's
designs, but it also has a certain affinity with representatives of Nordic national romanticism. Other elements and details, particularly the dome over the
sanctuary, the roofs covering the circular chapels, and the window treatment,
are articulated with a feel for Byzantine architecture. The interior is simple and
its solemnity is reinforced by a spectrum of subdued light.

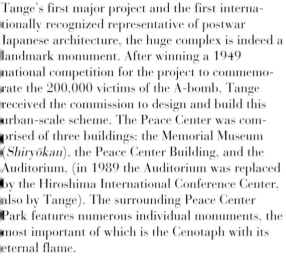

Tange's first major project and the first internationally recognized representative of postwar Japanese architecture, the huge complex is indeed a landmark monument. After winning a 1949 national competition for the project to commemorate the 200,000 victims of the A-bomb, Tange received the commission to design and build this urban-scale scheme. The Peace Center was comprised of three buildings: the Memorial Museum (*Shiryōkan*), the Peace Center Building, and the Auditorium, (in 1989 the Auditorium was replaced by the Hiroshima International Conference Center, also by Tange). The surrounding Peace Center Park features numerous individual monuments, the most important of which is the Cenotaph with its eternal flame.

Elevated on pilotis, the large horizontal volume of the Memorial Museum acts as the gateway to Peace Center Park. Cast solely in rough, exposed concrete with a skeletal presence, the structure, when built, resembled a burnt out, ruinous building like the Memorial Dome at the far end of the park. Tange combined the influences of Le Corbusier's plastic modern architecture with elements of traditional Japanese structures, particularly the *azekura-zukuri* style storehouse and *shinden-zukuri* style residential architecture, both characterized by their rather sturdy construction, horizontal disposition, and elevated floors over pilotis. In so doing, Tange also initiated a new trend in Japanese architecture which ruled the late 1950s and 1960s. This museum was renovated and its exposed surfaces refinished, thereby robbing the original architecture of some of its power.

Hiroshima Peace Center, 1955
Hiroshima Heiwa Kinen Kōen
Architect Kenzo Tange
Address Heiwa Kinen Kōen (Peace Center Park), Nakanoshima, Naka-ku, Hiroshima, Hiroshima Pref. (see map)
Transport From JR Hiroshima Station: south exit and streetcar to Heiwa-dōri and 8-minute walk to west; or 25-minute walk
Visitation Museum: 9:00–18:00 (May–November), 9:00–17:00 (December–April) (closed New Year's Day)

Hiroshima International Conference Center, 1989
Architect Kenzo Tange
Address Heiwa Kinen Kōen (Peace Center Park), Nakanoshima, Naka-ku, Hiroshima, Hiroshima Pref. (see map)
Transport From JR Hiroshima Station: south exit and streetcar to Heiwa-dōri and 8-minute walk to west; or 25-minute walk

Hiroshima Art Museum 1978
Hiroshima Bijutsukan
Architect Nikken Sekkei Co.
Address 3-2, Motomachi, Naka-ku, Hiroshima, Hiroshima Pref. (see map)
Transport From JR Hiroshima Station: south exit and streetcar to Kamiyachō stop and 5-minute walk north (south of Hiroshima Castle)

Motomachi and Chōjuen High-rise Apartment Blocks 1973

Hiroshima Motomachi to Chōjuen Danchi
Architect Masato Otaka
Address 16, 17, Motomachi, Naka-ku, Hiroshima, Hiroshima Pref. (see map)
Transport From JR Hiroshima Station: south exit and 10 minutes by bus to Motomachi (northwest of Hiroshima Castle)

These buildings are some of the most extensive urban developments in the city, and are excellent examples of late-Metabolist architecture. The high-rise blocks raised on pilotis form a zig-zag pattern along the Ōtagawa River and enclose the public facilities for residents: parks, playgrounds, schools, and shops. The structural and organizational systems of the residential blocks are similar to those of Kunio Maekawa's 1958 Harumi Apartments, block 15 in Tōkyō (see page 80), insofar as there is a primary structural steel two-story skeleton and a secondary concrete structure, arranged within the square modular zones of the primary system. Corridors are on every other level, where the elevators stop and from where stairs lead to the in-between levels. In spite of the large number of units, Otaka has infused the design with a sensible variety.

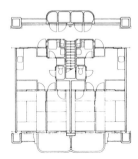
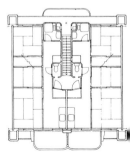

The museum, situated on the ridge of Hijiyama Hill, has been designed with great care to preserve the surrounding wooded areas. In order to keep the extensive program at a desirable height, more than half of the floor area is underground. Moreover, the above ground, longitudinally extruded wings frequently enclose open spaces wherein nature can penetrate the realm of architecture. In the center area, a circular plaza with a colonnade; it forms the public entry space. Other outdoor constructions include a system of ramps, a stone garden, and a stairway leading to the entrance. Everything is meticulously sculpted in materials as varied as roughly finished and highly polished stones, tile, and aluminum. This contemporary art museum is designed with numerous and varied architectural quotations that are filtered into the composition through important transformations, rendered as signs; they help Kurokawa achieve a subtle heterogeneity in design, what he calls an "architecture of symbiosis." Charles Jencks described the building as Kurokawa's "most mature and restrained work to date.... The Hiroshima Museum ... persuades one slowly, by stealth, without making any grand statements or propositions." (Charles Jencks, "Hiroshima Acropolis," in *Kisho Kurokawa: 1978–1989, Space Design* [June 1989]: 6)

Hiroshima City Museum of Contemporary Art 1988

Hiroshima-shi Gindai Bijutsukan
Architect Kisho Kurokawa
Address 1-1, Hijiyama Kōen, Minami-ku, Hiroshima, Hiroshima Pref. (see map)
Transport From Hiroshima Station: south exit and 8 minutes by taxi to Hijiyama Kōen (Park)
Visitation 10:00–17:00 (closed 29 December–3 January); tel: (082) 264-1121

Kure City Hall and Civic Center 1962

Kure Shichōsha and *Shimin Kaikan*
Architect Junzo Sakakura
Address 1, Chūō 4-chōme, Kure, Hiroshima Pref.
Transport From JR Hiroshima Station in Hiroshima: Train—JR Kure line to Kure Station: north exit and 8-minute walk

An excellent example of postwar modern Japanese architecture built within the governmental program to provide new municipal facilities across the country, the extensive complex consists of two major parts: the eight-story reinforced concrete, rectangular block of the city hall with the adjoining section of the assembly hall, and the large cylindrical volume of the civic center, whose softly curving but massive walls are covered with bluish-green mosaic tiles. The two parts are connected with an outdoor elevated platform directly accessible from the street and the small urban plaza in front. Sakakura was a disciple of Le Corbusier, whose influence can be traced in this project, insofar as the softly curving surfaces are remotely related to the forms of the Notre Dame du Haute in Ronchamp, France (1955).

🏙 **ASA-CHŌ**

Asa-chō Agricultural Cooperative Community Center, 1985
Asa-chō Nōkyō Chōmin Sentā
Architect Team Zoo— Atelier Zo
Address 1548-1, Ōaza-murō, Asa-chō, Asakita-ku,

Hiroshima Pref.
Transport From Hiroshima Station: Train—JR Kabe line to Aki-Imuro Station and 20-minute walk; or from Hiroshima Station: bus to Asahieigyōshō stop and 10-minute walk

市 TOTTORI

Tottori Prefectural Museum, 1972
Tottori Kenritsu Hakubutsukan
Architect Nikken Sekkei Company
Address 124, Higashi-chō 2-chōme, Tottori, Tottori Pref.
Transport From JR Kyōto Station in Kyōto City: Train—JR Sanin main line to Tottori Station: north exit and 15-minute walk or 5 minutes by taxi

Nifukaku House, 1907
Architect Tokuma Katayama and Heizō Hashimoto
Address 121, Higashi-chō 2-chōme, Tottori, Tottori Pref.
Transport From JR Kyōto Station in Kyōto City: Train—JR Sanin main line to Tottori Station: north exit and 15-minute walk or 5 minutes by taxi
The two-story, wooden building is an Important National Cultural Property.

市 KURAYOSHI

Kurayoshi City Hall 1957
Kurayoshi Shichōsha
Architect Kenzo Tange
Address 722, Aoi-chō, Kurayoshi, Tottori Pref.
Transport From JR Kyōto Station in Kyōto City: Train—JR Sanin main line to Utsubuki Station and 10-minute walk

One of Tange's first city hall projects, the four-story building is made of an exposed reinforced concrete post-and-beam skeletal structure, with a surrounding platform around the second floor and a balcony system around the fourth floor. The design is a forerunner of Tange's Kagawa Prefectural Office Building (1958) in Takamatsu (see page 263), a masterpiece by any standard.

市 KURAYOSHI

Kurayoshi Museum 1973
Kurayoshi Hakubutsukan
Architect Nikken Sekkei Company
Address 3-445-8, Nakano-chō, Kurayoshi, Tottori Pref.
Transport From JR Kyōto Station in Kyōto City: Train—JR Sanin main line to Utsubuki Station and 12-minute walk (2-minute walk from Kurayoshi City Hall)

市 SAKAIMINATO

Concert Hall in Sakaiminato 1994
Symphony Garden
Architect Shin Takamatsu
Address 2050, Nakano-chō, Sakaiminato, Tottori Pref.
Transport From JR Yonago Station: Train—JR Sakai line to Sakaiminato Terminal and taxi

---

Yonago Public Hall
1958

Yonago Kōkaidō
Architect Togo Murano
Address 61, Kakuban-chō 2-
chōme, Yonago, Tottori Pref.
Transport From JR Kyōto
Station in Kyōto City: Train—
JR Sanin line to Yonago
Station and 10-minute walk

There are several features that distinguish this project from other works by
Murano. The structural articulation is most pronounced here; the slanting concrete beams that support the spectators' seats in the auditorium cantilever
sharply from the front of the building, and the architecture is defined by the
slanting and slightly curving surfaces of the roof and the brick-covered walls.
At the lowest end of the roof the volume of the stage over the proscenium projects upward, thereby balancing the dynamic composition.

Hotel Tōkōen
1964

Architect Kiyonori Kikutake
Address 2-155, Kaike-Onsen,
Yonago, Tottori Pref.
Transport From JR Kyōto
Station in Kyōto City: Train—
JR Sanin line to Yonago
Station and 20 minutes by bus
bound for Kaike Onsen or 10
minutes by taxi

One of Kikutake's earliest and most powerful works, the Hotel Tōkōen is an
excellent representative of Metabolist architecture in the 1960s. The six-story
building is supported by an exposed reinforced concrete structural system,
whose articulation is reminiscent of some traditional wooden frame solutions
wherein the main posts are stabilized by interconnecting ones (*nuki*). Within
this large structural frame, Kikutake arranged the units of the prefabricated
guest rooms as if boxes on shelves, suggesting a flexibility or even interchangeability of the spatial units. While the lower floors are supported by the structural frame beneath them, the fifth and sixth floors are suspended from a pair
of enormous girders, leaving an open roof terrace above the third floor. The
interiors maintain an intimate relationship to the Japanese garden behind.

Kunibiki Messe, Convention Hall 1993

Shimane Kenritsu Sangyō Kōryō Kaikan—Kunibiki Messe
Architect Shin Takamatsu
Address 3-669, Nishikawatsu-chō, Matsue, Shimane Pref.
Transport Train—JR Sanin line to Matsue Station: north exit and 7-minute walk across Kunibiki Bridge

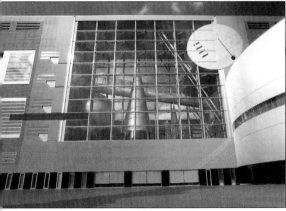

In the early 1990s Takamatsu introduced a new line of design. Prompted by the increasing scale of his commissions and an expanded design sensibility, many of his projects now feature large, "transparent," light-filled spaces and are less agitated by excessive detailings. The Kunibiki Messe is the most spectacular proof of the new direction's success. The composition is comprised of two adjoining simple rectangular volumes: a horizontal one for exhibitions, and a vertical one for offices. In addition, two cylindrical volumes contain multi-purpose spaces. The entire structure is shaped and/or wrapped in steel frame with stainless steel and aluminum panels; the facades are interrupted by flush-mounted glass windows. The most astonishing part of the design is a 79-foot/24-meter atrium space within the vertical block. Enclosed between two large glass walls this ethereal space features numerous geometric solids "floating" within. These volumes—cones, a globe, a horizontal oval cylinder, and a slanting glass tube—are constructed with an utmost precision and with the sensuality and "coolness" of space-age technology. Called by Takamatsu the "Garden of Abstract Forms," this atrium contributes greatly to the overall science-fiction quality of the architecture. The building is equally spectacular in the night, when lighting is both reflected on and emitted through the surfaces.

Shimane Prefectural Museum
1958
Shimane Kenritsu Hakubutsukan
Architect Kiyonori Kikutake
Address Tōno-machi, Matsue, Shimane Pref.
Transport Train—JR Sanin line to Matsue Station: north exit and 15 minutes by bus or 7 minutes by taxi

Shimane Prefectural Martial Arts Training Hall
1970
Shimane Kenritsu Budōkan
Architect Kiyonori Kikutake
Address Nakahara-chō, Matsue, Shimane Pref.
Transport Train—JR Sanin line to Matsue Station: north exit and 15 minutes by bus or 7 minutes by taxi (5-minute walk from Shimane Prefectural Museum)

Shimane Prefectural Library
1968
Shimane Kenritsu Toshokan
Architect Kiyonori Kikutake
Address 153, Nakahara-chō, Matsue, Shimane Pref.
Transport Train—JR Sanin line to Matsue Station: north exit and 15 minutes by bus or 7 minutes by taxi (3-minute walk from Training Hall or 7-minute walk from Shimane Prefectural Museum)

🏯 TAISHA-MACHI (IZUMO)
Izumo Shrine Office Building, 1963
Izumo Taisha Chonoya
Izumo Shrine Shinkōden Reception Hall, 1982
Izumo Taisha Shinkōden
Architect Kiyonori Kikutake
Address Kizukihara, Taisha-machi, Hikawa-gun, Shimane Pref.
Transport From JR Matsue Station in Matsue City or from Izumo Station in Izumo City: bus to Izumo Taisha Terminal and 12-minute walk
Visitation 8:30–16:30

The small buildings are within the compound of the famous Izumo Taisha Shrine (AD fifth century), second only to the Ise Shrine in importance for the Japanese within the Shintō religion. For this reason utmost care was taken in designing them. Replacing the previous wooden structure, which had burnt down in 1953, Kikutake's office building was constructed of prefabricated reinforced concrete elements. The primary structure is a pair of prestressed concrete beams, 165 feet/50 meters in length, supported by the rectangular shafts of the stairways at the two ends of the volume. The secondary structures of the slanting walls on the east and west sides lean against the beams, and are made up of louverlike concrete elements with stripes of glass between them. The overall design resembles the heavy roof structures of traditional architecture, yet the wall surfaces here are lacy and penetrated by light. The structural form also characterizes the interior space. Inside, an independent wooden mezzanine level increases the display and repository area where valuable archives are stored. The Shinkōden Reception Hall, facing the office building on the east side of the compound, is a much more traditional architectural design, highlighted by its large roof with softly curving surfaces.

Zeus, Nima Sand Museum
1990

Nima-chō Suna Hakubutsukan
Architect Shin Takamatsu
Address 975, Amagouchi,
Nima-chō, Nima-gun,
Shimane Pref.
Transport Train—JR Sanin
line to Nima Station and
8-minute walk west (along
Route 9)
Visitation 9:00–16:00 (closed
Wednesdays but open on
national holidays), tel:
(08548) 8-3776

The museum exhibits various materials related to sand and the sea. At the entrance there is an outdoor circular sandy "desert" followed by numerous scientific and historic displays. Some additional displays are also dedicated to the elucidation of the passing of time in the history of Earth. The museum is the first project that introduced Takamatsu's new line of designs characterized by simpler geometric forms and less decorative details than his earlier work. Partially inlaid in the sloping terrain, the unusual building is dominated by a long curving concrete wall in front, and two large and four small pyramidal structures of glass on top. Suspended under the sixty-nine-foot-/twenty-one-meter-high central glass pyramid is an enormous stainless steel mechanism with a one-year "hour glass" in it. In the basement Takamatsu designed a high-tech audio-visual auditorium lit by the second-largest pyramidal skylight, which can be completely closed by electronically operated blinds during slide shows. If one of the major purposes of the museum is to introduce the phenomenon of time to the visitors, Takamatsu has managed to choreograph for it an architectural setting that is timeless.

Nima Museum of Bohemian Art (MOBA)
1993
Architect Shin Takamatsu
Address 975 Amagouchi,
Nima-chō, Nima-gun,
Shimane Pref.
Transport Train—JR Sanin
line to Nima Station and
8-minute walk west (along
Route 9), adjacent to Zeus,
Nima Sand Museum

🜨 GŌTSU

Gōtsu City Hall
1962

Gōtsu Shichōsha
Architect Takamasa Yoshizaka
Address 1-525, Gōtsu-chō, Gōtsu, Shimane Pref.
Transport Train—JR Sanin line to Iwami Gōtsu Station and 3-minute walk (south of the train line)

The building consists of three parts, of which the office block is the most distinctive. The large-span, prestressed concrete structure is elevated above the ground on a pair of *A* pillars. This creates an open zone connected to a pine grove in front of the building and used as an entrance plaza. The other two parts of the building house conference rooms and the fire department.

🜨 HAMADA

Hamada Children's Museum
1995

Hamada-shi Sekai Kodomo Bijutsukan
Architect Shin Takamatsu
Address Nohara-chō, Hamada, Shimane Pref.
Transport Train—JR Sanin line to Hamada Station and bus to the Kodomo Bijutsu-kan Museum (near the seashore)

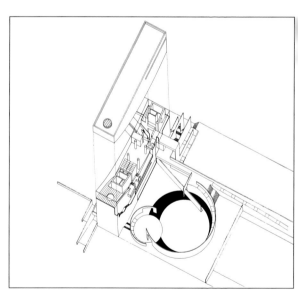

The first facility of an extensive "culture zone overlooking the sea," the Children's Museum accommodates two major programs: a museum/gallery in the upper part, and an atelier/creative center in the lower part. In between the two is a uniquely shaped, glass-walled atrium with wide stairways and a large, curving ceiling. The indoor activity places are complemented by outdoor ones, including a partially sunken performing area.

Hagi Civic Center 1968

Hagi Shiminkan
Architect Kiyonori Kikutake
Address 495-4, Emukai, Hagi, Yamaguchi Pref.
Transport Train—JR Sanin line to Higashi-Hagi Station and 8 minutes by taxi or 18-minute walk
Visitation 9:00–17:00

The Hagi Civic Center is the first of two major public buildings that form the city center of Hagi and were designed by Kikutake. The simple, large, rectangular volume houses two auditoria, conference rooms, a restaurant, a wedding ceremony room, and a small exhibition space, all accessible from an extensive lobby. The unusual exterior is derivative of the structural system behind it. The first floor is built of sturdy reinforced concrete walls. These walls support a light, steel space frame that, covered by metallic plates with white enamel finish, comprises the cantilevered upper section. The roofing is exposed completely to the spaces below, and accommodates myriads of small lighting fixtures in a radial configuration. The building was extended by Kikutake on its north side during the 1980s.

Hagi City Hall 1974

Hagi Shichōsha
Architect Kiyonori Kikutake
Address 510, Emukai, Hagi, Yamaguchi Pref.
Transport Train—JR Sanin line to Higashi-Hagi Station and 8 minutes by taxi or 18-minute walk (next to the Hagi Civic Center)
Visitation 8:30–17:00 on workdays

The Hagi City Hall is built on a site adjacent to the Hagi Civic Center. The careful arrangement of the two buildings defines a small civic plaza with some parking in front; the plaza in turn organizes the architectural elements into a coherent urban composition. The hall is laid out along a nine-square quadrilateral plan wherein steel posts mark the intersections of the grid. In order to provide extensive spaces for the citizen's reception halls on the first floor without frequent intermediary supports, the structural span is relatively large. This large span is made possible by a story-high steel lattice truss system, whose dark, metallic-plate-covered forms remind the observer of the impressively extensive roofs in traditional Japanese architecture. However, the structural frame of the "roof" here is not empty; constituting the second floor, it accommodates various departmental offices, the mayor's office, and conference halls.

Ube Public Hall 1937

Ube Shiminkan
Architect Togo Murano
Address 8-1, Asahi-chō, Ube, Yamaguchi Pref.
Transport Train—Sanyō Shinkansen line or JR Sanyō main line to Ogōri Station; change to Train—JR Ube line to Ube-Shinkawa Station and 5-minute walk; or Train—JR Sanyō line to Ube Station and bus or train to Ube-Shinkawa Station and 5-minute walk

🏫 YAMAGUCHI

Yamaguchi Civic Center 1971

Yamaguchi Shimin Kaikan
Architect Nikken Sekkei Company
Address 5-1, Chūō 2-chōme, Yamaguchi, Yamaguchi Pref.
Transport Train—JR Yamaguchi line to Yamaguchi Station and 10-minute walk to northwest (see page 21, figure 21)

A prewar masterpiece by Murano, this building is among the early representatives of modern Japanese architecture. The building is dedicated to Soko Watanabe, who developed Ube from a poor village to an industrial city; so the Ube Public Hall is also a memorial hall. Its symmetrical composition impresses one with its simple volumetric shapes; curving, brick-covered front facade; and six tall concrete pylons in front of the entrance plaza. The entrance hall and second-floor foyer have equally curving spaces whose simplicity is underscored by their sturdy cylindrical columns and their new and high-quality materials, including polished travertine and glass block. The huge auditorium features a large balcony and an undulating ceiling with a structure of uniquely shaped, reversed, coffered slabs with integrated lighting. The space was designed using the latest achievements in acoustics, and, in this regard, the building is the first of its kind in Japan. The quality of sound is excellent even today. The Ube Public Hall has recently been renovated, restoring its original architecture, including the high-quality detailing. It faces a large park and parking area to the south delimited by the tracks of the JR Ube railroad line.

⚓ NAOSHIMA-CHŌ (NAOSHIMA ISLAND)

Naoshima Municipal Gymnasium 1976
Naoshima Chōmin Taiikukan and *Budōkan*

Naoshima Municipal High School 1979
Naoshima Chōritsu Chūgakkō
Architect Kazuhiro Ishii (with Kazuhiko Namba)
Address 3601 and 1580, Naoshima-chō (Naoshima Island), Kagawa-gun, Kagawa Pref.
Transport From JR Okayama Station in Okayama City: Train—JR Uno line to Uno Port Terminal and Shikoku Ferry to Naoshima (20 minutes) and 10 minutes by bus

Part of a series of playfully investigative designs by Ishii in the late 1970s, the Naoshima Municipal Gymnasium and High School focus on a Western theme: the colonnade. The straightforward, rectangular volumes of the two main structures are lined and connected with an undulating row of small cubical elements that are reminiscent of the capsules Metabolist architects often used in their architecture. However, the emphasis of these capsules is not on their technological solution but, rather, on the language of architecture. The units are raised over pilotis that form a long, connected colonnade all along the buildings. This reinforced concrete structure plays out variations on the idea, role, and meaning of the column, with some solutions bordering on the joke; for example, at several places where a pair of columns are expected to be, only their broken bases and heads are provided. Equally playful is Ishii's articulation of the capsules; he varies their windows, replaces several with other elements, and removes some altogether. At the entrance to the training hall for traditional martial arts, a capsule is replaced by a gabled roof, similar to those seen on ancient Shintō shrines.

Naoshima Primary School 1970
Naoshima Shōgakkō

Naoshima Kindergarten 1974
Naoshima Chōritsu Yōji-Gakuen
Architect Kazuhiro Ishii (with Kazuhiko Namba)
Address 1841, Naoshima-chō (Naoshima Island), Kagawa-gun, Kagawa Pref.
Transport From JR Okayama Station in Okayama: Train—JR Uno line to Uno Port Terminal and Shikoku Ferry to Naoshima (20 minutes) and 10 minutes by bus (adjacent to Naoshima Municipal High School)

Naoshima Contemporary Art Museum 1992

Benesse House or *Naoshima Gindai Bijutsukan*
Architect Tadao Ando
Address Godanchi, Naoshima-chō (Naoshima Island), Kagawa Pref.
Transport From Okayama Station in Okayama City: Train—JR Uno line to Uno Port Terminal and Shikoku Ferry to Naoshima (20 minutes) and 10 minutes by taxi; or bus to Benesse Bunka-mura and 10-minute walk
Visitation 10:00–17:00, tel: (0878) 92-2030

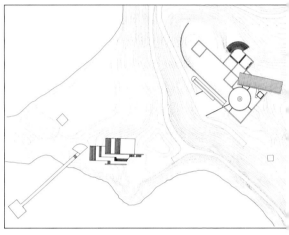

Naoshima Town Hall 1983

Naoshima-chō Yakuba
Architect Kazuhiro Ishii
Address 1122-1 Naoshima-chō (Naoshima Island), Kagawa-gun, Kagawa Pref.
Transport From JR Okayama Station in Okayama City: Train—JR Uno line to Uno Port Terminal and Shikoku Ferry to Naoshima (20 minutes) and 10 minutes by bus
Unlike Ishii's previous four projects in Naoshima-chō, this building was conceived in a more explicitly historicizing, postmodernist paradigm.

Located on sloping high grounds over the Seto Island Sea at the southern tip of Naoshima Island, the museum has a spectacular natural surrounding and a commanding view of the sea. The site can be approached also by boat, arriving at a small wharf. On the shore there is a stepped plaza, from which the visitor has to climb in order to reach the building. In order not to disturb the pristine landscape, Ando designed the reinforced concrete structure with half of its spaces underground. The main elements of the architectural parti are a two-story, rectangular, 164-by-26-foot/50-by-8-meter gallery and a large, cylindrical, top-lit main lobby with a diameter of 65.5 feet/20 meters; both of them have systems of long ramps. These two volumes intersect, thereby generating a varied spatial composition. A smaller, rectangular, two-story wing—housing ten guest rooms and a cafeteria, in addition to some service facilities—joins the parti at a slightly skewed angle.

TAKAMATSU

Kagawa Prefectural Office Building 1958

Kagawa Kenchōsha
Architect Kenzo Tange
Address 1, Ban-chō 4-chōme, Takamatsu, Kagawa Pref.
Transport From the Ferry Terminal in Takamatsu Port: 5-minute walk to JR Takamatsu Station and 10-minute walk to south

Unquestionably one of Tange's finest designs, this office building is a landmark in postwar modern Japanese architecture. Here Tange combined the virtues of Le Corbusier's exposed, reinforced concrete architecture with the structural clarity and elegance of traditional Japanese construction and structural form to achieve a synthesis between the present and the past. Composed of an eight-story quadrilateral office block and a longitudinal three-story auditorium and conference room block on pilotis, the complex soon became a prototype for similar public or governmental offices all over the country. In front, the pilotis shape the entranceway to the office block while providing from the street both good visibility of and accessibility to the attractive Japanese garden. This garden, with a pond, rocks, and gravel, is enclosed on two sides by the two wings.

The most impressive and innovative feature of the design is its structural/formal articulation. The concrete post and beam construction reinvents the simplicity of the rectangular wooden structural frame with a spatial quality that is as convincingly free flowing as its traditional counterpart. Enhancing the reference to historic solutions in Japan, Tange employed a system of balconies that surround the building on every level; like the engawa in the Japanese house, it both expands the interior and acts as an effective *brise-soleil.*

Kagawa Prefectural Gymnasium 1965
Kagawa Kenritsu Taiikukan
Architect Kenzo Tange
Address 18, Fukuoka-chō 2-chōme, Takamatsu, Kagawa Pref.
Transport From the Ferry Terminal in Takamatsu Port: 10-minute walk (first south then east).

Step 1980
Architect Tadao Ando
Address 9-1, Marugame-chō, Takamatsu, Kagawa Pref.
Transport From JR Takamatsu Station: 10-minute walk to south toward Kagawa Prefectural Office Building then east 3 blocks to shopping street (5-minute walk from Kagawa Prefectural Office Building)

Marugame Genichirō-Inokuma Museum of Contemporary Art 1991

Marugame Inokuma Genichirō Gendai Bijutsukan, or *MIMOCA*
Architect Yoshio Taniguchi
Address 80-1, Hamamachi, Marugame, Kagawa Pref.
Transport From JR Okayama Station in Okayama City: Train—JR Dōsan main line or Seto Ōhashi line to Marugame Station; or from Matsuyama and Takamatsu cities: Train—JR Yōsan main line to Marugame Station: south exit and few steps (on the west side of station plaza)
Visitation 9:30–17:00 (closed Mondays and 28 December–4 January), tel: (0877) 24-7755

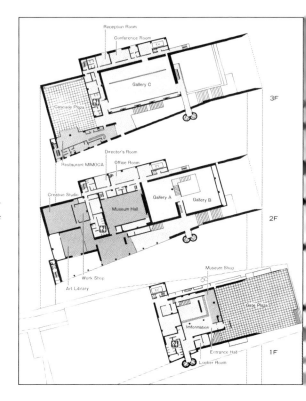

The museum is not only one of Taniguchi's largest works to date, but it is also one of his best. It was built as part of the city's ninetieth anniversary activities, and is dedicated in large part to the work of the internationally known modern painter Genichirō Inokuma, who spent much of his youth in the city, graduating from Marugame High School in 1921. Standing at the west edge of the station plaza, Taniguchi's building distinguishes itself with its powerful design that reinterprets the best legacies of modern architecture in both vocabulary and rationality of conception. Perhaps even more importantly, the overall scheme impresses the observer with its highly elegant response to the urban site. The simple volume of the three-story structure is articulated so as to continue the various activities and events that take place on the busy station plaza, while simultaneously providing the architectural definition of the large urban place. The gatelike front facade, with an extensive, free-standing, white wall featuring a mural by Inokuma, is recessed under the deep canopy of the protruding

flat roof, and, in between the two, equally deep, flanking sidewalls. This arrangement has assured a semi-covered entrance plaza, which, as the transformed continuation of the public square in front, acts as a stage for urban art. This cavernous intermediary space extends further in a long and wide stairway that, running through the building longitudinally like a stepped tunnel, reaches the Cascade Plaza, a public rooftop terrace with an outside cafe, and a curtain of cascading water on one of the four enclosing walls, on the third floor, at the opposite side of the museum. This stairway and its penetrating public space, in effect the transformed extension of the city within the realm of the building, provide access to such facilities as the museum hall, creative studio, art library, and workshop. The shaping of the interior spaces of the galleries on three floors are equally simple and elegant, and their qualities are vastly enhanced by the intricate introduction of diffused natural light.

Imabari City Hall and Public Hall
1958

Imabari Shichōsha and *Kōkaidō*
Architect Kenzo Tange
Address 4-1, Bekku-chō 1-chōme, Imabari, Ehime Pref.
Transport Train—Yōsan main line to Imabari Station: east exit and 2-minute walk

The two buildings of exposed reinforced structure, both oriented in the north-south direction, surround a public plaza on its two sides. In this way, the in-between urban space is open to the nearby bay and the port of Imabari, the city in which Tange was born. To the west, the three-story City Hall displays the geometric pattern of a latticelike concrete sun-shading device (*brise soleil*), behind which the facade is deeply recessed. The Public Hall to the north, employing a "folded" wall construction with a roof of 88.5-foot/26.6-meter span, has a monumental volume. This civic complex is one of Tange's most impressive early architectural and urban designs.

🏛 MATSUYAMA

Tokumaru Children's Clinic
1979

Tokumaru Shōnika
Architect Itsuko Hasegawa
Address 6-25, Ichiban-chō 1-chōme, Matsuyama, Ehime Pref.
Transport From JR Matsuyama Station: street car to Ōkaidō stop and 2-minute walk

Ehime Civic Hall
1953

Ehime Kenminkan
Architect Kenzo Tange
Address Horinouchi, Matsuyama, Ehime Pref.
Transport From JR Matsuyama Station: east exit and Street car 3 stops to Ehime-kenminkan stop
The partially circular structure is covered by a large dome.

Aono Building
1982

Architect Itsuko Hasegawa
Address 3-7, Chifune-chō
4-chōme, Matsuyama, Ehime
Pref.
Transport From JR Matsu-
yama Station: 5-minute walk

The multistory urban infill building, which replaced an old structure on the same site, is a mixed-use project with a music shop on the first floor, furniture store on the second, eye clinic on the third, music school on the fourth, and small concert hall on the fifth; the sixth and seventh levels are occupied by the owner's residence, complemented with a rooftop terrace. The building, located in a busy commercial area of the city, features an oxidized-aluminum-clad, delicately shaped facade with a pattern that looks like the silhouette of a building imprinted on its surface. The form of a gabled roof on part of the top denotes the presence of a "house." Much attention was paid to the residence to assure privacy in the functionally complex building. Natural illumination from sky lights and the terrace makes the dwelling bright and cheerful, even though the depth of the building is significant. The Aono Building is one of the first designs in which Hasegawa considered the nature of large urban structures in the contemporary city.

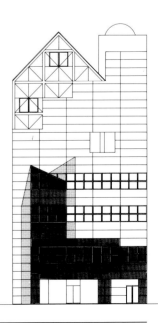

House at Kuwahara
1980

Architect Itsuko Hasegawa
Address 8-50, Kuwahara-chō
5-chōme, Matsuyama, Ehime
Pref.
Transport From JR Matsu-
yama Station: walk 4 minutes
east to Iyo Yokogawara
Ōtemachi Station: Train—Iyo
Yokogawara line to Fukuonji
Station and 3 minutes by taxi
(near Kuwahara-dera Temple)
Visitation Private residence;
seen only from the outside

The residence of a construction material dealer, the House at Kuwahara, upon its owner's request, was designed utilizing a broad range of materials from his dealership. These materials include steel elements, aluminum sheets, perforated metallic screens, glass block, and highly polished stone. The house has thus become a sort of showcase of these parts and related technologies, yet—in agreement with Hasegawa's design sensibility—without the need or even the possibility to synthesize them into some harmonious whole. Within the simple, gable-roofed volumes of the one- and two-story adjoining structures, recollecting a prototypical house with its "primitive" vernacular, all constituent elements have self-proclaimed independence as they are collaged into numerous surfaces, thin structures, and screens of different density. For example, the placement of the flush-mounted, various sized windows disregards the modular network of the aluminum panels, while steel diagonal braces cross within the openings of the porch and even the sliding glass doors. As such episodes abound, the house acquires not only some unpremeditated quality, but also a liberated, emotional, or "natural" predisposition.

ITM Building in Matsuyama 1993

Ichi-Roku Kaisha Biru
Architect Toyo Ito
Address 228-1, Higashi Ishii-chō, Matsuyama, Ehime Pref.
Transport From JR Matsuyama Station: 15 minutes by taxi to south on Road 33 (325 feet/100 meters east from the intersection of Road 33 and Ono River)
Visitation Open daily during working hours; tel: (0899) 57-0017

The ITM Building continues the line of Ito's recent small office buildings in which he pursues a simplicity of form and construction and the use of ordinary, mainly ferrous materials in conjunction with glass to achieve opacity and phenomenal lightness. Ito has designed the outer skin of this building with highly polished, corrugated aluminum panels, except for the three-story elevation that looks over two old houses next door, merely some three feet away. Here the wall is made entirely of glass. This large, virtually uninterrupted surface has been covered by a milk-white film to limit the influx of ultraviolet light. Behind this delicate, translucent screen there is a three-story atrium, whose space is connected directly to the entrance hall and the offices on each level. In this way the intricately modulated yet continuous interior is washed in soft, diffused light filtered through the large opaque glass wall. At the same time, the outside world, as if projected in the movies, emerges on this screen, but out of focus, diffused, and, as the shadowy silhouette of the two adjacent houses, tamed and rendered merely as a mirage.

The main facade softly curves as it tightly follows the path of a canal. On its other sides, the building is covered up by closely built residential structures from which only the narrow northwest entrance elevation emerges.

▣ UCHIKO-CHŌ

Ōse Secondary School
1992

Uchiko Chōritsu Ōse Chūgakkō
Architect Hiroshi Hara
Address 1328, Ōse 1-chōme, Uchiko-chō, Kita-gun, Ehime Pref.
Transport From JR Matsuyama Station: Train—JR Yōsan line to Uchiko Station and JR bus to Ōse (20 minutes)

The school is located in a luscious green valley, east of the small, well-known, traditional town of Uchiko. Responding to the spectacular setting, Hara designed the basic scheme as a cluster of three, elongated, parallel volumes that climb the sloping site at the northern foot of a densely wooded hill. These three sections enclose several long courtyards among them. Open stairways, covered walkways, arcades, terraces, a steel bridge, and "public" plazas help to form these attractive outdoor spaces. In addition, there are two large cylindrical volumes; the one to the east is the music room, while the smaller one in the southwest corner contains the art studios. The block occupied by the staff room, the principal's office, and other service facilities is located at the west end, near the entry to the compound.

The school comprises a terraced composition in which each layer of indoor and outdoor spaces occupies a level higher than the one before. Constructed largely of exposed reinforced concrete with many repetitive elements, the building displays a sensible unity. At the same time, as a result of Hara's sensitive articulation of the numerous components, the complex also appears as a system of individual, yet interconnected, architectural units. Almost like a small urban enclave, the school impresses the visitor most with its capacity to provide a range of intimate spaces with various internal foci, while remaining open to the outside, incorporating as many aspects of nature as possible.

KŌCHI

Sakamoto Ryōma Memorial Hall 1991

Kōchi Kenritsu Sakamoto Ryōma Kinen-kan
Architect Akiko and Hiroshi Takahashi
Address 830, Shiroyama, Urado, Kōchi, Kōchi Pref.
Transport From JR Marugame Station in Marugame City: Train: JR Dosan line to Kōchi Station: bus bound for Katsurahama to Katsuramatsukaku-mae stop (40 minutes) and 3-minute walk
Visitation 9:00–16:30 (closed 26 December–1 January)

The young couple Akiko and Hiroshi Takahashi were both students of Kazuo Shinohara while he was teaching at Tōkyō Institute of Technology. This competition-winning project of theirs reveals the influence of their master, yet not in any direct or formal way. This is an important achievement in that its design is articulated with a certain simplicity and an ability to directly respond to the given and perceived conditions of the would-be architecture. It is largely devoid of both dogmatic restrictions of any kind and of the now fashionable tendencies of image making. The site of the hall, south of Kōchi City, is on a high rim, overlooking the Pacific Ocean below; the designers took maximum advantage of this unique setting. In order to incorporate the presence of the infinite water and sky, the long volume of the exhibition hall is extensively cantilevered. The steel structure supported by internal suspension cables is covered by half-mirror glass that, from the outside, reflects the panorama, while from the inside it provides unrestricted views. There is a feeling of remarkable lightness that emanates from this design both inside and out. This long space with a level of small galleries in it is approachable by a covered ramp, whose long, boxlike structure is attached to the main volume at a skewed angle, is an integral part of the architectural parti. The roof terrace acts as an observation deck under an undulating canopy. This outstanding piece of architecture is the first work of the designers. (See also page 31, fig. 48.)

KYŪSHŪ AND OKINAWA REGIONS

Kyūshū is the third largest and southernmost of the four main islands of Japan. The majority of the land, like that of most other regions, is covered by mountains, many of them active volcanoes, such as Aso, Unzen, Kirishima, and Sakurajima. The climate in Kyūshū is similar to, yet even warmer than, that of Shikoku Island: mild and short winter with practically no snow, and long, hot, and humid summer; the southern part is rather Mediterranean. Spring and fall are complemented by the rainy season in May and the season of typhoons in September. In terms of historic significance, culture, industry, and economy, the region follows only Honshū, the main island, although it does so only at a sensible distance.

Kyūshū has always been a gateway to Japan. Foreign influences from the continent since prehistoric times arrived at the shores of this island. First came the Chinese and Korean civilizations, bringing Buddhism in the sixth century, then, in the thirteenth century, Mongol armadas made attempts to invade Japan off the coast at present-day Fukuoka, but finally failed because a strong typhoon, the "divine wind" (*kamikaze*), destroyed their fleet. In the sixteenth century the first Europeans, mainly Portuguese and Spanish traders accompanied by missionaries, landed near Kagoshima; beyond trying to spread Christianity, they introduced firearms as well as elements of Western knowledge to Japan. During the centuries of isolation from the rest of the world in the Edo Era (1603–1868), it was only in Nagasaki that the Dutch were allowed to maintain a small trading post. Then, after opening the country once again in the mid-nineteenth century, Kyūshū was among the first regions to welcome foreign visitors and residents. Nagasaki, therefore, is also among the places where the first examples of Western architecture in Japan were built, of which several remain extant.

Although the number of historic monuments documenting the region's past is rather small, there are a few that could be mentioned. In Kyūshū, as in other parts of Japan, there were numerous castles and castle towns, yet, with the exception of Kumamoto, they were small and today only a few are extant. The castle in Kumamoto (1607), while one of the largest in the country, is only a

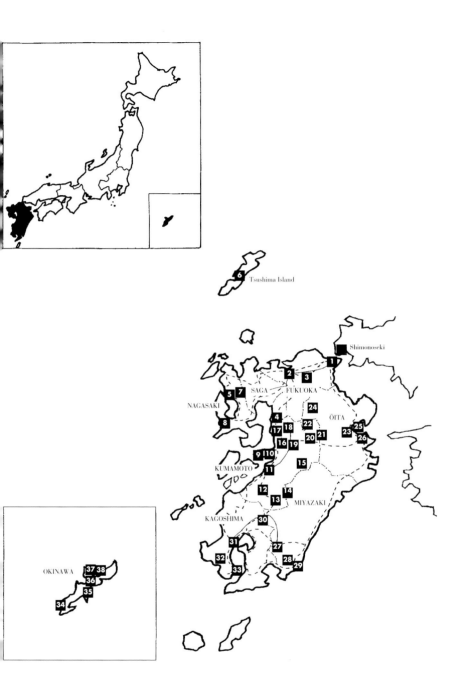

Tsushima Island

Shimonoseki

SAGA   FUKUOKA

NAGASAKI

ŌITA

KUMAMOTO

MIYAZAKI

KAGOSHIMA

OKINAWA

recent reconstruction of the original, which was destroyed in the 1877 Satsuma Rebellion. More remains, however, of the numerous, traditional towns, of which Nagasaki is both the largest and most famous; its fame today nevertheless is more associated with the tragic fate of becoming the site of the second A-bomb dropped on Japan in 1945. Other small, rural settlements with well-preserved, old districts are Arita, famous for its chinaware; Chiran, with numerous attractive samurai residences (*buke-yashiki*) and gardens; and Obi, a small, castle town.

The most popular stroll garden in the region, with a national reputation, is the Suizenji Kōen (1632) in Kumamoto. Buddhist temples and Shintō shrines are of course aplenty, yet only a few, such as the Usa Shrine (circa AD 720), the Dazaifu Tenmangū Shrine (rebuilt 1583) and Kanzeon-ji Temple (AD 746) in Dazaifu, and the Kōfuku-ji (1620) and Sōfuku-ji (1629) temples in Nagasaki, have historic significance. In Kyūshū, there are several ancient burial mound (*kofun*) sites as well, and Kumamoto Prefecture features a few near Kaō-machi.

While outstanding traditional architectural examples remain limited in number, contemporary ones are not in short supply in Kyūshū. As one of the regions where modernization and Westernization began soon after the country's opening in the late nineteenth century, Kyūshū took an early lead in industrialization and urbanization. Today the largest urban areas include Fukuoka (1.2 million), Kitakyūshū (1.02 million), Kumamoto (0.61 million), Kagoshima (0.53 million), and Nagasaki (0.44 million), with additional, though somewhat smaller, cities of Ōita, Miyazaki, and Sasebo.

This island was the first to be connected to the main island of Honshū by means of trains and vehicular traffic, both in tunnels under the sea and, later, by bridge; the huge Kaimon Ōhashi was completed in 1973. Today the Shinkansen super-express train also connects the two islands. Because of all these developments, the megalopolitan sprawl that initially extended from Tōkyō to only Ōsaka now stretches as far as Fukuoka. Thus, this northern part of Kyūshū is the most urbanized area in the region. With its fast progress in the past two decades—with such urban-scale developments as Seaside Momochi, Nexus Kashii, and the new Hakata Bayside projects—Fukuoka has by now acquired the status of an international city.

Nevertheless, Fukuoka is by no means alone in this respect; in the mid-1980s, Kumamoto launched one of the most uniquely innovative urban projects in Japan's postwar history. Upon the initiatives of Morihiro Hosokawa, then governor of Kumamoto Prefecture, and with the help of Arata Isozaki as commissioner, a large number of selected Japanese and foreign architects began working on the still on-going Kumamoto Art Polis (K.A.P.). What makes this *public* project unique is the mode in which the officials, organizers, and "planners" set out to promote high-quality public architecture and a new contemporary urban culture not only in Kumamoto City, but also throughout Kumamoto Prefecture. The vast majority of new public complexes has been designed for various small urban, and even smaller rural areas, to act as catalysts in a process of improving the quality of the built environment. The success of the already completed numerous pieces of architecture—often genuine masterpieces—as well as various structures—bridges, parks, public toilets, and dam and tunnel facilities—proves that the profit accumulated during the economic boom in the 1980s has been, and still is, well spent here.

Apart from the scores of well-known designers working within the Kumamoto Art Polis program—Tadao Ando, Toyo Ito, Kazuo Shinohara, Shōei Yoh, Team Zoo—Atelier Zo, Kazuhiro Ishii, Riken Yamamoto, Kunihiko Hayakawa, Kazuyo Sejima, and Yasumitsu Matsunaga—there are many more who have been active in Kyūshū from early times on. Kenzo Tange, Kiyonori Kikutake, Fumihiko Maki, Seiichi Shirai, Hiromi Fujii, Kisho Kurokawa, Itsuko Hasegawa, Hiroshi Hara, and Atsushi Kitagawara have all completed significant works on this island. Shōei Yoh is based in Fukuoka and has completed numerous projects not only in his hometown, but also in other parts of Kyūshū. Yet, the one architect who has done most for the cause of contemporary architecture here is Arata Isozaki. A native of Ōita City, Isozaki designed his first and startlingly powerful avant-garde projects for the cities of Ōita, Fukuoka, and Kitakyūshū, in the 1970s. Many of them are now among the most important representatives of modern Japanese architecture. Today an internationally accomplished architect with a growing number of celebrated buildings in the United States, Australia, Spain, and other countries, Isozaki continues to work for his homeland of Kyūshū with several major projects finished recently, or currently under construction.

Often called the "Hawaii of Japan," this southernmost region is more than 400 miles/600 kilometers south of Kagoshima. This tropical region, also known as Ryūkyū Islands, has its own distinct culture and unique dialect. The largest island is Okinawa-jima, which is about 68 miles/110 kilometers long and has an area of 458 square miles/1,185 square-kilometers. The annual average temperature here varies between sixty-one degrees Fahrenheit in January and eighty-three degrees in July. There are many beautiful, white sandy beaches and coral seas all around, while the hilly island is filled with tropical plants, such as palm trees and sugar cane.

Although the race and folklore of Okinawa have common origins with those of Japan, Okinawa was an independent kingdom until it became a domain of the Satsuma Clan of Kagoshima, and, in effect, a colony of Japan in 1609, during the Tokugawa Shōgunate (1603–1868). A strategic stronghold of the Japanese during the last years of World War II, Okinawa was eventually occupied by the advancing American forces; in the fierce battles nearly 250,000 Okinawans, Japanese, and Americans died, of which some 150,000 were civilians. American occupation here lasted until 1972, when the island was returned to Japan. Today an American military base remains in Okinawa, as it does in many other parts of Japan.

Largely because of the devastation inflicted upon the island in 1945, few original historical monuments are extant. What can be seen today are ruins like those of Shuri, the ancient royal city and castle (fifteenth century), and the

Nakagusuku (circa 1450) and Nakijin (fourteenth century) castles. One can also visit recent postwar reconstructions, including Kankai-mon, the magnificent gate (fifteenth to sixteenth century) to Shuri Castle, the Hōshō-kyō Bridge and Sō-mon Gate of Engaku-ji Ato, the memorial temple (1492) of the second Shō Dynasty kings, and some others. Nevertheless, there are many outstanding examples of traditional Okinawan houses built of wood and surrounded by either high hedges or wonderful, stone enclosures. One of the best preserved such structures is the Nakamura-ke, a mid-eighteenth-century farmhouse at the outskirts of Naha.

On Okinawa, the only major urban area is centered on Naha, the lively capital city of the prefecture. Significant pieces of contemporary architecture are similarly scarce, although some of them are among the major accomplishments of Japanese constructions of the 1975 Okinawa Marine Expo, held on Motobu Peninsula, some 31 miles/50 kilometers north of Naha. Several of the major pavilions or structures, like the Aquapolis, have been retained and are open to the public. Among the prominent architects who have completed buildings in Okinawa are Tadao Ando, Kiyonori Kikutake, Kisho Kurokawa, Fumihiko Maki, Hiroshi Hara, Team Zoo—Atelier Zo, and Shōei Yoh.

市 KITAKYŪSHŪ

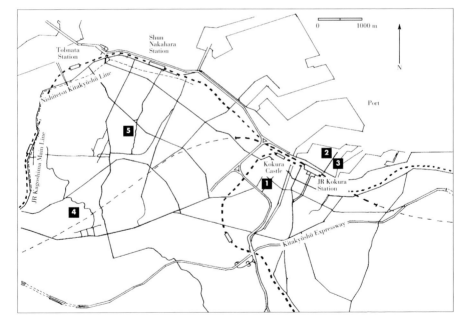

1 Kitakyūshū Central Library, page 277
2 West-Japan Exhibition Center, page 278
3 Kitakyūshū International Conference Center, page 279
4 Kitakyūshū City Museum of Art, page 280
5 West-Japan Industrial Club, page 280

Kitakyūshū Central Library 1975

Kitakyūshū Shiritsu Chūō Toshokan

Architect Arata Isozaki
Address 4-1, Jōnai, Kokura, Kita-ku, Kitakyūshū, Fukuoka Pref. (see map)
Transport From JR Kokura Station: south exit and 10-minute walk (entrance opposite to Kitakyūshū City Hall across a multi-lane road, south of Kokura-jō Castle)

Following the design of his Fujimi Country Clubhouse in Ōita (1974) (see page 314), the Kitakyūshū Central Library is derivative of cylindrical forms. Here the plan is generated by two curving, extruded volumes finished with copper-covered semicircular barrel vaults. The first volume, bent only once, houses the library, while the adjoining volume, bent twice, accommodates a historical museum. The two comprise an *L*-shaped configuration that defines a public plaza leading to the entrance of the complex. The walls of the building are constructed of reinforced concrete, and the roofs of a series of pairs of precast concrete panels, which are connected to each other at the top. The ribs of these panels are exposed to the spaces below, which generates an attractive rhythm inside and—where the space curves and the ribs run into a central cluster—an image of the ribbed structures in Gothic cathedrals. Historical quotations appear at several other places in the project. The barrel vault itself is reminiscent of Boullée's 1780 project for the National Library in Paris; the circular rose window is a mandala created by the Japanese philosopher Baien Miura; and in the undulating external forms of the restaurant one can discover one of Isozaki's favorite design motifs from the 1970s, the "Marilyn Monroe curves."

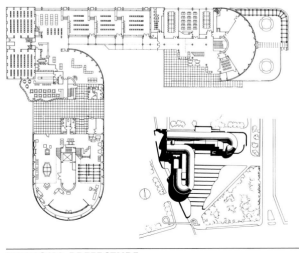

West-Japan Exhibition Center 1977

Nishi Nippon Sōgō Tenji-jō
Architect Arata Isozaki
Address 3-7-1, Asano, Kokura, Kita-ku, Kitakyūshū, Fukuoka Pref. (see map)
Transport From JR Kokura Station: north exit and 8-minute walk north

The West-Japan Exhibition Center occupies part of a previous port now being redeveloped. Its design was led by the architect's strong intention to relate the structure to the water. As Isozaki said, he wanted "to fill the building with metaphors of water." To this end he devised a unique suspension structure with rows of steel masts and slanting cables that is capable of bridging the large-span spaces while evoking the images of a group of sailboats resting at the port or the steel frames of a long-span bridge. At the same time these naked structural elements blend into the industrial environment replete with cranes, oil tanks, refineries, and warehouses. Moreover, the articulation of the plan and many details of the building is reminiscent of a large ship; one end of the long complex boasts a curving facade that recollects the captain's command post and bridge. Finally, Isozaki wanted to create, inside the large spaces, the feeling of being under water, as if looking up at the sparkling surface. He originally designed the roof with a thin, wavy covering, but for budgetary reasons this had to be abandoned. Instead he arranged a shallow pool of water in the courtyard between the office block and the exhibition halls to give the illusion that the building, like a ship, was adrift.

The Kitakyūshū International Conference Center stands at the wharf on the sea front. Isozaki's project continues his West-Japan Exhibition Center both literally and figuratively; the 600-seat conference hall wing of the complex mirrors the tract, width, height, and curving facade of the West-Japan Exhibition Center. The roof structures of the complexes, however, are different. While both relate to the notion of water, the roof over the conference center takes the undulating shapes of huge waves, cast in a 5-inch/12.8-centimeters thick, reinforced concrete shell and covered by corrosion-resistant metallic sheets. The other wing of the conference center features small meeting rooms and offices and is centered around an eight-story "leaning" tower. According to Isozaki, as the wavy roof accounts for the sea, the tower represents a ship that sails on it. The colorful composition is laid out along two axes: one defined by the exhibition center, the other by the edge of the waterfront. Isozaki's scheme takes advantage of the tension created by the shifting axes to form a dynamic architecture.

Kitakyūshū International Conference Center 1991
Kitakyūshū Kokusai Kaigi-jō
Architect Arata Isozaki
Address 3-9-30, Asano, Kokura, Kita-ku, Kitakyūshū, Fukuoka Pref. (see map)
Transport From JR Kokura Station: north exit and 8-minute walk north (across the road from West-Japan Exhibition Center)

Kitakyūshū City Museum of Art, 1974 addition, 1986

Kitakyūshū Shiritsu Bijutsukan
Architect Arata Isozaki
Address 21-1, Nishi-Sayaga-dani-chō, Tobata-ku, Kitakyū-shū, Fukuoka Pref. (see map)
Transport From JR Kokura Station: south exit and Street-car—Nishitetsu Kitakyūshū line to Edamitsu Station and 5 minutes by taxi or 25-minute walk east uphill; or 15 minutes by taxi from JR Kokura Station
Visitation 9:30–17:00 (closed Mondays); tel: (093) 882-7777

Outside of the densely built central urban area of Kitakyūshū, this museum occupies a hilltop among a rolling landscape and has a commanding view particularly toward the north, the direction of the city and its port. Designed within an orthogonal geometry, the first stage of the main gallery of 1974 is dominated by a pair of horizontally laid, large, tubular volumes with extensive cantilevers on both north and south sides. These 200-foot/60-meter structures, each with an identical square section and covered with die-cast aluminum panels, seem to float over their base structure of exposed reinforced concrete. The scheme is reminiscent of Isozaki's visionary project, the "City in the Air" (1961) (see page 20, fig. 19). Beneath the "flying tubes" the multistory entrance hall is rendered in white marble, with die-cast aluminum surfaces on the tubes that penetrate the space, creating a delicately modulated monotonicity of the softly lit interior. The 1986 addition is connected to the first stage by an open corridor. It is an elongated, rectangular, three-story volume, whose lower section is finished in rusticated concrete and upper section in brick facing. The articulation of both the facades and interior details here shows more affinity with classical architecture than the earlier main building. (See also page 24, fig. 30.)

West-Japan Industrial Club, 1911

Nishi Nippon Kōgyō Kurabu
Architect Kingo Tatsuno and Yasushi Kataoka
Address 4, Eda 1-chōme, Tobata-ku, Kitakyūshū, Fukuoka Pref. (see map)
Transport From JR Kokura Station: south exit and Street-car—Nishitetsu Kitakyūshū line to Kōdai-mae stop and 6 minutes by taxi
The building is an Important National Cultural Property.

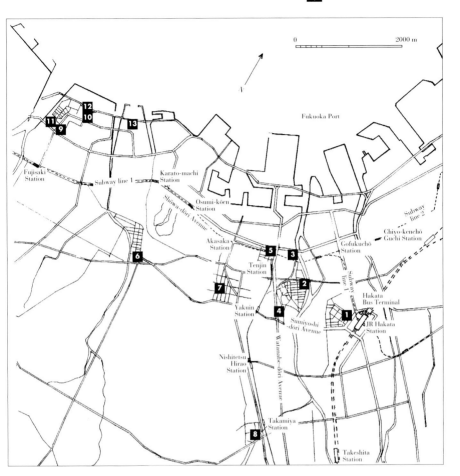

🏛 FUKUOKA

Fukuoka Sōgō Bank Home Offices (now Fukuoka City Bank), 1971 addition, 1983

Fukuoka City Ginkō Honten
Architect Arata Isozaki
Address 1, Hakata Eki-mae 3-chōme, Hakata-ku, Fukuoka, Fukuoka Pref. (see map)
Transport From JR Hakata Station: west exit and 2-minute walk across station square

In the 1960s Isozaki built a number of relatively small but very important structures, including the Old Ōita Prefectural Library (1966) (see page 312) and several branch buildings of the Fukuoka Sōgō Bank. Based on his success with these projects, he was commissioned to design the Sōgō Bank Home Offices in 1968. In this large work Isozaki could rely on the experiences he had gained in earlier projects, and so much of their structural/formal technique was reused here. The bank, like the library, is composed of a huge "space wall"—a pair of parallel walls with the space of offices in between them—and a low-profile extension on each side of the bladelike slab. The strongly manneristic architecture of Isozaki is demonstrated here with a vocabulary that is not only derivative of his previous projects, but is also new. There is a juxtaposition of various and often sharply contrasting forms, structures, materials, and colors. The high-rise section is entirely covered with rough, red, Indian sandstone; the horizontally extruded "flying square tubular beams" of the computer rooms are finished in highly polished red granite; the numerous metallic elements of the air-conditioning and other mechanical devices are shaped in sepia-colored Corten steel. As most architectural elements have been substantially distorted or transformed in the design process, so have the "columns" supporting the huge space-beams; they have been turned into stubby cylindrical shafts, finished in white marble. The interior is equally shaped with a combination of high-tech, popular, and some historicizing elements. As much as the architecture of this bank was influenced by many sources, including Seiichi Shirai's and Isozaki's own work, it has influenced many designs after its completion. Unfortunately, the addition, built to the west side of the complex, effectively diminishes much of the quality represented by the original design.

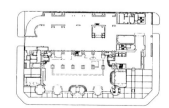
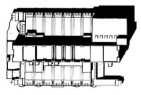

Hotel Il Palazzo
1989
Architect Aldo Rossi (Italy) (with Morris Adjmi, U.S.)
Address 13-1, Haruyoshi 3-chōme, Chūō-ku, Fukuoka, Fukuoka Pref. (see map)
Transport From JR Hakata Station: west exit and 20-minute walk or 8 minutes by bus to Minami Shinchō stop and 3-minute walk across Haruyoshi-bashi Bridge (hotel is along the west bank of Nakagawa River behind a row of old two-story houses)

Fukuoka Historical Records Repository
1909
Fukuoka Shiritsu Rekishi Shiryōkan or *Kyū Nihon Seimei Kyūshū Shiten*
Architect Kingo Tatsuno and Yasushi Kataoka
Address 15, Tenjin 1-chōme, Chūō-ku, Fukuoka, Fukuoka Pref. (see map)
Transport From JR Hakata Station: west exit and 27-minute walk or 10 minutes by bus; or Subway—Line 1 to Tenjin Station and

5-minute walk to north and then west; or 7-minute walk north from Hotel Il Palazzo to north, along the river (on northwest corner of Shōwa-dōri Avenue at Nishi Nakajima Bashi Bridge)
Visitation 9:00–17:00 (closed Mondays and New Year's Day)
The building is an Important National Cultural Property.

Shūkōsha Building
1975
Shūkōsha Biru
Architect Arata Isozaki
Address 14-9, Watanabe-dōri 5-chōme, Chūō-ku, Fukuoka, Fukuoka Pref. (see map)
Transport From JR Hakata Station: west exit and 18-minute walk, first west on Sumiyoshi-dōri Avenue, then north on Watanabe-dōri Avenue; or 6 minutes by taxi; or 7-minute walk south from Fukuoka Sōgō Bank Home Offices (on east side of Watanabe-dōri Avenue)

Housing the offices and showrooms of a small graphic design company, the Shūkōsha Building is a four-story structure designed with a rectangular reinforced concrete frame forming six large cubes. A scaled-down version of the same configuration, enclosing machinery and mechanical rooms, appears over the flat rooftop. Within this abstract framework Isozaki introduced numerous pop elements—painted surfaces, signs, and logos—many of which create optical illusions. One of these is the entrance; the semicircular niche in front features eight mirror glass doors, of which only two can be opened. In the top-floor reception/conference room, Aiko Miyawaki, Isozaki's wife, designed the managerial office as a stepped composition reminiscent of one of Escher's impossible stairways.

市 FUKUOKA

Fukuoka Bank Home Offices 1975

Fukuoka Ginkō Honten
Architect Kisho Kurokawa
Address 13-1, Tenjin
2-chōme, Chūō-ku, Fukuoka,
Fukuoka Pref. (see map)
Transport Subway—Line 1 to
Tenjin Station and 1-minute
walk; or 3-minute walk on
south side of Shōwa-dōri
Avenue, west from Fukuoka
Historical Records Depository
(between Shōwa-dōri and
Meiji-dōri avenues)

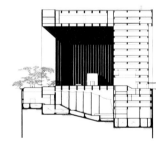

Occupying a corner site along a major road in the Tenjin area of Fukuoka, the huge, dark, granite-faced, solid building boasts an unusual multistory atrium. As if carved away from a solid block of stone, this atrium is completely open on the sides facing the streets. Between the two sides a rectangular stairway shaft defines the corner while supporting the top floor with large conference rooms and other spaces. As the atrium space, designed with an attractive public plaza at street level, is contiguous with the surrounding city, Kurokawa has called it an "urban hall" under an "urban roof." Under the plaza there is a large auditorium accessible from the street. Kurokawa's atrium solution, although much reminiscent of Kevin Roche's Ford Foundation Building in New York (1967), differs from this prototype by not being enclosed with glass walls; in this way it blurs any sharp boundary between outside and inside, as well as public and private spaces in the city.

Fukuoka Sōgō Bank Ropponmatsu Branch (now Fukuoka City Bank) 1971
Fukuoka City Ginkō Ropponmatsu Shiten
Architect Arata Isozaki
Address 1-1, Kusagae

2-chōme, Chūō-ku, Fukuoka, Fukuoka Pref. (see map)
Transport From JR Hakata Station: west exit and Bus to Ropponmatsu stop and 2-minute walk to west (on north side of Beppu-bashi-dōri Avenue, that is, Route 202) (see page 21, fig. 20)

Metrotristan Office Building
1991
Shinsei Jūtaku
Honsha-ya Biru
Architect Atsushi Kitagawara
Address 11-15, Yakuin 2-chōme, Chūō-ku, Fukuoka, Fukuoka Pref. (see map)
Transport Subway—Line 1 to Tenjin Station; change to Train—Nishitetsu line one stop to Yakuin Station; west exit and 10-minute walk west (300 feet/100 meters north of Fukuoka Teishin Byōin Hospital)

Nexus World Kashii Condominiums
1991
Architect Oscar Tusquets (Spain), block 1
Architect Christian de Portzamparc (France), blocks 2, 3, and 4
Architect Osamu Ishiyama, blocks 5, 6, and 7
Architect Mark Mack (U.S.), block 8
Architect Rem Koolhaas (Holland), blocks 9 and 10
Architect Steven Holl (U.S.), block 11

Address 4-11, Kashii-hama 4-chōme, Higashi-ku, Fukuoka, Fukuoka Pref.
Transport Train—JR Kagoshima main line to Kashii Station and 15-minute walk to west; or Subway—line 2 to Kashiinomiya-mae Station and 10-minute walk to northwest
Visitation Nexus Gallery (in block 11) 10:00–18:00, tel: (092) 673-1121

Konkokyō Church
1980
Konkokyō Fukuoka
Takamiya Kyōkai
Architect Kijo Rokkaku
Address 17-4, Takamiya 5-chōme, Minami-ku, Fukuoka, Fukuoka Pref. (see map)
Transport From Hakata Station Bus Terminal: bus to Takamiya and 2-minute walk to north; or Train—Nishitetsu line to Takamiya Station and 8-minute walk southwest
Visitation Open daily, tel: (092) 541-6317

Remarkably similar to Shin Takamatsu's Ark (Nishina Dental Clinic) in Kyōto (1983) (see page 199), the Konkokyō Church—the temple or, rather, the "house of worship" of an uncommon, syncretic Shintō Sect (as opposed to the traditional Shrine Shintō) established in 1859—features a huge cylindrical volume over a base. The meticulously symmetrical composition intends to symbolize the essence of the Konko teachings of Shintō religion, insofar as the circle implies presentations of the universe, rebirth by Karma, energy of life, and the harmonious world of humans.

The building's exterior is finished with brick over reinforced concrete, while the cylinder has a steel structure faced with Corten steel sheets joined with long seams. The interior is equally unusual in shape, suggesting that every element was designed to assist in a specific ritual. The first floor is occupied by the entrance hall, the worship hall, and the sanctuary; the second by a gallery around the temple; and the third by a multipurpose congregation hall and stage.

Kashiwara Duō Housing Community Facilities 1992

Kashiwara Duō Town Center
Architect Atsushi Kitagawara
Address 62, Kashiwara
6-chōme, Minami-ku,
Fukuoka, Fukuoka Pref.
Transport From Hakata
Station Bus Terminal: Bus 52
bound for Kashiwara to
Kashiwa Kōkō-mae stop (40
minutes) and 5-minute walk

Amidst uniform, although not necessarily unattractive, large housing units at the southwestern edge of Fukuoka, Kitagawara inserted a complex of colorful "stage sets." Comprised of several interconnected elements that form a small, urban enclave, the project provides various common facilities for all the neighboring residents of the Kashiwara Duō Housing.

Included is a five-story residential block that is decidedly different from the other buildings. This block is surrounded by three buildings: a traditional tea ceremony room—capped with a vaulted metallic roof—across a sunken, sloping, micro-garden; gymnasia with dressing and washing rooms in a black oval box; and the vaulted-roof volume of the swimming pool.

Further down on the sloping site Kitagawara arranged a two-story structure with shops and many walk-through spaces: a ramp, a stairway, and a balcony under a stretched, tentlike, translucent canopy, curving against the sky. All these elements are connected by a long walkway among a system of freestanding walls whose slanting edges and tilted, earth-tone-colored surfaces evoke the experience of either a narrow, Mediterranean street or a colorful gorge. In Kitagawara's words, "The composition of the whole—based as it is on the disposition of a variety of symbolic elements on the site—is determined by the 'exteriors' inserted in the intervals." ("Atsushi Kitagawara," *Japan Architect* 8 [1994]: 200)

Fukuoka Seaside Momochi 1989

Architect Kisho Kurokawa
Address 3, Momochi-hama
3-chōme, Sawara-ku,
Fukuoka, Fukuoka Pref.
(see map)
Transport Subway—Line 1 to
Fujisaki Station and 6-minute
walk to north

Saibu Gas Museum of Phenomenart 1989

Architect Shōei Yoh
Address 9-20, Momochi-hama 3-chōme, Sawara-ku, Fukuoka, Fukuoka Pref. (see map)
Transport Subway—Line 1 to Fujisaki Station and 5 minutes by taxi; or 14-minute walk from Seaside Momochi (next to Fukuoka Tower)
Visitation 10:00–17:00 (closed Mondays), tel: (092) 845-1410

The Saibu Gas Museum of Phenomenart introduces various features and uses of gas and other energies through exhibits and an hourly electronic show. The high-tech, steel and glass building is centered around a large, multistory, quadrilateral space. This so-called "media space" is surrounded by service walls, both structural and mechanical, which are covered by acrylic as well as perforated aluminum panels to both hide and reveal myriads of small lights in multiple layers.

These lights come alive with quickly changing, colorful patterns, along with electronic music, as the show begins. The floor surface, made of thick, dark glass, also becomes a part of the show. From the slopes and crossing bridges above, visitors can look through the glass at the multilayered and multicolored co-generation system in the basement, highlighted by various and rapidly oscillating illuminations. As a result of these special effects, the boundaries of the space seem to recede and disappear, or, alternatively, to expand and contract in unpredictable ways. Thus while losing its "everyday" reality, it conjures up another, virtual one.

In order to liberate the area around this first floor, the second and third floors and the roof slabs are suspended from outside supports by cables. The sloped galleries around the "media space" feature selected artworks based on various physical phenomena, which are called "Phenomenart." While the museum's structure and exterior are conceived of industrial "hardware" technology, the interior is operated by an electric "software" technology.

Fukuoka Seaside Momochi Condominiums 1989

Architect Michael Graves (U.S.) (corner unit); Stanley Tigerman (U.S.) (the block north of Graves's project)
Address 1, Momochi-hama 4-chōme, Sawara-ku, Fukuoka, Fukuoka Pref. (see map)
Transport Subway—Line 1 to Fujisaki Station and 6-minute walk north (across the street from Fukuoka Seaside Momochi)
Visitation 9:30–16:30 (office hours), tel: (092) 845-5305

🏯 FUKUOKA

Fukuoka Tower
1989
Architect Nikken Sekkei
Company
Address 3-26, Momochi-
hama 2-chōme, Sawara-ku,
Fukuoka, Fukuoka Pref.
(see map)
Transport Subway—Line 1 to
Fujisaki Station and 16-min-
ute walk or 7 minutes by taxi
(next to Saibu Gas Museum)
Visitation 10:00–21:00
(October–February); 10:00–
22:00 (March–July); 10:00–
23:00 (August–September)
(closed second Tuesdays and
Wednesdays of June and
December), tel: (092)
823-0234

Fukuoka Dome
1993
Architect Takenaka
Corporation (with Maeda
Corporation)
Address 2-2, Jigyō-hama 2
chōme, Chūō-ku, Fukuoka,
Fukuoka Pref. (see map)
Transport Subway—Line 1 to
Tōjinmachi Station and
18-minute walk north; or
6-minutes by taxi
The Fukuoka Dome is a
gigantic cylindrical baseball
stadium and multipurpose
arena with a unique
retractable roof structure.

Kinoshita Clinic
1985
Architect Shōei Yoh
Address 51-1, Nakama Aza,
Kota Ōaza, Nishi-ku,
Fukuoka, Fukuoka Pref.
Transport From JR Hakata
Station: Subway—Line 1 to
Meinohama Terminal: north
exit and bus bound for
Nishinoura to Chūkan stop
(20 minutes)
The clinic is a unique, elon-
gated, donut-shaped, silver-
painted volume on pilotis,
and seems to float above the
green hillock along the road.

Standing near the seashore on newly developed,
reclaimed land, the 500-foot/150-meter, triangular,
prismatic structure serves as both a radio and tele-
vision transmitter and an observation tower.
Similar to Nikken Sekkei's earlier Chiba Port
Tower (1986) (see page 74), this tessellated-glass-
covered, obelisk-like tower is constructed with a
hollow core that is surrounded by the lacy steel
frame of the structure. Through a skylight in the
first-floor lobby, visitors can look up into this
impressive light-filled space. At the top of the
building there are several floors with shops and
observation decks, from where the entire city of
Fukuoka, the port, and the Korean Strait unfold in
a spectacular panoramic view.

This small private residence, like Fujii's previous Gymnasium 2 of the Shibaura Institute of Technology in Ōmiya (see page 67) and the Ushimado International Arts Festival Building (see page 243) (both 1985), creates a new quality of multilayered space, and a new "inscription" of that quality. In so doing, Fujii has clearly rejected the compositional principles of classical architecture: balance, harmony, stability, and unity. The space in this two-story house is generated by four L-shaped walls that have been disassembled from a cube. The walls are covered by systems of grids of various sizes— 6 feet/1.8 meters, 3 feet/.9 meter, and 2 feet/.6 meter—to indicate the position and role of the spaces inside. Despite all the conceptual operations, or perhaps because of them, the experience of this project is remarkably exciting. While moving through and among these walls, the grids form multiple layers, shifting one's vision constantly. The changing light introduced into this architectural matrix helps this effect.

市 IIZUKA

Project Mizoe 1
1988

Architect Hiromi Fujii
Address 1342-16, Junno, Iizuka, Fukuoka Pref.
Transport Train—JR Chikuhō line to Shin-Iizuka Station and 6 minutes by taxi or Bus to Iizuka Bus Center and 3 minutes by taxi
Visitation Private residence; seen only from the outside.

Shiranui Stress Care Hospital
1991

Ōmuta Shiranui Byōin
Architect Itsuko Hasegawa
Address 1800, Tegama, Ōmuta, Fukuoka Pref.
Transport From JR Ōmuta Station: bus bound for Kurosaki Danchi to Tegama stop and 8-minute walk toward west (building is near the fishing port)

The hospital is situated near a fishing port along a small river in the western part of Ōmuta. Filled with the manifestations of nature, yet not devoid of human activity, the site is almost ideal for soothing the spirit and healing the mind. Taking advantage of the site, Hasegawa has arranged the two-story hospital with the patient rooms facing southeast towards the river. The design is articulated in opposition to the usual, institutionalized, and impersonal architecture of hospitals; in fact, the elongated and undulating composition has the explicit attributes of a series of row houses, displaying their own playful variations while adding up to a "natural" unity. The units are defined by their slightly pitched roofs, balconies, and large windows. Although utilizing a range of contemporary industrial materials—such as metallic sheets and perforated aluminum plates—and colorfully painted in pastel shades of earth tones, the complex displays an unmistakable affinity with vernacular architecture, one that has always maintained a close relationship with nature. Hasegawa, combining her "feminine" sensibility with the rejuvenating powers of nature, has created an intimate and informal piece of architecture.

Among Shirai's best works, the Shinwa Bank was designed and built in three stages over a period of almost ten years. Shirai's architecture, a complete antithesis of the principles of the modern movement, here reveals its full spectrum of mannerist idiosyncrasies. At the same time, his design has nothing to do with historicist or regional architecture. The early stages were shaped by juxtaposing uniquely articulated volumes: one covered with white travertine, the other with blackened bronze plates. The interiors of these two-story structures are equally extraordinary. The banking halls are dressed in green marble, while the conference rooms and lecture halls have mysterious reflective spaces like those of some solemn, religious place. This impression is fully reinforced by the high-rise block of the computer center, built in 1975. Here the eleven-story, massive, symmetrical tower is finished in rough, yellowish white, travertine blocks and highly polished, meticulously chiseled, red granite elements. An enormous-scale, central entrance, marked by a circular window above and a narrow vertical slit, contrasts with the rest of the building like an autonomous architectural fragment. The structure is covered with an umbrella-like roof with copper-plated rafters. The three-story entrance hall gallery space, carved in white, black, and green marble and reflected in a shallow pool, adds to the image of the building as the temple of a strange religious cult (perhaps the one that worships money itself).

Shinwa Bank
Building 1, 1967
Building 2, 1969
Building 3, 1975
Shinwa Ginkō Honten and *Kaishō-kan*
Architect Seiichi Shirai
Address 10-12, Shimanose-chō, Sasebo, Nagasaki Pref.
Transport From JR Sasebo Station: east exit and 6-minute walk

🏛 TOYOTAMA-CHŌ (TSUSHIMA-ISL.)
Tsushima Culture Complex 1990
Tsushima Bunka no Sato
Architect Toyokazu Watanabe
Address 370 Ōaza, Toyotama-chō (Tsushima Island), Shimogata-gun, Nagasaki Pref.
Transport From Hakata Port of Fukuoka: Ferry—Kyūshū-yūsen Ferry to Izuhara-chō Port and bus to Toyotama-chō

Memorial of the Twenty-six Martyr Saints
1962

Nihon Nijū-roku Seijin
Junkyō Kinen Shisetsu
Architect Kenji Imai
Address 7-8, Nishizaka-chō,
Nagasaki, Nagasaki Pref.
Transport From JR Nagasaki
Station: 10-minute walk
(north across station square
and uphill)

Dedicated to the memory of six Spanish friars and twenty Japanese Christians who were crucified here in 1597 and canonized in 1862, Imai's design is comprised of several distinct elements. The memorial chapel with two ceramic-tile-decorated concrete towers, colorful mosaic-covered exterior walls, and unfinished concrete interior surfaces, recalls Antonio Gaudi's Sagrada Familia in Barcelona (1890–1930). In front of the archives building, whose walls are also decorated with ceramics, the memorial wall, facing a small plaza, concludes the complex. The granite-covered wall displays a large bronze relief with statues of the martyrs.

Nagasaki Ferry Terminal
1995

Architect Shin Takamatsu
Address Nagasaki Port,
Motofune-chō, Nagasaki,
Nagasaki Pref.
Transport From JR Nagasaki
Station: 10-minute walk

Shinwa Bank Nagasaki Branch
1973

Shinwa Ginkō
Nagasaki Shiten
Architect Seiichi Shirai
Address 4-16, Gotō-machi,
Nagasaki, Nagasaki Pref.
Transport From JR Nagasaki
Station: Streetcar to Gotō-
machi stop and 5-minute
walk

Ōura Tenshudō Catholic Church
1864

Ōura Tenshudō
Katorikku Kyōkai
Architect Bernard T. Petitjean
(France)
Address 5-3, Minamiyamate-
machi, Nagasaki, Nagasaki
Pref.
Transport From JR Nagasaki
Station: Streetcar to Ishibashi
stop and 5-minute walk
uphill
The church is an Important
National Cultural Property.

Originally the site of a few residences for Western-ers living on the eastern hills of Nagasaki Harbor, the site has been converted into an open-air muse-um of early Meiji Era, Western-style buildings. Therefore, the museum, in addition to several resi-dences, features the Steele Memorial Academy (1880), the Mitsubishi 2 Dock House (1896), and other structures that have been moved here from other parts of the city. The oldest house in the com-pound—as well as the oldest extant Western-style building in Japan—is the Glover House, which gives its name to the open-air museum. Built in 1863 by the Scotsman Thomas Blake Glover, who came to Japan in 1858 as an arms merchant, the house is a wooden, bungalow-style structure with an attractive garden. It was designed by Glover with some help from his friend Thomas James Waters, and built by local carpenters. Other impor-tant residences on the site include the Alt House (1865), Ringer House (1865), and Walker House (mid-1860s). Complementing the buildings is the Nagasaki Museum of Traditional Performing Arts. The tale of Puccini's opera *Madame Butterfly* relates to this area of Nagasaki, and so there is a statue of Chocho-San in the compound.

Glover House and Gardens 1863–96

Gurabā-en

Architect Thomas Blake Glover (U.K.) (with Thomas James Waters, U.K.)

Address 8-1, Minami-Yamate-machi, Nagasaki, Nagasaki Pref.

Transport From JR Nagasaki Station: Streetcar to Ishibashi stop and 8-minute walk (3-minute walk from Ōura Tenshudō Catholic Church)

Visitation 8:00–16:00 (March–November); 8:30–17:00 (December–February)

The buildings are Important National Cultural Properties.

Misumi Ferry Terminal (K.A.P.) 1990

Misumi-kō Feri Tāmināru or *Umi no Piramiddo*
Architect Shōei Yoh
Address 1160, Misumi-ura, Misumi-machi, Uto-gun, Kumamoto Pref.
Transport From JR Kumamoto Station: Train—JR Misumi line to Misumi-kō Terminal and 3-minute walk (at Misumi Port)

Ishiuchi Dam Control Facility (K.A.P.), 1991

Architect Shigeru Aoki
Address Hachikubo, Nakamura, Misumi-machi, Uto-gun, Kumamoto Pref.
Transport From JR Kumamoto Station or Misumi Port: Train—JR Misumi line to Ishiuchi Dam Station and 20-minute walk

Museum of Ishiuchi Dam (K.A.P.), 1993

Ishiuchi Damu, Shiryō-kan
Architect Keiichi Irie
Address 3629-2, Hachikubo, Nakamura, Misumi-machi, Uto-gun, Kumamoto Pref.
Transport From JR Kumamoto Station or Misumi Port: Train—JR Misumi line to Ishiuchi Dam Station and 25-minute walk (164 feet/50 meters south from the Dam Control Facility Building)

A 82-foot/25-meter high reinforced concrete structure with a large conical tent shape, the Misumi Ferry Terminal is an unusual and easily identifiable landmark at the Misumi Port. The silhouette of the terminal stands as a symbol of the port and the town whose name, "Misumi," literally means "triangle." The building is constructed largely with prefabricated elements: ceramic-tile-finished panels attached to posts that converge into a sharp and open peak. An uncommon and highly successful feature of the design is a system of double ramps wrapping around the structure both inside and out and leading to the observation deck on top. Inside, the ramp is fully exposed in the large and fairly dark space. The spiraling line of the ramp increases visually the height of the building and adds a mysterious, almost archaic, quality to the space. The large first floor with stepped platforms contains a variety of services related to travel and local tourism. The terminal was built as part of the Kumamoto Art Polis Program.

市 YATSUSHIRO

Gallery 8 1991

Tori-chō Gyararī
Architect Toyo Ito
Address 7-63, Tori-chō, Yatsushiro, Kumamoto Pref.
Transport From JR Yatsushiro Station: 5 minutes by taxi

ACT 6 Complex 1985

Act 6 Hyakkaten Yatsushiro
Architect Shōei Yoh
Address 3-8, Hanazono-machi, Yatsushiro, Kumamoto Pref.
Transport From JR Yatsushiro Station: south exit and 6-minute walk to west (along National Road 3)

Yatsushiro Municipal Museum (K.A.P.), 1991

Yatsushiro Shiritsu Hakubutsukan
Architect Toyo Ito
Address 12-35, Nishi-Matsu-ejō-machi, Yatsushiro, Kumamoto Pref.
Transport From JR Yatsushiro Station: 8 minutes by taxi (3-minute walk from the Yatsushiro Municipal Cultural Center)

One of Ito's largest and most outstanding projects to date has been built a short distance from the remains of the old Matsue Castle compound. The site is part of a cultural and educational district and faces an Edo Period (1603–1868) house of a well-known local family. Since the vicinity has restrictions to the height and volume of new buildings, and since the program for the museum was rather extensive, Ito reduced its size by covering its first floor on the north side with an artificial hillock. Thus the curving ramp leading to the entrance reaches the second floor where a lobby, a cafe, a lecture room, and a small exhibition hall are located. The majority of the display areas are one level below, that is, on the "underground" first floor. The repository is on the third floor, within the "floating" volume of a bubble-shaped horizontal cylinder. While the base structure is solid reinforced concrete—partially covered by the berm—the upper sections are constructed with light steel frames and surfaces. In order to diminish the volumes and imposing monumentality of the structures, Ito used stainless steel (for a series of rhythmically vaulted roofs), thin perforated metallic screens, and glass. In this way the structure both fuses and contrasts with the landscape in an attempt to create a new environmental architecture. The project continues Ito's efforts to engender an "architecture as light as the wind," which began in his "Silver Hut" in Tōkyō (1984). When the reflective metallic surfaces begin to sparkle in the changing light conditions, they appear as a mirage or the image of an astonishingly large and futuristic hang glider that has just landed on top of the softly curving green hillock.

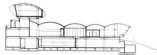

市 YATSUSHIRO

Yatsushiro Municipal Cultural Center 1962
Yatsushiro Kōseinen-kan
Architect Yoshinobu Ashihara
Address 1-47, Nishi-Matsuejō-machi, Yatsushiro, Kumamoto Pref.
Transport From JR Yatsushiro Station: 8 minutes by taxi (3-minute walk from the Yatsushiro Municipal Museum)

Yatsushiro Fire Station 1995
Yatsushirojō Shōbō Honbu Chōsha
Architect Toyo Ito
Address 970, Ōmura-machi, Yatsushiro, Kumamoto Pref.
Transport From JR Yatsushiro Station: bus or taxi (along the main harbor highway that links Yasushiro interchange of the expressway to the downtown and port)

Home of the Elderly in Yatsushiro, 1994
Yōgo Rōjin Hōmu—Yatsushiro Shiritsu Hosuryō
Architect Toyo Ito
Address 1, Hinagu-heisei-machi, Yatsushiro, Kumamoto Pref.
Transport From JR Yatsushiro Station: Train—JR Kagoshima main line to Hinagu Station and bus or taxi (near seashore at fishing harbor of Hinagu)

村 KUMA-MURA

Kyūsendō Forest Museum 1984
Kyūsendō Shinrinkan
Architect Yasufumi Kijima
Address 1122-1, Hirano, Ōse-Aza, Kuma-mura, Kuma-gun, Kumamoto Pref.
Transport From JR Yatsushiro Station: Train—JR Hisatsu line to Kyūsendō Station and 10 minutes by taxi (along Road 219 or Hitoyoshi Kaidō Road)

This museum is located on a steep slope of the Kumagawa River's gorge in a remote and uniquely picturesque area of Kyūshū. The building is the center of numerous educational and recreational facilities in the area, all related to a nearby limestone cavern and the surrounding forestry. Kijima's scheme is built upon seven intersecting cylindrical volumes of various heights, two of them set on pilotis over an open terrace. The steel-framed, reinforced concrete cylinders are all capped by intersecting hemispherical domes finished in asphalt shingles with a thin copper coating. One's first impression of the building is the softly undulating shapes of its domes; they have been designed to reinterpret, and so to blend into, the surrounding rolling mountain ranges, and they achieve this rather well. On the other hand, this spectacular piece of architecture, as Hiroshi Watanabe has pointed out, "suggests a cross between a Byzantine church straight out of the Kremlin and a cliff-style Buddhist temple." (*Amazing Architecture from Japan* [Tokyo: Weatherhill, 1991], 55.)

Kuma High School of Industry, Traditional Architecture Workshop (K.A.P) 1991

Kuma Kōgyō Kōtō Gakkō Dentō Kenchiku Jisshū-to
Architect Team Zoo— Atelier Zo
Address 800, Shiromoto-chō, Hitoyoshi, Kumamoto Pref.
Transport Train—JR Hisatsu line to Hitoyoshi Station and 12-minute walk north uphill

The program for the Traditional Architecture Workshop and the designers who were selected to realize it found a perfect match in each other. The Kuma High School of Industry is one of the few places where students are taught the traditional techniques and craftsmanship of Japanese wooden architecture. Team Zoo—Atelier Zo has long been emphasizing the qualities of locally inflected vernacular architecture, imbued with a feel for playful details, and local and natural materials; in short, theirs is a uniquely organic, often explicitly anthropomorphic architecture. The high school called for several new buildings and facilities, which the designers successfully turned into a small vernacular "village" around a colonnade-lined, circular, open court—a kind of commons. While some of the structures are concrete painted in earth tones (pink, orange, and red), most of them are constructed of wood. The roofs over the buildings are gabled and covered with tiles. Detailing of the structures is exemplary; some of the exposed roof works are outright spectacular, such as the one in the large hall. Ferrous materials are not completely excluded, however; some of the roofs are constructed with steel frames and/or lattice girders, whereas certain facades of the covered walkways are made of perforated metallic screens, providing sun protection as well as ventilation. Altogether the design assures a most appropriate setting for the kind of program the school offers.

市 YUNOMAE-MACHI

Yunomae Cartoon Museum and Community Center (K.A.P.) 1992
Yunomae Manga Bijutsukan and *Kōminkan*
Architect Hideaki Katsura
Address 1834-1, Kami Makibaru, Yunomae-machi, Kuma-gun, Kumamoto Pref.

Transport From Hitoyoshi: Train—JR Kumagawa line to Yunomae-machi Terminal Located in the center of a small town, the project is part of the revitalization program here. The complex is comprised of five unusual wooden volumes covered with aluminum plates. The units are connected by a curved wall.

Seiwa Bunraku Puppet Theater (K.A.P.) 1992

Seiwa-mura Bunrakukan
Architect Kazuhiro Ishii
Address 152, Ohira, Seiwa-mura, Kamimashiki-gun, Kumamoto Pref.
Transport From Kumamoto Kōtsu (Bus) Center: Bus (bound for Mamehara) to Seiwa-mura stop (about 1.5 hours; along Route 218)

The small complex was constructed to foster the tradition of *bunraku*, the old Japanese puppet theater, which is popular in the region. Ishii's architecture uses several attributes of traditional structures, including a wooden framework and tiled roofs. The meticulously symmetrical composition consists of two parts: a rectangular section with a *T* plan housing the theater and spectator hall for 120 people, and a "cylindrical" volume accommodating an exhibition space. In both sections the highlight of the interiors is the wonderful wooden roofing for which Ishii is well known. This roof structure, exposed to the spaces below, is different in each part of the complex. The spiral layering of the wooden beams over the exhibition hall is reminiscent of the technique employed by the Buddhist monk Chogen (1121–1206).

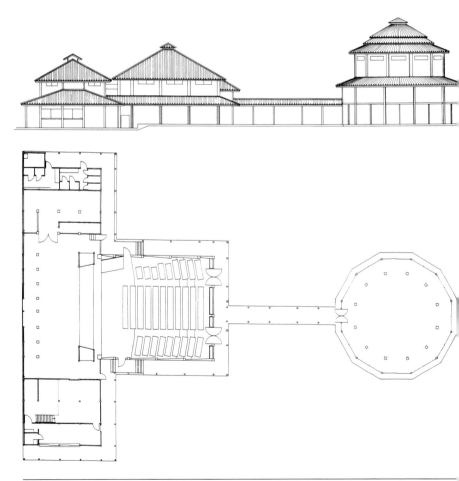

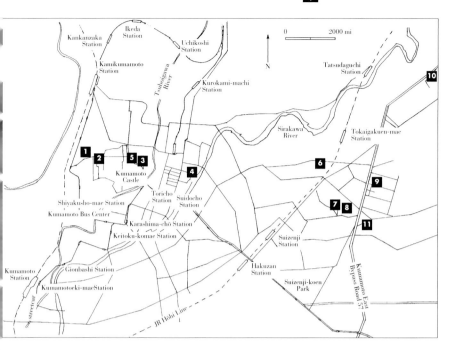

Kumamoto Municipal Museum
1977
*Kumamoto Shiritsu
Hakubutsukan*
Architect Kisho Kurokawa
Address 3-2, Kōkyō-machi,
Kumamoto, Kumamoto Pref.
(see map)
Transport From JR Kuma-
moto Station: Streetcar to
Sugidomo Station and
5-minute walk (northwest of
Kumamoto Castle)
Visitation 9:00–16:30 (closed
Mondays, national holidays,
and at the new year)

Kumamoto Prefectural Art Museum
1977
*Kumamoto Kenritsu
Bijutsukan*
Architect Kunio Maekawa
Address 2, Ninomaru,
Kumamoto, Kumamoto Pref.
(see map)
Transport From JR Kuma-
moto Station: Streetcar to
Sugidomo Station and 7-
minute walk (2-minute walk
from Municipal Museum)
Visitation 9:00–16:30 (closed
Mondays, national holidays,
and at the new year)

Kumamoto Prefectural Art Museum Chibajōchō Branch (K.A.P.)
1992
*Kumamoto Kenritsu
Bijutsukan Chibajōchō Shiten*
Architect Elias Torrez and
Jose Lapena (Spain)
Address 2-2, Chibajō-chō,
Kumamoto, Kumamoto Pref.
(see map)
Transport From JR Kuma-
moto Station: Streetcar to
Kumamoto-Shiyakushō-Mae
Station and 5-minute walk to
north (northwest of
Kumamoto Castle)

Kumamoto North Police Headquarters (K.A.P.) 1991

Kumamoto Kita Keisatsu-shō
Architect Kazuo Shinohara
Address 5-13, Kusaba-chō, Kumamoto, Kumamoto Pref. (see map)
Transport From JR Kumamoto Station: streetcar to Suidō-chō Station and 5-minute walk to north (on the north side of Shirakawa Kōen Park)

One of the first projects completed within the Kumamoto Art Polis (K.A.P.) program, the Kumamoto North Police Headquarters building is situated at the edge of Shirakawa Park in downtown Kumamoto. Shinohara's intentions with the design were to deviate as much as possible from the official or authoritarian formalism that generally characterizes government buildings. For this reason, the structure is horizontal rather than vertical, and the west facade facing the park, parking, and Kumamoto Castle in the distance is made of reflective mirror-glass curtain wall. This part of the building, formed as a five-story front section with the entrance and public reception hall, is cantilevered symmetrically in a step-by-step fashion at each floor, leaving more open exterior space at street level. Adjoining to this section, the horizontally extruded volume on the east is relatively simple and straightforward in articulation. Only one element breaks the rectangular disposition here; on the northern elevation a horizontally laid, large, cylindrical volume containing part of the mechanical installations is attached at the fifth floor. This cylinder is wrapped in perforated highly polished metallic sheets. Like many of Shinohara's recent works, this building uses complex structural solutions. This is particularly so in the case of the stepped front-section, where the steel skeleton features substantial diagonal elements that run the entire height of the building and that are visible in the two-story public lobby. Rendered in a spectrum of pastel colors (yellow, green, blue, etc.), with polished, light gray, marble floor, this well-lit space is more friendly and inviting than awe-inspiring or gloomy, as it is in many other police stations.

Kumamoto Arts and Crafts Center
1982
Kumamoto-ken Dentō Kogei-kan
Architect Kiyonori Kikutake
Address 3-35, Chibajō-chō, Kumamoto, Kumamoto Pref. (see map)
Transport From JR Kumamoto Station: Streetcar to Kumamoto-Shiyakushō-Mae Station and 7-minute walk to north; or 10-minute walk from Kumamoto Prefectural Art Museum; or 2-minute walk from Kumamoto Prefectural Art Museum Chibajōchō Branch (north of Kumamoto Castle)

Shintoroku Public Housing (K.A.P.)
1993
Kōen Shintoroku Danchi
Architect Akira Komiyama
Address 854-1, Toroku 3-chōme, Kumamoto, Kumamoto Pref. (see map)
Transport From Kumamoto Kōtsu (Bus) Center: bus to Hotakubo Iriguchi stop and 5-minute walk northeast under the train tracks
The eleven-story block of box-frame construction is elevated on pilotis. The long, bladelike building is painted gray with red accents on its metallic structures.

Obiyama A Public Housing (K.A.P.)
1992
Kumamoto Kenei Obiyama Danchi
Architect Shimon Nino
Address 28, Obiyama 1-chōme, Kumamoto, Kumamoto Pref. (see map)
Transport From Kumamoto Kōtsu (Bus) Center: bus to Obiyama Chūgakkō stop and 6-minute walk to west (adjacent to Hotakubo Housing)

Hotakubo Public Housing (K.A.P.)
1991
Kumamoto Kenei Hotakubo Daiichi Danchi
Architect Riken Yamamoto
Address 28, Obiyama 1-chōme, Kumamoto, Kumamoto Pref. (see map)
Transport From Kumamoto Kōtsu (Bus) Center: bus to Obiyama Chūgakkō stop and 6-minute walk to west

Bolstered by the K.A.P.'s enthusiasm for an unprecedented solution, Yamamoto proposed a truly new work for this low-cost public housing. His scheme is innovative both in terms of the apartment units themselves and in the mode in which they are assembled into a larger urban composition. Yamamoto aimed to provide the residents with as much contact with the outside as possible. Of the four types of apartments, three have partially enclosed outdoor spaces within their configurations. There are also large terraces in each section. The bedroom sections (facing the residential streets) and the living room/kitchen sections (overlooking a large plaza) are pulled apart and then connected by a covered bridge. The 110 units surround a plaza with a small community facility on its south side. This plaza is accessible only through the apartments, so outsiders cannot get there. In order to achieve this solution, each residential unit has two stairways: one on the street side, and one attached from the living sections to the plaza. Stairways are covered with canopies of translucent acrylic sheets, and uppermost units are roofed with vaulted metallic plates, both of which enhance the attractive character of the complex.

Saishunkan Seiyaku Women's Dormitory (K.A.P.) 1991

Saishunkan Seiyaku Joshiryō
Architect Kazuyo Sejima
Address 323-1, Obiyama
4-chōme, Kumamoto,
Kumamoto Pref. (see map)
Transport From Kumamoto
JR Station: Train—Hōhi line
to Tōkaigakuen Station and
8 minutes by taxi; or from
Kumamoto Kōtsu (Bus) Cen-
ter—Bus to Hotakubo Hon-
chō stop (15 minutes) and
2-minute walk (near NTT
Building and Obiyama Shō-
gakkō Elementary School;
1-minute walk east from
Kumamoto East Bypass or
Road 57)
Visitation Private residence;
seen only from the outside

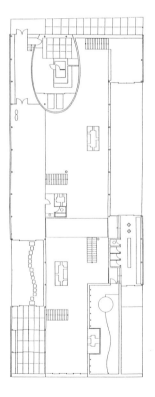

The largest work to date of the young female architect, the dormitory is an exceptional achievement.
The building provides accommodation for eighty
female employees of a local pharmaceutical company who, in the first year of their employment, live
and study together. Therefore, more emphasis was
given to the joint community space than to the living units themselves. The twenty small rooms for
four are arranged on the first floor at both east and
west sides of the slightly elongated rectangular
building. Ventilation and service shafts with toilets
inside them are wrapped with large mirrors and
translucent acrylic sheets above. In between the
east and west sections, the public space is modulated so as to create a large indoor atrium.

The experience of this light-washed and elusive
space is truly phenomenal. A gallery level over the
east row of rooms contains a small open courtyard
featuring a Japanese garden. On the other side of
the large space, over the western rooms, washroom
facilities and a lounge enclose a generous, second-
floor, outside terrace. "Floating" in the central
space is a corrugated-metal-plate-wrapped oval
volume that houses the manager's studio apartment. After scaling a gently sloping outside stairway, one enters the building on the second level
adjacent to the manager's room, then proceeds to
the entrance gallery on the same level. From here a
slender, steel bridge leads to the western side; stairways on both sides descend to the lower level. The
exterior of the structure features numerous perforated aluminum screens finished with polished
metallic and glass surfaces for privacy.

Takuma Public Housing (K.A.P.) 1992–94

Kumamoto Shiei Takuma Danchi

Architect Yasumitsu Matsunaga. blocks 1, 5, and 9
Architect Kazunari Sakamoto, blocks 2, 4, 6, and 10
Architect Itsuko Hasegawa, blocks 3, 7, and 8
Address 33, Shin-Nabe-chō, Kumamoto, Kumamoto Pref. (see map)
Transport From JR Kumamoto Station: bus to Hirano-shita stop (30 minutes) and 5-minute walk southeast, uphill; or from Kumamoto Airport: bus to Nishi-Bara stop (30 minutes) and 12-minute walk (up on a hill, south of Kumamoto East Bypass or Road 57)

Located in the northeastern part of Kumamoto, this large housing complex provides accommodations for 375 households. The several three-to-five-story blocks are loosely arranged along a north-south central promenade lined with greenery and parks. These residential blocks, designed by three different architects, display a desirable variety and deviate from any preconceived, arbitrary, or rigid ordering system; they take up different positions and undulate and enclose open spaces in various ways depending on their topography, need for public space, accessibility, and orientation. This development is an excellent example of how the quality of public housing can be improved with the concerted effort of local government, the thoughtful selection of architects, and the effective collaboration among designers. (The photo shows block 1.)

Ryujabira Public Housing (K.A.P.) 1993

Kumamoto Kenei Ryujabira Danchi

Architect Makoto Motokura
Address 1, Obiyama 3-chōme, Kumamoto, Kumamoto Pref. (see map)
Transport From Kumamoto Kōtsu (Bus) Center: bus to Higashi Suizenji stop and 5-minute walk northeast

Kamimuta Matsuo Shrine 1975

Kamimuta Matsuo Jinja
Architect Yasufumi Kijima
Address 623-5, Kamimuta, Ezu-machi, Kumamoto, Kumamoto Pref.
Transport From JR Kumamoto Station: streetcar to Suizenji Kōen Mae stop and 10 minutes by taxi

Kijima added to a small, old, wooden shrine a new section, whose parts resembles an ancient Roman sanctuary, thus creating an altogether radical juxtaposition.

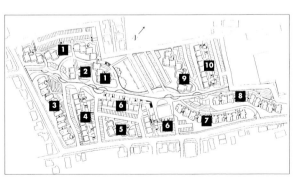

1 Block 1, Y. Matsunaga
2 Block 2, K. Sakamoto
3 Block 3, I. Hasegawa
4 Block 4, K. Sakamoto
5 Block 5, Y. Matsunaga

6 Block 6, K. Sakamoto
7 Block 7, I. Hasegawa
8 Block 8, I. Hasegawa
9 Block 9, Y. Matsunaga
10 Block 10, K. Sakamoto

Shinchi Public Housing (K.A.P.) 1991–95

Kumamoto Shiei Shinchi Danchi

Architects Hajime Yatsuka, masterplan; Kunihiko Hayakawa, phase 1, 1991; Riichiro Ogata, phase 2, 1992; Yuzuru Tominaga, phase 3, 1993; Hiroshi Nishioka, phase 4, 1995; Kenjiro Ueda, phase 5, 1994

Address 1917-58, Shinchi, Shimizu-machi, Kumamoto, Kumamoto Pref.

Transport From Kumamoto Kōtsu (Bus) Center (near Kumamoto Castle): bus bound for Shinchi-danchi to Sugishita stop

1 phase 1, K. Hayakawa
2 phase 2, R. Ogata
3 phase 3, Y. Tominaga,
4 phase 4, H. Nishioka
5 phase 5, K. Ueda

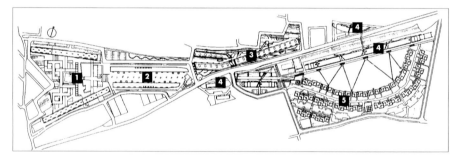

Even larger in scale than the Takuma Public Housing, the Shinchi project will accommodate some 4,000 people in 1,078 apartment units. Laid out along Hajime Yatsuka's master plan—which includes ample open space, parks, a reflective pool, and numerous public amenities—this housing is decidedly linear in its composition, which is rather unusual in Japan. The site is divided into three zones: a dense, urban, west zone with medium-rise buildings; a central zone that conforms in scale to the adjacent prefectural highway; and a less dense, urban, east zone with low-profile buildings. The individual units, to be constructed in five phases, have been designed by five architects. With the first stages complete, it is safe to say that not only the master plan but also the concrete design of the buildings is of a high standard that provides a remarkable sense of urban quality while assuring a variety. (The photos show phase 1.)

This unusual tower surrounded by an attractively paved outdoor community plaza crowns a hillock within the extensive Momota Sports Park in the western suburbs of Tamana, across the Kikuchi River. Although Takasaki's design features open observation decks on two levels, it is only with a stretch of imagination that one can call it a "tower." This reinforced concrete structure is rather a construct of posts, beams, frames, a few walls, and, of course, the decks. It is apparently a disordered porous matrix of various parts, wherein each element—including a large egg-shaped shell within the structural fabric—are symbolic in form and seem to comply with some unknown rituals. These elements represent lotus flowers, stars, arrows, earth, and sky energy; the egg-shaped structure, an enclosed hall, denotes "Zero Cosmology." Takasaki shares with Günther Domenig, with whom he worked in Austria in the late 1970s, a certain inclination toward an organic architecture, perhaps in the vein of Rudolf Steiner's anthroposophy; yet Takasaki's design also displays features that characterize Kiko (Monta) Mozuna's architecture of cosmic mythology.

Tamana City Observation Tower (K.A.P.) 1992
Tamana-shi Tembōdai
Architect Masaharu Takasaki
Address Momota Undō Kōen-nai, 1144, Takada, Okura Aza, Tamana, Kumamoto Pref.
Transport From JR Tamana Station: 15 minutes by taxi (within Momota Undō Kōen Park)

Tamana Museum of History 1994
Tamana-shi Furusatō Hakubutsu-kan
Architect Kiko (Monta) Mozuna
Address 117, Iwasaki, Tamana, Kumamoto Pref.
Transport From JR Tamana Station: 10 minutes by taxi
Visitation Open daily, tel: (0968) 74-3989

Forest of Tombs Museum (K.A.P.) 1992

Kumamoto Kenritsu Sōshoku Kofunkan
Architect Tadao Ando
Address 3085, Iwabara, Kaō-machi, Kamoto gun, Kumamoto Pref.
Transport From JR Kumamoto Station: Bus—Nihon Tsu line to Yamaga Onsen Terminal (1 hour) and 10 minutes by taxi
Visitation 8:30–17:00 (closed on Mondays and 25 December–4 January); tel: (0968) 36-2151

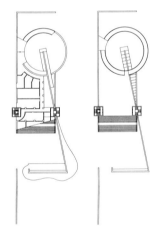

North of Kumamoto City, in the area of Kaō-machi, there are several extant ancient burial mounds (*kofun*). Within the Kumamoto Art Polis program, Ando was commissioned to design a small museum that would introduce the culture and artifacts of these so-called Iwabara *tumuli*, famous for having one of the largest and most impressive mounds. In order not to disturb the natural site, parking was placed far from the building, and most exhibition rooms were arranged underground to create an association with the burial mounds. Visitors approaching the museum on foot scale a wooded slope before arriving at a wide, paved courtyard that is partially surrounded by concrete walls, one with a waterfall and pool. Ando created a raised rooftop platform from which the tombs can be viewed. Wide stairs between two shafts of emergency stairways topped with skylights lead to the platform. From here to the entrance, one takes a long ramp descending into a circular courtyard, itself a display area for some of the artifacts. Ando's overall design recalls the "keyhole" shape of the large mound.

🏢 KIKUYŌ-MACHI

House in Kumamoto
1986
Architect Itsuko Hasegawa
Address 2303, Tsukurei Ishizaka, Kikuyō-machi, Kikuchi-gun, Kumamoto Pref.
Transport From JR Kumamoto Station in Kumamoto: Train—JR Hōhi line to Sanrigi Station and taxi
Visitation Private residence, seen only from the outside

🏢 ASO-CHŌ

Kumamoto Grasslands Agricultural Institute (K.A.P.), 1992
Kumamoto-ken Kusachi Chikusan Kenkyūjō
Architect Tom Heneghan and Inga Dagfinnsdottir (U.K.)
Address 1454, Nishi-yuura Ōaza, Aso-chō, Aso-gun, Kumamoto Pref.
Transport Train—JR Hōhi line to Aso Station and 40 minutes by taxi

🏘 UBUYAMA-MURA

Ubuyama Community Center (K.A.P.)
1993
Ubuyama Hana no Onsen-kan
Architect Workshop
Address Aza-Shimokama-buta, Ōaza-Tajiri, Ubuyama-mura, Aso-gun, Kumamoto Pref.
Transport Train—JR Hōhi line to Miyaji Station and bus for Ubuyama-mura

🏢 OGUNI-CHŌ

Oguni Glass Station 1993
Cosmo (Harada) Gasu Stando
Architect Shōei Yoh
Address 2311, Miyanohara, Oguni-chō, Aso-gun, Kumamoto Pref.
Transport From Kumamoto Kōtsu (Bus) Center: bus to Oguni Kōtsu Center (1.5 hours) and 8 minutes by taxi; or Train—JR Hōhi line to Aso Station and bus bound for Oguni-chō to Sekita teiryūjō stop and 5-minute walk to north (on the corner of bifurcating road)
Visitation Open daily, tel: (0967) 46-4149

This small gas and service station is covered with a unique glass canopy suspended from arched concrete frames. The building's new material—a thin membrane of glass plates with an inlayed layer of perforated aluminum sheet—comes alive with sparkling brilliance when the sun shines through it.

Oguni Dome
1988
Oguni Chōmin Taiikukan
Architect Shōei Yoh
Address 214-2, Miyanomu-kai Aza, Miyanohara Ōaza, Oguni-chō, Kumamoto Pref.
Transport From Kumamoto Kōtsu (Bus) Center: bus to Oguni Kōtsu Center (1.5 hours); or Train—JR Hōhi line to Aso Station and bus for Oguni-chō Kōtsu Center and 5 minutes by taxi
This large sports arena is covered with a spectacular dome of wooden space-frame structure over reinforced concrete grandstands and walls.

Oguni-chō Bus Terminal
1987
Oguni-chō Kōtsu Sentā
Architect Shōei Yoh
Address 1754-17, Shimo-yuhara Aza, Miyanohara Ōaza, Oguni-chō, Kumamoto Pref.
Transport From Kumamoto Kōtsu (Bus) Center: Bus to Oguni Kōtsu Center (1.5 hours); or Train—JR Hōhi line to Aso Station and bus to Oguni Kōtsu Center

JR Yufuin Railway Station 1990

JR Yufuin Eki
Architect Arata Isozaki
Address JR Yufuin Station, Yufuin-chō, Ōita Pref.
Transport Train—JR Kyūdai line to Yufuin Station

An impressively simple and meticulously symmetrical wooden structure, the station centers on a multistory, quadrilateral, public lobby and waiting room, whose facades are made entirely of glass. As the towerlike central section of the station is also centered on the main street running to the building, visitors who get off the train can see through the lobby and all the way down the road, right into the small hot spring resort town and toward the mountains that surround it. Two short vaulted canopies provide protection for the two entrances/exits, and the building is extended by two identical wings that run along the railroad tracks. In one of the wings all the facilities relate to the station, while in the other a small conference room is located. In this conference room the second international architectural symposium of "ANYwhere"—organized by Arata Isozaki and Peter Eisenman—was held in June 1992. The building is finished with darkened wooden clapboards with vaulted roofs over the wings and a shallow dome on the tower, and thus reveals influence on its design by both European classicist and Japanese vernacular architectures. In this respect this station is reminiscent of Arata Isozaki's Hara Museum ARC in Shibukawa (1988) (see page 62).

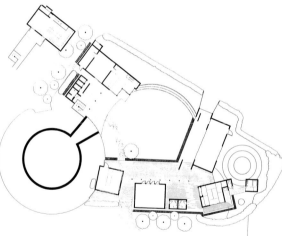

Yufuin Art Museum
1991
Yufuin Bijutsukan
Architect Team Zoo—
Atelier Zo
Address 2995, Iwamuro,
Kawakami, Yufuin-chō, Ōita
Pref.
Transport From JR Yufuin
Station: 10-minute walk; or
Bus—Kamenoi Bus to Yufuin
stop and 5-minute walk
Visitation 9:00–18:00 (closed
Tuesdays), tel: (0977) 85-
3525

One of the most remarkable recent structures of Team Zoo—Atelier Zo, the
museum is designed in a vernacular vein that is as simple as it is natural. The
small complex, comprised of a cluster of spaces of "pure [and] free spirit without restraint," displays the work of Kei Sato, a wanderer, poet, and painter
who died in Yufuin in 1960. Situated at the edge of a small creek, the picturesque ensemble of "huts" is constructed entirely with natural materials: wood,
bamboo, earth, and tiles. The pavilion-type arrangement provides plenty of
open space, either covered or in a courtyard. One of the exhibition rooms is a
cylindrical space completely covered by earth in the form of an attractive
mound with greenery on it. The compound is complemented with a second-
floor cafe and an observation tower.

Sueda Art Gallery 1982

Sueda Bijutsukan
Architect Hiroshi Hara
Address 1834, Tsue, Kawa-
kami, Yufuin-chō, Ōita Pref.
Transport From JR Yufuin
Station: 5 minutes by taxi or
25-minute walk
Visitation 9:00–18:00 (open
daily, year round), tel: (0977)
85-3572

村 KAMITSUE-MURA

**Autopolis Art Museum
1991**
Architect Hiroshi Naito
Address Ueno-Aso Racing
Park, Uenoda, Kamitsue-
mura, Hita-gun, Ōita Pref.
Transport From Kumamoto
or Ōita City: Train—JR Hōhi
line to Higo-Ōtsu Station and
30 minutes by taxi

市 BEPPU

**B-con Plaza/Ōita
Convention Center
1994**
Architect Arata Isozaki
Address Noguchi-Hara,
Beppu Aza, Beppu, Ōita Pref.
Transport From JR Beppu
Station: bus for Beppu Kōen
(15-minutes); next to Beppu
Kōen Park

Hiroshi Hara investigated extensively the indige-
nous architecture of many cultures. This project—
like many of Hara's previous residential designs,
such as the Hara House in Machida, Tōkyō (1974)
(see page 24, fig. 29), Kudo Village in Karuizawa
(1976), the Niramu House in Ichinomiya (1978),
and the Shokyodō Museum for Wood Block Prints
in Toyoto (1979) (see page 169)— was inspired by
the vernacular of traditional Japanese storehouses.
The darkened clapboard-covered, wooden building
is both a small private museum and the residence
of a couple of artists—the sculptor Ryūsuke Sueda
and his wife Shiori Sueda, a designer of hand-
woven tapestries, both natives of Kyūshū. A separate structure with a square plan and a skylight on
top houses Ryūsuke's studio. Behind the building a
small but beautiful garden extends as an open-air
gallery. Along the exterior wall Hara designed several round niches with openings to the garden,
while at the opposite side a second-floor gallery
with additional spaces both below and above, for
display. The complex is designed with an extensive
system of pitched and gabled tiled roofs. As
opposed to the dark exterior, the interior of the
two-story exhibition space is rendered entirely in
white, with intricate lighting fixtures, many of
which are shaped as prismatic permanent floor
lamps. The attractive architectural setting here is
matched by one of the most exquisite small exhibitions inside and out—abstract sculptures of stone,
metal, glass, and many other materials—and complemented by the hospitality of the owners.

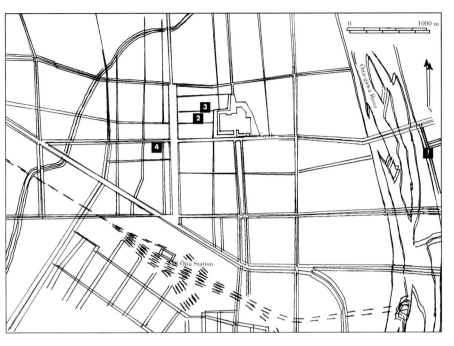

☗ ŌITA

1 Iwata Girls' High School, Gymnasium, and Dormitory, page 311

2 Old Ōita Prefectural Library, page 312

3 Ōita Medical Hall, page 312

4 Fukuoka Sōgō Bank Ōita Branch (now Fukuoka City Bank), page 313

Iwata Girls' High School, 1964
Iwata Girls' High School Gymnasium and Dormitory, 1985
Iwata Gakuen
Architect Arata Isozaki
Address 1-1, Iwata-chō 1-chōme, Ōita, Ōita Pref. (see map)
Transport From JR Ōita Station: 6 minutes by taxi; or 15-minute walk from Old Ōita Prefectural Library to the east across Ōita-gawa River

The bold composition of the school consists of two parts: a five-story classroom and a two-story staff and service block, both of unfinished reinforced concrete structure. These are connected by a bridge over an elevated-ground-level "walk-up" platform.

Old Ōita Prefectural Library 1966

Kyū Ōita Kenritsu Toshokan
Architect Arata Isozaki
Address 2-2, Niage-chō, Ōita, Ōita Pref. (see map)
Transport From JR Ōita Station: 10-minute walk (3-minute walk from Fukuoka Sōgō Bank Ōita Branch)

The Old Ōita Prefectural Library is an early but impressively powerful design that established Isozaki as an avant-garde architect both in Japan and abroad. Although a sympathizer with the ideas of the Metabolists, he was by this time more interested in exploring the expressive potentials of a formal language in architecture than the technological possibilities of design. The library displays many features that characterized Isozaki's visionary urban schemes for the Joint Core System (1960) and the City in the Air (1961) (see page 20, figs. 18 and 19), but here these features are forwarded with a manneristic exaggeration. Among them the most dominant are the hollowed space beams or "flying tubes" that, in addition to a pair of "space walls," generate the structural/spatial matrix of this building. The dynamic composition is distinguished by its brutal exterior, yet has a more accommodating and colorful interior whose spaces are highlighted by bridges and natural light.

Ōita Medical Hall, 1960 addition, 1972

Ōita-ken Ishi-Kaikan
Architect Arata Isozaki
Address 6-23, Niage-chō, Ōita, Ōita Pref. (see map)
Transport From JR Ōita Station: 11-minute walk (4-minute walk from Fukuoka City Bank; next to the Old Ōita Prefectural Library)

Ōita Prefectural Library 1994

Ōita Shin Kenritsu Toshokan
Architect Arata Isozaki
Address Minami-Ōji-chō, Ōita, Ōita Pref. (see map)
Transport From JR Ōita Station: 10-minute walk or bus bound for the library (.6 mile/1 kilometer west of station)

Ōita Audio-Visual Center 1979

Ōita Shichōkaku Center
Architect Arata Isozaki
Address 3-1, Oishi-chō, Ōita, Ōita Pref. (see map)
Transport From JR Ōita Station: bus bound for Ikadai, Kokubu Kōnohara via Kaku to Oishi-chō-Itchōme stop and 5-minute walk
Visitation Open daily, tel: (0975) 45-8616

Fukuoka Sōgō Bank Ōita Branch (now Fukuoka City Bank) 1967

Fukuoka City Ginkō
Ōita Shiten
Architect Arata Isozaki
Address 5-18, Chūō-chō
1-chōme, Ōita, Ōita Pref.
(see map)
Transport Train—JR Nippō,
JR Hōhi, or JR Kyūdai line to
Ōita Station and 8-minute
walk to north

The first among numerous small branch offices
that Isozaki designed for the Fukuoka Sōgō Bank,
this building stands on the corner of a major intersection in Ōita. The bank consists of two sections: a
solid, almost windowless high-rise volume supported by four reinforced concrete columns, and a low-
profile wing whose roof structure and skylights
take a forty-five-degree disposition relative to the
rectangular geometry of the tower and the street.
This architectural parti finds its predecessor in
James Stirling's Leicester University Engineering
Building (1963). In addition to the in-situ reinforced concrete structure, the bank building also
utilizes precast concrete panels on the high-rise
block. Rather than strive for a technological
achievement—according to the prevailing trend of
Metabolism—this project explores an innovative
approach to spatial and formal articulation.

神 ŌITA

Fujimi Country Clubhouse, 1974

Architect Arata Isozaki
Address 1473, Tsujita,
Yokose, Ōita, Ōita Pref.
(see map)
Transport From JR Ōita
Station: 30 minutes by taxi
along Route 210 toward
Yufuin (.5 mile/.8 kilometer
south of the highway)
Visitation Closed on the last
Monday of the month,
tel: (0975) 41-5252

In the 1970s, when Isozaki's uniquely manneristic architectural "rhetoric" was based on his manipulation of the basic elements of Cartesian geometry, the Fujimi Country Clubhouse represented the first example that used the circle and the cylinder. The building was designed with a copper-covered, concrete, semicylindrical, vaulted roof whose long, extruded, continuous form is bent twice horizontally. Using the associative power of the vault, Isozaki shaped the white stuccoed sections beneath the roof with references to Renaissance architecture, particularly the manneristic designs of Andrea Palladio, such as the Villa Poiana in Vicenza (c. 1549–56). These references are most evident in the treatment of the facades where the barrel vault comes to an abrupt end, practically revealing the section of the long space. The somewhat classical impression of the design disappears from the two ends of the vault. Where the vault takes a 180-degree turn, the roof structure, supported by a series of columns, doubles in width. The interconnected spaces here flow freely and, through the panoramic, almost cinematic glass walls, merge with the softly undulating landscape of the golf course. In this way outside and inside sceneries join in imparting a spatial experience that is as wonderfully ambiguous as it is non-classical.

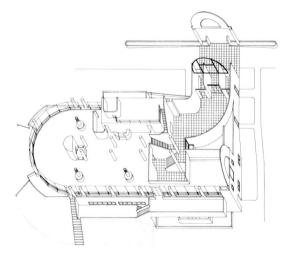

As the Metabolist architects correctly perceived, some parts of a building or an urban environment may change rapidly while others remain relatively stable for a long period of time. Trying to build upon such principles and determined to foster the process of change, many designers conceived their buildings with a clear, often contrived, distinction between permanent and impermanent, or rather, interchangeable elements. The odd shape and over-all organization of the Miyakonojō Civic Center reflects this mode of thinking and process of design. The lower section of the complex, which includes the lobby, the stage, and the entire seating area, has been made of solid reinforced concrete structures. Over this section the roof structure covering the large auditorium has been designed with a system of radially arranged steel frames and a steel plate shell. This suspended, dark colored shell, which resembles the cover of a baby carriage, was presumed to be subject to change as theater technology developed at a fast pace. The prefabricated metallic structure thus could be rebuilt or reconfigured according to future needs. It is ironic that, while changes to the center have indeed been necessary, these changes (by Kikutake) have involved the expansion and rebuilding of the "permanent" lower section rather than the metallic shell.

Miyakonojō Civic Center 1966

Miyakonojō Shimin Kaikan
Architect Kiyonori Kikutake
Address Sangai-ku, Hachiman-chō, Miyakonojō, Miyazaki Pref.
Transport Train—JR Nippō main line to Nishi-Miyakonojō Station: east exit and 5-minute walk
Visitation 9:00–17:00

市 NICHINAN

Nichinan Cultural Center 1962

Nichinan-shi Bunka Sentā
Architect Kenzo Tange
Address 14, Miyamae-Higashi, Tokada, Nichinan, Miyazaki Pref.
Transport Train—JR Nichinan line to Nichinan Station: west exit and 3-minute walk

⬛ MAKIZONO-CHŌ

Kirishima International Concert Hall
1994
Kirishima Kokusai Ongaku Hōru or *Miyama Konsēru*
Architect Fumihiko Maki
Address Takachihō-Deguchi, Makizono-chō, Gōra-gun, Kagoshima Pref.
Transport From Kagoshima City: highway bus to Miyama Konseru Mae stop (60 minutes); or From JR Kagoshima Station: Train—JR Nippo main line to Kirishimajingū Station and 15 minutes by taxi; or From Kagoshima Airport: 25 minutes by taxi
Visitation Open daily, tel: (0992) 24-7691

帀 KAGOSHIMA

Shūseikan Old Machine Factory
1865
Shokō Shūseikan or *Kyū Shūseikan Kikai Kōjō*
Kagoshima Spinning Mill Housing
1867
Kagoshima Bōseki-shō Gishikan
Architect Anonymous
Address 120, Yoshino-chō, Kagoshima, Kagoshima Pref.
Transport From JR Kagoshima Station—Bus to Shūseikan or 6 minutes by taxi
The buildings are Important National Cultural Properties.

帀 IBUSUKI

Iwasaki Museum
1979
addition, 1987
Iwasaki Bijutsukan
Architect Fumihiko Maki
Address 3-755, Juni-chō, Ibusuki, Kagoshima Pref.
Transport Train—JR Ibusuki-Makurazaki line to Ibusuki Station and bus or taxi for Ibusuki Kankō Hotel (adjacent to the hotel)

The two reinforced concrete structures, although built eight years apart, complement each other and, like yin-yang, form a unity of opposites. The original museum was modeled on the image and type of a villa, while the addition suggests a more self-enclosed house. The two buildings explore contrasting themes: lightness versus darkness, verticality versus horizontality, and Mediterranean versus Japanese. The first—exhibiting primarily modern Japanese paintings and Western Fauvist works—is designed along the themes of stairstepped volumes and cruciform steel elements; the addition—displaying traditional Japanese-style paintings, calligraphy, ceramics, and folk art—is shaped with a post-and-beam framework, stepped floor areas, and several layers of vertical planes to give space a greater sense of depth. The two structures are connected by an underground passage. While small by the standard of Maki's other projects, these two museums equal, and even surpass, many larger ones, with their sensitivity to the program, sophisticated articulation of form and structure, siting, spatial experience, and, despite all these, sensible simplicity.

Festival
1984
Architect Tadao Ando
Address 8-19, Matsuo 2-chōme, Naha, Okinawa Pref.
Transport From Naha City Hall: 15-minute walk on Kokusai-dōri Avenue toward Mitsukoshi Department Store

Okinawa Prefectural Government Headquarters
1989
Okinawa Kenchōsha Gyōseito
Architect Kisho Kurokawa
Address 2-2, Izumi-saki 1-chōme, Naha, Okinawa Pref.
Transport From Airport: 15 minutes by bus to Kenchō-mae stop; or 10 minutes by taxi

Jōsei Primary School
1987
Jōsei Shōgakkō
Architect Hiroshi Hara
Address 1-5, Mawashi machi, Shuri, Naha, Okinawa Pref.
Transport From Naha City Hall: bus bound for Shuri-jō to Sekiyama-iriguchi stop (25 minutes) and 5-minute walk on Samukawa-dōri Street (near the ruins of Shuri-jō Castle)
A group of pavilion-type buildings—covered by red tiled roofs—are arranged around a system of small courtyards.

🏙 **ISHIKAWA**

Ishikawa Municipal Park
1980
Ishikawa-shi Shirahamahara Kōen
Architect Team Zoo—Atelier Zo
Address Shirahamahara, Ishikawa, Okinawa Pref.
Transport From Naha Bus Terminal: bus to Ishikawa City Hall (along the seashore)

This eight-story building is the largest commercial complex by Ando to date. Facing a major thoroughfare and adjacent to a covered shopping street (*shōtengai*), the building was designed so as to continue the street space around; one might say, the Festival is a three-dimensional street in itself. The structure comprises a large cube of 118 feet/36 meters to a side, and is made of an exposed concrete frame. The exterior wall is made of concrete blocks between the concrete skeleton; the porous surfaces temper the scorching heat of the sunshine by filtering it, and at the same time let the breeze coming from the sea penetrate the interior "open" spaces of the complex. In so doing, these perforated walls, in conjunction with the concrete frame, engage their environment in the most poetic way and manifest the rich variations of light and shadow. Within this orthogonal matrix Ando has inserted an open atrium that penetrates the entire height of the building. Here escalators transport people up and down to the various levels and the rooftop plaza, with its huge tree and stage for outdoor festivities. Open spaces continue throughout the building in the form of open-air walkways, galleries, bridges, and stairways for pedestrians. Ando said: "I always wanted to build a building which blends with the climate of the region, utilizes features of the site, and yet is autonomous based on strict logic." ("Festival, Tadao Ando 1981–1989, *SD* 9 [1989]: 152.) In the Festival he fully succeeded.

市 NAGO

Nago City Hall
1981

Nago Shichōsha
Architect Team Zoo—
Atelier Zo
Address 1-1, Minato 1-chōme,
Nago, Okinawa Pref.
Transport From Naha Bus
Terminal: Bus 20 or 21 for
Nago City (2.5 hours) and
10-minute walk

Not far from the seashore, the Nago City Hall is located along an important highway in Okinawa. The three-story building is a rectangular matrix with a stepped contour and a profile that zig-zags, particularly on the side opposite the road. The building extensively utilizes the products of local concrete industry: high quality, high strength concrete blocks for pillars; hollowed, decorative blocks for walls and handrails; and reinforced concrete for floor structures. The color variation of the blocks gives an interesting "checker-board" look to the building. Like Ando's Festival, the city hall has an interconnected fabric of closed spaces and open spaces (such as terraces, walkways, and bridges), whereby there is a sensible continuity between interior and exterior as well as private and public areas. The city hall's playful design has acquired the qualities of the Okinawa vernacular to best address the climatic conditions (temperature, humidity, velocity and direction of wind, and intensity and reflection of light) not just as measurable data, but also as human experience.

町 MOTOBU-CHŌ

National Aquarium
of Okinawa Marine
Expo '75, 1975

Kaiyō Hakurankai Kinen
Kōen—Suizokukan
Architect Fumihiko Maki
Address 424, Aza Ishikawa,
Motobu-chō, Okinawa Pref.
Transport From Naha
Airport: Bus 93 to Kaiyō-
Hakurankai-Kinen-Kōen-
mae stop (3.5 hours); From
Nago: Bus 70 (45 minutes)

This large structure was built for the Okinawa Marine Expo '75. Along with Kiyonori Kikutake's Aquapolis, it is a facility that continues to serve both the local citizens of this tropical island and many of its visitors. Maki designed the aquarium with on-site prefabricated reinforced concrete slabs, each cut out with a simple half circle to form a system of two-dimensional arches. These elements create extensive, shadowy arcades on two levels to tame the constantly strong sunshine around the huge enclosed aquariums. In addition, they layer the space from the exterior to the interior. Playing out the possible combinations of connecting the basic elements, Maki has been able to achieve unexpected formal associations, one of them being the image of Gothic arches in a sequence. Yet the forms are also reminiscent of the powerful compositions of Louis Kahn.

Aquapolis of Okinawa Marine Expo '75, 1975

Kaiyō Hakurankai Kinen Kōen—Akuaporisu
Architect Kiyonori Kikutake
Address 424, Aza Ishikawa, Motobu-chō, Okinawa Pref.
Transport From Naha Airport: Bus 93 to Kaiyō-Haku-rankai-Kinen-Kōen- mae stop (3.5 hours); From Nago City: Bus 70 (45 minutes)
Visitation 9:30–17:00

Although most of the futuristic urban schemes of the Metabolists remain unbuilt, some of their visions were given a chance to be realized, even if in scaled down versions, by the repeated occurrences of major world expositions organized by the Japanese. Kenzo Tange used the Ōsaka Expo '70 to build a version of his "city in theair" as the huge space frame of the Theme Pavilion (see page 19, fig. 15), while Kikutake used the opportunity of the Okinawa Marine Expo '75 to build one of his early "floating city" projects. The strange-looking structure anchored at the shores of Motobu Peninsula is not an industrial installation or an oil-drilling rig, though it may look like one; it was built as an exhibition facility and pavilion to introduce the idea of future urban communities living over the sea. Constructed in one of Hiroshima's shipyards and towed to its present location, the Aquapolis is an enormous steel structure that floats on the water. Twelve large cylindrical shafts connected to buoys support a multistory deck with extensive exhibition spaces and service facilities, plus a flat rooftop area that serves partially as a heliport. The Aquapolis, after the demise of the Tange's Space Frame in 1978, remains the only monument to represent on an "urban" scale the heroic age of Metabolism in Japan.

村 NAKIJIN-MURA

Nakijin Village Center 1975

Nakijin-mura Chūō Kōminkan
Architect Team Zoo—Atelier Zo
Address 232, Nakasone, Nakijin-mura, Kunigami-gun, Okinawa Pref.
Transport From Nago City: Bus 66 (30 minutes); or from Kinen Kōen (Expo '75): Bus 65 (15 minutes) to Mura-yakuba stop

Arashiyama Golf Club 1991

Architect Shōei Yoh
Address 654-32, Aza Kure Wagayama, Nakijin-mura, Kunigami-gun, Okinawa Pref.
Transport From Nago City or Nakijin-mura: bus to Azakure Wagayama; or taxi

LIST OF ARCHITECTS AND THEIR BUILDINGS

Note: entries set in bold type are pictured in this book.

Mozuna, Kiko (Monta) (b. 1941)
—Anti-Dwelling Box (Mozuna House),
Kushiro, Hokkaidō, 1972, p. 48
—Ainu Ethnic Museum, Kussharō-
kotan, Teshikaga-chō, Hokkaidō,
1982, p. 51
—**Kushiro City Museum, Kushiro,
Hokkaidō, 1984, p. 50**
—**Kushiro Marshland Museum and
Observatory, Kushiro, Hokkaidō,
1984, p. 48**
—Kushiro Castle Hotel, Kushiro,
Hokkaidō, 1987, p. 48
—**Kushiro Fisherman's Wharf Moo,
Kushiro, Hokkaidō, 1989 (with
Nikken Sekkei Company), p. 49**
—**Notojima Glass Art Museum,
Notojima-chō, Ishikawa Pref., 1991,
p. 179**
—**Noto Monzen Family Inn, Monzen-
chō, Ishikawa Pref., 1991, p. 180**
—Shimokawa City Tower, Shimokawa-
chō, Hokkaidō, 1991, p. 51
—Nishiwaki Earth Science Museum,
Nishiwaki, Hyōgo Pref., 1992, p. 233
—Tamana Museum of History,
Tamana, Kumamoto Pref., 1994,
p. 305
Murakami, Toru (b. 1949)
—Nakagawa Photo Gallery, Kyōto City,
1993, p. 194
Murano, Togo (1891–1984)
—Morigō Shōten Office Building (now
Kinsan Building), Tōkyō, 1931,
p. 90
—Sōgō Department Store, Ōsaka City,
1935, p. 211
—**Ube Public Hall, Ube, Yamaguchi
Pref., 1937, p. 260**
—**World Peace Memorial Cathedral,
Hiroshima, Hiroshima Pref., 1953,
p. 248**
—**New Kabuki Theater, Ōsaka City,
1958, p. 213**
—**Yonago Public Hall, Yonago, Tottori
Pref., 1958, p. 254**
—Yokohama City Hall, Yokohama,
Kanagawa Pref., 1959, p. 151
—Nissei Hibiya Building (Theater),
Tōkyō, 1963, p. 85
—Chiyoda Life Insurance Building,
Tōkyō, 1966, p. 118
—**Takarazuka Catholic Church,
Takarazuka, Hyōgo Pref., 1967,
p. 223**
—**Industrial Bank of Japan, Tōkyō,
1974, p. 89**
—Takarazuka City Hall, Takarazuka,
Hyōgo Pref., 1980, p. 223
—**Tanimura Art Museum, Itoigawa,
Niigata Pref., 1983, p. 175**
Nagano, Uheiji (1867–1937)
—**Heian Museum (now Museum of
Kyōto), Kyōto City, 1907 (with K.
Tatsuno), p. 194**
—Bank of Japan Otaru Branch, Otaru,
Hokkaidō, 1912 (with K. Tatsuno),
p. 39
—Daiichi Kangyō Bank Kōbe Branch
(now Mitsui Bank), Kōbe, Hyōgo
Pref., 1916, p. 231
—Bank of Japan Okayama Branch
Office, Okayama, Okayama Pref.,
1922, p. 242

Naito, Hiroshi (b. 1950)
—Autopolis Art Museum, Kamitsue-
mura, Ōita Pref., 1991, p. 308
—Sea Folk Museum, Toba, Mie Pref.,
1992, p. 187
—Shima Art Museum, Toba, Mie Pref.,
1993, p. 187
Negishi, Kazuyuki (b. 1947)
—Maruzen Bakery Yamashina, Kyōto
City, 1992, p. 198
Nikken Sekkei Company (est. 1951)
—**San-Ai Dream Center, Tōkyō, 1963,
p. 82**
—Kōbe Port Tower, Kōbe, Hyōgo Pref.,
1964, p. 231
—**Palaceside Building, Tōkyō, 1966,
p. 101**
—IBM Japan Head Office, Tōkyō, 1971,
p. 108
—Japan Cycle Sports Center, Shūzenji-
chō, Shizuoka Pref., 1971, p. 167
—**Pola Home Offices, Tōkyō, 1971,
p. 116**
—Yamaguchi Civic Center, Yamaguchi,
Yamaguchi Pref., 1971, p. 260
—Tottori Prefectural Museum, Tottori,
Tottori Pref., 1972, p. 253
—Kurayoshi Museum, Kurayoshi,
Tottori Pref., 1973, p. 253
—**Nakano Sun Plaza, Tōkyō, 1973,
p. 138**
—Sanwa Bank, Tōkyō, 1973, p. 89
—Hiroshima Art Museum, Hiroshima,
Hiroshima Pref., 1978, p. 249
—Bank of Japan Ōsaka Branch, addi-
tion, Ōsaka City, 1980, p. 207
—**Shinjuku NS Building, Tōkyō, 1982,
p. 137**
—Ōsaka-jō Hall, Ōsaka City, 1983,
p. 216
—Mitsui (Taishō) Insurance Company
Building, Tōkyō, 1984, p. 94
—Chiba Port Tower, Chiba, Chiba
Pref., 1986, p. 74
—Ōsaka City Hall, Ōsaka City, 1986,
p. 207
—Twin 21 Office Towers, Ōsaka City,
1986, p. 215
—Tōkyō Dome, Big Egg, Tōkyō, 1988,
(with Takenaka Corporation), p. 98
—**Fukuoka Tower, Fukuoka, Fukuoka
Pref., 1989, p. 288**
—NEC Corporation Headquarters,
Tōkyō, 1990, p. 110
—Meguro Gajō-en Hotel, Tōkyō, 1991,
p. 117
—Pacifico Yokohama, Yokohama,
Kanagawa Pref., 1991, p. 150
—Long Term Credit Bank of Japan,
Tōkyō, 1993, p. 108
Nino, Shimon (b. 1961)
—Obiyama A Public Housing (K.A.P.),
Kumamoto, Kumamoto Pref., 1992,
p. 301
Nippon Sogo Architectural Office
—Telecom Center, Tōkyō, 1996 (with
Helmuth Obata Kassabaum [U.S.]),
p. 77
Nishioka, Hiroshi (b. 1945)
—**Shinchi Public Housing (K.A.P.),
phase 4, Kumamoto, Kumamoto
Pref., 1995, p. 304**
Ogata, Riichiro (1941–90)
—**Shinchi Public Housing (K.A.P.),**

phase 2, Kumamoto, Kumamoto
Pref., 1992, p. 304
Okada, Shinichi (b. 1928)
—**Supreme Court Building, Tōkyō,
1974, p. 103**
Okada, Shinichirō (1883–1932)
—**Nakanoshima Central Auditorium,
Ōsaka City, 1918 (with K. Tatsuno
and Y. Kataoka), p. 208**
—**Kabuki Theater, Tōkyō, 1924, p. 82**
—Meiji Life Insurance Building, Tōkyō,
1934, p. 87
Otaka, Masato (b. 1923)
—Chiba Prefectural Cultural Center,
Chiba, Chiba Pref., 1967, p. 74
—Chiba Prefectural Central Library,
Chiba, Chiba Pref., 1968, p. 74
—**Tochigi Prefectural Conference Hall,
Utsunomiya, Tochigi Pref., 1968,
p. 61**
—Motomachi and Chōjuen High-rise
Apartment Blocks, Hiroshima,
Hiroshima Pref., 1973, p. 250
—Gumma Prefectural Museum of
History, Takasaki, Gumma Pref.,
1979, p. 62
Otani, Sachio (b. 1924)
—**Kyōto International Conference Hall,
Kyōto City, 1966; addition 1973,
p. 197**
Pelli, Cesar (b. 1926), U.S.
—United States Embassy, Tōkyō, 1976,
p. 107
—NTT Headquarters Building, Tōkyō,
1995, p. 137
Pesce, Gaetano (b. 1939), Italy
—Organic Building Ōsaka, Ōsaka City,
1993, p. 211
Petitjean, Bernard T. (1829–84),
France
—Ōura Tenshudō Catholic Church,
Nagasaki, Nagasaki Pref., 1864,
p. 292
Piano, Renzo (b. 1937), Italy
—Kansai International Airport, Tajiri-
chō, Ōsaka Pref., 1994, p. 222
Raymond, Antonin (1888–1976), U.S.
—Saint Anselm Meguro Church, Tōkyō,
1956, p. 117
—Gumma Music Center, Takasaki,
Gumma Pref., 1961, p. 62
Roche, Kevin (b. 1922) (U.S.)
—Yūrakuchō 1-chōme Building, Tōkyō,
1994, p. 85
Rogers, Richard (b. 1933), U.K.
—Kabuki-chō Tower, Tōkyō, 1993,
p. 135
Rokkaku, Kijo (b. 1941)
—**Zassō Forest Kindergarten, Tanabe-
chō, Kyōto Pref., 1977, p. 200**
—**Konkokyō Church, Fukuoka,
Fukuoka Pref., 1980, p. 285**
—Tōkyō Budōkan, Tōkyō, 1989, p. 143
Rossi, Aldo (b. 1931), Italy
—Hotel Il Palazzo, Fukuoka, Fukuoka
Pref., 1989 (with M. Adjmi, U.S.),
p. 283
—Ambiente Showroom, Tōkyō, 1991
(with M. Adjmi, U.S.), p. 128
Rudolph, Paul (b. 1918), U.S.
—Daiei Building, Nagoya, Aichi Pref.,
1973, p. 171
Sadachi, Shichijiro (1856–1922)
—Old Japanese Mail Shipping Company

CHRONOLOGICAL LIST OF BUILDINGS

Note: entries set in bold type are pictured in this book.

329

CHRONOLOGICAL LIST OF BUILDINGS

Kumamoto, Kumamoto Pref.,
K. Maekawa, p. 299
—Zassō Forest Kindergarten, Tanabe-
chō, Kyōto Pref., K. Rokkaku, p. 200
—Sōgetsu Art Center, Tōkyō, K. Tange,
p. 107
1978
—Kamioka Town Hall, Kamioka-chō,
Gifu Pref., A. Isozaki, p. 174
—PMT Building, Nagoya, Aichi Pref.,
T. Ito, p. 172
—Hiroshima Art Museum, Hiroshima,
Hiroshima Pref., Nikken Sekkei
Company, p. 249
—House on a Curved Road, Tōkyō,
K. Shinohara, p. 123
—Koboku Lighting Showroom, Kyōto
City, S. Takamatsu, p. 190
—109 Building, Tōkyō, M. Takeyama,
p. 121
—Hanae Mori Building, Tōkyō,
K. Tange, p. 127
1979
—Toy Block House 2, Yokohama,
Kanagawa Pref., T. Aida, p. 150
—Mochida Building, Tōkyō, H. Fujii,
p. 136
—Shokyodō Museum for Wood Block
Prints, Toyota , Aichi Pref., H. Hara,
p. 169
—Tokumaru Children's Clinic, Matsu-
yama, Ehime Pref., I. Hasegawa,
p. 266
—Naoshima Municipal High School,
Naoshima-chō (Naoshima Island),
Kagawa Pref., K. Ishii (with
K. Namba), p. 261
—Kindergarten (54 Roofs), Takebe-
chō, Okayama Pref., K. Ishii, p. 242
—Ōita Audio-Visual Center, Ōita, Ōita
Pref., A. Isozaki, p. 312
—Iwasaki Museum, Ibusuki, Kagoshima
Pref., F. Maki, p. 316
—Royal Danish Embassy, Tōkyō,
F. Maki, p. 121
—Gumma Prefectural Museum of
History, Takasaki, Gumma Pref.,
M. Otaka, p. 62
1980
—Step, Takamatsu, Kagawa Pref.,
T. Ando, p. 263
—House at Kuwahara, Matsuyama,
Ehime Pref., I. Hasegawa, p. 268
—NEG Employee Service Facilities,
Ōtsu, Shiga Pref., A. Isozaki, p. 187
—Takarazuka City Hall, Takarazuka,
Hyōgo Pref., T. Murano, p. 223
—Bank of Japan, Ōsaka Branch, addi-
tion, Ōsaka City, Nikken Sekkei
Company, p. 207
—Konkokyō Church, Fukuoka,
Fukuoka Pref., K. Rokkaku, p. 285
—Shōtō Museum, Tōkyō, S. Shirai,
p. 122
—Nakamura Memorial Hospital, Sap-
poro, Hokkaidō, M. Takeyama, p. 43
—Ishikawa Municipal Park, Ishikawa,
Okinawa Pref., Team Zoo—Atelier
Zo, p. 317
—Miyashiro Municipal Center,
Miyashiro-chō, Saitama Pref., Team
Zoo—Atelier Zo, p. 64
—Kurashiki New City Hall, Kurashiki,
Okayama Pref., S. Urabe, p. 245

1981
—Rin's Gallery, Kōbe, Hyōgo Pref.,
T. Ando, p. 229
—House at a Bus Stop in Seijō, Tōkyō,
K. Hayakawa, p. 142
—LP House 1, Tōkyō, A. Komiyama,
p. 127
—Keiō University Library, Tōkyō,
F. Maki, p. 111
—Studio Ebis, Tōkyō, M. Suzuki,
p. 121
—Origin 1, Kyōto City, S. Takamatsu,
p. 195
—Musashino Art University Building 10,
Kodaira, Tōkyō Pref., M. Takeyama,
p. 146
—Nago City Hall, Nago, Okinawa Pref.,
Team Zoo—Atelier Zo, p. 318
1982
—Hillport Hotel, Tōkyō, H. Hara,
p. 121
—Sueda Art Gallery, Yufuin-chō, Ōita
Pref., H. Hara, p. 121
—Aono Building, Matsuyama, Ehime
Pref., I. Hasegawa, p. 267
—Toga Sanbō Theater and Amphi-
theater, Toga-mura, Toyama Pref.,
A. Isozaki, p. 175
—Izumo Shrine Shinkōden Reception
Hall, Taisha-machi, Shimane Pref.,
K. Kikutake, p. 256
—Kumamoto Arts and Crafts Center,
Kumamoto, Kumamoto Pref.,
K. Kikutake, p. 301
—Saitama Prefectural Museum of
Modern Art, Urawa, Saitama Pref.,
K. Kurokawa, p. 65
—Ainu Ethnic Museum, Kussharō-
kotan, Teshikaga-chō, Hokkaidō,
K. Mozuna, p. 51
—Shinjuku NS Building, Tōkyō, Nikken
Sekkei Company, p. 137
—Ukiyoe Museum, Matsumoto, Nagano
Pref., K. Shinohara, p. 165
—Origin 2, Kyōto City, S. Takamatsu,
p. 195
—Pontochō-no-Ochaya (Yoshida
House), Kyōto City, S. Takamatsu,
p. 192
—Akasaka Prince Hotel, Tōkyō,
K. Tange, p. 103
—Ginza Sukiyabashi Police Box, Tōkyō,
K. Yamashita, p. 84
—Japan Folk Craft Museum, addition,
Tōkyō, K. Yamashita, p. 123
1983
—Toy Block House 7, Tōkyō, T. Aida,
p. 119
—Bigi Atelier, Tōkyō, T. Ando, p. 121
—Rokkō Housing 1, Kōbe, Hyōgo Pref.,
T. Ando, p. 227
—House at a Crossroad in Seijō, Tōkyō,
K. Hayakawa, p. 142
—Naoshima Town Hall, Naoshima-chō
(Naoshima Island), Kagawa Pref.,
K. Ishii, p. 262
—Fukuoka Sōgō Bank Home Offices
(now Fukuoka City Bank), addition,
Fukuoka, Fukuoka Pref., A. Isozaki,
p. 282
—Tsukuba Center Building, Tsukuba
Science Center, Ibaraki Pref.,
A. Isozaki, p. 71
—National Bunraku Theater, Ōsaka

City, K. Kurokawa, p. 213
—YKK Guest House, Kurobe, Toyama
Pref., F. Maki, p. 176
—Tanimura Art Museum, Itoigawa,
Niigata Pref., T. Murano, p. 175
—Ōsaka-jō Hall, Ōsaka City, Nikken
Sekkei Company, p. 216
—House in Higashi-Tamagawa 2,
Tōkyō, K. Shinohara, p. 118
—Ark (Nishina Dental Clinic), Kyōto
City, S. Takamatsu, p. 199
—Mikakuto Candy Factory, Yamatō-
kōriyama, Nara Pref., M. Takeyama,
p. 203
—Ken Dōmon Museum of Photography,
Sakata, Yamagata Pref., Yoshio
Taniguchi, p. 56
—Municipal Kasahara Elementary
School, Miyashiro-chō, Saitama Pref.,
Team Zoo—Atelier Zo, p. 64
1984
—Toy Block House 10, Tōkyō, T. Aida,
p. 125
—Festival, Naha, Okinawa Pref.,
T. Ando, p. 317
—Melrose, Tōkyō, T. Ando, p. 118
—Time's 1, Kyōto City, T. Ando,
p. 193
—N.C. Housing, Tōkyō, I. Hasegawa,
p. 139
—Tanabe Agency Building, Tōkyō,
K. Ishii, p. 118
—Okanoyama Graphic Arts Museum,
Nishiwaki, Hyōgo Pref., A. Isozaki,
p. 233
—Kyūsendō Forest Museum, Kuma-
mura, Kumamoto Pref., Y. Kijima,
p. 296
—LP House 2, Tōkyō, A. Komiyama,
p. 127
—Roppongi Prince Hotel, Tōkyō,
K. Kurokawa, p. 108
—Wacoal Kōjimachi Building, Tōkyō,
K. Kurokawa, p. 102
—Fujisawa Municipal Gymnasia,
Fujisawa, Kanagawa Pref., F. Maki,
p. 154
—Kushiro City Museum, Kushiro,
Hokkaidō, K. Mozuna, p. 50
—Kushiro Marshland Museum and
Observatory, Kushiro, Hokkaidō,
K. Mozuna, p. 48
—Mitsui (Taishō) Insurance Company
Building, Tōkyō, Nikken Sekkei
Company, p. 94
—Pharaoh (Asano Dental Clinic), Kyōto
City, S. Takamatsu, p. 198
1985
—Eishin Higashino High School, Iruma,
Saitama Pref., C. Alexander (U.S.),
p. 64
—Atelier Yoshie Inaba (Bigi 3), Tōkyō,
T. Ando, p. 121
—Jun Port Island Building, Kōbe,
Hyōgo Pref., T. Ando, p. 230
—Gymnasium 2 of Shibaura Institute of
Technology, Ōmiya, Saitama Pref.,
H. Fujii, p. 67
—Ushimado International Arts Festival
Building, Ushimado-chō, Okayama
Pref., H. Fujii, p. 243
—Iwata Girls' High School Gymnasium
and Dormitory, Ōita, Ōita Pref.,
A. Isozaki, p. 311

CHRONOLOGICAL LIST OF BUILDINGS

—YKK Research Center, Tōkyō,
F. Maki, p. 92
—Station Pavilion, Takaoka, Takaoka,
Toyama Pref., E. Miralles (Spain)
(with Total Architecture of Toyama),
p. 178
—Ryujabira Public Housing (K.A.P.),
Kumamoto, Kumamoto Pref.,
M. Motokura, p. 303
—Nakagawa Photo Gallery, Kyōto City,
T. Murakami, p. 194
—Shima Art Museum, Toba, Mie Pref.,
H. Naito, p. 187
—Long Term Credit Bank of Japan,
Tōkyō, Nikken Sekkei Company,
p. 108
—Organic Building Ōsaka, Ōsaka City,
G. Pesce (Italy), p. 211
—Kabuki-chō Tower, Tōkyō, R. Rogers
(U.K.), p. 135
—Museum for Woodcarving, Inami-
machi, Toyama Pref., P. Salter (U.K.)
(with K. Tohata Architects), p. 175
—Observation and Rest Pavilion,
Kamiichi-machi, Toyama Pref.,
P. Salter (U.K.) (with Tamura Archi-
tects), p. 177
—**Pachinko Parlor Kinbasha, Hitachi,
Ibaraki Pref., K. Sejima, p. 68**
—Landmark Tower, Yokohama,
Kanagawa Pref., H. Stubbins (U.S.)
(with Mitsubishi Real Estate
Architectural Office), p. 150
—**Kunibiki Messe, Convention Hall,
Matsue, Shimane Pref.,
S. Takamatsu, p. 255**
—Nima Museum of Bohemian Art
(MOBA), Nima-chō, Shimane Pref.,
S. Takamatsu, p. 257
—Ueno Green (Bonsai) Club, Tōkyō,
S. Takamatsu, p. 97
—Fukuoka Dome, Fukuoka, Fukuoka
Pref., Takenaka Corporation (with
Maeda Corporation), p. 288
—Takenaka Research and Development
Institute (R-90), Inzai-machi, Chiba
Pref., Takenaka Corporation, p. 75
—**Shinchi Public Housing (K.A.P.),
phase 3, Kumamoto, Kumamoto
Pref., Y. Tominaga, p. 304**
—Observation and Rest Pavilion,
Shōgawa-machi, Toyama Pref.,
C. Villanueva (Spain), p. 175
—Aobadai Tōkyū Department Store,
Yokohama, Kanagawa Pref., J. M.
Wilmotte (France), p. 150
—Ubuyama Community Center
(K.A.P.), Ubuyama-mura, Kumamoto
Pref., Workshop, p. 307
—Galaxy 92 and Prospecta 92, Kosugi-
machi, Toyama Pref., S. Yoh, p. 177
—**Oguni Glass Station, Oguni-chō,
Kumamoto Pref., S. Yoh, p. 307**
1994
—**Chikatsu-Asuka Historical Museum,
Minami-Kawachi-gun, Ōsaka Pref.,
T. Ando, p. 221**
—Garden of Fine Arts, Kyōto City,
T. Ando, p. 196
—Santory Museum-Tempōzan, Ōsaka
City, T. Ando, p. 214
—Picture Book Museum in Ōshima,
Ōshima-machi, Toyama Pref.,
I. Hasegawa, p. 178

—**Sumida Cultural Center, Tōkyō,
I. Hasegawa, p. 93**
—B-con Plaza/Ōita Convention Center,
Beppu, Ōita Pref., A. Isozaki, p. 310
—Nagi Museum of Contemporary Art,
Nagi-chō, Okayama Pref., A. Isozaki,
p. 244
—Ōita Prefectural Library, Ōita, Ōita
Pref., A. Isozaki, p. 312
—Home of the Elderly in Yatsushiro,
Yatsushiro, Kumamoto Pref., T. Ito,
p. 296
—Tsukuba South Parking Building,
Tsukuba, Ibaraki Pref., T. Ito, p. 71
—Kirishima International Concert Hall,
Makizono-chō, Kagoshima Pref.,
F. Maki, p. 316
—Tamana Museum of History, Tamana,
Kumamoto Pref., K. Mozuna, p. 305
—Kansai International Airport, Tajiri-
chō, Ōsaka Pref., R. Piano (Italy),
p. 222
—Yūrakuchō 1-chōme Building, Tōkyō,
K. Roche (U.S.), p. 85
—**Kanematsu Building, Tōkyō, Shimizu
Corporation, p. 85**
—**Sagishima "RING" Guest House,
Mihara (Sagi Island), Hiroshima
Pref., R. Suzuki, p. 246**
—Concert Hall in Sakaiminato,
Sakaiminato, Tottori Pref.,
S. Takamatsu, p. 253
—YKK Okayama 1, Okayama, Oka-
yama Pref., S. Takamatsu, p. 242
—**Shinjuku Park Towers, Tōkyō,
K. Tange, p. 137**
—**Shinchi Public Housing (K.A.P.),
phase 5, Kumamoto, Kumamoto
Pref., K. Ueda, p. 304**
1995
—Kyōto Symphony Hall, Kyōto City,
A. Isozaki, p. 196
—Yatsushiro Fire Station, Yatsushiro,
Kumamoto Pref., T. Ito, p. 296
—**Shinchi Public Housing (K.A.P.),
phase 4, Kumamoto, Kumamoto
Pref., H. Nishioka, p. 304**
—NTT Headquarters Building, Tōkyō,
C. Pelli (U.S.), p. 137
—Hamada Children's Museum, Gōtsu,
Shimane Pref., S. Takamatsu, p. 258
—Nagasaki Ferry Terminal, Nagasaki,
Nagasaki Pref., S. Takamatsu, p. 292
1996
—Ariake Clean Center, Tōkyō,
K. Kobayashi (with Takenaka
Corporation), p. 77
—Telecom Center, Tōkyō, Nippon Sogo
Architectural Office with Helmuth
Obata Kassabaum (U.S.), p. 77
—Tōkyō International Exhibition
Center and Congress Tower, Tōkyō,
Sato Architectural Office, p. 77
—World City Exposition Tōkyō '96,
Urban Frontier (March–October),
Tōkyō, Tōkyō Metropolitan
Government and Tōkyō Frontier
Association, p. 77
—Tōkyō International Forum, Tōkyō,
R. Vinoly (U.S.), p. 86
1997
—**JR Kyōto Station, Kyōto City,
H. Hara, p. 189**

LIST OF MAPS

BIBLIOGRAPHY

Arata Isozaki: Architecture 1960–1990. New York: Rizzoli, 1991 (with essays by David Stewart and Hajime Yatsuka).

Arata Isozaki 1976–1984, Space Design 1 (1984), Tōkyō.

Ashihara, Yoshinobu. *The Hidden Order: Tōkyō Through the Twentieth Century.* Tōkyō and New York: Kōdansha International, 1989.

Atelier Zo, Space Design 11 (1985), Tōkyō.

Barthes, Roland. *Empire of Signs.* R. Howard, trans. New York: Hill and Wang, 1982.

Bognar, Botond. *Contemporary Japanese Architecture: Its Development and Challenge.* New York: Van Nostrand Reinhold, 1985.

——. "Critical Intentions in Pluralistic Japanese Architecture," *Free Space Architecture, Architectural Design Profile* 96, vol. 62, no. 3/4 (1992): 72–96, London.

——. *The New Japanese Architecture.* New York: Rizzoli, 1990.

——. *Togo Murano: An Architect for All Seasons.* New York: Rizzoli, 1996.

—— (ed.). *Japanese Architecture, Architectural Design Profile* 73, vol. 58, no. 5/6 (1988), London.

—— (ed.). *Japanese Architecture 2, Architectural Design Profile* 99, vol. 62, no. 9/10 (1992), London.

Bognar, Botond, Kenneth Frampton, and Sandy Heck. *Nikken Sekkei: Building Modern Japan 1900–1990.* New York: Princeton Architectural Press, 1990.

Boyd, Robin. *New Directions in Japanese Architecture.* New York: George Braziller, 1968.

Drew, Philip. *The Architecture of Arata Isozaki.* New York: Harper and Row, 1982.

Fawcett, Chris. *The New Japanese House.* New York: Harper and Row, 1980.

Frampton, Kenneth (ed.). *The Architecture of Hiromi Fujii.* New York: Rizzoli, 1987.

—— (ed.). *Kazuo Shinohara.* New York: IAUS Catalogue 17, 1982.

—— (ed.). *A New Wave of Japanese Architecture.* New York: IAUS, 1978.

—— (ed.). *Tadao Ando: Buildings Projects Writings.* New York: Rizzoli, 1984.

Friedman, Mildred, (ed.). *Tōkyō: Form and Spirit.* Minneapolis: Walker Art Center and New York: Abrams, 1986.

Fumihiko Maki 1979–1986, Space Design 1 (1986), Tōkyō.

Fumihiko Maki 1987–1992, Space Design 1 (1993), Tōkyō.

Futagawa, Yukio (ed.). *Tadao Ando.* Tōkyō: A.D.A. Edita, 1987.

Global Architect Houses, no. 4., *Japanese Houses* 1 (1978).

Global Architect Houses, no. 14., *Japanese Houses* 2 (1983).

Global Architect Houses, no. 20., *Japanese Houses* 3 (1986).

A Guide to Japanese Architecture. Tōkyō: Shinkenchiku-sha, 1984.

Itsuko Hasegawa, Space Design 4 (1985) Tōkyō.

Japan: Climate, Space and Concept, Process Architecture 25 (1981), Tōkyō.

Kestenbaum, Jackie. *Emerging Japanese Architects of the 1990s.* New York: Columbia University Press, 1991.

Kinoshita, Jun and Nicholas Palevsky. *Gateway to Japan.* Tōkyō and New York: Kōdansha International, 1992.

Kisho Kurokawa 1978–1989, Space Design 6 (1989) Tōkyō.

Kulterman, Udo. *New Japanese Architecture.* New York: Praeger (1960).

Kurokawa, Kisho. *From Metabolism to Symbiosis.* London: Academy Editions and New York: Saint Martin's Press, 1992.

——. *Intercultural Architecture: The Philosophy of Symbiosis.* London: Academy Editions, 1991.

Maki, Fumihiko. *Investigations in Collective Form.* Saint Louis: University of Washington Press, 1964.

Muramatsu, Teijiro, Hiro Sasaki, and Hiroki Onobayashi. "History of Modern Japanese Architecture, 1840–1945." *Japan Architect* 6 (1965).

Polledri, Paolo (ed.). *Shin Takamatsu.* San Francisco: Museum of Modern Art and New York: Rizzoli, 1993.

Popham, Peter. *Tōkyō: The City at the End of the World.* New York and Tōkyō: Kōdansha International, 1985.

Ross, Michael Franklin. *Beyond Metabolism: The New Japanese Architecture.* New York: McGraw-Hill, 1978.

Roulet, Sophie and Sophie Soulie. *Toyo Ito: Architecture of the Ephemeral.* Paris: Editions due Moniteur, 1991.

Shin Takamatsu. JA Library 1 (1993), Tōkyō.

Shin Takamatsu. Space Design 1 (1988), Tōkyō.

Stewart, David. *The Making of a Modern Japanese Architecture.* Tōkyō and New York: Kōdansha International, 1987.

Suzuki, Hiroyuki. *Shin Takamatsu. Global Architect* 9 (1990), Tōkyō.

Suzuki, Hiroyuki, Reyner Banham, and Katsuhiro Kobayashi. *Contemporary Architecture of Japan.* New York: Rizzoli, 1985.

Tadao Ando, Space Design 6 (1981), Tōkyō.

Tadao Ando 1981–1989, Space Design 9 (1989), Tōkyō.

Takashina, Shūji (ed.). *Tōkyō: Creative Chaos, Japan Echo* 14 (1987).

Takefumi Aida: Buildings and Projects. New York: Princeton Architectural Press, 1989.

Telescope. Tōkyō: Workshop for Architecture and Urbanism, 1989.

Tempel, Egon. *New Japanese Architecture.* New York: Praeger, 1969.

Toyo Ito. JA Library 3 (1993) Tōkyō.

Toyo Ito, Space Design 9 (1986) Tōkyō.

Waley, Paul. *Tōkyō: City of Stories.* Tōkyō and New York: Weatherhill, 1991.

Watanabe, Hiroshi. *Amazing Architecture from Japan.* Tōkyō and New York: Weatherhill, 1991.

World Architecture 16 (special Japanese issue) (1992) (with a profile of Fumihiko Maki).

Yatsuka, Hajime. "Architecture in the Urban Desert: A Critical Introduction to Japanese Architecture After Modernism." *Oppositions 23* (winter 1981): 3–35.

——. "Post-Modernism and Beyond." *Japan Architect* (February 1986): 59–66.